THE SENSORY STUDIES MANIFESTO

Tracking the Sensorial Revolution in the Arts and Human Sciences

The senses are made, not given. This revolutionary realization has come as of late to inform research across the social sciences and humanities, and is currently inspiring groundbreaking experimentation in the world of art and design, where the focus is now on mixing and manipulating the senses.

The Sensory Studies Manifesto tracks these transformations and opens multiple lines of investigation into the diverse ways in which human beings sense and make sense of the world. This unique volume treats the human sensorium as a dynamic whole that is best approached from historical, anthropological, geographic, and sociological perspectives. In doing so, it has altered our understanding of sense perception by directing attention to the sociality of sensation and the cultural mediation of sense experience and expression.

David Howes challenges the assumptions of mainstream Western psychology by foregrounding the agency, interactivity, creativity, and wisdom of the senses as shaped by culture. *The Sensory Studies Manifesto* sets the stage for a radical reorientation of research in the human sciences and artistic practice.

DAVID HOWES is a professor of anthropology and co-director of the Centre for Sensory Studies at Concordia University.

T0385486

DAVID HOWES

The Sensory Studies Manifesto

Tracking the Sensorial Revolution
in the Arts and Human Sciences

UNIVERSITY OF TORONTO PRESS
Toronto Buffalo London

© University of Toronto Press 2022
Toronto Buffalo London
utorontopress.com
Printed and bound by CPI Group (UK) Ltd, Croydon, CR0 4YY

ISBN 978-1-4875-2861-4 (cloth)   ISBN 978-1-4875-2864-5 (EPUB)
ISBN 978-1-4875-2862-1 (paper)   ISBN 978-1-4875-2863-8 (PDF)

Library and Archives Canada Cataloguing in Publication

Title: The sensory studies manifesto : tracking the sensorial revolution in the arts and
    human sciences / David Howes.
Names: Howes, David, 1957– author.
Description: Includes bibliographical references and index.
Identifiers: Canadiana (print) 2022024099X | Canadiana (ebook) 20220241139 |
    ISBN 9781487528621 (paper) | ISBN 9781487528614 (cloth) |
    ISBN 9781487528645 (EPUB) | ISBN 9781487528638 (PDF)
Subjects: LCSH: Senses and sensation – History. | LCSH: Senses and sensation –
    Social aspects. | LCSH: Senses and sensation – Case studies. | LCSH: Senses
    and sensation in art. | LCSH: Aesthetics.
Classification: LCC BF233 .H69 2022 | DDC 152.109–dc23

We wish to acknowledge the land on which the University of Toronto Press
operates. This land is the traditional territory of the Wendat, the Anishnaabeg,
the Haudenosaunee, the Métis, and the Mississaugas of the Credit First Nation.

University of Toronto Press acknowledges the financial support of the Government of
Canada, the Canada Council for the Arts, and the Ontario Arts Council, an agency of
the Government of Ontario, for its publishing activities.

Canada Council   Conseil des Arts
for the Arts   du Canada

ONTARIO ARTS COUNCIL
CONSEIL DES ARTS DE L'ONTARIO
an Ontario government agency
un organisme du gouvernement de l'Ontario

Funded by the   Financé par le
Government   gouvernement
of Canada   du Canada

For my children

Contents

Figures

Acknowledgments

The reflections on the social and cultural life of the senses offered here were elaborated in the context of a long series of highly stimulating conversations with fellow sensory studies scholars. Constance Classen, with her exceptional mastery of the history of the senses, has played a vital part throughout. Other key interlocutors include Dor Abrahamson, Jennifer Biddle, Mikkel Bille, Rosabelle Boswell, Michael Bull, Fiona Candlin, Mónica Degen, Jennifer Deger, Sandra Dudley, Kathryn Earle, Tim Edensor, Elizabeth Edwards, David Garneau, Marie-Luce Gélard, Kathryn Linn Geurts, Bianca Grohmann, Sheryl Hamilton, Anna Harris, Michael Herzfeld, Caroline A. Jones, Carolyn Korsmeyer, Michael Lambek, David Le Breton, Fiona McDonald, Richard Newhauser, Mark Paterson, Marina Peterson, Sally Promey, Chris Salter, Mark M. Smith, Charles Spence, Paul Stoller, David Sutton, Anthony Synnott, and Boris Wiseman.

I wish to thank the many students who have served as research assistants on the diverse projects I have directed or otherwise participated in stretching back to 1988, and "The Varieties of Sensory Experience" project. These projects would not have been possible without the generous financial assistance of the Social Sciences and Humanities Research Council of Canada and the Fonds de Recherche du Québec – Société et Culture. I am also mindful of the tremendous debt I owe to my family for their continuous support and encouragement.

This book presents an analysis of the progress that has been made over the last decades in the cross-disciplinary study of the senses and offers guidelines for the future development of the field. Parts of this work were published previously, though they have been revised substantially for inclusion here. Chapters 1, 2, 3, and 6 began as the introductory chapters to the four-volume *Senses and Sensation: Critical and Primary Sources* compendium originally published by Bloomsbury in 2018 and later transferred to Routledge. Chapter 4 is taken mostly unaltered from my introduction to *A Cultural History of the Senses in the Modern Age, 1920–2000*, part of a multivolume series on the history of the senses edited by Constance Classen, and published by Bloomsbury in 2014.

The opening section of chapter 6 was first published as the introduction to a special issue of *The Senses and Society* on "Sensory Museology" (vol. 9, no. 3). The middle section of chapter 8 is derived from an essay called "Immersion and Transcendence: Some Notes on the Construction of Performative Sensory Environments" in *Par le prisme des sens: Mediation et nouvelles réalités du corps dans les arts performatifs*, edited by Isabelle Choinière, Enrico Pitozzi, and Andrea Davidson, and published by Presses de l'Université du Québec in 2019. I am grateful to the above-mentioned publishers for permission to reuse this material here. I also wish to express my thanks to the Office of the Vice-President Research and Graduate Studies of Concordia University and the Centre for Sensory Studies for grants in aid of publication of this book.

It is important to acknowledge that Concordia University is on land that has long served as a site of meeting and exchange amongst Indigenous peoples, including the Haudenosaunee and Anishnaabeg nations. My work has involved engaging with Indigenous scholars and artists, and I am acutely conscious of the need to attend to Indigenous perspectives and histories in our contemporary world.

The two anonymous reviewers chosen by the press provided insightful comments on an earlier draft of the manuscript. They enabled me to better see the overarching narrative of this treatise, and I am deeply appreciative of their input. I am grateful to the artist-designer Erik Adigard for his compelling cover art for the book. The medallions that adorn the front and back covers convey the experience of intersensoriality discussed inside the book in a striking visual form. Other variations from Adigard's "Collideroscope series" can be seen on the half-title pages that divide this book into three parts.* Finally, to the editorial team at the University of Toronto Press, and especially Jodi Lewchuk, I wish to say that it is ever so good to be working with the Press again, thirty years after UTP first published *The Varieties of Sensory Experience*!

*For full-colour reproductions of the medallions designed by Erik Adigard used on the half-title pages of this Manifesto see the "Collideroscope" entry on the Picture Gallery page of the Sensory Studies website (http://www.sensorystudies .org/picture-gallery/). There you will also find an animated version of the cover illustration.

THE SENSORY STUDIES MANIFESTO

Prologue: Coming to Our Senses

If a revolt is to come, it will have to come from the five senses!

Michel Serres

An intense new focus on the cultural life of the senses has swept over the social sciences and humanities. With its roots in the disciplines of history and anthropology, this transformation in the study of perception has directed attention to how the senses are constructed and lived differently across cultures and periods, and thus disrupted the monopoly that the discipline of psychology formerly exercised over this domain. The burgeoning literature on the cultural mediation of "sensory processing" has resulted in a drive to liberate the senses from the artificial confines of the psychology laboratory and explore how they function "in the wild," as Michel Serres[1] would say, or "everyday life" (de Certeau 1983b; Seremetakis 2019). The multi- and interdisciplinary approach to the analysis of sense experience that has emerged out of this "sensory turn" in the human sciences goes under the name of *sensory studies* (Bull et al. 2006). Sensory studies involves a cultural approach to the study of the senses and a sensory approach to the study of culture. It treats the senses and sensations as both object of study and means of inquiry.

The first two chapters of this Manifesto survey how geographers, anthropologists, historians, and sociologists have come to train their disciplinary skills on documenting and analysing the varieties of sensory experience across cultures and over time. Various foundational late twentieth-century texts will be identified and discussed in this survey. As regards anthropology and geography, these include Paul Stoller's *The Taste of Ethnographic Things: The Senses in Anthropology* (1989) and *The Varieties of Sensory Experience: A Sourcebook in the Anthropology of the Senses* (Howes 1991); Yi-Fu Tuan's *Passing Strange and Wonderful: Aesthetics, Nature, and Culture* (1993) and Paul Rodaway's *Sensuous Geographies: Body, Sense and Place* (1994). As regards history, we will examine

Alain Corbin's extensive corpus of works on "the history of the sensible" (e.g., Corbin [1982] 1986, [1994] 1998) and Constance Classen's *Worlds of Sense* (1993) and *The Color of Angels: Cosmology, Gender and the Aesthetic Imagination* (1998); within sociology, we will touch on *The Body Social: Symbolism, Self and Society* (1993) by Anthony Synnott and *The Senses in Self, Society and Culture: A Sociology of the Senses* (Vannini, Waskul, and Gottschalk 2012). First, however, a few words are in order concerning the genesis of this paradigm shift in the conceptualization and approaches to studying the life of the senses.

The sensory turn in anthropology and cognate human sciences arose after the *linguistic turn* of the 1960s and '70s, which privileged language-based models of culture (e.g., culture as "language game" or as "structured like a language," culture "as text" or "discursive formation").[2] It also succeeded the *pictorial turn* of the 1980s, which gave rise to visual culture studies and the steady proliferation of image-based models of meaning and communication (e.g., culture as "world view" or "world picture," "the image society," "visual literacy"). The emergent field of sensory studies, with its emphasis on *sense-based* inquiry, both critiques and seeks to correct for the *verbocentrism* of language-based models and the *ocularcentrism* of image-based models by analysing the sensorium as a whole and striving to articulate the sensory order – or "model" (Classen 1993b, 1997) – that informs how people in different cultures and historical periods *sense* the world. Crucially, sensory studies plays up the double meaning of the term "sense." This term encompasses both sensation *and* signification, feeling *and* meaning (as in the "sense" of a word) in its spectrum of referents. *Sensation-signification* is seen as forming a continuum, which is modulated by the sensory order. In this regard, the field of sensory studies can be seen as charting a middle course between cognitivism and empiricism. The former treats perception as determined by cognition. The focus is on analysing the "cognitive map" of the individual subject that is supposed to dictate how their senses function. The latter views the mind as a *tabula rasa* and the senses as passive receptors of the impressions made on them by the exterior world. The former is too top-down, and the latter too bottom-up. Both approaches ignore the mediating role of culture and the socialization of the senses in addition to overlooking the agency and interactivity of the people sensing and of the senses themselves.

The sensory turn also figures as a successor to the *corporeal turn* of the 1980s (Csordas 1990). The latter turn was predicated on affirming the unity of mind and body. It gave rise to such theoretical constructs as "the embodied mind" and "mindful body." The sensory turn complicates this merger, by redirecting attention to the mix. For example, in Buddhist philosophy the mind is regarded as a sixth sense, hence on a par with the other senses rather than occupying a privileged position over and above the body and senses (Howes 2009, 27); some traditions do insist on a bipartite (body/mind), tripartite (body/mind/soul), or quadripartite, etc., schema. What is more, sensory studies scholars are interested in investigating how the senses are distinguished from one another and how they may conflict, and not simply how they merge in some putative "synergic system" or "prereflective unity" (Merleau-Ponty 1962; Ingold 2000). Thus, sense-based inquiries attend to the differential elaboration or hierarchization and modulation of the senses in history and across cultures.

Finally, the sensory turn crystalized at roughly the same time as two other paradigm shifts – namely, the *material turn* and the *affective turn*. The former emphasized the material underpinnings of social life and has important things to say about the agency of objects, materials, and environments (Appadurai 1983; Dant 1999, 2005; Tilley et al. 2006). The latter undermined the hegemony of reason in social and political life and has unleashed a torrent of speculation concerning precognitive triggers and affective intensities – or, in short, the *visceral* (Manalansan 2005; Longhurst, Johnston, and Ho 2009; Panagia 2009; Trnka et al. 2013). It can prove difficult to disentangle the material, affective, and sensory shifts. For example, the term "feeling" resonates in both sensory studies (as tactility) and affect studies (as affectivity). Unpacking the meaning and spelling out the implications of this amorphous and highly fluid notion of "feeling" is best approached from both of these perspectives – the affective and the sensitive.

Summing up all these strands of thought, in "Foundations for an Anthropology of the Senses," Constance Classen observed that when we examine the meanings vested in different sensory faculties and sensations across cultures

> we find a cornucopia of potent sensory symbolism. Sight may be linked to reason or to witchcraft, taste may be used as a metaphor for aesthetic discrimination or for sexual experience, an odour may signify sanctity or sin, political power or social exclusion. Together, these sensory meanings and values form the *sensory model* espoused by a society, according to which the members of that society "make sense" of the world ... There will likely be challenges to this model from within the society, persons and groups who differ on certain sensory values [and practices], yet this model will provide the basic perceptual paradigm to be followed or resisted. (Classen 1997, 402)

Classen's introduction of the seminal concept of the *sensory model* dovetails with the recent recuperation of another notion – that of the *sensorium*. This notion had been obscured beneath the neurological reductionism and mentalism that took hold as a result of the cognitive revolution in modern psychology (as will be discussed in chapter 3). The idea of the sensorium was both physiological and cosmological in its original definition. It referred primarily to the "percipient centre," or "seat of sensation in the brain," and still carries this sense today. But it also extended to include what could be called the circumference of perception. In illustration of the latter point, the *Oxford English Dictionary* quotes one usage from 1714: "The noblest and most exalted Way of considering this infinite Space [referring to 'the Universe'] is that of Sir Isaac Newton, who calls it the *Sensorium* of the Godhead"; and another from 1861: "Rome became the common sensorium of Europe, and through Rome all the several portions of Latin Europe sympathized and felt with each other." This expanded sense (cosmological and social) of the term "sensorium" had been all but lost until the media theorist Walter J. Ong retrieved it in a little section of *The Presence of the Word* (1967) entitled "The Shifting Sensorium," which was in turn reprinted as the lead chapter in *The Varieties of Sensory Experience* (Howes 1991). Building on Marshall McLuhan's notion of cultures as manifesting contrasting "sense-ratios" in accordance with the prevailing media of communication (e.g., speech that privileges the ear versus writing or print that privilege the eye), Ong proposed that "given sufficient knowledge of the sensorium exploited within a specific culture, one could probably define the culture as a whole in all its aspects," including its cosmology or "world view" (Ong 1991, 28). The implication is that perception is not just "down to our DNA" (Hollingham 2004), nor does it just go on "in some secret grotto in the head" (Geertz 1986, 113). It is also up to our culture, for as Oliver Sacks once said, "culture tunes our neurons" (cited in Howes 2005b, 22). Hence, as Ong (1991, 26) proposed in "The Shifting Sensorium": "the sensorium is a fascinating focus for cultural studies."

Ong's remark hints at an alternative genealogy of and for the sensory turn in contemporary scholarship. In addition to unfolding along the disciplinary trajectories discussed above, which gave rise to such subfields as the anthropology of the senses, history of the senses, sociology of the senses, and so forth, sensory studies can be conceptualized along sensory lines as divisible into visual culture, auditory culture (or sound studies), smell culture, taste culture, and the culture of touch. There is much to commend the latter framework, as we shall see, though it also raises certain questions.

The "fascination" (Ong 1991) that the study of the sensorium holds for cultural studies is exemplified by the rich profusion of readers, handbooks, and introductions that started appearing in the 1990s and continues unabated. A key text in this connection is *Aroma: The Cultural History of Smell* (Classen et al. 1994), which advanced the history, anthropology, and sociology of olfaction in one comprehensive and groundbreaking move. We shall come back to this work presently, after noting how the other senses were stirring.

The publication of *Visual Culture: The Reader* (Evans and Hall 1999) started a trend that generated *Visual Sense: A Cultural Reader* (Edwards and Bhaumik 2008), *Practices of Looking: An Introduction to Visual Culture* (Sturken and Cartwright 2008), *The Handbook of Visual Culture* (Heywood and Sandywell 2011), and *Global Visual Cultures: An Anthology* (Kocur 2011), among other works. The publication of *The Auditory Culture Reader* (Bull and Back [2003] 2016) opened the way for *The Oxford Handbook of Sound Studies* (Pinch and Bijsterveld 2011), *The Sound Studies Reader* (Sterne 2012), *The Routledge Companion to Sound Art* (Cobussen et al. 2017), *The Routledge Companion to Sound Studies* (Bull 2018), and *The Bloomsbury Handbook of the Anthropology of Sound* (Schulze 2021).

Tracing the genealogy of the sense-specific subfields of sensory studies brings out a different array of foundational works, or "overtures." For example, the origin of visual culture studies is usually traced either to John Berger's *Ways of Seeing* (1972), or to Michael Baxandall's *Painting and Experience in 15th Century Italy* (1972) and Svetlana Alpers' *The Art of Describing: Dutch Art in the Seventeenth Century* (1983) (see further Sturken and Cartwright 2009; M. Smith 2007b). From its cradle in art history, visual culture quickly spread to encompass film, television, fashion, advertising, and architecture. The invention of visual culture was famously responsible for toppling the hierarchical division between "high" and "low" (or "popular") culture. What is not so often recognized is how visual culture studies contributed to reproducing and further entrenching the hierarchical division of the senses. The rapid uptake and exponential growth of visual culture can be explained in part by reference to vision being first among the senses in the West. If an attack on "the hegemony of the text" or "the prisonhouse of language" was to come, it was (culturally) inevitable that it would come from the angle of vision. Paradoxically, however, the vaunted status of vision also smuggled in a certain blindness with respect to the multisensory character of most human experience: vision, being the paragon sense, could stand for all the senses, with the result that the "other" senses were easily ignored or assimilated to a visual model. Indeed, the proliferation of visual culture studies has been challenged by some. For example, there are those who question the ranging of architecture with visual culture because of how this deflects attention from the acoustic, tactile, thermal, and other sensory qualities of buildings (Palasmaa 1996; Blesser and Salter 2009; Ong 2012).

The subfield of sound studies can be seen as having its origin in the notion of the "soundscape," which was coined by the maverick Canadian composer and "acoustic ecologist" R. Murray Schafer in the 1970s (Schafer 1977). The idea of an "auditory turn" was theorized by art historian Douglas Kahn in "Digits on the Historical Pulse" (2002). In an essay entitled "How Sound Is Sound History?" Renaissance literary scholar Bruce R. Smith reflected on the principles that hold the field of sound studies (or auditory culture) together:

> At least three principles in particular seem to unite [sound studies practitioners] across their disciplinary differences: (1) They agree that sound has been neglected as an object of study; (2) they believe that sound offers a fundamentally different knowledge of the world than vision; and (3) they recognize that most academic disciplines remain vision-based, not only in the materials they study, but in the theoretical models they deploy to interpret them. (2004, 390–1)

All three of Smith's points are valid. At the same time, his account occludes the deeper historical reasons for the momentum behind the auditory turn. Hearing is "the second sense" (after sight) in the conventional Western hierarchy of the senses (Burnett, Fend, and Gouk 1991). Thus, if an attack on "the hegemony of vision" or "precession of the image" (vis-à-vis reality) was to come, it was (culturally) inevitable that it would come from the angle of sound and hearing. Put another way, were it not for the pictorial turn, there might have been no auditory turn: for just as the pictorial turn questioned the privileging of linguistic models and the idea of culture "as text" by exposing the increasing salience of visual cognition and communication in contemporary culture, so the auditory turn arose as a corrective to the overemphasis on the visual entrained by the pictorial turn – that is, it was motivated in no small part by a "critique" or "rejection of visualism." Thus, we can discern a constant jostling among the faculties in the development of sensory studies, as each faculty hove into view only to become a target for critique from the standpoint of the next faculty in the hierarchy.

There is no Archimedean point, independent of any culture or period, from which to conceptualize the bounds of sense, or assess the different senses' contribution to the advancement of knowledge. This makes it a matter of first importance to reflect on the sensory biases embedded in mainstream Western thought and culture, instead of taking such biases, or essentialisms, as given. The influence of these biases can be rendered perceptible and moderated to a significant degree by cultivating the capacity to "be of two sensoria" – one's own and that of the culture or period under study, and continuously tacking back and forth between them (Howes 2003, 10–14). To develop such a hyperacute awareness of sensory difference does not come easily. It requires a high degree of discipline, attunement, and reflexivity, or being in and out of one's own body and senses at once. But for all the cognitive dissonance that being of two sensoria might entail, it is crucial to the successful pursuit of "sensuous scholarship" (Stoller 1997).

The field of tactile culture studies was nurtured by Ashley Montagu's *Touching: The Human Significance of the Skin* ([1971] 1986), even with all that work's shortcomings from a historical and cross-cultural perspective. These lacunae, which stemmed from Montagu's overemphasis on physiology, were corrected in Claudia Benthien's *Skin: On the Cultural Border between Self and the World* (2002), Constance Classen's *The Book of Touch* (2005a) and *The Deepest Sense* (2012), and David Parisi's *Archaeologies of Touch* (2018), thanks to these authors' resolutely cultural approach to the description and analysis of haptic experience. The field of "skin studies" (which overlaps to a considerable extent with the culture of touch) has also blossomed in the ensuing period (see Lafrance 2012 and 2018 for an overview).

It is more difficult to pinpoint an urtext for the domain of taste culture studies, although Pierre Bourdieu's *Distinction: A Social Critique of the Judgment of Taste* ([1979] 1984) and the chapters on food in Mary Douglas' *In the Active Voice* (1982) would certainly figure in any such genealogy (see Sutton 2010). The philosopher Carolyn Korsmeyer consolidated the field of taste culture studies by editing *The Taste Culture Reader* ([2005] 2016) in which she expanded her earlier work on taste and philosophy (Korsmeyer 1999) into a sociology, anthropology, and history of gustation. The companion interdisciplinary field of food studies, which was strangely oblivious to considerations of taste in its first two decades (see Sutton 2010 and Hamilakis 2014), has also become significantly more flavourful in recent years (e.g., Bégin 2016; Rhys-Taylor 2017; Counihan and Høglund 2018).

Smell was first constituted as an object of multidisciplinary investigation in *Aroma: The Cultural History of Smell* (Classen et al. 1994). *Aroma* devoted equal space to the history, anthropology, and sociology of olfaction. Part 1 of *Aroma*, which is entitled "In Search of Lost Scents," delves into the significance of odour in antiquity (ch. 1) and then "follows the scent" from the Middle Ages to modernity (ch. 2). Part 2, "Explorations in Olfactory Difference," investigates the universes of odour or "osmologies" of a range of African, Asian, Melanesian, and Indigenous Latin American societies (ch. 3) before turning to consider the ritual uses of smell (ch. 4). Part 3, "Odour, Power, and Society," brings a critical perspective to bear on the politics of smell. It highlights how olfaction is mobilized in the interests of social inclusion and exclusion and also analyses the unevenness to its distribution – smell pollution (ch. 5). The final chapter is entitled "The Aroma of the Commodity: The Commercialization of Smell." It addresses such topics as the problematization of body odour, gender stereotyping and perfumery, the fragrancing of products, and the trademarking of scents.

Aroma concludes by offering a series of reflections on the connection between olfaction and the postmodern condition. It notes the manner in which smell, denied and ignored by scholars of modernity, has attained a new lease on life in late modernity. For example, odour, being by nature personal and local, enables olfactory values to be used to reinforce social intimacy and distancing. Another key feature is that smells resist containment in discrete units, "they cross borders, linking disparate categories and confusing boundary lines" (Classen et al. 1994, 205) in a manner consistent with the privileging of pastiche and promiscuity under postmodernism. Finally, the exponential growth of the artificial flavour and fragrance industry betokens the arrival of the "Age of the Simulacrum" wherein the world has come to be "completely catalogued and analyzed and then artificially revived as though real" (Baudrillard 1983, 16). Yet,

> Postmodernity ... in no way allows for a full range of olfactory expression. Odours are rather eliminated from society and then reintroduced as packaged agents of fantasy, a means of recovering or recreating a body, an identity, a world, from which one has already been irrevocably alienated. The question is, will smell, seduced by an endless procession of olfactory simulacra, succumb to its postmodern fate, or will it – ever elusive – transcend its postmodern categorization to remind us of our organic nature and even hint at a realm of the spirit. (Classen et al. 1994, 205)

Aroma opened the way for numerous subsequent sociohistorical studies of the power of smell. These include Jim Drobnick's *The Smell Culture Reader* (2006), Kelvin Low's *Scent and Scent-sibilities* (2009), Holly Dugan's *The Ephemeral History of Perfume* (2011), James McHugh's *Sandalwood and Carrion* (2012), William Tullett's *Smell in Eighteenth-Century England: A Social Sense* (2019), Mark Smith's *Smell and History: A Reader* (2019), and Hsuan Hsu's *The Smell of Risk: Environmental Disparities and Olfactory Aesthetics* (2020b).

This alternative genealogy of sensory studies (by sense rather than by discipline) is provisional. It will require further elaboration. Even in this provisional form, however, it raises interesting questions. Why the unevenness to the development of these subfields – that is, why are some senses (e.g., sight, hearing) better represented than others (e.g., smell, touch)? What is the role of institutions in maintaining and/or changing the current "distribution of the sensible" (Rancière 2004)? How else might the sensorium be divided for purposes of cultural analysis? What of the senses beyond the customary five, such as the sixth sense (Howes 2009), the seventh sense (Kivy 2003), etc.? And, perhaps most pressing, while it remains customary to speak of "turns" when describing these openings – as in "the pictorial turn" (Mitchell [1992] 1994; Curtis 2010), "the auditory turn" (Kahn 2002), and so on – might it not be time to think of this quickening of the senses as more in the nature of a revolution (Howes 2006)?

While it is only possible to recognize visual culture, sound studies, taste culture, etc., as flowing into sensory studies in retrospect (since the term "sensory studies" did not exist, or was not used in this way, prior to 2006 [see Bull et al. 2006]), it is nevertheless apparent that these previously independent streams now form a vast, fast-flowing river. Indeed, it could be argued that the sensory turn now rivals the aforementioned linguistic, pictorial, corporeal, and material turns in terms of its impact on scholarship in the humanities and social sciences. Rather than being just another turn, then, the uptake of the senses across the humanities and social sciences *is* revolutionary.

Insofar as one major impetus behind the sensory revolution was to liberate the study of sense perception from the psychology laboratory and insert it (back) into society by insisting on the historicity and sociality of sensation, it has succeeded, as the wealth of literature surveyed in the chapters that follow will attest. However, there remain many important issues to be addressed. One of these concerns theorizing the interactivity of the senses. This problem can be illustrated by considering an observation Bruce R. Smith makes in passing in *The Acoustic World of Early Modern England* (1999) to the effect that, in the early modern period, it was thought that a person's handwriting might carry the sound of the writer's voice. This observation illustrates how the interface of the senses (here, sight and hearing) deserves no less attention than their specificity as modalities of perception.

To cite another example, many premodern thinkers (following Aristotle) viewed taste as "a form of touch" whereas in the modern period taste is commonly seen as most closely connected to smell (i.e., a fellow chemical sense). To add a cross-cultural twist: among the Dogon of Mali, sound and odour are understood to have a common origin in vibration (Howes and Classen 1991, 268), and the "vibration theory" of olfaction also has a few proponents in contemporary Western culture (e.g., Turin 2006; Burr 2002). However, it is sound and touch, the audible and the palpable, that are now seen as having the greatest overlap, in terms of vibration (Connor 2004; Trower 2012; Eidsheim 2015). Finally, there is the example of synaesthesia, the "union of the senses," which takes many different forms, and also scrambles conventional notions of the senses as discrete channels. Thus, charting the relations among the senses, and how these relationships shift over time, should occupy us no less than seeking to fathom the depths of each of the senses in any given historical period or culture.

All of these variations to the individuation and/or integration of the senses underscore the importance of adopting a *relational* approach to the study of the divisions of the sensorium and attending to the role of culture in shaping how the senses are constructed and lived. This was, in fact, the starting point of *Empire of the Senses: The Sensual Culture Reader* (Howes 2005b), the inaugural volume of the Sensory Formations series, and it is also the premise underpinning this Manifesto. This relational focus is given in the notion of "intersensoriality." This term refers to how the relations between the senses, and the correspondence or conflicts amongst their deliverances (colours, sounds, perfumes, etc.), are constituted differently in different societies and epochs. It bears noting that this focus on intersensory relations dovetails with an important opening in contemporary experimental psychology. Alongside the traditional unimodal or one-sense-at-a-time, one-sensation-at-a-time approach to the study of sense perception, there has emerged a new focus on the interaction and integration of the senses in perceptual processes. This multimodal approach has been pioneered by Charles Spence, who heads up the Crossmodal Research Laboratory at Oxford University. Spence's work will figure centrally in the discussion in chapter 3.

Sensualizing Theory

The senses are our means of perception. As the psychologist Rudolf Arnheim (1969) showed in *Visual Thinking*, they are also our means of cognition. In contrast to the view that vision is the handmaiden of cognition, in this book Arnheim advanced a theory of thinking as a continuation of seeing. This interpretation holds well for Western thought and culture, but as the sensory anthropologist would be quick to point out, it immediately comes to grief when it is extended to such other, more "ear-minded" cultures as that of the Suyà of Brazil, who associate knowing with hearing (Seeger 1975, 1981), or "nose-minded" cultures like that of the Ongee of the Andaman Islands (Classen

1993b, ch. 6). The Ongee will refer to themselves by pointing to their nose and ask "How is your smell?" when they greet each other. They navigate the forest by sniffing and are careful to "bind" their smell to their bodies (so as not to attract the attention of jealous spirits, themselves scentless). Furthermore, their calendar is "a calendar of scents." Thus, personhood, space, and time are all theorized through the sense of smell among the Ongee.

The orchestration of the senses in Suyà as in Ongee culture does not line up with any of the customary ways in which the senses have been arranged in the history of Western culture. Recognizing this fact and striving to "lead with the senses" in our research, rather than some hypostatized notion of cognition and the primacy of vision, can open our minds to myriad other ways of sensing and making sense of the world.

Leading with the senses also has implications for how we theorize the senses (and much else, for that matter). The term "theory" comes from the Greek *theōria*, which means "a beholding, speculation" according to the *Concise Etymological Dictionary of the English Language* – that is, theory means "to look at." This imports a visual bias into the basis of theory-building, whatever its object (e.g., the senses, society, the cosmos). What if theorizing had to do with sensualizing rather then visualizing phenomena? To sensualize theory would involve opening a space in which other senses could come to the fore. It would mean upending the conventional Western hierarchy of the senses and establishing a democracy of the senses, or, if that is too much to hope for, at least a heterarchy of the senses, in its place. The time has come for overhauling theory in the interests of sensualizing its practice – that is, for acknowledging the senses (all of them, not just vision) as potentially "direct theoreticians in practice."[3]

Manifesto for Sensory Studies

To pursue this notion of the senses as theoreticians, I would like to propose a set of twelve propositions for sensory studies (inspired by Heywood and Sandywell's example in *The Handbook of Visual Culture* [2011, ch. 29]). The first few propositions are expressed negatively to underscore the extent to which they depart from the received wisdom about the senses (and language) in Western philosophy and culture. The last few propositions are expressed in the active (and also affirmative) voice. They bring out the sociality of sensations, and highlight a series of topics in the expanding field of sensory studies to be explored in depth in the chapters that follow.

1 The senses are not simply passive receptors. They are *interactive*, both with the world and each other.
2 The senses overlap and collaborate, but they may also conflict. The unity of the senses should not be presupposed.[4]

3 Language influences perception, but it is equally true that the senses infuse language with sense. The senses come before language and also extend beyond it.[5]

4 Perception is not solely a mental or neurobiological or individual phenomenon. "The perceptual is *cultural and political*."[6]

5 There is no Archimedean point, independent of culture or history, from which to gauge the bounds of sense or assess the different senses' contribution to the advancement of knowledge.

6 The rise of sensory studies has precipitated a shift from a focus on the organs of perception to *practices* of perception, or *techniques* of the senses, *ways* of sensing. Approached from this standpoint, "the senses are infinite and innumerable."[7]

7 "*The senses are everywhere.*"[8] They mediate the relationship between idea and object, mind and body, self and society, culture and environment.

8 Every society and historical period elaborates its own ways of understanding and using the senses. No one sensory model will fit all.

9 No account of the senses in society can be complete without due attention being paid to sensory discrimination. It is here, in particular, that the necessity of going beyond an examination of sensory techniques to investigate underlying sensory models and social systems is revealed to be essential.

10 Sensory critique is the beginning of social critique.[9]

11 The methodologies of sensory studies are grounded in "feeling along with others what they experience" (sensory ethnography), "sensing between the lines" (sensory history), and "research-creation" (or arts-based research), which is situated "between art and science." All of these sense-based methods and others disturb our conventional habits of perception, and lead to the discovery of other modes of being and knowing.[10]

12 As advocated throughout this Manifesto, there is a growing urge and increasing need for more crosstalk among the disciplines regarding the culture-nature of sense perception and action.

Origin of This Work

The idea for this Manifesto was first planted in my head at a talk I attended in the Senior Common Room at Trinity College, Toronto, in 1979. The talk was presented by Marshall McLuhan and was entitled "Laws of Media." I was intrigued by McLuhan's notion of cultures as embodying contrasting "sense-ratios" determined by the prevailing medium of communication (most notably speech, which privileges the ear vs. writing and print, which privilege the eye). A decade later, when I went to Papua New Guinea, I had the opportunity to explore the relevance of McLuhan's hypothesis within the context of two predominantly "oral" communities (as will be recounted in chapter 5).

That initial idea has been nurtured by my collaboration with diverse scholars, most notably the cultural historian Constance Classen, co-author of *Aroma* (1994) and *Ways of Sensing* (2014), among other works; the sociologist Anthony Synnott, co-founder of the Concordia Sensoria Research Team (1988–); the media theorist Michael Bull, co-founding editor of *The Senses and Society* (2006–); Chris Salter (Design Art), co-creator of a series of "performative sensory environments"; and Bianca Grohmann (Marketing), co-director of the Centre for Sensory Studies (2016–).

Chapters 1 and 2 build on the survey of research in the anthropology and geography, and history and sociology, of the senses that I posted on the Sensory Studies website in 2013 under the title "The Expanding Field of Sensory Studies" (www.sensorystudies.org). This overview was keyed to book-length studies published or translated into English and the occasional synthetic journal article.[11] This material was reworked to form the subject matter of the introductions to the first two volumes of the *Senses and Sensation: Critical and Primary Sources* compendium (originally published by Bloomsbury in 2018 and later transferred to Routledge). The other two volumes in the *Senses and Sensation* set include one on "Biology, Psychology and Neuroscience" and one on "Art and Design." The introductions to all four volumes of *Senses and Sensation* have been reprised and revised to form the basis of chapters 1, 2, 3, and 6 of this Manifesto.[12]

Outline of the Book

Part 1 of this Manifesto consists of three chapters. Chapter 1 documents the sensorial revolution within the disciplines of anthropology and geography. Chapter 2 traces how this paradigm shift unfolded within the disciplines of history and sociology. Chapter 3 interrogates the disciplining of the senses within experimental psychology and cognitive neuroscience from an orthogonal angle, informed by the insights of sensory studies. Each of the aforementioned chapters is divided into two sections. The first section is called "Laying the Foundations" and presents a genealogy of sensory studies by discipline. The second is called "Probes," on which more in a moment. Read together, these chapters offer a Grand Tour of research in sensory studies, which is also quite intense, due to the formidable dynamism of sensuous scholarship in the humanities and social sciences since the 1990s.

Part 2, "Case Studies," opens with a chapter entitled "The Modern Sensorium," which presents a case study in the cultural history of the senses, with a particular focus on how the senses were fashioned and refashioned during the period 1920–2001. The ensuing chapter, "Melanesian Sensory Formations," offers a comparative case study in the anthropology of the senses, centring on the field research that I carried out in two regions of Papua New Guinea in the early 1990s. In effect, these two chapters substantiate the theoretical reflections of previous chapters by engaging in what Michael Herzfeld (2001) calls "a practice of theory" or "theoretical practice." Their focus is on research "with" the senses instead of "on" or "about" the senses – that is, on "doing sensory history" by sensing between the lines of historical sources and on "doing sensory ethnography" by striving to sense and make sense together with others (which is one way of describing the methodology of *participant sensation* employed here).

Part 3, "Multisensory Aesthetics," also consists of three chapters. The discussion in chapter 6 links back up with the discussion in the chapters of Part 1. It offers a genealogy of research on the senses in the history of art and design. The two ensuing chapters introduce a further shift – from research (Herzfeld's "theoretical practice" or "practice of theory") to *research-creation*. Research-creation "combines discursive, analytic and critical theories and methods from the social sciences and humanities with the embodied, experimental and situated practices of creative artistic expression producing new ways of knowing and being."[13] By uniting artistic expression, scholarly investigation, and material experimentation, research-creation opens up a space "between art and science" (Born and Barry 2010; Sormani et al. 2018; Galison and Jones 2014) or "between art and anthropology" (Schneider and Wright 2010; Elliott and Culhane 2017).

The museum has emerged as a prime site for such experimentation, as recounted in chapter 7, "Sensory Museology." Curators use the medium of objects in place of monographs or films to engage not only the intellects but also the senses of their visitors in knowledge production and/or transfer. Chapter 8 shifts the focus from curating to creating. Among other things, it recounts my experience of the end-of-term production put on by the Fine Arts students in a course directed by R. Murray Schafer called "The Theatre of the Senses"; of creating a scent called "Sacred Now" in collaboration with a perfumer at International Flavors and Fragrances. Inc. (not your ordinary academic output); and of collaborating with new media artist Chris Salter to design and evaluate audience response to a series of "performative sensory environments" (i.e., multimodal installation artworks). In the performative sensory environment, art comes off the wall, immersion takes the place of representation, the senses are rearranged, and the visitor gets to try out new ways of knowing and being.

Probing the Senses, the Senses as Probes

One of the novel features of this Manifesto is the "Probes" sections that take up the latter half of chapters 1, 2, 3, and 6. There is some resemblance in the architecture of these sections to such works as *Key Debates in Anthropology* (Ingold 1996) or Raymond Williams' *Keywords* (1976). However, I chose to call these sections "Probes" with a tip of the hat to Marshal McLuhan. In my estimation, with some caveats (to be discussed later), McLuhan theorized the senses more capaciously than any other scholar. The probes also evince McLuhan's style of thinking, which he described as "mosaical." Indeed, McLuhan railed against the strictures of linear perspective vision in painting just as he railed against the linealization of thought brought on by the technology of repeatable type – both inventions of the Renaissance. His alternative model of the "collideroscope" of the sensorium can only be evoked mosaically. Expanding on that model, through and by bringing multiple disciplinary lenses to bear on the study of the senses and sensation, holds great promise for advancing the extrapsychological take on "sensory processing" advocated in this Manifesto.

In these sections, then, my aim is to probe the wisdom on the senses that has been built up within each of the disciplines concerned, and also use the senses as probes to trouble that wisdom. The selection of topics is based on my first-hand knowledge of the field, as co-director of the Concordia Centre for Sensory Studies and chief organizer of the Uncommon Senses conference series, general editor of the Sensory Formations and Sensory Studies book series, and managing editor (a mission I share with Michael Bull) of *The Senses and Society*, the premier journal in the field.

Here is an overview of the topics to be probed.

1   *Ontology.* The "ontological turn" in the human sciences, particularly within anthropology, has resulted in the jettison of the idea of there being one nature and many cultures and introduced the notion of "multinatures" in its place. While this shift has generated many keen insights, the precession of ontology (or science of "what is") has precipitated a recession in reflection on just "how" we know what is (i.e., epistemology or "know-how"). This subsection argues for the reintroduction of a concern with sensuous epistemologies and sensory cosmologies.

2   *Emplacement.* The notion of emplacement is of central concern to geography, where it goes under the name of landscape studies. This probe argues that it could usefully be taken up by other disciplines for the way this notion directs attention to the *situatedness* of the mind-body in a particular locale (mind-body-environment) and brings out how context alters perception.

3   *Materiality.* The understanding of materiality that has emerged out of studies in material culture has brought to light the social agency of objects, infrastructures, and environments. This probe argues that the focus on materiality needs to be augmented by attention to the sensoriality of things to arrive at a full-bodied understanding of living in the material world.

4   *Memory.* Memory emerged as a prime topic for sociological, and not just psychological, investigation with the publication of *How Societies Remember* (Connerton 1989). In addition to foregrounding the sociality of

memory, this subsection pries open the materiality of memory. Probing the sociality and materiality of memory explodes the supposition that memory is basically a cognitive faculty. It should rather be regarded as embedded in the distribution of the sensible.

5 *Alterity*. Othering by means of the senses (i.e., sensory discrimination) is at the core of processes of social inclusion and exclusion. It therefore calls out for sociological investigation. This probe brings out the role of perception – socially conditioned perception, that is – in the constatation of alterity.

6 *Mediation*. McLuhan sent communication studies off in some highly productive directions by suggesting that media be regarded as "extensions of the senses." But there are difficulties with the technological determinism and essentialism of his position. This probe will seek to expose and resolve them.

7 *Affect*. The affective turn crystalized at roughly the same time as the sensory turn. There is both overlap and antagonism to the way these two paradigms – namely, affect studies and sensory studies – approach diverse phenomena. This subsection probes how the two schools can be reconciled.

8 *Movement*. There is an overwhelming stillness to the way in which the perceiving subject has been pictured in the largely spectatorial tradition of Western philosophy. This stillness, and the focus on the individuation of the senses, has been shattered by an emergent focus on the motility of the body and senses, and the idea of perception as enaction (not representation), which constitutes the focus of discussion in this subsection.[14]

9 *Representation*. An intense focus on representational practices and issues of "authority" erupted in the 1980s, and a "crisis of representation" ensued. It is not so well recognized how this crisis also precipitated a crisis in sensation, as documented in this subsection. The subsequent rise of "nonrepresentational theory," as treated in this probe, may be read as an effort to bring the senses back in.

10 *Gustation*. The emergence of taste culture studies together with the science of "gastrophysics" as theorized by Charles Spence has exploded the idea of taste as a singular sense. The experience of flavour has been shown to be a product of the conjunction of tasting with the tastebuds and retronasal olfaction and is also modulated by sound, visual presentation, and mouth feel. Further, taste is a social sense. Taste, then, turns out to be the *intersensorial* sense par excellence, and therefore a fitting focus for reflecting on the varieties of sensory/social interaction. It has its own epistemology, which can be called "gustemology" (Sutton 2010).

11 *Synaesthesia*. The phenomenon of synaesthesia – "secondary sensation caused by stimulation of another part of the body, such as accompanying sensations of colour with given sounds [i.e., coloured hearing]" (Rodaway 1994, 6) – has attracted a flurry of attention in recent years. The idea of the "union of the senses" has also generated a lot of confusion. Some scholars

maintain that it is congenital, others that it is cultural. This probe will examine both sides of the debate, and advance an intermediate position.

This assortment of probes is far from exhaustive of the range of current debates in the human sciences, though it is reasonably representative. At the same time, there is much that remains to be done and that needs to be done within sensory studies, including delving into the senses of non-human animals and, more generally, the "more-than-human sensorium."[15] It is also imperative to undertake a sense-based approach to the greatest crisis of our times – namely, the climate emergency. I humbly submit that this assortment of probes can provide a springboard for further reflection and directions for research into these and other areas.

Concluding Notes

Writing this Manifesto has proved to be tremendously rewarding. Practising what the anthropologist Paul Stoller (1989) calls "sensuous scholarship" is formidably illuminating and exhilarating, particularly when it simultaneously involves attending to what fellow scholars in related disciplines (history, geography, sociology, etc.) have accomplished in their own sensorial investigations. In my experience, disciplinary specialization always stands to be enriched when paired with a commitment to engaging in conversation across disciplines, since this in turn leads to the "enlargement of mind" that the philosopher Hannah Arendt extolls in her critique of judgment:

> Judgment, according to Hannah Arendt, is genuinely subjective ... But judgment is not therefore merely arbitrary or simply a matter of preference. Judgments, properly understood, are valid for the judging community ... What makes it possible for us to genuinely judge, to move beyond our private idiosyncrasies and preferences, is our capacity to achieve an "enlargement of mind." We do this by taking different perspectives into account. This is the path out of the blindness of our subjective private conditions ... we imagine trying to persuade others. (Nedelsky 1997, 107)

Exploring the senses across disciplines and cultures involves just such an "enlargement of mind" – to accommodate other ways of making sense.

In this Manifesto, I have aspired to be judicious to the senses, to sense-based research across the human sciences, and to the recent surge in sensory experimentation in the studio and the museum. When the life of the senses is examined from all these different angles, the sensible is rendered that much more intelligible, but without losing any of its sensuousness.

This Manifesto, then, is at once a call for more correspondence among the disciplines concerning the senses and an inquiry into the correspondences of the senses themselves. It follows in the footsteps of the poet Baudelaire who, when he walked "the forest of symbols," discovered that "sounds, fragrances and colours correspond." Indeed, it would be "really surprising," the author of "Correspondences" proclaimed elsewhere, "if sound could *not* suggest color, if colors could *not* suggest a melody … things being always expressed by a reciprocal analogy." Nonetheless, "modern professors of aesthetics," according to Baudelaire (1978, 30), had "forgotten the color of the sky, the form of plants, the movement and odor of animals," and their "rigid fingers, frozen to their pens" were unable "to play over the immense keyboard of correspondences." It is important to be mindful of Baudelaire's rebuke to the professors – and to take up his challenge of becoming sensors – as we embark on this inquiry into the genealogy of sensory studies.

Sensory studies is not just a branch of aesthetics in the rarefied sense, however. It encompasses the full range of social practices and sites. Furthermore, sensations do not always correspond; oftentimes they clash and conflict. This contestation is analysed and described in the recent article "What does poverty feel like? Urban inequality and the politics of sensation" (Jaffe et al. 2020), which is all about "sense disruption," and *transgressing* "established hierarchies of socio-spatial value."

The social life of the senses is complex and diverse, and it requires a kaleidoscope of approaches to match the kaleidoscope of its modes of expression. The present work aims to bring out the correspondences and the congeries of this dynamic heterarchy of approaches and expressions, while presenting crucial guidelines for ensuring that the "sensorial revolution" achieves its full potential within both the human sciences and the creative arts.

PART ONE

The Sensorial Revolution in the Human Sciences

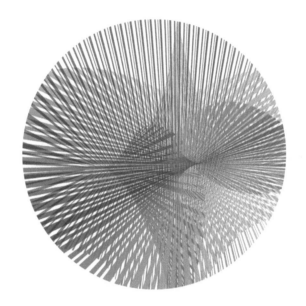

Collideroscope series (2022) © Erik Adigard, M-A-D

CHAPTER ONE

On the Geography and Anthropology of the Senses

The first two disciplines to be considered in this genealogical survey of the sensory revolution in the human sciences are geography and anthropology. The geography of the senses is concerned with mapping sensory diversity in space, while the anthropology of the senses traces the varieties of sensory experience across cultures. In the former, the focus is on how different environments shape perception, and how space becomes place through sensory interaction with differing surroundings, both natural and built. In the latter, the emphasis is on the enculturation of the senses, and how the differing ways in which the senses are constructed and lived generate distinct sensory worlds.

In section 1, the focus will be on identifying the foundational texts that framed the senses as both object of study and means of inquiry from the early 1990s on. However, it would be remiss to overlook what could be called the "overtures" to the senses in the geographical and anthropological literature of earlier decades. As we shall see, an interest in the senses and sense perception dates back to the very origins of the two disciplines, only to be discarded and then revived on an altogether different, more cultural footing in the 1990s.

In section 2, a series of eleven probes is offered. The discussion in these subsections is keyed to such concepts as *ontology* and *affect* and such topics as *alterity* and food or *gustation* as framed in the human sciences with a view to disclosing what sensory ethnography and sensuous geography bring to their critique, or better, their *sensualization*. This move contrasts with the abiding interest in "visualizing theory" in contemporary scholarship (e.g., Taylor 1994), which only compounds the visual bias inherent in "theory" (from *theoria*, looking at, gazing at) itself. We are familiar with the nexus between seeing, knowledge, and power or *voir, savoir, pouvoir* in French (after Foucault 1973, 1979). Digging deeper etymologically, we are able to unlock the connection between *saveur* and *savoir* in French, or *sapore* and *sapere* in Italian (Calvino 2005), which is actually integral to the archaic, more flavourful definition of humanity as *Homo sapiens* (Onians 1951, 61–3). Our collective theorizing stands to be enriched significantly by extending the practice of theorization to other senses besides sight.

I. Laying the Foundations

Geographical Overtures

The first scholar to explicitly theorize the senses in geography was Paul Rodaway in *Sensuous Geographies* (1994), though he himself points to the "perception geography" of the 1960s and 1970s as antecedents.[1] Actually, the history of geography's entanglement with the senses extends much further back than that. Indeed, the distinguished Irish geographer Anne Buttimer (2010, 12) has suggested that "multi-sensory attunement to the environment itself" can be seen to have informed the work of the discipline's two most illustrious founders: Alexander von Humboldt (1769–1859) and, a century later, Johannes Gabriel Granö (1882–1956). These two geographers were not regarded as founders at the time, of course, but only in retrospect.

Coincidentally, both Humboldt and Granö started out in botany, and both traversed Siberia (Granö repeatedly). However, it was the sensuousness of their approaches that truly distinguished the geography they practised. Buttimer quotes the following passages from Humboldt's *Ansichten der Natur* (1808) by way of illustration:

> The goals for which I strove were to depict nature in its prime traits, to find proof of the interworking of (natural) forces, and to achieve a sense of enjoyment which the immediate view gives to *sensitive man* … descriptions of nature impress us more or less according to the degree to which they agree with the needs of our feelings; for the physical world is mirrored vividly and truly in the *inner feelings*. Whatever is essential for the character of a landscape – the outlines of the mountains which limit the horizon in bluish, fragrant distance, the darkness of the fir forests, the forest-streams which rush between overhanging cliffs – all that is in old mysterious contact with the *inner life* of man. (quoted in Buttimer 2010, 22; emphasis added)

The Finnish scholar J.G. Granö's *Reine Geographie* (*Pure Geography*), published in 1929, was even more explicit (if rather less feelingful or Romantic) in its focus on the sensory as *the* medium of geography. In "The Background to *Pure Geography*" (1997), Olavi Granö (the son) and Anssi Paasi bring out well how, for J.G. Granö, the "real object" of geographical research is the environment that a human being perceives with the senses. Granö distinguished between the "proximity" or close-up environment, which is perceived and to be charted or described through multisensory modes (visual, auditory, olfactory, kinetic), and the distant environment or "landscape," which is perceived primarily through the visual sense. "If smells belong to a geographical complex, be it a landscape or a proximity, they must be studied and their value assessed" J.G. Granö insisted ([1929] 1997, 128). The same with sounds, textures, sights, and so on, he maintained, for only in this way could a geographical complex or "region" be delimited.

It is important to note that the one doing the sensing was not just any ordinary person, nor Humboldt's "sensitive man," but the "pure geographer" with scientifically disciplined senses, which Granö assumed would guarantee the objectivity of the observations. Alas, or perhaps fortunately, he was not always successful at upholding his own first principles, as Olavi Granö and Paasi note, and there are places in his writings where he waxed as eloquent as Humboldt. Also of note: Granö took his understanding of how the senses function directly from the psychophysics of his day. He did not question the account of perception that comes out of psychophysics, and so missed the opportunity to explore either how context alters perceptions, or all that the discipline of geography could have brought to psychology as regards the understanding of the spatial formation of the sensorium.

Granö's work, most notably his *Atlas of Finland* (1925), contributed substantially to the establishment of geography as a discipline in Finland and the German-speaking world. However, his insistence on the primacy of the sensate (i.e., the perceived environment as the basis for geographical study) was not well received, and even rebuffed. His sensorially grounded approach accordingly lay fallow for many decades, until the senses came back into focus in the 1990s, with the publication of Rodaway's *Sensuous Geographies*. Even then, the recovery of the senses within geography owed more to the influence of thinkers from other disciplines, such as the composer and "acoustic ecologist" R. Murray Schafer (1977), than to Granö himself. This is apparent in a seminal article by Douglas Pocock, "The Senses in Focus" (1993), that took many of its cues from Schafer's work. In an expansive move, Pocock also suggested that geographers should explore the wonderment of the child, the sensibilities of non-Western peoples, and the alternative sensoria of the blind and the deaf. Granö, with his idea of the "pure geographer," would probably have been perplexed at this suggestion, but as we shall see presently, sensory and cultural pluralism has become the touchstone of geography going forward.

Disciplining the Senses in Geography

Other factors that contributed to the (re)discovery of the senses in geography, according to Rodaway (1994, 6–9), included the rise of human or humanistic geography (the brainchild of Yi-Fu Tuan); the adoption of cultural, phenomenological, and ecological models of perception – all of which pointed to perception being "more qualitatively variable and creative than mechanistic stimulus-response models might suggest"; and the debates about postmodernism that convulsed academia in the 1980s, such as the controversy over "the redefinition of the 'real' and the position of the 'sign'" that was sparked by the writings of French postmodern theorist Jean Baudrillard.

The key insight of the geography of the senses is that the senses mediate the apprehension of space and in so doing contribute to our sense of place. Yi-Fu Tuan (1974) was the first to call attention to the spatiality of the senses and their role in shaping the affective relation of people to their habitat. "What begins as undifferentiated space becomes place as we get to know it better [through our senses] and endow it with value" (Tuan 1977, 6).

Primed by Tuan's work, some geographers started questioning the (presumed) transparency of concepts like that of landscape, and techniques of data gathering, like that of remote sensing (i.e., satellite-generated imagery). As regards the latter, J. Douglas Porteous (1990, 201) ventured that "Remote sensing is clean, cold, detached, easy. Intimate sensing ... is complex, difficult, and often filthy. The world is found to be untidy rather than neat. But intimate sensing is rich, warm, involved." For Porteous there was no question as to which methodology – remote sensing or intimate sensing – is more grounded in geographic reality and therefore to be trusted.

The concept of landscape was also interrogated. As the work of Denis Cosgrove ([1984] 1998), among others, had shown, the idea of landscape is rooted in a particular Western painterly and literary tradition – namely, the picturesque, with its reliance on the Claude glass and other technologies of vision (Maillet 2004; see further Broglio 2008). This ostensibly visualist bias led to the concept of landscape being bracketed and replaced by the more neutral term "sensescape." The latter concept was in turn broken down into "soundscape," "smellscape," "bodyscape," and so forth (Porteous 1990). This refinement stemmed from the recognition that "Each sense contributes [in its own way] to people's orientation in space; to their awareness of spatial relationships; and to the appreciation of the qualities of particular micro- and macro-spatial environments" (Urry [2003] 2011, 388). As a corollary to this, following Rodaway's lead in *Sensuous Geographies*, a number of geographers started taking note of the distinct ways in which different senses are "interconnected" with each other to produce a sensed environment. These ways include

cooperation between the senses; a *hierarchy* between different senses, as with the visual sense during much of the recent history of the West; a *sequencing* of one sense which has to follow on from another sense; a *threshold* of effect of a particular sense which has to be met before another sense is operative; and *reciprocal* relations of a certain sense with the object which appears to "afford" it an appropriate response. (Urry 2011, 388, summarizing Rodaway)

These reflections concerning the multiple modes of sensory interconnection are noteworthy for the way they highlight the relations *among* the senses, above and beyond their informational content.

The sensory turn in geography, signalled by Pocock and Rodaway and anticipated by Tuan, in turn precipitated a shift within the discipline from a focus on "spatial organization" (which mainly meant visualization) to one on "activity." Hayden Lorimer (2005) holds up Lisa Law's account of the sensory practices of migrant Filipino women in Hong Kong's domestic labour economy by way of example. Every Sunday the off-work domestic workers flock to Hong Kong Central (the vacated banking district) and literally occupy that space with their pop-up food stands, hair salons, etc. Hong Kong Central becomes "Little Manilla," if only for a day (Law 2005). As Lorimer observes, "it is [the *activity* of] sharing in the taste, smell and texture of food that offers comforting reminders of home and bonds of friendship. However, the practice of food preparation, its odours and eventual consumption in public spaces also offer grounds for ethnic discrimination and a contested urban geography" (H. Lorimer 2005, 87). Indeed, the Chinese citizens of Hong Kong look askance and turn up their noses at the weekly occupation of the banking district by their household servants. The point here is that the space remains the same, but it is reconstituted by the sensory *activity* that goes on within it.

Another emergent area is the "geography of rhythm" or "rhythmanalysis," which augments the conventional focus on the spatial within geography by attending to the interpellation of the temporal (e.g., the seasonal, or more broadly, the repetitional): "every rhythm implies the relation of a time with space, a localized time, or if you wish, a temporalized place" (Lefebvre cited in Edensor 2012, 57; Edensor 2010). A third especially salient overture in geographical study is the burgeoning interest in the idea of "atmosphere" (McCormack 2018). The term "atmosphere" foregrounds the multisensory character and experience of *lived* space (elemental envelopment) while downplaying the more formal aspects of environments.

This attentional shift has spilled over into cognate disciplines, such as architecture and urbanism (Palasmaa 1996; Zardini 2005). Designing buildings and planning cities has accordingly morphed from a visual-technocratic art into a sensuous science of creating atmospheres or (to use another current term) "ambiances."[2] Geographers have followed suit by devising ever more sensitive methods for registering sensescapes and also of critiquing the political and commercial interests that drive schemes of "urban renewal," gentrification, and the like (Degen 2008, 2014). The methods in question are typically of a populist, participatory nature and centre on walking (e.g., the soundwalk, smellwalk, touch tour, etc.) as opposed to the God's-eye view of the city planning bureaucrat (Paterson 2009; Degen and Rose 2012; Henshaw 2013; Polli 2017; Springgay and Truman 2019).

Another area of geography where a sensory studies approach has made inroads since the 1990s is that most venerable of geographical practices – mapmaking. The practice of cartography has metamorphosed from the production of two-dimensional scalar projections into cybercartography or "multisensory mapping." This development is partly due to advances in technology. But it is also inspired by a growing awareness of what the study of Indigenous knowledge systems, such as Inuit wayfinding (Aporta 2005, 2006), can contribute to our understanding of human spatial orientation. At the Geomatics and Cartographic Research Centre at Carleton University, under the direction of D.R. Fraser Taylor, there are many innovative cybercartographic forms being developed, which take their inspiration from Indigenous practice (see Taylor et al. 2018; Taylor and Lauriault 2013).

Two further developing areas of research include the geography of displacement and the geography of the insensible.[3] These areas have been pioneered by Joy Parr, who is the Canada Research Chair in Technology, Culture and Risk in the Department of Geography at the University of Western Ontario. Parr is the author of *Sensing Changes: Technologies, Environments and the Everyday, 1953–2003* (2010). In it she writes, "Our bodies are archives of sensory knowledge that shape how we understand the world. If our environment changes at an unsettling pace, how will we make sense of a world that is no longer familiar?" The geography of displacement concerns how people cope sensorially with being uprooted and relocated to make way for state-sponsored megaprojects such as hydroelectric dams (Parr 2010, ch. 2) as well as by war (Bunkše 2007). The geography of the insensible concerns how workers in nuclear power plants, for example, try in their own way to detect and protect themselves against radiation using their own un-aided senses in place of Geiger counters and other such devices (Parr 2010, ch. 3).

The emergence of "non-representational" – or better, "more-than-representational" – theory has also had a catalyzing effect on the deployment of the senses and sensory analysis in geographical study. Hayden Lorimer explains what the "more-than" here entails:

> To summarize lots of complex statements as simply as possible, it is multifarious, open encounters in the realm of practice that matter most. Greatest unity is found in an insistence on expanding our once comfortable understanding of "the social" and how it can be regarded as something researchable. This often means thinking through locally formative interventions in the world. At first, the phenomena in question may seem remarkable only by their apparent insignificance. (Lorimer 2005, 84)

This apparent insignificance or "everydayness" is, however, key. Lorimer continues:

> The focus [in sensory geography] falls on how life takes shape and gains expression in shared experiences, everyday routines, fleeting encounters, embodied

movements, precognitive triggers, practical skills, affective intensities, enduring urges, unexceptional interactions and sensuous dispositions. Attention to these kinds of expression, it is contended, offers an escape from the established academic habit of striving to uncover meanings and values that apparently await our discovery, interpretation, judgement and ultimate representation. In short, so much ordinary action gives no advance notice of what it will become. Yet, it still makes critical differences to our experiences of space and place. (Lorimer 2005, 84, citing Thrift 2004)

In addition to focussing attention on practices and ephemera, the more-than-representational turn has entrained a shift from the exteroceptive to the interoceptive or "visceral" (see Longhurst, Ho, and Johnston 2008; Longhurst, Johnston, and Ho 2009), as will be discussed below. It is an interesting question whether the emergent focus on the visceral recycles Humboldt's archaic notion of "the inner life of man" or represents a new departure.

Ethnological Overtures

The first scholar to theorize the senses in anthropology was Paul Stoller in *The Taste of Ethnographic Things* (1989). However, there were various overtures to the senses in the anthropological literature of previous decades. Indeed, these openings date back to the very foundations of the discipline. For example, a major preoccupation of the Société d'Anthropologie de Paris, led by Paul Broca, was the "measurement of the senses" of Indigenous peoples and mapping the supposedly innate differences in "sensory acuity" between "primitives" and moderns onto the brain (Dias 2004). The 1898 Cambridge Anthropological Expedition to the Torres Strait, led by A.C. Haddon and W.H.R. Rivers, was animated by a similar purpose: to verify the sundry reports of missionaries and colonial officials to the effect that "the black man could see and hear, etc., better than the white man" (Rivers 1901, 3). Meanwhile, Franz Boas, the founder of American anthropology, started out as a physicist and went to the Canadian Arctic to explore a range of questions having to do with the psychophysics of vision among the Inuit but there underwent a "conversion" to ethnology. This led him to reject the psychophysical, evolutionist, and racist perceptual theories of his contemporaries, and set anthropology on a different trajectory (Howes et al. 2018).

Claude Lévi-Strauss is another anthropologist who broke to some extent with evolutionist assumptions, and whose work is noteworthy for its *relational* approach to the study of the sensorium. In *The Savage Mind* ([1962] 1966), he introduced the notion of a "science of the concrete" – that is, a science of "tangible qualities" characteristic of the classificatory systems of traditional societies in contrast to the abstractions of modern physics, though no less rigorous. In the four-volume *Mythologiques*, he sought to decipher the "sensory codes" of Amerindian myth by tracing all the homologies and transformations within and between sensory registers that attended the transmission of myths across cultural borders from Tierra del Fuego to Vancouver Island (see especially the section called "Fugue of the Five Senses" in *The Raw and the Cooked* [1969] 1979).

In a conversation with Didier Eribon centring on the topic of "sensible qualities," Lévi-Strauss set out the "basic principle" of his approach (structural analysis) as follows:

> In order to be able to speak of structure, it is necessary for there to be invariant relationships between elements and relations among several sets, so that one can move from one set to another by means of a transformation ... [C]omponent parts have no intrinsic meaning: it [i.e., meaning] arises from their position. (Lévi-Strauss and Eribon 1988, 113)

This is the essence of "structural thinking." As we shall see presently, it is also the way sensual thinking works.

In "The Meaning of Body Ornaments" (1975), Anthony Seeger fleshed out the social concomitants of Lévi-Strauss' combinatorial understanding of the sensorium.[4] He found that among the various tribes of the Mato Grosso region of Brazil, the ornamentation of a sense organ (by means of ear-disc, lip-plug, eye makeup, nose pendant, penis sheath, etc.) was normally related to the symbolic meaning of the related faculty (hearing, speaking, seeing, etc.). The presence (suggesting elaboration) or absence (suggesting suppression) of these accoutrements or "extensions of the senses"[5] provided an index of the enculturation of the component parts of the sensorium. For example, among the Suyà, adult men wear ear-discs and lip-plugs and either blacken the occiput (which makes the eyes appear to recede) or leave them unadorned. This reflects the positive social valence attached to hearing and speaking and the mistrust or devaluation of sight. Significantly, witches are said to be possessed of extraordinary visual powers, hear poorly, and tend to mumble. Their sensorium is the inverse of that of the big man or chief who literally embodies the normative "sensory model" (Classen 1993b, 1997) through his adornments – the painted lip-plugs and ear-discs that extend his speech and hearing – and his diminished vision due to age.

Steven Feld's ethnomusicological writings, beginning with *Sound and Sentiment* (1982), anticipated both the sensory and affective turns in the human sciences by close to a decade. Feld (1996) introduced the concept of "acoustemology" by way of summing up his practice of listening in to the culture and environment of the Kaluli people of Papua New Guinea. By training his ears to pick up on all the nuances of local ways of producing and perceiving sound, he was able to discern the capital cultural importance of such auditory motifs as "lift-up-over sounding" and even hear the "inside" of a drumbeat (Feld 1991,

91–4). Feld is also the author of the theory of the "iconicity of style" or cross-modal correspondence and transposability of perceptual schema. (This theory could be read as a variation on Lévi-Strauss' notion of "invariants.") For example, he discerned a link between the layering of sound in the Kaluli singing style and the layering of paint and other accoutrements in their ceremonial costumes. Finally, Feld has produced many fine recordings of sounds ranging from the voices (both human and non-human) of the rainforest to bells, car horns, and glaciers melting. It was out of this shift in registers that an "anthropology of sound" was born (Feld and Brenneis 2004; Rice 2013).

Disciplining the Senses in Anthropology

Turning now from these overtures to a consideration of the foundational texts of the anthropology of the senses, we come to Paul Stoller's *The Taste of Ethnographic Things* (1989). Stoller is a master raconteur who, rather like Clifford Geertz in his famous Balinese cockfight article (Geertz 1973), typically starts with an incident and then puzzles over it, trying to make sense of it. For example, he relates an incident that involved him being served a bad-tasting sauce, *fukko hoy*, by the disgruntled daughter-in-law of one of his hosts: though the sauce tasted horrible, the incident made for "good ethnography" since it alerted him to the culinary codes of the Songhay (see Stoller and Olkes 2005). In another incident, Stoller confesses that he failed to hear the sound that a sick man's wayward soul supposedly made when the attendant sorcerer liberated it from a pile of rubble, and he relates how he was berated by the sorcerer for his inattention. Stoller cites the case of the inaudible (to him) sound that the soul gave off on being liberated to underscore the fundamental aurality of Songhay modes of perception and cultural expression. This led him to underscore the importance of transcending the "visualist" bias of Western thought and culture in order to connect with the cultural experience of non-Western subjects (see further Fabian 1983). The anthropology of the senses was thus initially inspired by a desire to explore under-investigated, non-visual modes of experience. It would later draw attention to the varying ways in which sight too is configured differently in different cultures (Howes 1991, chs. 13, 16, 17 and 2003, ch. 5; see also Eck 1998) including Western cultures (Grasseni 2007; Goodwin 1994). Thus, contrary to the picture some have painted (e.g., Ingold 2000), sensory anthropology does not involve mounting "a case against vision," nor does it entail shutting one's eyes, though it typically requires focussing them differently.[6]

The cultural anthropology of the senses as framed by Stoller stands in sharp contrast to the physical anthropology of the senses of the late nineteenth century – that is, the work of Broca in France and Haddon and Rivers in England. For one, the evolutionist and racist biases of Victorian anthropology had been exposed and extirpated (thanks to Boas' influence); for another, a focus on meaning supplanted the former fixation on measurement; third, attunement to the politics of perception took the place of psychophysics; and it is reflexivity rather than (supposedly) innate reflexes that occupy the contemporary sensory anthropologist's attention (Howes et al. 2018).

In its initial stages, during the closing decades of the twentieth century, sensory anthropology was also animated by a critique of the "verbocentrism" and "textualism" of then current anthropological theory. Anthropology had always been "a discipline of words" (Grimshaw 2001) insofar as anthropologists relied on interviews to gather data, and on monographs and journal articles to disseminate their findings. However, this bias was exacerbated in the anthropology of the early 1980s by the emphasis on "text" (e.g., cultures "as texts" or "discourse," ethnography "as a process of textualization," and so forth). The focus on the "interpretation of culture" (Geertz 1973) and *a fortiori* "writing culture" (Clifford and Marcus 1986) distracted attention from *sensing* cultures. A growing number of anthropologists felt the latter should take priority (Jackson 1989, ch. 3; Stoller 1989, 1997; Howes 1990a, 2003, ch. 2; Stahl 2008).

The introduction of "embodiment" as a paradigm for anthropology (Csordas 1990, 1994) together with Paul Stoller's (1997) call for "sensuous scholarship" helped galvanize the sensory turn by attuning anthropologists that much more acutely to how they could use their own bodies and senses as means of ethnographic analysis, and then write about their experience.[7] Various electronic devices, such as audio tape recorders and camcorders, also came to figure more and more centrally in the practice of ethnography during the last decades of the twentieth century and on into the twenty-first. While this development dealt a further blow to the language- and text-based models and methods of previous decades, it also imported a new set of biases to anthropological knowledge, giving it an audiovisual cast (though this is not often recognized). It had to be acknowledged that we make sense of the world not just through language, not just by talking about it, however "performative" such utterances may be, but *through all our senses*, and their *extensions* in the form of diverse media (Munn 1986; Taylor 1994; Seremetakis 1994b; Finnegan 2002; MacDougall 2005 and 2019; Howes 2016b). Furthermore, there are some places and some matters that the senses and sense-based media can reach that words cannot.

The liberating effect of this recognition is evident in the ensuing explosion of interest in "sensorial fieldwork" (Robben and Slukka 2007, part 8) or "sensory ethnography" (Pink 2009), as it is also known. Sensory ethnography experiments with multiple media for the registration and communication of cultural facts and theories (see Cox, Irving, and Wright 2016; Elliott and Culhane 2017; Collins, Durington, and Gill 2017; Howes 2019a). There is a lively internal debate over the limits and potentialities of, for example, the medium of film compared to that of writing (MacDougall 2005, 52; Howes 2003, 57–8 and 2012, 637–42), installation art compared to the conventional ethnographic exhibit (Grimshaw 2007; Schneider and Wright 2010; Drewal 2012; Howes and Salter 2015), and the medium of performance compared to the public lecture (Schechner 2001; Elliott and Culhane 2017, ch. 6).

The term "sensory ethnography" has come to cover a wide spectrum of research and knowledge mobilization practices. It figures in the name of an ethnographic film lab at Harvard University directed by Lucien Castaing-Taylor, which is committed to expanding the frontiers of media anthropology. It appears in the title of a manual of fieldwork practice by Sarah Pink (2009), which advocates intensive use of audiovisual media but also acknowledges the usefulness of the unaided senses. It applies to Anthony Seeger's work among the Suyà of Brazil (see above) and Kathryn Geurts' (2002) in-depth ethnographic study of the enculturation of the senses among the Anlo-Ewe of Ghana. The term "sensory ethnography" could equally well be predicated of the intensely sensorial prose of Kathleen Stewart in *Ordinary Affects* (2007), which conjures multisensory images of everyday "happenings" that seem (almost) to lift off the page (see also Peterson 2016, 2021). In Stewart's work, as in that of Nadia Seremetakis (1994a, 2018), representation and sensation blend.

In my own work, beginning with *The Varieties of Sensory Experience* (1991), the emphasis has been on taking a relational approach to the study of the senses, using the comparative method to highlight the contrasts between the sensory orders of different cultures (see *infra*, chapter 5), developing the power of language to analyse and express sensory nuances, critiquing the essentialism of phenomenology, and challenging the dictates and assumptions of Western sensory psychology and neuroscience. Other sensory anthropologists have embraced phenomenology or sought explanations for cultural practices in neuroscience (see Pink and Howes 2010; Ingold and Howes 2011; Lende and Downey 2012). Some have opted for film and sound recordings in preference to writing, or elected to concentrate on a specific sense, such as sound or "the visual," rather than the relations among the senses. As well, some sensory anthropologists prefer single- or multi-site ethnography to using the comparative method. There exists, then, a wide spectrum of approaches within the anthropology of the senses, and they continue to multiply. This plurality of sensory modes of engagement, and the liveliness of the discussions over their respective merits, are signs of the methodological and epistemological vigour of the sensory revolution in anthropology.

In the wake of all the different works mentioned above, the standards of ethnography have changed. Having an "experimental style" of writing (Clifford and Marcus 1986) is fine, but good ethnography, increasingly, is seen as going beyond semiotics, beyond poetics, beyond representation,[8] and engaging with culturally mediated sensory experiences and expressions (Stoller 1997; Herzfeld 2001, ch. 11; Howes 2003; Pink 2006; Howes and Classen 2014; Cox, Irving, and Wright 2016; Elliott and Culhane 2017; Howes 2019a).

II. Probes

The subsections of this section take stock of the contributions of sensory ethnography and sensuous geographies to the exploration of a range of topics and
debates in the human sciences. Such key theoretical concepts as *materiality* and
affect, and such topics as *gustation* and *representation*, are approached differently
when one leads with the senses. Acknowledging the primacy of perception results in a more nuanced and context-sensitive appreciation of what's at stake in
these debates. As noted in the prologue, the following probes can be read longitudinally (i.e., sequentially) or latitudinally (i.e., across the chapters of this part).

1   *Ontology*. The ontological turn has attracted many subscribers across numerous disciplines (for an account of its uptake in philosophy, see Kane
2015). Within anthropology, it arose as a counterpart to interpretive or
"symbolic" approaches of earlier decades (e.g., Geertz 1973), or what could
be characterized as social constructionist paradigms. In place of there being one world and many cultures (i.e., points of view or interpretations), it
posits the existence of "multinatures" or "naturecultures" (Descola 2013;
P. Heywood 2017). This elision of interpretation represented an important
advance according to some anthropologists, such as Tim Ingold (2018)
with his doctrine of "direct perception." However, it is vulnerable to criticism for having reinstated the notion of cultures as isolated wholes (albeit
now naturecultures) and for leaving its epistemological foundations un-
examined. For example, in the literature on Amazonian societies this construct is often paired with the idea of "perspectivism" (all subjects, human
and animal, share the same soul, culture, or point of view, but they possess
different bodies, and so what they see is different). This emphasis on the
ocular is problematic, however, since a careful reading of the ethnographic
record reveals that mind and cosmos are often understood on the model
of sound and hearing, or in more synaesthetic terms, as among the Desana
(Reichel-Dolmatoff 1981; Gearin and Sáez 2021). Thus, the ontological
turn needs to be tempered by attending to the sensory underpinnings, or
"sensuous epistemologies" (Feld 2005), that inform different ways of "being in the world," or "that which is."
   Constance Classen's notion of "sensory cosmology" is useful here (i.e.,
as qualifying the understanding of ontologies). In *Worlds of Sense* (1993b,
ch. 6), she devoted a chapter to analysing the thermal cosmology of the
Tzotzil of the Chiapas Highlands of Mexico, for whom heat (not light) is
the ordering principle of the cosmos as of society, and the osmology of the
Ongee of Little Andaman Islands in the Bay of Bengal, for whom the experience of space, time (or the seasons), and personhood are all mediated by
olfaction, as well as the synaesthetic cosmology of the Desana.

Following Classen, the idea of a sensory cosmology is brilliantly exemplified by anthropologist Marina Roseman's description of the "ecological environmental awareness" of a Malayan forest people, the Temiars, in "Blowing 'cross the Crest of Mount Galeng" (2008). Fundamental to Temiar physics and cosmology is the notion of a cool, moist liquid or vital energy that is condensed to different degrees and mobilized by the winds of the landscape, winds of the spirits, voices of mediums, the movements of trance-dancers, and the beat of the bamboo stampers. In healing ceremonies these sensuous resources are channelled by the shaman to attract a wayward soul back to the body in which it belongs.

Classen's theory of sensory cosmologies was foreshadowed in the work of the geographer Yi-Fu Tuan. For example, there is a little section on mountains in *Topophilia*, where he explores how the aesthetic response to mountains has varied from culture to culture, and over time within the same culture: in the case of Western cultures, for instance, the perception of mountains has changed "from a religious attitude in which awe was combined with aversion, to an aesthetic attitude that shifted from a sense of the sublime to a feeling for the picturesque; to the modern evaluation of mountains as a recreational resource" (1974, 70–4).

2 *Emplacement.* The concept of embodiment crystalized as a paradigm for research within anthropology in the 1980s, and the body was hailed as the "existential ground" of culture itself (Csordas 1990). This ushered in an important shift since prior to that the body had been viewed as the target of collective representation (e.g., M. Douglas 1973), not a pre-existing condition. The embodiment paradigm has inspired lots of groundbreaking research, but it is seen as wanting from a sensory studies perspective because, while it may overcome the longstanding split between mind and body, it often fails to *situate* the subject adequately (i.e., it can prove somewhat impervious to context). Enter the paradigm of emplacement, which foregrounds "the sensuous interrelationship of body-mind-environment" (Howes 2005b, 7; Pink 2009, 25) and extends well beyond such limit constructs as the "mindful body" or "embodied mind."

While still comparatively novel in anthropology, the notion of emplacement is not foreign to geography, though it goes under a different name – landscape. (Sensescape would be a more apt term, as discussed previously.) In "Feeling is Believing" (2007), one of the great "landscape geographers," Edmunds Valdemārs Bunkše, offers a range of reflections on his formation both as a person and as a geographer – the books he read, the people he met, the encounters he had with diverse physical terrains. Upon reflection, he noted his predisposition (present since childhood) to make sketches of landscapes, and how he was initially impressed by his teacher Carl Sauer's idea of landscape as "the visual, material impress of culture on land," but gradually veered off down "a path away from the visual," and came to pay increased attention to the "earth senses," as he calls them, of touch, smell, and hearing. This culminated in his definition of landscape as "*a unity in one's surroundings, perceived through all the senses*" and realization that his personal and professional mission in life involved "harmonizing interior-exterior landscapes" (2007, 114) – echoes of Humboldt. On Bunkše's account, then, landscapes constitute "a way of being in the world" with all the senses.

3 *Materiality*. Much has been written on the social life of things, less on their sensory life, although this is changing (e.g., Edwards et al. 2006; Classen 2017). The material turn, by virtue of its emphasis on materiality *tout court*, has tended to deflect attention from the fact that it is only by virtue of their sensible qualities that things impinge on the consciousness and actions of social subjects. The theory of "vibrant matter" (Bennett 2010) needs to be rejigged so that account is taken of the extent to which "vibrant matter" is first and foremost "sentient matter."

The indigenous Anlo-Ewe understanding of sentience (*seselelame* or "feeling in the body") is at the heart of anthropologist Kathryn Linn Geurts' *Culture and the Senses: Bodily Ways of Knowing in an African Community* (2002) and her and Elvis Gershon Adikah's (2006) account of diverse transformations in the experience of material culture in West Africa. The case studies in what could be called "the sensori-social life of things" presented by Geurts and Adikah include drinking water from a calabash instead of an industrially manufactured glass, which takes two hands instead of one, and thus imparts balance to the act of drinking in addition to being "associated with an overall sense of pleasure and rejuvenation"; wearing *kete* (strip-woven cloth) in place of sewn-clothing (e.g., trousers) for the "spiritual work" it does and the way it elevates one's gait, compelling one to walk "a chief's walk"; and the "feeling of how you sleep" on a thick straw mattress, which is said to impart a sense of "solidity and security" in contrast to the experience of "bouncing up and down" on a foam mattress (Geurts and Adikah 2006, 35, 43–4, 53).

The concept of materiality has been subjected to a withering critique by Tim Ingold as part of his "efforts to restore anthropology to life" in *Being Alive* (2011) and other works. According to Ingold, by focussing on the made instead of the making, and the "social life of things" over and above the "liveliness" of the materials from which they are wrought (i.e., all the processes of deterioration, transformation, etc. that go on continuously at the material level), material culture scholars unduly "objectify" things. Ingold's polarization of materials and materiaity has been questioned by some, however, such as Carl Knappett (2007) in "Materials *with* Materiality?" (i.e., the issue is not either/or) and by others who would insist on attending to the *sensori-social* life of things as opposed to Ingold's exclusive focus on the liveliness of materials and the responsiveness of the artisan in the individual-material dyad.

4 *Memory*. "Memory cannot be confined to a purely mentalist or subjective sphere," writes the anthropologist Nadia Seremetakis (1994a, 9) in the opening chapter of her edited collection *The Senses Still: Memory and Perception as Material Culture in Modernity*: "It is a culturally mediated material practice that is activated by embodied acts [of commensal exchange] … and artifacts laden with perceptual recall." Seremetakis illustrates her material-interactive theory of memory by reflecting on her nostagia for "the breast of Aphrodite," a locally grown peach of her native Greece, which "disappeared," like many other regional products, under the joint expansion and centralization of EEC food marketing regulations. In the course of her exposition, she expounds on the original Greek meaning of such terms as "aesthetics" (*aisthēsis*) and "nostalgia" (*nostalghia*). These are vital definitions to bear in mind in any study of memory and the senses in everyday life. The geographer Tim Edensor (2007) presents a similarly rich "sensory description" of an environment. In his article, the environment is an industrial ruin in Manchester, with all its unbidden sights, textures, sounds, and smells. The jarring sensual effects of the ruin stand in stark contrast to the hypercontrolled, secure, and sanititized "blandscapes" of the high modern city. For Edensor as for Seremetakis, memory is embedded in the sensory strata of the material environment.

5 *Alterity*. The vogue for conceptualizing community as "imagined" following Benedict Anderson (1983) has been supplanted by a more pressing concern with analysing how community is "sensed" (Trnka et al. 2013; Howes and Classen 2014; Lamrani 2021). Processes of social inclusion and exclusion are intimately bound up with sensory processing – sensory discrimination, to be exact. The expression of sensory discrimination takes many forms, one particularly virulent manifestation being the trope of the "smelly immigrant." In "Immigrant Lives and the Politics of Olfaction in the Global City" (2006), anthropologist Martin F. Manalansan IV highlights the opposition in the sensory imaginary of New York City between the gleaming Manhattan skyline, symbolic of that city's modernity and financial prowess, and the outer boroughs, perceived by some as "enclaves of smelly immigrants." He goes on to complicate this image of the "dual city" (financier/service-worker, inodorate/odorous) by taking the reader on a ride on the Number 7 train, which connects the boroughs and downtown,

with its forced intimacies and jumbled aromas that transgress the private/public boundary. Manalansan also documents how immigrant peoples cope with their olfactory stereotyping: "ethnic odors" are regarded by the Asian Americans he interviewed both as markers of identity and belonging *and* a source of anxiety as they seek to fashion themselves as "modern," too. Manalansan's ethnography, which he frames as a "new anthropology of the visceral," is a brilliant testimony to the political life of sensation.

6 *Mediation.* One key point that Rodaway makes in *Sensuous Geographies* is that "perception is corporeal; it is mediated by our bodies and the techno- logical extensions employed by the body (such as walking sticks, specta- cles and hearing aides, even clothes)." There are actually two points here. The first is that geography arises "out of the disposition of the body, that is the way in which our bodies give us orientation in and a measure of the world … In fact, without our bodies we would have no geography – orien- tation, measure, locomotion, coherence" (Rodaway 1994, 31). Rodaway's second point is that the body is "extended" by diverse media (i.e., media further mediate the mediation of the body). Here he is actually channel- ling McLuhan, whose definition of media extended beyond "the media" to include clothing, for example, though he ended up directing most of his analytic attention to the effects of the technologization of the word (in its being spoken or written) on cognition and society, as in *The Gutenberg Galaxy* (1962).

   In "Literacy as Anti-Culture: The Andean Experience of the Written Word" (1991), Constance Classen engages with the theory of the "Great Divide" between orality and literacy that comes out of media studies (McLuhan's writings in particular), refining, critiquing, politicizing, and complexifying it. She argues that writing, by disembodying knowledge (through the separation of the writer from the written and the writer from the reader), engenders a "devitalized, depersonalized and reified" cos- mos. When oral and literate cultures collide, the effect on the sensorium of the oral culture can be deeply alienating. She illustrates her thesis by reference to the violent encounter between the civilizations of the Inca and the Spanish. She discloses how the Andeans experienced writing as "a demonic instrument of destruction" – that is, as anti-culture. (This percep- tion of writing is unthinkable from within a literate mindset.) The vibrant aurality of the Andean cosmos was subdued. In addition to exposing the dark side of the medium of writing, Classen nuances her analysis of the clash of media (in ways that McLuhan and his followers failed to do) by exploring how the Inca negotiated the regime of written documents the Spanish foisted on them, and appropriated writing to their own ends (see further Classen 1993a).

7 *Affect.* In "Materialist Returns," geographer Sarah Whatmore (2006, 604) identifies one of the prime openings within the new cultural geography as being "a shift from an onus on *meaning* to an onus on *affect*."

> Affect refers to the force of intensive relationality – intensities that are felt but not personal, visceral but not confined to an individuated body. This shift of concern from what things mean to what they do has methodological consequences for how we train our apprehensions of "what subjects us," "what affects and what effects us," or "learn to be affected."

This opening is reflected in the anthropologist Kathleen Stewart's *Ordinary Affects* (2007), which pays minute attention to the sensual forces that precipitate an awareness of "something/happening" (Whatmore 2006), without "it" (either the process or the "something") being susceptible to conscious or rational reflection. It is also manifest in the geographers Robyn Longhurst, Elsie Ho, and Lynda Johnston's (2008) use of "the body" as an "instrument of research" when they staged a cook-in with immigrant women in Hamilton, New Zealand. In a hyperreflexive move, they further examine their own visceral reactions to such foodstuffs as kimchi and pavlova. This self-questioning, which, incidentally, is motivated by a wish to grapple with the "more-than-human" (Whatmore 2006), chimes with Manalansan's call for a "new anthropology of the visceral." Cooking (and tasting) together also chimes with another opening identified by Whatmore (2006, 604): "a shift in analytic focus from *discourse* to *practice*."

8 *Movement.* Western philosophers have not been much inclined to dance or move about (Vinge 1975; Sheets-Johnstone 1999).[9] The perceiving subject has typically been pictured as a still spectator (Rorty [1979] 2017). The long-standing understanding of perception as proceeding from a still point of view was shattered by the psychologist J.J. Gibson (1979), with his dynamic theory of the senses as "perceptual systems" and focus on the motility of the perceiver. It changed again by virtue of the shift from viewing perception "as representation" to conceiving it as "enaction" in contemporary cognitive science (Noë 2006). In step with this development is the entertaining account of the world perceived through the feet presented by Tim Ingold, a follower of Gibson, in "Culture on the Ground" (2004). In it, Ingold traces the "detachment" and "groundlessness of modern society," the separation of thought from action (or cognition from locomotion) and mind from body, and the privileging of sight over touch to "the bias of head [and hands] over heels." Ingold's (2004, 227) ultimate point is that "Locomotion, not cognition, must be the starting point for the study of perceptual activity," and "walking is itself a form of circumambulatory knowing." Ingold's doctrine of pedestrianism,

which reshuffles many of the time-honoured dichotomies of Western thought, is heady stuff.

9 *Representation*. On the eve of the sensorial revolution in anthropology circa 1990, as the "writing culture" movement (Clifford and Marcus 1986) reached its zenith, the discipline was gripped by a "crisis of representation." Attention came to focus on "the poetics of ethnography" (or "process of textualization") and the problem of how to write with "authority." What was missing from this moment, however, was any real awareness of, or attempt to theorize, the burgeoning "visualization" of anthropology, which is a very different mode of representation to textual description. This endured despite the vociferous protests of, for example, Lucien Taylor (1996, 1998), who contested the "linguification of meaning" ushered in by the textual turn (see also Grimshaw 2001).

Visual anthropology has been expanding steadily since the 1990s, and, arguably, reached its apogee in 2012 with the release of Lucien Castaing-Taylor (as he is known following his name change) and Véréna Paravel's visceral and highly disturbing documentary film about the North American fishing industry, entitled *Leviathan*. In "*Leviathan* and the Experience of Sensory Ethnography" (2015), Christopher Pavsek lauds the film for "the seemingly immersive experience the film offers as well as its ability to supplant contemporary documentary [which remains obsessed with 'telling stories'] ... by way of a fuller rendering of the sensory encounter with the profilmic world." In lieu of the "hyperdiscursivity" that came over anthropology in the wake of the textual revolution, Castaing-Taylor and Paravel's brand of sensory ethnography

> offers a cinema of sensuous plenitude and perceptual richness, embodied experience, and visceral immediacy, which ... includes a near-total eschewal of textual devices, be they in the form of explanatory or expository voiceover ... and, in many cases, even much comprehensible dialogue from its human subjects. (Pavsek 2015, 5)

However, Pavsek is rightly critical of the film for failing to adequately problematize the scenes of callous butchery or the harsh working conditions it depicts. This is a serious lacuna, and signals the importance of bringing ethical and political considerations into sensory ethnography, lest it lapse into sensationalism. This issue is especially acute due to the fact that animals, such as the fish depicted in the film, are completely and utterly vulnerable to exploitation, since they have no legal standing, no "representation," as the legal expression goes. John Shiga presents a poignant analysis of the struggle to represent cetaceans in the courtroom, and defend them from the disabling effects of sonar (used indiscriminately by the U.S. Navy) on the grounds that they are sentient creatures, too in "An Empire of Sound: Sentience, Sonar and Sensory Impudence" (2017).

In (profilmic) sensory ethnography, as represented by *Leviathan*, voluminous depiction takes the place of "thick description" and also (as noted above) edges out conversation and commentary. Pavsek is critical of the film for its "eschewal of the conceptual" (or "semiotic") as when Castaing-Taylor and Paravel claim that "the film exists before interpretation" and offers "an experience of an experience" (quoted in Pavsek 2015, 6). What the film fails to do, according to Pavsek, is *contextualize* its depiction, for this would be to introduce a degree of "semiotic coding and decoding" that Castaing-Taylor and Paravel flatly reject. Pavsek also problematizes the filmmakers' use of the relatively new, but now ubiquitous, GoPro camera technology, which, for all the novel perspectives and images it can generate, has nevertheless become "a constitutive a priori of experience today." In other words,

> the GoPro has not only become a central part of the way in which experience is enframed, rendering whatever immediacy it conveys of experience deeply historical [ironically] but the GoPro has become … the horizon of experience, both medium of experience and the final measure whereby one can confirm that experience has been had, that, indeed, one has experienced an experience. (Pavsek 2015, 9)

Within geography, a parallel to the practice of (filmic) sensory ethnography may be seen in the emergence of multimodal mapmaking as a counterpoint to the fixation on *visualizing* landscape in conventional cartography. In "Cybercartography" (2018), D.R. Fraser Taylor and co-authors present an overview of the sensational representational possibilities opened up by the incorporation of extravisual modalities into the geographic study of environments:

> The main reason for developing multimodal interfaces [is] to help users achieve more efficient, "natural," usable and easy to learn ways of interacting with computer applications, such as electronic maps. Furthermore, … multimodal interfaces permit more empowering applications relative to traditional interfaces. Such empowerment would be exemplified by a dynamic electronic map system, which could be interacted with using auditory, touch, and visual senses. (Taylor et al. 2018, 269)

It is an interesting question whether J.B. Granö would regard the technologization of geographic perception instituted by D.R. Fraser Taylor and associates as vindication for his project in *Pure Geography*, or as a development in a different direction.

10 *Gustation*. Curiously, considerations of taste and the sensory experience of food were largely absent from research in the anthropology of food and food studies generally until recently, though there were some notable exceptions

(e.g., Kuipers 1991; Weismantel 1988). In a landmark article in the *Annual Review of Anthropology*, David Sutton (2010) called attention to this lacuna and set the stage for future research by introducing the term "gustemology" to highlight the "gustemic" ways of knowing, living, and interacting that different cultures have elaborated. The idea of "food worlds" as a counterpoint to "world views" has proved highly productive, as has Sutton's suggestion that more attention should be paid to the interplay of the senses in the production of gustatory experience. In "The Sensory Experience of Food" (Korsmeyer and Sutton 2011), Sutton joins forces with the philosopher Carolyn Korsmeyer to argue the point that the exclusionary approach to gustation as exemplified by the blind taste test of mainstream food science is fundamentally misguided, since it cancels *anticipation*, which actually plays a key role in the appreciation of a meal. This point is further explored by Korsmeyer in her (re)appreciation of how Dutch still life painting sets up a "synaesthetic exchange," and by Sutton when he poses the question, "What would it mean for our studies of food if we thought of memory itself as a sense?" In answering this question, Sutton brings out well how "both memory and the senses are now being conceptualized as active, creative and even transformative cultural processes" rather than passive receptors of data (Korsmeyer and Sutton 2011, 470–1). He also shakes up conventional understandings of temporality itself – specifically, the notion of the present as temporally flat, by injecting the idea of "polytemporality" into the way we theorize the remembrance and immediate enjoyment of repasts.

11 *Synaesthesia*. The term "synaesthesia" refers to a condition in which the stimulation of one sensory mode, such as vision or taste, activates another, such as hearing or touch, thus resulting in "coloured hearing" or "tasting shapes" and all sorts of other intersensorial experiences. Various tests have been devised by neuropsychologists to determine whether an individual is a "true" (i.e., congenital) synaesthete (Baron-Cohen and Harrison 1997). According to the prevailing view, the phenomenon of synaesthesia is to be explained as an effect of "the cross-activation of brain maps" *tout court* (Ramachandran et al. 2004).

Yi-Fu Tuan challenges and also broadens this definition by situating synaesthesia in cultural context rather than confining its analysis to the study of neural networks. In his exploration of cross-sense linkages in the chapter entitled "Synesthesia, Metaphor and Symbolic Space" in *Passing Strange and Wonderful* (1993), Tuan moves from synaesthesia to "synesthetic tendency," and from synaesthetic tendency to "metaphorical perception" as expressed in language (i.e., figures of speech, such as "sharp sound"), and from metaphorical perception to "symbolic space," which he defines as "geography elevated and transfigured" (i.e., a product of culture). He illustrates his argument by reference to the sensory cosmologies of the Oglala Sioux and imperial China. The linear progression of Tuan's exposition makes synaesthesia sound like a one-way street, but in a radical and truly illuminating about-face towards the end of his exposition, he recasts it as a two-way street: "Metaphor reaches backward into synesthetic tendency and forward into symbol: in one direction it becomes an automatic response; in the other a product of culture and the active imagination" (Tuan 1993, 171).

Another way in which synaesthetic experiences can be entrained is through the ingestion of hallucinogens. However, Ramachandran, the doyen of neuropsychology, discounts the study of psychedelics-induced synaesthesia because it is "far less organized than congenital synaesthesia," and, in his view, amounts to nothing more than "sensory confusion" (2004, 868). But Ramachandran's dismissal is belied by the ethnographic record, particularly Gerardo Reichel-Dolmatoff's richly detailed account of the use of the *Banisteriposis caapi* plant among the Desana of Colombia. In his classic article, "Brain and Mind in Desana Shamanism" (1981), Reichel-Dolmatoff shows that synaesthetic perceptions are very well organized among the Desana, precisely because they are *culturally* modulated. The Desana shaman administers the hallucinogen and also manipulates various kinds of external stimulation (e.g., music) so that people are made to "see, and act accordingly," "hear, and act accordingly," "smell, and act accordingly," and "dream, and act accordingly" (Reichel-Dolmatoff 1981, 76–7, 90–5): their meditation is not just some random "trip" – it is structured.

The Desana have a highly elaborate theory of the brain and its functions, based partly on observing people with brain injuries and partly on their introspective experience of the hallucinogen. Thus, in one image

> the human brain is compared to a huge rock crystal subdivided into many smaller hexagonal prisms, each containing a sparkling element of color energy ... In another image a brain consists of layers of innumerable hexagonal honeycombs; the entire brain is one huge, humming beehive ... each tiny hexagonal container holds honey of a different color, flavor, odor, or texture. (Reichel-Dolmatoff 1981, 83)

fMRI brain imaging pales in comparison. Studying the brain science of the Desana could teach neuropsychologists like Ramachandran a thing or two, if only they were open to considering the Indigenous psychologies of the world (see further Heelas and Lock 1979). This aporia highlights a fundamental tenet of sensory studies: Western science is but one field of knowledge among others, just as congenital synaesthesia is but one variety of intersensoriality, among countless others.

Even when psychologists do take drug-induced synaesthesia seriously, in keeping with the current vogue for psychedelic experimentation (Pollan 2018), their investigations are often marred by another, equally pernicious, species of reductionism: pharmacological reductionism. It is assumed that the perceptual effects or "vision" induced by the hallucinogen will be the same the world over. This assumption has been challenged by anthropologists A.K. Gearin and Oscar Calavia Sáez. In "Altered Visions" (2021), the authors present a comparative sensory ethnography of the use of hallucinogens in Amazonian shamanism and Australian Ayahuasca Neo-shamanism (a New Age movement). They note that while the experience of ayahuasca registers as a "vision" in the Australian context, in the Amazonian context there are all manner of crosmodal connections, which are typically of cosmological import; that while Amazonian shamans transform into animals, such as jaguars, the boundary between humans and animals is never breached in the Australian neoshamanic context; and that in the latter context the experience of ayahuasca is privatized (becoming "my truth") or "owned," and the ego expands (even as it is supposed to be eclipsed) through becoming "one" with the universe. It is only by reference to a theory of the cultural mediation of perception, and not the (alleged) intrinsic properties of some drug, that any of these effects (the predominance of vision, the human exceptionalism, the focus on and expansion of the ego in the Australian context) can be explained.

Concluding Note

This chapter has shown how some of the key founders of geography (Humboldt, Granö), as of anthropology (Broca, Rivers, Boas), went about their research with the senses in mind. In most cases, Granö and Broca especially, their senses were fettered by the psychophysical and evolutionary doctrines of their day, but not all (Boas being the prime exception). Then, after a lengthy fallow period, with certain notable exceptions (Tuan, Lévi-Strauss, Seeger, Feld), geographers and anthropologists came into their senses again, this time with a more concerted emphasis on the cultural than the natural, and on practice in place of physiology. Allowing the senses back in has in turn generated many keen insights into processes of social inclusion and exclusion (i.e., sensory discrimination), qualified the focus on embodiment, and challenged the reductionism of the ontological turn by shifting the focus to sensuous epistemologies and sensory cosmologies. So too have sense-based approaches enlivened the study of material culture by redirecting attention to the sensori-social life of things. In the next chapter, we consider the repercussions of the sensorial revolution in history and sociology.

CHAPTER TWO

On the History and Sociology of the Senses

This chapter takes up the notion of the sensorium as a historical formation and also addresses sense experience from a sociological angle. As with the previous chapter, the research reported on in this chapter challenges the monopoly that the discipline of psychology has traditionally exercised over the study of the senses and sensation. As cultural historian Constance Classen (1997, 401) observes, "sensory perception is a cultural, as well as a physical, act ... sight, hearing, taste, touch, and smell are not only means of apprehending physical phenomena, but also avenues for the transmission of cultural values." In *The Senses in Self, Culture and Society* (2012), sociologists Phillip Vannini, Dennis Waskul, and Simon Gottschalk make the point that as we humans sense we also make sense, which implies both that the senses are made, not given, and that the senses are full of sense or "meaning," both linguistic and extralinguistic.

The history of the senses is concerned with charting and analysing sensory diversity in time. The sociology of the senses looks at diversity within contemporary society. In sensory historiography, the emphasis is on the historicity of perception, how sensory values and practices made sense within a particular historical period, and how the balance of the senses and meaning of particular sensations have shifted over time. In sensory sociology, the focus is on the socialization of the senses, and how sensory values and social values intertwine. As regards writing the history and sociology of the senses, the guiding idea is that the senses are "produced relationally" in everday life (Dawkins and Loftus 2013; Jaffe et al. 2020) as well as in extraordinary contexts, such as times of conflict or celebration.

I. Laying the Foundations

Historical Overtures

The first scholar to theorize the senses in history, by imagining a "history of the sensible" (Corbin and Heuré 2000) was Alain Corbin in "Anthropologie et histoire sensorielle" (1990; Corbin 2005 in English translation). However, there were various overtures to the senses in the historical literature of previous decades. Indeed, when one considers the work of two of the discipline's most prominent modern practitioners – Johan Huizinga, author of "The Task of Cultural History" ([1929] 1984) and Lucien Febvre, co-founder (with Marc Bloch) of the journal *Annales d'Histoire Economique et Sociale* (1929) – one sees that sense experience constituted a foundational terrain of exploration within the fields of cultural history and social history, when those fields were first assuming their current definition.[1]

In *The Autumn of the Middle Ages* ([1919] 1996), Huizinga sought to convey not merely the "historical experience" but the "historical sensation" of the late medieval period. Among his sources of inspiration for this move were, first, his work as a linguist, which revealed to him the influence of the senses on language; and second, the Dutch literary genre known as Sensitivism, which promoted a sensitive and sensuous approach to writing. In the introductory chapter of *Sublime Historical Experience* (2005), the philosopher of history Frank Ankersmit enucleates how Huizinga "moved outside himself" and made contact with history – specifically, the history of the late Burgundian Moyen Age – and sought to intimate this in his writing. The Huizingan overture is summed up by Ankersmit (2005, 121) in the line "Historical experience pulls the faces of past and present together in a short but ecstatic kiss." (Huizinga called this *Ahnung* [or "inkling" in German] and at other times *ekstasis*.) Later on, Ankersmit (2005, 122) alludes to the differences between seeing and hearing to help illuminate the nature of Huizinga's phenomenology of historical sensation: "as we know from music, the world of sounds may sometimes give us an understanding of the *condition humaine* that we can never expect from the world of visual forms." Parenthetically, Ankersmit (2005, 130) defines *sensation* as the "other" of observation and impression, because sensation connotes "the most intimate contact with reality that we can have" whereas the concept of observation is too objective and the idea of impression is too beholden to the individual's own subjectivity. This definition of *sensation* also provides a vital antidote to the psychophysical definition of sensation, which is largely denuded of sense (in the sense of "meaning").

In a little section entitled "The Underdevelopment of Sight" towards the end of his classic work on the mentality of sixteenth-century France, Lucien Febvre ([1942] 1982) observed that the sixteenth century was more attentive to smells and sounds than sights, and he went on to suggest that "a fascinating series of studies could be done of the sensory underpinnings of thought in different periods" (quoted and discussed in Classen 2001). Febvre's ode to the non-visual senses in *The Problem of Unbelief in the Sixteenth Century* (1982) is a key overture, which would serve to inspire many future historians of the senses.

Disciplining the Senses in Historical Writing

In the 1980s Alain Corbin broke with the focus on "mentalities" in the work of Febvre and the Annales School and also with the focus on "discourse" in the work of Foucault and the post-structuralists to write a "history of the sensible" (see Corbin and Heuré 2000). The French term *sensible* is difficult to translate into English. In contemporary English usage, the emphasis is on practicality or common sense, as when the term is used in the phrase "sensible shoes." This lacks the sensitivity that the French term connotes, and this discrepancy points to just how *uncommon* the senses are across cultures. When the term "sensible" is used in what follows, it will help to think of it as delimiting "the sensate," "the perceptible," or "the sensorium" (in the archaic sense of this term).

Corbin's *The Foul and the Fragrant* ([1982] 1986) explored the social life of smell in nineteenth-century France. It was followed a decade later by *Village Bells: Sounds and Meanings in the 19th-CenturyFrench Countryside* ([1994] 1998). In the interim, Corbin initiated a dialogue with anthropology in a piece called "Histoire et anthropologie sensorielle" (1990; for the English translation, see Corbin 2005).[2] This essay contains numerous keen suggestions regarding sensory studies methodology. For example, Corbin urges us to "take account of the *habitus* that determines the frontier between the perceived and the unperceived, and, even more, of the norms which decree what is spoken and what left unspoken"; he also highlights the dangers of "confusing the reality of the employment of the senses and the picture of this employment decreed by observers" (2005, 135, 133). In other words, the key to writing the history of the senses lies in sensing between the lines of written sources.

The pioneering work of the cultural historian Constance Classen helped to define the fields of both the history and anthropology of the senses (1997, 2001). In *Inca Cosmology and the Human Body* (1993b) she investigated how the Inca made sense of the world and ordered their imperial state through corporeal and sensory metaphors and practices. Classen went on to describe and analyse a wide range of other temporally specific sensory models and practices in such works as *Worlds of Sense: Exploring the Senses in History and across Cultures* (1993b), *The Color of Angels: Cosmology, Gender and the Aesthetic Imagination* (1998), and *Aroma: The Cultural History of Smell* (Classen et al. 1994). One particularly trenchant example of Classen's sensuous historiography is her account in *Worlds of Sense* of the "olfactory decline" of the West as figured by one minor but significant object of cultural interest: the rose (Classen 1993b, ch. 1). Prior to the Enlightenment, the most salient feature of the rose was customarily taken to be its scent ("A rose by any other name would smell as sweet"). Afterwards, the visual appearance of the rose began to attract more attention, as can be seen both in literary references and in gardening practices, which sacrificed scent in the quest to breed showier blooms. Classen argues that the sensory history of the rose reflects a general tendency to downplay olfaction in favour of vision in modernity.

In her subsequent work, Classen has continued to expand the field of sensory history, analysing, for example, how changing tactile practices shaped the transition from premodern to modern culture in *The Deepest Sense* (2012) and how the senses were engaged by artworks and collections from the Middle Ages to modernity in *The Museum of the Senses* (2017). The latter work offers a history of art "with the fingerprints left on." In a recent piece, "The Senses at the National Gallery" (2019), she examines art as recreation and regulation in Victorian England, bringing out the contrast between representations of the ideal sensory role of the National Gallery as purveyor of civilized and civilizing sensations and its somewhat chaotic actual sensory life. The National Gallery, like other public art institutions, was "imagined to function as the soft fingertips of the long arm of the law, transforming social disorder into social order and destructive sensuality into compliant sensitivity" (Classen 2019, 85), but this agenda was subverted in various ways by boisterous and picnicking visitors, much to the consternation of the middle- and upper-class "observers."

The British social historian Roy Porter was an early supporter of sensory history. He was instrumental in seeing Corbin's work translated into English, co-edited *Medicine and the Five Senses* (Bynum and Porter 1993) and was working on *Flesh in the Age of Reason* (2003), a profound contribution to the history of sensibilities, at the time of his premature death in 2002. Porter was also responsible for coining the term "cultural anthropology of the senses," which he used in his foreword to Corbin's *The Foul and the Fragrant* (1986).

One highly influential early text in sensory history is *Sweetness and Power* (1985) by the anthropologist Sidney Mintz. This book traces the social, political, and economic impact of a gustatory sensation: that of sugar. Mintz shows how capitalism thrived on the sugar trade while wreaking misery on the African slaves who worked the sugar plantations, how sugar insinuated itself into the rhythms of the British workday via its use in tea and coffee as well as jam, and how it ultimately came to be classified as a health risk (an ironic twist, since sugar was initially touted as a cure-all). *Sweetness and Power* opened a space within the nascent field of sensory history for researching and writing the history of *particular* sensations, or sensuous substances. This subfield has expanded dramatically in the ensuing decades to include such topics as the social history of spices (Schivelbusch 1992), salt (Kurlansky [2002] 2010), chocolate (Off 2006), colours (Findlay 2002; Pleij 2004), perfume (Dugan 2011), and other stimulants, along with the cultural history of darkness and light (Schivelbusch 1995), noise (Mansell 2017), stench (Barnes 2006), and dust (Amato 2001) as well as visceral responses, such as disgust (Miller 1997, chs. 1, 4).

Within the United States, George Roeder Jr. is often credited with being the first to call historians to their senses. In a 1994 review article, Roeder recounted the results of his analysis of the sensory content of sixteen U.S. history text-books published during the previous forty years. He found few references to the senses and little use being made of sensory materials, such as photographs, in the earlier texts but noted a slight increase in the attention paid to "the sensory dimension of history" in the more recent texts, and urged that this trend continue, for: "When we write about the senses with the same fullness and precision that we demand of ourselves when discussing politics, philosophy or social movements, we *enlarge our audience, our field of study* and *our understanding of the past*" (Roeder 1994, 1122; emphasis added).

   The field of U.S. sensory history has definitely come into its own since Roeder's summons, thanks to the contributions of Leigh Schmidt (2000), Donna Gabaccia (2000), Emily Thompson (2002), Peter Charles Hoffer (2005), Sally Promey (2006, 2012, 2014), and, particularly, Mark M. Smith (2001, 2006, 2007a, 2007b, 2008). By attending to "the sensate" (M. Smith 2007b) in their explorations of social processes, these scholars have reshaped the *way* the U.S. past is understood. Thus, Hoffer held that sensation and perception played a "causal role" in the conflicts between Indigenous peoples and settlers in *Sensory Worlds in Early America* (2005). Schmidt (2000) delved into the heated debates over the meaning of divine signs and the rationalization of listening in the American Enlightenment. Gabaccia (2000) recounted how "crossing the boundaries of taste" and savouring (as well as experimenting with) the cuisine of the "other" became the norm in interethnic relations in late nineteenth- and twentieth-century United States, giving new meaning to the notion of America as a melting pot. Promey (2006, 2012) has explored the "taste evangelism" of American liberal Protestantism in the mid-twentieth century and the reform of visual habits as religious dispositions. In *The Soundscape of Modernity* (2002), Thompson brings out how the silence that resulted from the "quest for quiet" that drove the invention of various sound-insulating materials during the first decades of the twentieth century was then filled by the sounds of radio, which in turn produced a new "culture of listening" and national consciousness.

   The most prominent historian of the senses in the United States, Mark Smith, began his work in the field by examining the clash between the soundscapes of the Northern (industrial) and Southern (pastoral) United States in the first half of the nineteenth century, and the role this clash may have played in the lead-up to the American Civil War (M. Smith 2001). He went on, in *How Race Is Made* (2006), to expose the sensory dynamics of racializing processes in the Southern United States and concluded that racial issues were never black and white, but instead involved a range of emotionally charged sensory stereotypes, which he proceeded to deconstruct. In addition to these detailed studies, Smith edited a round table entitled "The Senses in American History" for the the *Journal of American History* (Smith 2008),[3] and proposed a charter for sensory history in

Sensing the Past (2007b). His latest offering is entitled *A Sensory History Manifesto* (2021).

In 2011, the *American Historical Review* came out with an issue entitled "The Senses in History." The introduction to this issue was written by the intellectual historian Martin Jay, author of *Downcast Eyes* (1993). He begins by quoting Frederic Jamieson: "The scandalous idea that the senses have a history is, as Karl Marx once remarked, one of the touchstones of our historicity" (in Jay 2011, 63). He then proceeds to rattle off a range of questions with far-reaching implications, such as

> Have all cultures posited the same five senses, or have others been included? … Are the differentiation and uneven development of the senses, however many we may posit, legislated by nature or the product of historical forces? … How has culture developed technologies to extend and enhance the senses, creating an 'exosomatic' array of devices that compensate for the limits of our creaturely nature? … How has the loss or impairment of the senses been understood, lamented, and alleviated historically? … How can we plausibly periodize and narrate changes in the sensorium in different contexts?

Jay concludes that, with all these questions – and more – being avidly pursued by contemporary historians, "the history of the senses, it is now fair to say, has become far less of a scandal than a vigorous mainstream enterprise with a bright future ahead of it" (Jay 2011, 66).

A sensory history approach is now being applied to numerous geographical regions. One of these is Russia, as evidenced by the publication of *Russian History through the Senses: From 1700 to the Present* (Romaniello and Starks 2016) and the work of the Cambridge Russian Sensory History Network (or CRUSH). The Romaniello and Starks edited collection is remarkably varied in the range of topics it covers, from the politics of deafness and hearing (Stalin was notoriously opposed to the use of sign language) to the acquired gastronomic appreciation for the rotted, and from the memorialization of martyrs to how wartime nurses coped with the sensory onslaught of wounded bodies. The work of CRUSH (e.g., Widdis 2017) is more focused on early twentieth-century projects, and the new models of human subjectivity they created. Its members see their task as one of counterbalancing the "emotional turn" that has dominated much scholarship on Russian and Slavic culture by promoting a corresponding sensory turn.

Another is Latin America. Latin American sensory studies introduces a perspective on the sensorium from the Global South that is particularly attuned to the politics of perception. For example, Dylon Robbins' *Audible Geographies* (2019) interrogates the connection between the colonization of place and the racialization of sound; Francine Masiello's *The Senses of Democracy* (2018) explores the possibilities for embodied resistance in the face of dictatorial discipline and

Eurocentric constructions of civilization vs. barbarism. These two works, among numerous others, point the way for a decolonization of the senses.

A third is ancient Greece and Rome. The sensorial revolution is particularly far advanced in classics. The Senses in Antiquity series, under the general direction of Mark Bradley and Shane Butler, is similar in structure to the Sensory Formations series. It is composed of six volumes: one on each of the canonical five senses, and a sixth on synaesthesia and the ancient senses (Butler and Purves 2013). Of particular note is the book *Senses of the Empire: Multisensory Approaches to Roman Culture* (2017), edited by Eleanor Betts. The rule in this book is that each contributor must explore whatever object, event, or site they have chosen (signet ring, votive object, pantomime, funeral, cityscape). This is a significant methodological advance, as will become apparent in the discussion that follows.

While sensory history has typically been organized along specific sensory and national lines, there is a growing interest in forging a more synthetic (not to say synaesthetic), multisensory, and comparative or transnational understanding of the sensorium as a historical formation. The first intimations of such an integrative approach are to be found in such works as literary scholar Louise Vinge's *The Five Senses: Studies in a Literary Tradition* (1975) and Classen's *Worlds of Sense* (1993b) and *The Color of Angels* (1998) as well as geographer Yi-Fu Tuan's *Topophilia* (1974) and *Passing Strange and Wonderful* (1993) and philosopher Jonathan Rée's *I See a Voice* (1999). This trend continued with the publication of the German medical historian Robert Jütte's *A History of the Senses: From Antiquity to Cyberspace* (2005) and Mark Smith's *Sensing the Past* (2007b). Of particular note is the six-volume *Cultural History of the Senses* set, under the general direction of Constance Classen (2014b), which was published in 2014. Its six volumes explore Western sensory culture from antiquity (Toner 2014), through the Middle Ages (Newhauser 2014), the Renaissance (Roodenburg 2014), the Enlightenment (Vila 2014), the nineteenth and early twentieth century (Classen 2014c), and the twentieth century (Howes 2014a). Each volume explores a range of cultural domains, including urban life, the marketplace, the arts, religion, and science, etc. in keeping with the brief for the *Cultural Histories* series from Bloomsbury. This domain-based approach makes it possible to develop a fuller sense of the differential elaboration and interplay of the senses within each of the periods covered as well as across them.

One of the domains covered in each of the volumes in the *Cultural History of the Senses* set centres on the interconnections between sensory modalities and media of communication. An emergent field of inquiry that contributes to our understanding of these interconnections is "media archaeology." This approach seeks to consider the social dimensions (or impacts) of the development of new media of communication, and to "construct alternate histories of suppressed, neglected, and forgotten media" (Huhtamo and Parikka 2011, 3). Pursuant to the latter point, history is littered with devices that never quite caught on, like the "Baby Talkie" of 1930s Japan. This variation of the optical toy known as the zoetrope was to be placed at the centre of a gramophone turntable so that the consumer could enjoy animations accompanied by sound. Produced when silent films were being transformed into "talkies," it was perhaps the earliest form of "multimedia" home entertainment (i.e., a "home movie machine"). One ad for the "Baby Talkie" suggested that if you buy the device "at the cost of one record, any old record will become really interesting and lively, pleasing both your eyes and ears as if you were watching a real talkie" and went on to clinch the argument by claiming: "You will no longer be satisfied with a gramophone which is merely for listening" (Kusahara 2011, 127). The Baby Talkie quickly became a relic, partly due to the attractions of the cinema. However, this device, and numerous other devices across cultures, endure as signals of the popular interest in reuniting sensations that had been severed by the proliferation of monosensory (single-sense) media, such as photography and telephony.

The study of the relationship between the senses and media has become a subject of intense interest for contemporary historians and cultural theorists. As Huhtamo and Parikka (2011) note, it was prefigured in the work of such theorists as Walter Benjamin, Michel Foucault, and (in the German context especially) Friedrich Kittler. The Canadian media guru Marshall McLuhan is particularly significant in this connection for his groundbreaking enucleation of media as "extensions of the senses" with concomitant social and cognitive effects. McLuhan's approach, however, had certain limitations, one of which was its technological determinism, and another, its essentialist understanding of the senses (e.g., positing seeing as intrinsically more rational and linear than hearing). More recent work in the history and sociology/anthropology of the senses has insisted on inquiring into the cultural *construction* of the senses and examining the differing *combinations* of the senses in different cultures and historical periods, in place of emphasizing the contest between the eye and the ear alone. Thanks to such work it is now clear that the sensorium of a given period cannot be read from its prevailing technology of communication (speech, writing, print, electronic) in a McLuhanesque fashion, but instead demands a more contextual or constructionist analysis (see Howes 1991; Classen 1993b and 2005b; Schmidt 2000; Smith 2007b; Howes and Classen 2014).

Sociological Overtures

The first intimations of a sociology of the senses can be found in the work of one of sociology's founders, Georg Simmel. In a pair of essays that date from the first decades of the twentieth century, Simmel drew attention to how the senses and sense experience impact social attitudes and interaction: "That we get involved in interactions at all depends on the fact that we have a sensory effect upon one another," he wrote (Simmel [1907] 1997, 110).

In "The Metropolis and Mental Life" ([1903] 1976), Simmel attributed the "blasé outlook" of the modern city dweller to the need to develop a "protective organ" in the form of intellectual distance so as not to be overly affected by the constant barrage of sensations that is characteristic of life in the metropolis. In "Sociology of the Senses" ([1921] 1997), he related the confusion and loneliness of the modern urban subject to the greater preponderance of occasions to *see* rather than to *hear* people. Contrary to the country village, where people typically exchange glances and greet each other when out walking, in the city people are forced to spend long periods staring absently and keeping silent while riding on a streetcar or other public transport.

In her book *Shock and the Senseless in Dada and Fluxus* (2010) in the chapter entitled "Shock and Distraction," the German art historian Dorothée Brill makes a valuable contribution to the history of sensory studies by bringing out how Simmel's social theory, perceptual theory, and especially his concept of "shock," reflected his experience of his native city, Berlin. Often regarded as the paradigmatic twentieth-century metropolis, on account of its crowding, rapid expansion and restless transformation,[4] Berlin both formed the crucible of Simmel's thought and gave its stamp to sociology, for it was "reflection on the metropolitan experience that generated and shaped modern sociology in the first place" (Brill 2010, 32, quoting Srubar).

In "Shock and Distraction," Brill also examines the work of Simmel's fellow Berliner, the Marxist philosopher and cultural critic Walter Benjamin. Though thirty-four years Simmel's junior, Benjamin grew up under much the same intense urban conditions as his countryman, and this imprinted itself on his social and aesthetic theories.[5] Like Simmel, Benjamin grappled with shock, but proposed a different theory of coping – the theory of distraction (the reverse of contemplation) as a semi-conscious mode of perception, or infrastructural way of sensing.

Simmel's insights into the link between the senses and sociality lay fallow for much of the twentieth century or were taken up only partially. For example, Deena Weinstein and Michael Weinstein in "On the Visual Constitution of Society" (1984) investigated "the constitution of intermental relations through vision" as though the sensory foundations of society were solely visual and could be reduced to "intermental relations." Simmel, by contrast, advocated a *relational* approach to the study of the senses and society, one which was as attuned to sound and smell as to sight, and sought the explanation for social change in the changing ratio or balance of the senses (rather like McLuhan).

Disciplining the Senses in Sociology

Simmel's insights were finally recovered and expanded by a number of sociologists working in the area of the sociology of the body in the 1990s. For example, Anthony Synnott explored the "sociological function" of touch and smell as well as sight in *The Body Social: Symbolism, Self and Society* (1993). In *Flesh and Stone* (1994), Richard Sennett proposed that the blasé attitude of the city dweller was prompted by the "tactile sterility" of the modern urban environment. According to Sennett, urban sprawl disperses the population – thus increasing interpersonal distance – while the various modern "technologies of motion," such as cars, elevators, and movie theatres, provide "freedom from resistance" by insulating bodies from their surroundings and whisking them from point to point. This "freedom from resistance" increases passivity, diminishes empathy, and undermines meaningful engagement in public life (the domain of alterity) by dulling touch. Sociologist Lisa Blackman's *Immaterial Bodies* (2012) extends the study of embodiment to include various extrasensory phenomena, such as telepathy and hearing voices. Blackman is also concerned with how the mobilization of the senses impacts the genesis and circulation of affect, creating an intersection between the sensory turn and the affective turn in the social sciences.

Pierre Bourdieu opened a different perspective from both Simmel and Benjamin on the senses in society in *Distinction: A Social Critique of the Judgment of Taste* ([1979] 1984). There he documented how, in bourgeois society, attending to the senses and acquiring the capacity to make fine discriminations can be a source of cultural capital, contrary to Benjamin's theory of distraction or Simmel's theory of the blasé attitude as coping mechanism. A further departure from Simmel's take on the senses can be seen in a series of postmillenial studies of clubbing that have revealed the sensation-*seeking* side of modern life. The club is a zone of sensory and social experimentation, where the rigours of the *habitus* of everyday life are suspended. Transgression is the order of the night, and this can unleash new forms of social intimacy (Jackson 2004). It is an interesting question whether the clubbing literature cycles back to Benjamin's theory of distraction or represents a new departure.

Phillip Vannini, Dennis Waskul, and Simon Gottschalk's *The Senses in Self, Society and Culture: A Sociology of the Senses* (2012) offers the first general overview of the sociology of the senses. They begin by identifying a "crypto-sociology of the senses" in the sociological theories of G.H. Mead on "the act," John Dewey on "experience," and William James on "the emotions," and also tip their hats to the work of Howard Becker on jazz and marijuana-smoking and Irving Goffman on the visual construction of gender. All of these theories come together in the paradigm of Symbolic Interactionism, which constitutes Vannini and company's point of departure for theorizing the social life of sensation – and, in particular, their notion of "somatic work," defined as quotidian "sense-making activity," which implies that we continuously fashion (and refashion) the senses in the never-ending process of sensing the world. Or, as Vannini and his co-authors succinctly (2012, 15) put it: "*humans sense as well as make sense.*"

In their work, Vannini, Waskul, and Gottschalk have also brought a sensory sociological approach to bear on the analysis of one of the defining phenomena of "hypermodernity" (a term they use in preference to postmodernity) – namely, hyperconsumption. "Intent on fueling our appetite for consumption," they write, contemporary communication media and cultural industries are "in the business of producing a material culture – a panoply of objects, services, and fantasies – that more than ever before in the history of civilization depends on catering to the human quest for sensuous pleasures." The hypermodern regime of consumption unleashes the forces of "intensity, instantaneity, urgency, instant gratification and excess." In this connection, it is quite striking that while sociologists of the senses analyse "the new immediacy of consumption" from a critical standpoint, which emphasizes the constructed or mediated nature of even the most apparently "immediate" stimuli in the "experience economy," most affect theorists take all these forces as givens. As we will see when we get round to probing the concept of affect in chapter 6, affect theorists conceive of themselves as delving beneath representation and beyond mediation. The situation is analogous to the one decried by Zygmunt Bauman (1988), writing at the height of postmodernism, who contested the rise of "postmodern sociology" by arguing that what was truly needed was a "sociology of postmodernism." Affect theorists are similarly caught up in the moment, or rather instant, since they believe that affective forces hit us even before we perceive them with our senses, they are that "immediate." Bauman's observation remains relevant today.[6]

II. Probes

Continuing on from the corresponding section in the previous chapter, here we take stock of the contributions of sensory history and the sociology of the senses to a range of contemporary discussions in the human sciences, centring on such theoretical concepts as *materiality* and *affect*, and such topics as *representation* and *gustation*. The reader is reminded that they might want to read these probes latitudinally (i.e., across the chapters of part 1 and the first chapter of part 3) instead of longitudinally (i.e., sequentially), the better to arrive at a holistic or "mosaical" appreciation of the correspondence among disciplines that this Manifesto enacts.

1 *Ontology.* The philosopher Aristotle is commonly touted (or blamed) for being the author of the five-sense model of the sensorium. He posited that each sense has its "proper object" or sphere: colours in the case of vision, sounds in the case of audition, smells in the case of olfaction, and so forth. What is not so commonly recognized is that his scheme, while ostensibly grounded in anatomy, was also dictated in no small part by cosmology: each sense was matched up with one of the elements. (As the senses were

five, however, and the elements four, this required a certain amount of creative thinking; see Vinge 2009.) Also missing from many contemporary critiques of Aristotle's legacy is any awareness of how Aristotle not only delimited the five senses but also posited the existence of "the common sense" (as will be discussed in the next chapter).

"On the Color of Angels: The Sensory Cosmologies of St. Hildegard, Boehme, and Fourier" is the lead chapter of Constance Classen's *The Color of Angels: Cosmology, Gender and the Aesthetic Imagination* (1998). It examines and compares the cosmological designs of three extraordinary visionaries from three different periods of Western history: Hildegard of Bingen (Middle Ages), Jacob Boehme (Renaissance), and Charles Fourier (nineteenth century). Their writings are exemplary for the richness of their sensory imaginings and for the distinctive ways in which each thinker engaged with the outlook of their respective epoch. According to Classen, St Hildegard elaborated a divine "geography of the senses," dividing the cosmos into five parts and allotting a different sense to each; Boehme invented a mystical "chemistry of the senses," inspired by Renaissance alchemy; Fourier crafted a "political economy of the senses," critiquing the "abuse of the senses" in the civilization of his day and envisioning a utopia in which each of the senses could flourish. As Classen's work shows, the "whatness" (ontology) of the universe can only ever be grasped as such through know-how – that is, through the mediation of the senses.

2   *Emplacement.* In "The Everyday City of the Senses" (2014), cultural sociologist Mónica Degen presents an overview of research in the geography, anthropology, and history of the senses and then applies the insights she derives from this survey to the analysis of urban sensations and contemporary urban development policies. Her account highlights the importance of the senses in "structuring and mediating" the everyday life and experience of the city. Degen (2014, 99) describes the aim of her method – the "walk-along" – as being to gain access to others' "immediate sensing and embodiment in spaces ... and to consider this experience reflexively." Of particular note is her analysis of the racial, gendered, and class-based sensory ideologies that inform the planning of cities, and the shift from managerial forms of governance to an "entrepreneurial approach," as can be seen in the way cities increasingly strive to brand themselves and promote their unique "place differentiating qualities" to investors, residents, and visitors alike.

3   *Materiality.* The field of the material and visual culture of religion has been enlivened in recent years by the adoption of a sensory studies approach. In her landmark 2006 *Art Bulletin* article entitled "The Performative Icon" (2006) and again in *The Sensual Icon* (2013), medieval art historian Bissera Pentcheva

explores the "original setting" of the icon in Byzantine culture. She highlights the performativity of the materiality of the icon – specifically, its "textured surfaces." She also emphasizes the multisensory dynamism of the icon's display and veneration (which involve incense, chants, the flickering light of candles, and the act of kissing the icon). Icons were not solely addressed to the eye (as we moderns assume): their effectiveness as channels of and for the experience of the divine was a function of their *intersensoriality* and "exuberant materiality." Pentcheva (2006, 631) holds that the sensory multiplicity of Byzantine ritual produces "synesthesis," defined as "simultaneity of sensation," but not "synaesthesia" – that is, "the experience of one sense through the stimulation of another." This distinction between synesthesis and synaesthesia is extremely useful. It can be applied to many situations in which multiple senses are mobilized. It helps foster more refined attention to how the senses are joined.

Art historian and religious studies scholar Sally M. Promey, the director of Material and Visual Culture of Religion (MAVCOR) at Yale University, offers an eminently sensible, materialist critique of modernization and secularization theory in her introduction to *Sensational Religion* (2014). Secularization theory foretold the disappearance of religion, while modernization theory posited the "progression" of religion to "an 'advanced' private and dematerialized state of interiority and invisibility" – i.e., "modern religion" (as prefigured in the restricted sensory regime of Protestant Christianity that crystallized during the Reformation). As Promey (2014, 6–7) brings out, the latter (restrictive) sensibility spilled over into the Modernist (high formalist) conception of art, a point also taken up by art historian Caroline A. Jones (2006a, 2006c, 2017). In any event, neither vision has come to pass. On the contrary, many religions now assert themselves publicly and sensuously as never before (see Weiner 2014). Promey (2014, 7) adduces a number of reasons for why the "supersessionary binaries" of secularization theory (e.g., primitive/modern, sacred/secular, concrete/abstract, sensation/cognition) have ended in an impasse. Primary among these reasons is secularization theory's failure to grapple with the *materiality* of religious practices and objects due to the presupposition of religion being a metaphysical affair. Religion is never just a matter of belief, Promey argues. She concludes by stating that "We need new stories, adjusted to different sorts of material and sensory reality" to make sense of religious pluralism in the present (Promey 2014, 13).

4 *Memory.* "The Proust Effect" takes its name from the author *of À la recherche du temps perdu*. Everyone is familiar with the incident involving the madeleine cake dipped in tea: the crumbly savour of the madeleine precipitated a moment of "total recall" in the novelist, suffused with the sentiments of childhood, and gave rise to the doctrine of smell being the sense of memory

and emotion. The transformation of Proust's anecdote into scientific "fact" and artistic commonplace is a fascinating history in itself. So is its operationalization. In *The Proust Effect* (2014),[7] Cretien van Campen, an accomplished author and researcher with the Netherlands Institute for Social Research, devotes a chapter to the operationalization of the doctrine of "the memory of the senses" in the therapeutic culture of late modernity. As he relates, the Dutch have long been at the forefront of research into how the construction of environments that facilitate sensory reminiscence can function as a means to counteract dementia, depression, and other egodystonic states (such as isolation) in older people. Van Campen surveys this development from the creation of the Snoezelen room back in the 1970s through to the present. His account of the evolution of these therapeutic chambers provides a critical framework for the evaluation of the burgeoning literature on Autism, which has been recast as a "sensory processing disorder" in recent years (see also Rourke 2019), and the huge industry that has grown up around creating environments that modulate sensations in the interests of enabling non-neurotypical individuals to "adjust" (see further Grace 2020).

5 *Alterity.* In the previous chapter, we saw how the racialization of the senses contributes to the othering of immigrants in New York City. Other "others" include persons living with disabilities, such as blindness or deafness. The latter persons have been discriminated against historically for not conforming to the sensory model of the dominant society or "able" body (Barasch 2001; Rée 1999). What happens when the clines of sensory and social differentiation intersect? Sociologist Asia Friedman takes up the question of racial attribution by the visually impaired in a seminal article in *The Sociological Quarterly* (2016). Racial discrimination in America is a reflex of discrimination based on skin colour (or so it is assumed), but if a person cannot see then how can they tell another person's race? Fascinatingly, Friedman brings out how there is a process of *deliberation* involved in racial attribution by the blind, which gives the lie to racialization being a reflex. As she shows, racialization, in fact, depends on the prior cultural construction of a sense of difference. Friedman's study has profound implications for our understanding of the "sensorial construction of reality" as an integral aspect of the "social construction of reality" (Berger and Luckman 1966; Friedman 2016).

Friedman's article is of a piece with the burgeoning literature in Critical Disability Studies that seeks to probe beyond the representation of alterity (where the emphasis is always on the *projection* of able-bodied schemas onto "others") by tapping into the lived experience of those othered in this way. This helps to unsettle many stereotypes (Hammer 2019; Graif 2018).

6 *Mediation.* In another chapter of *The Color of Angels*, entitled "Pens and Needles" (1998, ch. 4), Constance Classen explores the gender coding of

the senses in Western history, and how this served to explain and legiti-
mate the assignment of men and women to different social spheres. Men
have traditionally been associated with the "higher," "spiritual," "distance"
senses of vision and audition while women were conventionally identified
with the "lower," "animal," "proximity" senses of gustation, olfaction, and
touch. Within the context of this *socially* gendered sensorium:

> Men's star-set mastery of the distance senses ... empowered them to travel,
> to read and write, to conquer and govern. As the guardians of the proximity
> senses ... women's place was in the home, cooking, sewing, and taking care of
> families. (Classen 1998, 6–7)

Thus, the hierarchy of the sexes, the hierarchy of the senses, and the hierarchy
of media (i.e., writing as a male and primarily visual activity vs. sewing or
needlework as a female and primarily tactile activity) correspond. Such was
the power of this sexual division of labour, media, and the senses that those
women who sought to read instead of cook, or take up the pen instead of the
needle, faced severe social opprobrium until well into the twentieth century.

Margaret Cavendish, Duchess of Newcastle, was one of the rare early
modern women who managed to crack the mould, by schooling herself
and penning treatises and fictional works. The latter, notably *Blazing
World*, offer a startlingly different take on the sexes, the senses, and the
cosmos compared to the world views of Cavendish's seventeenth-century
male contemporaries. For example, she disagreed with the opinion (articulated most forcefully by Descartes) that "all knowledge is in the Mind
and none in the Senses":

> Cavendish argued that each part of the body and each sense has its own
> knowledge: "the Eye is as knowing as the Ear, and the Ear as knowing as the
> Nose, and the Nose as Knowing as the Tongue." She similarly stated in favor of
> a bodily intelligence that, "the Heads Braines cannot ingross all knowledge to
> themselves." (Classen 1998, 101)

This is a stunning charter for a democracy of the mind and senses.

In the notes accompanying *Blazing World*, which is pure science fiction, Cavendish went so far as to suggest that experimental science is a
more suitable field for housewives, given how they employ their time "in
Brewing, Baking, Churning, Spinning, Sowing" (all very experimental)
than for philosophers, with their overreliance on "Optick Glasses." Cavendish (quite rightly) argued that examining the world through telescopes
and microscopes engendered a grossly distorted image of it: "lenses can
produce a magnified image of a louse, but not of a whale, they can operate in light but not in darkness, they can enhance one sense but are of no
use to any of the others," and, worst of all, they "reveal only surfaces, and
not interiors or 'the obscure actions of Nature'" (104). Little wonder that

Cavendish's copious and somewhat formless writings (which she, not insignificantly, preferred to think of as "spinnings") were not well received: "Mad Madge," some of her contemporaries called her, and she was repeatedly attacked for her heretical opinions and lack of "female modesty."

Summing up, Classen's chapter is noteworthy for bringing to light how Cavendish penned the first feminist epistemology of the senses, and for its "archaeology" of the sensory and social foundations of such enduring commonplaces as "the male gaze" and "the female touch." Particularly moving is her account of how Cavendish boldly imagined a female-centred community in her play *The Convent of Pleasure*, where women achieve fulfilment though gratifying their senses, instead of subordinating them to men's desires.

Circling back to sociology, Vannini, Waskul, and Gottschalk, in addition to problematizing hyperconsumption (see above), devote a section of *The Senses in Self, Society and Culture* to "Virtualization: Sensory Atrophy and Disconnection." There, the authors examine "computer-mediated communication" (CMC) involving personal computers, cellphones, and suchlike in today's society, and reflect on how our sensory orientations and psychosocial dispositions have been "reconfigured" by these electronic technologies. Echoing McLuhan, Vannini, Waskul, and Gottschalk argue that CMC creates "environments" that extend and enhance the sensorium, but there is also an underside to this development: "the virtual environment atrophies and disconnects the sensorium" at the same time. In tracing the complex social and cognitive effects of the electronification of the senses with a critical eye, Vannini and company exemplify how "sensory critique is the beginning of social critique" – one of the key "Propositions for Sensory Studies" laid out in the prologue to this Manifesto.

7 *Movement.* "Grasping the Phenomenology of Sporting Bodies" (2007) by sociologists John Hockey and Jacquelyn Allen-Collinson (both avid runners) is a landmark article in the sociology of sport and physical activity. The authors examine the personal narratives of athletes and employ autoethnography to arrive at minute descriptions of what they style the "ceaseless stream of kinesthesias, cutaneous and visceral sensations" of the body in motion; they also evoke such outward manifestations as the smell of exertion and sounds of respiratory patterns. Hockey and Allen-Collinson bring out well the importance of timing and rhythm in sport, and at the same time highlight the need for the athlete to attend to the total "sporting environment" (the equipment, the terrain, other players). In this way, the authors lay the sensorial/phenomenological groundwork for approaching and theorizing athletic competence as embodied skill. Their articulation of a program for research, centring on the "sensory intelligence" of the sporting body, has given the sociology of sport a second wind, as can be seen in

the plethora of studies that engage with more extreme forms of sport, such as mixed martial arts (Spencer 2014; Sparkes 2017). This body of research puts the endurance of the researcher to the test: for example, Dale Spencer's research method is largely non-discursive insofar as it involves entering the ring and mixing it up with fellow mixed martial arts enthusiasts. Doing sensory sociology in the no-holds- (and no-kicks-) barred way Spencer does puts the body and senses at risk. It is "somatic work" (as Phillip Vannini would say) which borders on "edgework" (Lyng 2004).

In today's society of "hyperconsumption," being a sports fan vies with (and often eclipses) being an athlete oneself. In "Sporting Sensation" (2006), marketing professor John F. Sherry Jr. examines how the senses are engaged in the brandscaped sports bar – specifically, ESPN Zone Chicago, which he characterizes as a "two-story sensory inundation tank." Here is his description of the "sanctum sanctorum" of the Zone – the "Ultimate Viewing Area," the Throne:

> Ensconced in a luxurious La-Z Boy, enveloped in surround-sound audio feeds of live sports matches broadcast on a bank of enormous screens and controlled by a finger panel on the arm of the recliner, served by women who ensure constant delivery of food and drink, the rapt consumer may experience many a slip between cup and lip as the images wash over him, or as an eerily authentic crack of a bat and the reflexive expectation of a line drive to the head startles him from reverie … "Eat. Drink. Watch. Play. What More Could You Want?" (Sherry 2006, 246)

Sherry's case study reveals the extent to which *hyperaesthesia* has become the new normal with the rise of the so-called experience economy (Howes 2005c; Mack 2012).

8 *Affect*. "Listening-Touch: Affect and the Crafting of Medical Bodies through Percussion," which first came out in *Body & Society* in 2016, is written by Anna Harris of the Department of Society Studies, Maastricht University. Harris undertook her medical education to find out how the senses of the novice physician are "produced" through training (i.e., her investigation started not with the anatomy of the senses but with the analysis of sensory practice). She relates how she first concentrated on the stethoscope and auscultation (the fourth step in the the basic clinical examination), but after one of her instructors pointed out that percussion (the third step) is "a form of sound" too, she started following it, until another doctor declared that the practice was not about sound but about touch. "I know this is contrary to your study," he drawled, "but I could do percussion if I was deaf – its about the feel of the percussion rather than the sound" (Harris 2016, 35). Probing further, Harris discovered that percussion is neither just about hearing nor only about touch, but both: listening-touch, hearing fingers.

In the course of her study Harris had a further revelation: there are "three kinds of bodies" that are "produced" in the course of learning and teaching percussion: the enskilled body (after Tim Ingold), the body "trained to be affected," which is important to the discernment of differences and similarities (after Bruno Latour), and the resonating body (new), which emerges "when practitioners attend to their own sensations and the sensory aspects of their interior" (34) – that is, when they practise percussion on their own bodies, and thereby render the latter "both perceiver and perceived." All of these concatenations of listening-touch, and particularly the last, point to how percussion is intersensory, in the final analysis. Reflecting on the import of her experience of the "dissolution" of the perceiver and the perceived through self-touch, Harris came round to the view that "Knowing and being cannot be separated." This affirmation relativizes ontology in the very act of sensing it.[8]

Self-perception – or, as here, "self-touch" – is rarely examined in conventional accounts of diagnostic practice (where the focus is on the body of the patient, not the expert clinician). However, one thing Harris found in looking at self-perception was that "students not only develop the muscles, nerves and body parts needed for percussion (wrists, fingertips, ears) but also livers and spleens and hearts and lungs" (2016, 34). This is a lovely example of the extent to which touch is, indeed, "the deepest sense" (Classen 2012). Tellingly, it was most often during after-hours conversations with her classmates, when they compared notes, rather than in the lecture hall or the tutorial, that Harris arrived at her insights. For example, one fellow student confided to her: "I walk around tapping myself all the time" (Harris 2016, 47). Eliciting insights like this admission is the mark of a true ethnographer – the anthropologist who "follows the ethnography" wherever it may take her, instead of subordinating her inquiry to theory (Ingold, Latour). In Harris' account, the senses become directly in their practice theoreticians. Rather than concentrate only on the education *of* the senses in medicine, what she (and her classmates) did was to allow themselves to be educated *by* the senses.

Harris pursues these lines of inquiry further in her recent book, *A Sensory Education* (2020), which extends her sensorial investigations from medical training and practice to the cultivation or "crafting" of the faculties in the practices of everyday life, such as cooking and knitting. In this book, Harris crosses sensory studies and affect studies, and enriches both fields immeasurably in the process.

9 *Representation.* The early modern period is a fascinating epoch in the history of the senses due to all the social transformations that took place, such as the European encounter with the Americas, which brought with it

a range of new sensations; the transition from feudalism to capitalism; and the Reformation, which precipitated a massive sensorial as well as spiritual transformation (Milner 2011). Scholars of this epoch were among the first to delve into the historicity of the senses and perception in a meaningful way; for example, the groundbreaking work of Witse de Boer (2013) on the "moral economy of the senses," and the work of diverse literary scholars and cultural critics on the representation of the senses in literature (e.g., Harvey 2003).

In "Take Five" (2009), English professor Patricia Cahill surveys the many lively debates and discussions in this burgeoning field of inquiry. She traces how disputes over the relative dominance of the eye have steadily been supplanted by research into the contours of early modern aurality, the centrality of touch, and the popular motif of the "Banquet of Sense." The hierarchy of the senses turns out to have been far less stable (and more open to contestation) than is commonly thought, as illustrated most poignantly by the play *Lingua, or the Combat of the Tongue and the Five Senses for Superiority* (Tomkis 1607) and other dramas (see further Mazzio 2005).

Cahill concludes her survey by framing a series of questions that prompt a radical rethinking of the role of the senses, especially touch, in performance, both historically and up to the present, such as, "If we scrutinize historical narratives about touch, then perhaps we will be better able to understand, in a more expansive, historicized, and searching manner than existing scholarship offers: what might it mean to be 'touched' by a play? What happens when we move beyond spectacle and soundscape to explore the tactile dimension of theatricality?" (Cahill 2009, 1026; see further Banes and Lepecki 2007). Going to the theatre was a full-contact sport in Shakespeare's day, particularly for those in the pit at the Globe Theatre. Literary scholars and historians have also found in Shakespeare's plays a treasure trove of sensuous representations, including such tropes as "to see feelingly" and "the key of green" (Dundas 1985; B. Smith 2009). These explorations rattle the foundations of the order laid down by E.M. Tillyard in his classic *The Elizabethan World Picture* ([1942] 2011) by sensing between the lines of historical sources and redirecting attention from the period eye to the period sensorium.

10 *Gustation.* Michael Pollan's account of the meaning of sweetness for the European settlers of North America in a little section of his bestselling book *The Botany of Desire* (2001) is a tantalizing example of the subgenre of the history of the senses referred to earlier as the "history of *particular sensations.*" "It wasn't until late in the nineteenth century," Pollan writes "that sugar became plentiful and cheap enough to enter the lives of many Americans; before then the sensation of sweetness in the lives of most

people came chiefly from the flesh of fruit" and this usually meant the apple. As Pollan goes on to observe, during the colonial era and prior:

> The experience of sweetness was so special that the word served as a metaphor for a certain kind of perfection. When writers like Jonathan Swift and Matthew Arnold used the expression "sweetness and light" to name their highest ideal … they were drawing on a sense of the word sweetness going back to classical times, a sense that has largely been lost to us. The best land was said to be sweet; so were the most pleasing sounds, the most persuasive talk, the loveliest views, the most refined people, and the choicest part of any whole … Lent by the tongue to all the other sense organs, "sweet," in the somewhat archaic definition of the *Oxford English Dictionary*, is that which "affords enjoyment or gratifies desire." Like a shimmering equal sign, the word sweetness denoted a reality commensurate with human desire. Since then sweetness has lost much of its power and become slightly … well, saccharine. (Pollan 2001, 12)

Pollan suggests that we need to recuperate this lost usage of the word "sweet" if we are ever to appreciate the apple's former power as the embodiment of a sensation bordering on perfection that resonates across and in multiple modalities. He neglects to mention that we also need to further consider the role of slave plantations in making sugary sensations widely available in the nineteenth century (Mintz 1985).

Luca Vercelloni is a cultural historian and brand analyst (the president of Brandvoyager Corp., in fact). In *The Invention of Taste: A Cultural Account of Desire, Delight and Disgust in Fashion, Food and Art* (2016), he zeroes in on the origin of gastronomy. According to Vercelloni, the invention of gastronomy can be traced to the heady days in the aftermath of the French Revolution when restaurants sprang up all over Paris, manned by the chefs who had been put out of work by the execution of many of their patrons. These restaurants provided the emergent bourgeoisie with an institutional context for self-fashioning, and the gastronome provided them with a compass and language in which to speak of their desires. While most accounts of the process of individuation in modernity link it to the birth of the "surveillance society" (Foucault 1979), Vercelloni (2016) offers an alternative account, showing how the "appetising eloquence" of the discourse of gastronomy provided "a way of enclosing individual sensibility" for the bourgeoisie.

11 *Synaesthesia*. The Western imagination has long harboured the dream of transcending the limits of the senses and achieving a state of "universal harmony" or union with the cosmos. The origins of this dream are divine – that is, religiously inspired as Pentcheva and Classen have shown (see also Jørgensen, Laugerud, and Skinnebach 2015) – but the underlying notion of a fusion of the senses has also been a topic of scientific

investigation and artistic experimentation since the late 1600s. Of particular interest in this connection is the phenomenon of colour-sound synaesthesia, which involves the merging of sight and hearing.

In a seminal essay entitled "Color and Sound: Transcending the Limits of the Senses" (2013), cultural historian Fay Zika describes three "periods of discussion" surrounding the phenomenon of colour-sound synaesthesia led by particular scientific discoveries. In the late seventeenth century, before colour-sound synaesthesia was systematically categorized, the idea was entertained that it is possible to perceive an analogy between colours and sounds due to their common vibratory nature. Sir Isaac Newton codified these correspondences with his theory of the seven primary colours being in accord with the seven musical tones of the Western seven-tone scale. In the second half of the nineteenth century, spurred by advances in the study of human psychology, colour-sound synaesthesia (still typically known under other names, such as "synopsia" or "photism") came to be studied as an "actual" perceptual phenomenon, and the focus shifted from analogy to physiology. In the twentieth century, the discussion shifted yet again, from physiology to the plasticity of the brain, and the possibility of experiencing the content of one sensory modality by means of another was "actually" realized in the context of various experiments with prosthetic devices. These devices included the tactile-visual substitution system (TVSS) invented by Paul Bach-y-Rita, a complex apparatus involving a head-mounted television camera linked to electrically driven vibrators attached to a square of skin on the back of a blind person. The TVSS "throws" an image of the objects in the blind person's surroundings onto the patch of skin, and this tactile stimulation is transposed into visual information in the brain, thereby enabling the person to move in space without bumping into things. Another such device is the "eyeborg," which harnesses different colours (as light reflected from surfaces at different frequencies) to different sound frequencies, so the blind person is able to "see with their ears."

Zika discusses how the understanding of synaesthesia has been dogged by the suspicion that it is but a "figment of the imagination" – motivated by sensory association, metaphorical transfer, or simply hallucination. (This suspicion is indicative of the countervailing force of the five-sense model of the sensorium, or "modular" theory of the brain and perception.) She herself cleaves to the neurological definition but makes a point of documenting how the *idea* of synaesthesia spurred numerous artists and inventors to attempt to *induce* synaesthetic perceptions in their audiences, whence the "ocular harpsichord" developed by the French Jesuit Louis Bertrand Castel in the 1720s, the "colour organ" invented by the British painter Alexander Rimington in 1895, or the abstract paintings of Wassily Kandinsky in the early twentieth century. Nevertheless, according to Zika, all such artistic attempts were bound to come up short, because synaesthesia (the neurological condition) is not widely distributed, and it is highly idiosyncratic to boot.

Zika's suggestion that the problem of transcending the limits of the senses of sight and sound can and has been solved through sensory substitution systems (e.g., TVSS, the eyeborg) is an ingenious one, but it founders on account of her deference to the restricted definition of synaesthesia as a neurological condition. Enter anthropologist Silvia Casini, who boldly proclaims, "we are all synesthetes" (just not in a strictly neurological sense): "we can feel goose bumps not only when it is chilly but also in the presence of disturbing or emotional images or when hearing the sudden scratch of chalk across the blackboard." In "Synesthesia, Transformation and Synthesis" (2017), Casini approaches synaesthesia "as a cultural phenomenon," and focusses on the art of synaesthesia, though without ignoring the science. She notes that the root meaning of the term suggests a form of "feeling in common" or "common-sensing," and thus has a social dimension (i.e., synaesthesia is not confined to the individual brain), which may in turn ground "a politics of perception" with transformative potential. Casini illustrates her thesis via an analysis of three works by the contemporary German cross-media artist Johannes Deutsch: 1) an interactive multimodal garden for the blind and sighted, 2) a multimedia visualization of Gustav Mahler's second symphony, and 3) a multisensory interactive opera inspired by Ovid's *Metamorphoses*. By taking the study of synaesthesia out of the psychology laboratory and into the art gallery and elaborating a "pedagogy of the image" grounded in intersensory relations, Casini takes us a considerable way towards realizing McLuhan's vision for an "education of the senses" (see Friesen [2011] 2018).

Concluding Note

This chapter has shown how the twin founders of cultural history (Huizinga) and social history (Febvre), as of sociology (Simmel) and critical theory (Benjamin), were positively attuned to the life of the senses. The beachheads they established were soon abandoned, however, and psychology reasserted its dominion. Theoretical and more-than-theoretical interest in the senses revived in the 1990s, thanks to the interventions of Corbin, Classen, and (latterly) Smith in history, and Synnott, Sennett, and (latterly) Vannini and company in sociology. The sense-centred inquiries that have ensued have yielded many profound insights into the sociality of sensation and contingency of perception. It remains to be seen how this groundswell of sensuous scholarship has impacted psychology and the neurosciences – the focus of the next chapter.

CHAPTER THREE

On the Psychology and Neurobiology of the Senses in Historical and Cross-Cultural Perspective

In his account of "normal science" in *The Structure of Scientific Revolutions* (1970), the historian of science Thomas Kuhn (1970, 138) encapsulated his theory with a somewhat unsettling quote from the philosopher Alfred North Whitehead: "A science that hesitates to forget its founders is lost." By quoting Whitehead, Kuhn sought to underline the dependence of scientific knowledges on sets of assumptions or "paradigms" that are historical, yet ignore their own historicity. Indeed, forgetting earlier paradigms is the condition of success for "normal science." As Steve Fuller puts it, "science cannot progress unless its practitioners *take for granted* that it rests on secure epistemic foundations ... they should be willing to 'forget' the past in the sense of *discarding* it when necessary" (2000, 302n89). Only in "revolutionary" moments, when the "exceptional phenomena" pile up and can no longer be boxed in by the prevailing paradigm, does (veritable) innovation take precedence over repetition and tradition, according to Kuhn, and this is usually thanks to a few stalwart individuals who – at the risk of being branded misguided, unscientific, lunatic, or worse – propose new paradigms that can accommodate the recalcitrant phenomena.

The approach advocated in this chapter is "revolutionary." Contrary to the above-mentioned prescription for scientific advancement, however, it insists on *remembrance* and *cross-cultural comparison*. Thus, in what follows, the prevailing assumptions regarding the nature and function of the senses within "normal science" (contemporary Western psychology and neuroscience) will be confronted with historical facts (i.e., allegedly outmoded paradigms going back to Aristotle) and with cross-cultural data (i.e., Indigenous biologies, psychologies, and neurologies). This chapter's objective is to arrive at a resolutely historical and cross-cultural, multimodal, and intermodal theory of "sensory processing." This will in turn bring the genealogical trajectory of the previous two chapters to its climax, at least for the time being, since in Parts 2 and 3 of this Manifesto shall be shifting tracks yet again.

In "Overture I: "Sensory Individuation," the boundaries of the five-sense model of the sensorium are exposed and unsettled by examining the postulate of "the sixth sense," which has assumed many different guises through history. In "Overture II: Sensory Interaction," we turn to explore breaking research within psychology and neuroscience on the sensory integration of the brain. This research calls into question the whole project of individuating the senses, and institutes a radically relational, interactive understanding of how the senses function in its place. The latter understanding is consonant with the emphasis on relationality and the interactivity of the senses within sensory studies.

I. Laying The Foundations

Overture I: Sensory Individuation

REFIGURING THE SENSORIUM

As discussed in the prologue, in the early modern period the term "sensorium" was used to denote the "percipient centre," or "seat of sensation in the brain" (and is still used in this sense today), but also extended to include what could be called the circumference of perception. We see this in the usage from 1861: "Rome became the common sensorium of Europe, and through Rome all the several portions of Latin Europe sympathized and felt with each other."

The notion of the *sensorium* is thus a very capacious or *holistic* one. Thanks to its holism it can stand for "the five senses," which is one way of construing the totality of percipience, but nothing prevents it from being extended to other constructions, other models, such as "the two senses" (see below) or "the seven senses" (see Jütte 2005, 54–60), and so forth. This is a major advantage from the historical and cross-cultural (i.e., sensory studies) standpoint advocated in this Manifesto, since it enables us to incorporate the concepts and practices of other cultures and other historical periods into our discussion of the varieties of "sensory processing." For example, the Hausa of Nigeria have one word for sight (*gani*) and another for hearing, smelling, tasting, and touching, understanding, and emotional feeling (*ji*), "as if all these functions formed part of a single whole" (Ritchie 1991, 194). The Javanese "have five senses (seeing, hearing, *talking*, smelling and feeling), which do not coincide exactly with our five" (Dundes 1980, 92). The Cashinahua of Peru hold that knowledge resides in the skin, the hands, the ears, the genitals, the liver, and the eyes, hence six "senses" – or better, "percipient centres." "Does [the] brain have knowledge?" their ethnographer, Kenneth Kensinger (1995, 239), asked, assuming that the brain must constitute some sort of processing centre or "data-bank": "'*Hamaki* (it doesn't),' they responded ... 'the whole body knows.'"

Among the Cashinahua, "skin knowledge" (*bichi una*) is the knowledge of the environment (including the behaviour patterns of animals and other persons) that people acquire through their skin – through the *feel* of the sun, the wind, the rain, and the forest. It is the sense of presence. Skin knowledge is what enables people to find their way through the jungle or a hunter to locate prey. "Hand knowledge" (*meken una*) is what enables a man to shoot an animal with bow and arrow or chop down a tree and a woman to weave, make pottery, and cook. The eyes are the locus of the "eye spirit," which enables a person to see the spiritual insides or substance of persons, animals, and things as opposed to their surface (which is the domain of skin knowledge). "Social knowledge is gained through and resides in the ears and therefore is called *pabinki una*, ear knowledge" (241). This last usage could be taken to reflect the centrality of aurality in Cashinahua social life. "It is in one's liver that one feels joy and sorrow, fear and hope, distrust and pleasure," whence the term "liver knowledge" (*taka una*) to refer to knowledge of emotions (243). Finally, knowledge of one's mortality and immortality, or "life force," has its seat in the genitals.

The Hausa, Javanese, and Cashinahua perceptual paradigms all challenge the conventional Western model of "the five senses." In contemporary Westerrn society, we are not accustomed to thinking of speech as a sense as do the Javanese; unlike the Hausa we think of perception and emotion as separate functions; and we balk at the Cashinahua suggestion that the brain is not the seat of cognition. If we were more conscious of the history of the senses in the West, however, we would not be so dismissive. It could be argued that we moderns have been blinded to sensory diversity by an overexposure to the now standard fivefold arrangement of the sensorium, which can be found everywhere, from children's books on "The Five Senses" to the compartmentalization of the senses in and by the discipline of psychology, as reflected in most introductory textbooks on perception (e.g., Goldstein 2002; Bossomaier 2012; Mather 2016; DeSalle 2018).

Just as it is necessary to bracket the assumptions of the psychology of perception to make any headway in the study of the sensorium across cultures, so an awareness of the cultural contingency of sensory categorizations is the indispensable starting point of any inquiry into the varieties of sensory (and extrasensory) experience in Western history. As Louise Vinge observes in "The Five Senses in Classical Science and Ethics,"

> Sight, hearing, smell, taste and touch: that the senses should be enumerated in this way is not self-evident. The number and order of the senses are fixed by custom and tradition, not by nature. The regular order being subject to occasional change proves its arbitrariness. (2009, 107)

One way to imagine the ever-shifting divisions and relations among the senses in different cultures and historical periods is by analogy to a kaleidoscope. With each twist of its shaft, the kaleidoscope reveals a different alignment of shapes and colours.[1] Another analogy for imagining the composition of the sensorium would be by reference to a fugue, such as J.S. Bach's *Goldberg Variations* (particularly as interpreted by Glenn Gould). The essence of a fugue consists in the simultaneity of voices:

> a melody is always in the process of being repeated by one or another voice ... Any series of notes is thus capable of an infinite set of transformations, as the series (or melody or subject) is taken up first by one voice then by another, the voices always continuing to sound against, as well as with, all the others. (Said 1983, 47)

The medallions designed by Erik Adigard for the front and back covers of this book blend these two analogies – kaleidoscope and fugue – in a singularly compelling and dynamic fashion: you can virtually see the fugue and hear the kaleidoscope – or "collideroscope" of the sensorium (McLuhan 1962: 75 after Joyce). (See further "collideroscope," http://www.sensorystudies.org/picture-gallery/.)

THE SENSE OF SPEECH

With this image of the revolving sensorium in mind, let us consider the case for speech as a sensory faculty. The idea of speech as a sense, akin to sight or touch, has surfaced repeatedly in the history of the Western sensorium. One of the first to champion it was Philo in the first century (Classen 1993b, 2).[2] It reappears from time to time, explicitly or implicitly, in the Middle Ages: for example, in confessional manuals, where there is the occasional reference to "the five senses and speech," as if they formed a set (Woolgar 2006, 11–12). One source in which there is no ambiguity as to the sensory status of speech is the work of the fourteenth-century Catalan philosopher Ramon Llull. Llull wrote a Catalan book on the subject of the sixth sense (translated as *Liber de sexto sensu* in 1294), where he writes that "we call the previously mentioned sixth sense the affatus [speech and voice]" (Llull 2014, 128). In his *Ars breuis, quae est de inuentione iuris* (Brief art that concerns the discovery of law), Llull confirmed the standing of speech as a sense: "The common sense contains within itself six particular powers coessential to it, but remains substantially undivided. These powers, each different in its organs, objects and figures are the following, namely: the powers of touch, taste, smell, sight, hearing and speech and voice (affatiua)" (Llull 1984, 300).[3]

The seventeenth-century play *Lingua, or the Combat of the Tongue and the Five Senses for Superiority* (Tomkis 1607) played on speech's liminal position as a sense. In the play, female Lingua (Speech) is painted as "an idle prating dame," ever "babbling" by male Auditus (Hearing) and denounced for her presumption (i.e., wanting to be considered a sense): "We were never accounted more than five," Auditus asserts. Common Sense, who is called on to judge the dispute, rules that Speech is not a sense, except in the case of women: "all women for your sake shall have six senses – that is seeing, hearing, tasting, smelling, touching, and the last and feminine sense, the sense of speaking" (quoted and discussed in Classen 1998, 74–5; see further Mazzio 2005). This remark implies, albeit in jest, that the number of sensory faculties varies between women and men.

In the twentieth century, the notion of speech – or rather, "language" – being a natural faculty once again attracted a champion in the person of Noam Chomsky. He argued that the human capacity for language is innate. Chomsky's hypothesis of the existence of a "language organ" in the human brain is now widely accepted by linguists (Anderson and Lightfoot 2002), though they tend to see it as a cognitive faculty, not a sensory organ.

THE PSYCHIC SENSE (EXTRASENSORY PERCEPTION)

While the idea of speech or language as a sense continues to percolate (see, e.g., Truss 2003), by far the most common current usage of the phrase "sixth sense" concerns what is known as extrasensory perception. ESP regroups many different powers (to be discussed presently), including "seeing spirits." The latter notion was popularized in the 1999 Hollywood blockbuster film *The Sixth Sense*. The idea of "seeing spirits" (or rather "dead people") as portrayed in that film can be traced back to the Spiritualist movement of the late nineteenth century with all its séances (though the Spiritualists were more concerned with "hearing spirits," interestingly). That movement resulted in the creation of learned societies in both Britain and North America dedicated to the investigation of "psychic phenomena" (e.g., the British Society for Psychical Research, founded in 1882). The leaders of these societies went to extraordinary lengths devising protocols to test the powers of their research subjects (who were typically female spirit mediums) in an effort to winnow "scientific fact" from "superstitious nonsense," and outright fraud (Thurschwell 2001; Robertson 2016). The interests of psychical researchers went beyond spirit mediumship to encompass such extrasensory capacities as thought transference or "telepathy," premonitions or "precognition," and clairvoyance or "remote-viewing," among others. Generally speaking, these psychic "senses" are scientized versions of the occult powers known to the Spiritualists, with the main difference being that they were deemed to be mental rather than spiritual faculties.

The scientization of so-called occult powers began with the establishment of the above-mentioned societies for psychic research. In the early twentieth century, psychic research spread to universities and government research laboratories. The substitution of technical terms such as "precognition" for premonitions and "psychokinesis" for levitation was an important component of the process of rationalizing the occult. It created the impression that all of these historically disparate phenomena had a common denominator, and so could be jointly analysed in the present. For example, "Second Sight," a peculiarly Scottish phenomenon (Feibel 2000), was abstracted from its original context and became a generic term (Cohn 1999), interchangeable with precognition and remote viewing – the new common denominators.

This process came to a head in 1934. It was in that year that the psychologist J.B. Rhine of Duke University published *Extra-Sensory Perception* – a book which, somewhat surprisingly for an academic treatise, was picked up on by millions of readers. In this book, Rhine reported the results of a wide (and often ingenious) array of experiments that tested the psychic abilities of his research subjects. The most famous of these tests involved a pack of twenty-five cards, known as Zener cards, with each card displaying one of five symbols. Subjects were asked to predict the order of all twenty-five cards when spread before them on a desk, face down. If a subject consistently guessed more than five cards correctly, thereby defying the law of averages, this was taken to be evidence of psychic ability.

By taking the study of psychic abilities out of the darkened séance parlour and into the light of the laboratory; by replacing anecdotal accounts with statistical tables; by controlling for trickery; and by devising numerous quite ingenious and – most importantly – *repeatable* experimental procedures, Rhine managed to attract an aura of scientificity to the investigation of psychic powers. Plain, dry statistics produced in a laboratory setting enabled the murky powers of the occult to be garbed in the robes of scientific fact. But it was by coining the term "extra-sensory perception" for the title for his book that Rhine showed the greatest ingenuity, as the following account illustrates:

> [Rhine] told a friend that he wanted "to make it sound as normal as may be." Perception was an established subject of psychology by that time, and Rhine hoped psychologists would recognize ESP as a branch of perception, rather than as some otherworldly, nonprofessional pastime. (Kagan, Daniels, and Horan 1987, 54)

The strategy worked. The discipline of parapsychology (another of Rhine's neologisms) was born, and thanks to the lobbying efforts of a host of prominent intellectuals, including Margaret Mead, the American Association for the Advancement of Science was persuaded to admit the Parapsychological Association as an affiliate in 1969.

ESP, also known as "the psi faculty,"[4] thus became the *next* sixth sense (see, e.g., Pearson 2003; Jütte 2005, ch. 16), an umbrella term for a wide range of "inexplicable" mental powers and "paranormal" experiences, including all those listed above, and others which Rhine had no time for, such as "Out-of-Body Experiences" (OBE), "Near-Death-Experiences" (NDE), and reincarnation or "retrocognition," to name but a few. These further additions to the "additional faculty" of perception invented by Rhine reflect the inability of the discipline of parapsychology to control the destiny of its brainchild. Indeed, the founding and institutionalization of parapsychology played a decisive role in the emergence of what David Hess (1993) has called a new "paraculture," referring to the "arena of debate" that crystallized in the 1960s (and continues to escalate)

in which New Agers, debunkers, or sceptics and parapsychologists argue endlessly over the *meaning* of the paranormal.

Why did the postulation of ESP as an "additional faculty" of perception
attract so much popular and scientific interest? The notion of "extrasensory"
perception arguably responded to a perennial sense of there being a gap in the
human sensorium. We can find this perceived gap expressed, for example, in
the following seventeenth-century quotation from the *Oxford English Dictionary*: "It has been thought that we want a sixth Natural sense, by which we might
know many things more than we do." The mysterious "psychic sense" was thus
postulated to fill the supposed lacuna in human perception and open up hidden worlds of experience.

THE CONTINUUM OF PERCEPTION

The foregoing account of the diversity of supposed sensory powers highlights
the extent to which our understanding and employment of the senses is mediated by social and cultural schemas. It is this social dimension of perception
that makes the combined anthropological-historical approach to the study of
the sensorium advanced in this Manifesto so necessary. In order to appreciate
how this approach differs from the prevailing psychological and neurobiological theories of perception enshrined in the textbooks, let us posit a continuum
with the idea of perception as a neurobiological process at one end and the
notion of perception as a cultural process at the other.

The neurobiological perspective is aptly summed up in the following quotation from a work by Howard C. Hughes (2001, 7):

> The events that culminate in perception begin with specialized receptor cells that
> convert a particular form of physical energy into bioelectric currents. Different
> sensors are sensitive to different types of energy, so the properties of the receptor
> cells determine the modality of a sensory system. Ionic currents are the currency
> of neural information processing, and current flows that begin in the receptors are
> transmitted through complex networks of interconnected neurons and, in the end
> result in a pattern of brain activity we call perception.

Thus, perception is understood to be a matter of "information processing." It
begins at the edge of the CNS (central nervous system) and is conditioned exclusively by the properties of the receptor organs (Keeley 2002). On this account, perception is "all down to our DNA" (Hollingham 2004).

The historical-anthropological approach to the senses, as formulated by the
critical theorist Max Horkheimer, goes as follows:

> The objects we perceive in our surroundings – cities, villages, fields, and woods –
> bear the mark of having been worked on by man. It is not only in clothing and

appearance, in outward form and emotional make-up that men are the product of history. Even the way they see and hear is inseparable from the social life-process as it has evolved over the millennia. The facts which our senses present to us are socially preformed in two ways: through the historical character of the object perceived and through the historical character of the perceiving organ. (quoted in Levin 1997, 63n1)

On this account, the sensorium is an historical formation. Human perception begins at the edge of the humanly constructed environment and is conditioned by the "social preformation" of the senses. A broader study of the subject, how-ever, tells us that there are *multiple* sensory histories – or better, trajectories – not just one for all humanity (*pace* Horkheimer). The social sensorium *revolves* historically and across cultures as much as it "evolves" over the millennia.[5]

The cultural anthropologist, like the sensory historian, would have it that any account of perception must be keyed to the cultural organization of the sensorium. The neuroscientist would consider this unnecessary as perception is basically a matter of physiological functioning. Is it possible for these two approaches to be integrated? The transcultural psychiatrist Laurence Kirmayer suggests that it may indeed be possible, if one is willing to link neural processes with the social and material environment. He describes what is known as the "hierarchical systems view of neural organization" as follows:

> Contemporary cognitive neuroscience understands mind and experience as phe-nomena that emerge from neural networks at a certain level of complexity and organization. There is increasing recognition that this organization is not con-fined to the brain but also includes loops through the body and the environment, most crucially, through a social world that is culturally constructed. On this view, "mind" is located not in the brain but in the relationship of brain and body to the world. (Kirmayer, quoted in Howes 2009, 15)

Ideally, Kirmayer states, "we want to be able to trace the causal links up and down this hierarchy in a seamless way."

For all their talk of the "plasticity" of the brain, however, neuroscientists are remarkably insensitive to cultural influences, and therefore not very inclined to follow Kirmayer's lead. They rarely consider cultural factors, and when they do invoke them, it is in terms that anthropologists would typically regard as too simplistic. Conversely, some anthropologists have attempted to trace the links (and the loops) between the cultural and the physiological (see, e.g., Laugh-lin 1994; Lende and Downey 2012), but their attempts generally fail to attract interest beyond their own discipline due to the perception that such accounts are fundamentally unscientific. The matter is further complicated by the fact that the understanding of physiology itself varies from one society to another (see Kuriyama 1999 and Niewöhner and Lock 2018 on "divergent" and "local biologies"), making it problematic to link specific cultural practices with a supposedly acultural and universal (but in fact largely Western) "scientific" model of perception.

Plainly, there is a need for more crosstalk, more correspondence among the disciplines. I submit that recuperating the notion of the sensorium can help direct this conversation. But before reintroducing it, we need to examine how the senses came to be compartmentalized in the Western tradition, and perception reduced to "patterns of brain activity."

THE COMMON SENSE

As will be recalled, the Cashinahua reject the idea that the brain has any role to play in cognition – or "consciousness" for that matter. According to them, "the whole body knows." The modern idea of consciousness was similarly foreign to Aristotle and his contemporaries (see Heller-Roazen 2007, 38–9), who spoke instead in terms of *sentience* and tended to think of the heart, rather than the brain, as the seat of intelligence.

According to Aristotle, all living beings are animated by a "soul" or vital spirit. He argued that plants have only a nutritive soul, allowing them to nourish themselves, grow, and reproduce; animals have a soul that is nutritive and sensitive, or capable of perceiving; and humans possess a soul that is nutritive, sensitive, and rational. It is the sensitive powers of the human soul that concern us in what follows.

Aristotle held that every "affection of the soul" (or act of perception) involves the "alteration" of one or more of the five sense organs by some object through the medium that conjoins them. (The trinity of organ, object, medium is integral to Aristotle's account of perception.) The objects of perception are not things as such but *provinces* of sensation. The province or "proper object" of vision is colour, that of hearing is sound, that of smell is odour, that of taste is flavour. (The complexities of touch made it less amenable to such schematization, however much Aristotle tried to treat it as a unity: see Vinge 2009.) Within each province – and *exclusively* within each province, it must be stressed – sensation takes the form of "a kind of mean" between the two extremes of the pair of contraries proper to that province: sight between white and black, hearing between shrill and dull, and so on (with the province of touch left somewhat vague due to its complexity). The implication is that we perceive by means of differences, without positive things.[6] Each province of sensation has its own spectrum or ratio of sensible differences, defined as that which cannot be perceived by any other sense.

The provinciality (or exclusivity) of Arisotle's theory of the sensory functions of the soul posed certain difficulties, however. What of those objects, such as figure, number, and motion, known as the "common sensibles," which are perceived by more than one sense (for example, figure is perceived by vision and by touch)? What of complex sensations, such as the experience of eating grapes that are both red and sweet? Given that a sense cannot perceive itself, how is it that we perceive *that* we see and hear? In his attempt to answer these questions, Aristotle reasoned that there must be yet another sense, a shared sense, responsible for unifying, distinguishing and coordinating the five senses and their deliverances. This power of the sensuous soul he called "the common sense" (*koinē aisthēsis*, or *sensus communis* in Latin translation). For Aristotle, "this 'sense' constitutes a power of perception that is common to all the five senses yet reducible to none of them" (Heller Roazen 2007, 35). Is this then our mysterious sixth sense? Apparently not, for

> Strictly speaking, the common sense [on account of its commonality and ir-reducibility] is ... not a sixth sense ... it is nothing other than the sense of the difference and unity of the five senses, as a whole: the perception of the simul-taneous conjunction and disjunction of sensations in the common sensible, the complex sensation, and finally, the self-reflexive perception [or, sense of sensing]. (Heller-Roazen 2008, 35)

The idea of the common sense was pregnant with significance. This signif-icance was elaborated on by countless thinkers over many centuries. All this thinking is lost on us moderns, though, for whom common sense means simply sound judgement or shrewdness (see Heller-Roazen 2007; Geertz 2000) and has nothing to do with sensitivity or sentience per se. Tracing the successive elaboration and gradual dismemberment of the *sensus communis* would take a whole book, and indeed has: Daniel Heller-Roazen's marvellous book, *The Inner Touch: Archaeology of a Sensation*. But even that comprehensive treatise has its lacuna. In essence, the common sense is (or rather *was*) the relational sense *par excellence*, the ratio of ratios, the medium of media. The last modern thinker to understand this was Marshall McLuhan (an Aristotelian at heart).[7] Unfortunately, as McLuhan's writings are often elliptical, they do not provide much guidance, and we are forced to rely on our own wits to proceed, while leaning heavily on Heller-Roazen's archaeology of a sensation.

If we wished to visualize the relations between the common sense and the five senses, one possible image is that of the "Wheel of the Senses" in the wall paint-ing at Longthorpe Tower, Peterborough, UK, which dates from the mid-four-teenth century (see the image of this painting in the Picture Gallery at www. sensorystudies.org). The painting depicts a wheel with five beasts representing the five senses positioned at the end of each of its spokes: the cock stands for sight; the boar for hearing; the vulture for smell; the monkey for taste; and a spider in its web for touch. A king is shown behind the wheel, with his hand resting on one of its spokes. The king, who is emblematic of the common sense, exercises his dominion (and judgment) over the beasts, the senses. In another image, proposed by the great Persian philosopher of the early eleventh century Avicenna, the relation is expressed thusly: "This power which is called the common sense is the center from which the senses ramify, and to which the senses return, like rays; and it is in truth that which senses" (quoted in Heller-Roazen 2007, 42). It must be emphasized that both of these images are overstatements of Aristotle's notion of the common sense, as we shall see presently.

When modern thinkers criticize Aristotle for the dogmatism of his assertion that "There is no sixth sense in addition to the five enumerated – sight, hearing, smell, taste, touch," and for his hierarchical ranking of the senses with vision at the apex, they are forgetting that he was also the inventor of "the common sense," and that he did not just privilege vision unlike, for example, Plato (Keller and Grontkowski 1983). It is true that he dubbed sight "the most informative of the senses." But what to make of how he treated hearing as essential to reasoning, or of his declaration that "the well-developed sense of touch is the condition of man's intelligence" (Vinge 2009, 110)? One could say that he distributed (different) laurels to each of the senses.

It is only in retrospect that one can read anything of import to modern physiology, psychology, theology, or other disciplines, such as sociology, into Aristotle's writings. At the same time, because his treatises enjoyed such authority for so many centuries they constituted the touchstone, the foundation, for the anatomization, psychologization, spiritualization, and socialization of the senses. For example, Louise Vinge (2009) relates how the early Church Father Origen read the Bible in light of the Greek philosophy of *aisthēsis* (sense perception) and invented the doctrine of the "spiritual senses." This doctrine underwent extensive elaboration in the Middle Ages (Gavrilyuk and Coakley 2011; Rudy 2002; Classen 1998) and would later be developed even further by the eighteenth-century natural-philosopher-turned-Christian-visionary Emmanuel Swedenborg in his theory of the "celestial sensorium," or "spiritual anatomy of the senses" (see Schmidt 2000).

The psychologization of the common sense has a particularly convoluted history due to the liminality of its position at the interface of the five senses, and at the interface of the corporeal and the incorporeal, or sensual and rational, soul. In origin, it was not the king of the senses, as in the medieval elaboration (the wall painting at Longthorpe Tower) mentioned earlier, but rather *primus inter pares*, or "first among equals." It was also largely on a par with the other three functions of the sensuous soul identified by Aristotle: imagination, the cogitative function, and memory. Being situated on the boundary of the five senses, and the boundary of the sensuous and rational soul, the common sense was a two-faced faculty. But it did not remain in this liminal position for long due to a couple of incidental observations by Aristotle, which inflected the whole subsequent history of its elaboration (and eventual dismemberment).

In its apparent multiplicity, the common sense could be seen as analogous to the sense of touch, which Aristotle at one point allowed might be "more than one sense." (This observation was motivated by the constatation of the multiplicity of its objects.) Elsewhere, Aristotle characterized touch as the "inward sense." (This observation was, in turn, motivated by the difficulty of identifying its medium.) Subsequent commentators, poring over Aristotle's writings, seized on these remarks and fused them to form the basis of the doctrine of the "inner senses." The first intimation of this doctrine is given in the following line, which is commonly attributed to the Stoics: "the common sense is a kind of inner touching, by which we are able to grasp ourselves" (quoted in Heller-Roazen 2008, 37). It is doubtful whether Aristotle would have agreed with this line, any more than he would have agreed to the transplant of the seat of the soul from the heart to the brain. The latter migration resulted from Aristotle's writings being read in light of those of the prominent second-century Greek physician Galen. This (con)fusion was, however, fundamental to the doctrine of the inner senses as Simon Kemp points out in *Medieval Psychology*:

> The inner senses or inward wits were psychological faculties that, throughout the Middle Ages, were assumed to be located in the ventricles of the brain. These ventricles were supposed to be sense organs performing functions such as remembering or imagining in the same way that the eye was responsible for seeing or the ear for hearing. The theory was created by assigning the various perceptual and cognitive [faculties] identified by Aristotle in his *De Anima* to the spirit-filled cerebral ventricles described by Galen in his discussion of the anatomy of the brain. (Kemp 1990, 53)

According to Kemp, the doctrine of the inner senses received its most complete expression in the works of Avicenna. Avicenna apportioned the common sense and imaginative faculty to the front and rear, respectively, of the front ventricle, the cogitative faculty and estimative faculty (or instinct) to the front and rear of the middle ventricle, and the memory to the rear ventricle of the brain. Two further observations are in order at this juncture, the first being that, in earlier iterations, the common sense is sometimes included among the inner senses, and sometimes left out (see Ryan 1951; Heller-Roazen 2007). This history of flitting in and out of focus may be attributed to the common sense being neither "external" nor "internal" but rather *relational*, the boundary sense, in Aristotle's *own* writings. It was given an internal slant by some of Aristotle's commentators (most notably the Stoics), not Aristotle himself. Second, Avicenna, by characterizing the common sense as the "central power" (as noted above), basically inverted Aristotle's conception of it as shared – that is, as parted, not centred (see Heller-Roazen 2008, 40–5).

Kemp goes on to observe that the doctrine of the inner senses, thanks to its *linear* arrangement of the ventricles, anticipated the "information-processing" model of modern psychology: "incoming sensory information is transformed or processed in stages, and the output of each stage or level of processing becomes the input for the next" (1990, 60). But this was purely by chance, Kemp says, since, from a contemporary perspective, "Not only is the doctrine completely false in its physiological aspects – the ventricles of the brain fulfil no psychological functions at all – but also the adoption of the doctrine meant that the rational soul had many of its psychological [read: cognitive] functions stripped from it" (Kemp 1990, 58).

Stripped? Not from an Aristotelian perspective. One could argue that it was rather the sensuous soul that was stripped of its faculties by the development of modern psychology, for the five external senses and the five internal senses (including imagination and memory) were all *sensory* powers, not cognitive powers, in the periods of which we speak. The amount of mental or "cognitive" space that sensing, as opposed to thinking (the function of the rational soul) occupied in medieval psychology is indeed astounding. *Sentio ergo sum* (or "I sense therefore I am") was the watchword of the medieval conscience. It is appropriate to speak of "conscience" here since the potential for using the senses immoderately was always very much on the classical mind, while the potential for using them sinfully weighed just as heavily on the medieval Christian and early modern mind (Newhauser 2007; de Boer 2013). The birth of "consciousness" or cognition as we know it would have to await Descartes, who famously "called away" all his senses to discover the truth of his own existence: *cogito ergo sum*, "I think therefore I am" (quoted and discussed in Synnott 1993, 70).

Even so, aspects of the Aristotelian account of sentience survived the Cartesian censure of the senses and were (re)affirmed with a vengeance during the Age of Reason, which was also, it should be remembered, the Age of Sensibility. One of those aspects was the common sense, *sensorium commune*, which was transmuted by the thinkers of the time into a generalized notion of "sensibility" (Barker-Benfield 1992; Vila 2014; Riskin 2002).

SENSES WITHOUT ORGANS: THE MULTIPLICATION OF THE SENSES
IN THE EIGHTEENTH CENTURY

The eighteenth century was something of a watershed in the history of the senses in view of the number of new senses that were put forward for discussion during this period – common sense being just one of them. My colleague James Moore, in one of our many memorable conversations, summarized for me how

the Irish/Scottish philosopher Frances Hutcheson, for example, argued for the existence of both a moral sense, which would present the mind with an idea of virtue when perceiving a benevolent act, and an analogous sense of beauty, which would call up notions of beauty when perceiving harmonious configurations. To these, he later added an eighth "public" sense, which responded to the happiness and suffering of others, and a ninth – the sense of honour. (Moore, personal communication)

In these sensory multiplications Hutcheson was influenced by contemporary notions of an innate sense of public good or private virtue as formulated by such writers as the third Earl of Shaftsbury and the Cambridge Platonist Henry More. As Moore went on to elucidate for me, these notions were taken up by a series of philosophers, particularly those associated with the Scottish Enlightenment:

> David Hume agreed that virtues and vices are determined by a moral sense; but Hume resolved the moral sense into sympathy with others, with qualities of character that are useful and agreeable to self and to others. Hume's scepticism with regard to the moral sense was repudiated by Henry Home, who offered his own theory of the moral sense as a sense of remorse and dread of merited punishment. Adam Smith followed Hume in making sympathy, not the moral sense, the source of moral distinctions; but Smith considered utility to be merely one of the considerations that prompt us to sympathize with others. Adam Ferguson disagreed with his friends Hume and Smith; he agreed rather with Hutcheson in locating the origin of moral distinctions in a moral sense; he thought that the quality most esteemed by the moral sense was active intelligence, particularly when intelligence is exercised in the service of the public. Other Scottish philosophers – Thomas Reid, Dugald Stewart, and Sir William Hamilton – replaced the moral sense by a more general theory of common sense. This was not a sixth sense or a special faculty of perception; it referred rather to the human capacity to apprehend reality unmediated by ideas; it was the precondition of perception, memory, and the exercise of all the intellectual and active powers. (James Moore, personal communication; see further McCosh 1875; Broadie 2003; Moore 2004; Kivy 2003)

Without trying to fathom all the intricacies of these "internal senses" (as they may be called to distinguish them from the "inner senses" of the Middle Ages), a few general observations may be made. The inwardness of the "internal senses" points to a deepening sense of the interiority of consciousness, of the self. Furthermore, they are all forms of "feeling" rather than thinking or reason, which is consistent with the "sentimental empiricism" of the period in contrast to the rational empiricism of today (see Riskin 2002). Third, they are all very sociable rather than physical, particularly the moral sense and that of the public good. However, the eighteenth-century understanding of the *sociability* of the senses (and perception) did not endure for long, and it is the Scottish thinkers who were responsible for this. Whereas the moral *valuation* and moral *use* of the senses was intrinsic to classical and medieval sensory practice, the Scottish philosophers divorced the moral sense from perception generally by constituting it as a distinct modality. This opened the way for the amoralization of perception – that is, the reduction of sensation to "information processing," or, simply, "patterns of neural activity."

BENEATH THE FIVE SENSES

Apart from the world "beyond the five senses" (e.g., ESP), there is a world "beneath the five senses" (i.e., the visceral, the molecular) to which modern science has increasingly sensitized us.[8] Here is how Howard C. Hughes describes that world:

> There is also the world inside our bodies, and there are sensory organs that provide information crucial to internal bodily states. Our senses of balance, of body motion, and of posture, depend on sensory organs in the inner ear, in our joints, and in muscles. There are even organs that monitor such things as the levels of carbon dioxide in the blood, blood pressure, and blood glucose levels. These organs provide the brain with information essential to life, but they do not produce conscious sensory experiences (otherwise, people would be aware of the onset of hypertension, and it would less frequently go undetected). (Hughes 2001, 5)

An account of how this inner world was produced – that is, of the scientific practices which generated the physiological discoveries that gave definition to what we shall here call the "interoceptive" (as distinct from "inner" or "internal") senses of balance, body motion, etc. – is provided by Nicholas Wade in his classic essay "The Search for A Sixth Sense" (2009). These discoveries were perhaps inevitable, for we saw how Aristotle blurred certain distinctions in his account of the sense of touch, and already by the eleventh century there were suspicions (voiced by Avicenna) concerning the unity of the haptic sense (Kemp 1990, 46). Forced unions are bound to dissolve in time, especially when the cosmology that made them sensible or necessary no longer holds. There were but four elements in ancient Greek cosmology (Earth, Air, Fire, and Water). Each element was distinguished by a different combination of the hot and the cold, the wet and the dry. That arrangement (with minor variations, such as the postulation of a fifth element, Aether) held for centuries. However, in the nineteenth century this sensuous understanding of the elements was definitively dissolved and replaced by the sixty-three (now 118) elements of Mendeleev's Periodic Table of Elements, distinguished on the basis of atomic number and recurring chemical properties. Any intrinsic connection between the senses and the elements was henceforth severed (see Lévi-Strauss and Eribon 1991; Atkins 1997; Illich 2000; and Howes 2016a on the significance of this renumeration).

While there are a number of earlier intimations of the "interoceptive senses" (see Heller-Roazen 2007, 163–78, 237–51), it appears to have been the eighteenth century's intense focus on *feelings* that brought the matter to a head and precipitated the physiological discoveries of the nineteenth century (see Paterson 2021). Take the case of kinaesthesia:

> Kinaesthesia, the sense of bodily movement, had been studied before the nineteenth century under a variety of other names, including "inner sense" and "organic" or "visceral" sensibility – all referring to those unclassifiable sensations that could not be traced accurately to one of the five known sense organs, but seemed to originate from the undifferentiated mass of the viscera. It was not until the early nineteenth century, however, that "muscle sense" was officially declared a "sixth sense" in its own right. (Çelik 2006, 159)

The dissolution of the sense of touch into a panoply of senses – pressure, temperature, pain, as well as kinaesthesia, proprioception, balance, and so on – was only to be expected. Not so expected, perhaps, is the way vision has come to be dismembered by contemporary scientists into separate senses for light and colour (and arguably, separate senses for red, green, and blue); or the way taste has fragmented into separate receptor organs for sweet, salt, sour, bitter (and for the fifth flavor, umami); or the way smell has been broken down into multiple receptors (see Jones 2006a, 45n26). "The more we study the structure of our sense organs, the more senses we appear to have" (Durie 2005, 35). A conservative estimate would put the number of senses at ten, but it is generally accepted by neurobiologists that our senses number twenty-one, while more radical estimates put the number at thirty-three or higher (see figure 1).

These figures confirm Vinge's point: "The number and order of the senses are fixed by custom and tradition, not by nature" (2009, 107). There is a widespread tendency to privilege the sensory models of our own time and place over those of other cultures and epochs. In contemporary Western culture, this generally means favouring biomedical accounts. But the question arises: Should the neurobiologists necessarily have the last word on what counts as a faculty of perception? Might not each of the "alternative" perceptual paradigms we have been considering (Cashinahua, ancient Greek, medieval Christian, Scottish Enlightenment) have something to teach us about the sensorium? Of course they do, from the standpoint of sensory studies, and it is only by approaching the study of perception with open senses and an open mind that we can arrive at a composite understanding of the changing *contexts of perception* that give the senses their meaning.

Overture II: Sensory Interaction

The modern subdivision of the sensorium can be seen as leading to a finer appreciation of the biological substrate of perception. The ten (or twenty-one or thirty-three) sense model is consistent with the modular conception of the sensorium that is otherwise reflected in the analytic orientation of most

Figure 1. How many senses are there? Ten (conservative estimate), twenty-one (possibly), thirty-three (radical estimate). But if you really want to know, the senses are innumerable. Credit: Table adapted from Durie (2005, 36).

SENSORY MODALITY			
	Conservative	Accepted	Radical
Vision	■	□	□
Light	□	■	■
Color	□	■	□
Red	□	□	■
Green	□	□	■
Blue	□	□	■
Hearing	■	■	■
Smell	■	■	□
2,000 or more receptor types	□	□	■
Taste	■	□	□
Sweet	□	■	■
Salt	□	■	■
Sour	□	■	■
Bitter	□	■	■
Umami	□	□	■
Touch	■	■	□
Light touch	□	□	■
Pressure	□	□	■
Pain	■	■	□
Cutaneous	□	□	■
Somatic	□	□	■
Visceral	□	□	■
Mechanoreception	■	□	□
Balance	■	■	□
Rotational acceleration	□	□	■
Linear acceleration	□	□	■
Proprioception—joint position	□	■	■
Kinaesthesis	□	■	□
Muscle stretch—Golgi tendon organs	□	□	■
Muscle stretch—muscle spindles	□	□	■
Temperature	■	□	□
Heat	□	■	■
Cold	□	■	■
Interocepters			
Blood pressure	■	■	□
Arterial blood pressure	□	□	■
Central venous blood pressure	□	□	■
Head blood temperature	□	□	■
Blood oxygen content	□	■	■
Cerebrospinal fluid pH	□	■	■
Plasma osmotic pressure (thirst?)	□	■	■
Artery-vein blood glucose difference (hunger?)	□	■	■
Lung inflation	□	■	■
Bladder stretch	□	□	■
Full stomach	□	□	■

current research in the psychology of perception with its "sense-by-sense" - or one sensory modality at a time – approach to the study of perceptual processes (even as the number of named senses has expanded beyond the canonical five). However, in recent decades, a more interactive, relational approach to the understanding of how the senses function has begun to take shape as a result of the growing body of evidence that points to the "multisensory organization" or "integration" of the brain. As Gemma Calvert, Charles Spence, and Barry E. Stein point out in their introduction to *The Handbook of Multisensory Processes*,

> even those experiences that at first may appear to be modality-specific are most likely to have been influenced by activity in other sensory modalities, despite our lack of awareness of such interactions ... [To] fully appreciate the processes underlying much of sensory perception, we must understand not only how information from each sensory modality is transduced and decoded along the pathways primarily devoted to that sense, but also how this information is modulated by what is going on in the other sensory pathways. (2004, vi–xii; see further DeSalle 2018)

Examples of such modulation include the well-documented fact that, in noisy surroundings, speakers can be understood more easily if they can be seen as well as heard. This finding is readily explicable in terms of the redundancy hypothesis of classic information theory: two pathways or "information channels" are better than one. However, the new multisensory psychology of perception probes deeper to explore the *relationships* among the component parts of a multisensory signal. For example, in the case of animal and human communication, redundant multisensory signals can be subclassified into those that produce responses in the receiver equivalent to the response to each unisensory component (and are hence called *equivalent* or *additive*), and those where the overall response is enhanced – that is, greater than the response to the unisensory components (hence, *superadditive*). Multisensory signals may also be made up of stimuli that convey different (i.e., non-redundant) information. In such cases, the relationship between the component parts may be one of *dominance* as in the ventriloquism effect, where the seen lip movements of the dummy alter or "capture" the apparent location of the speech sounds.

A further, particularly intriguing pattern of intersensory relations is that of *emergence*, as exemplified by the McGurk effect. In the McGurk experiment, a research subject is shown a dubbed video of an actor's face pronouncing syllables. It would appear that the seen lip movements can alter which phoneme is heard for a particular sound (e.g., a sound of /ba/ tends to be perceived as /da/ when it is coupled with a visual lip movement associated with /ga/). In this instance, the response to the multisensory signal is new, qualitatively different from the response to either of the unisensory components (see figure 2), and thus demonstrates *emergence*. It is a perception without any direct basis in sensation.

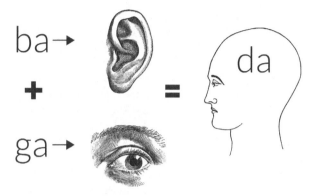

Figure 2. The McGurk effect. Illustration courtesy of Shannon Collis.

Many of the studies in the *Handbook* use modern neuroimaging techniques to reveal the multiple sites of multisensory processing in the brain, including many regions long thought to be modality specific or "primary sensory" areas as distinct from the so-called higher order "associative areas" traditionally assumed to be responsible for the formation of unified percepts out of the diversity of inputs. In addition to demonstrating the functional *interdependence* of the modalities, a number of these studies point to the functional equivalence or *adaptability* of the modalities. For example, it is now clear that sensory-specific areas can be "recruited" or "remapped" by other sensory-specific areas in situations of sensory deprivation or intensive perceptual training. Thus, the visual cortex in blind individuals has been found to show activation in auditory tasks while the auditory cortex in deaf individuals can be activated by visual tasks (Sur 2004; Röder and Rösler 2004). Such evidence of adaptive processing, or "cross-modal plasticity," underscores the importance of adopting a relational approach to the study of the sensorium in place of assuming that the senses are structurally and functionally distinct.

Other studies in the *Handbook* explore such issues as whether the sensory integration involved in speech perception is fundamentally the same or different from other kinds of multisensory integration (the same); whether the senses are differentiated at birth and become coordinated through experience – the developmental integration hypothesis – or are relatively unified at birth and become differentiated through development – the developmental differentiation hypothesis (neither – the formation of percepts in early development involves the joint action of developmental integration and differentiation processes); and whether the phenomenon of synaesthesia (i.e., the union or crossing of the senses) might not provide a better model for conceptualizing perceptual processes than the conventional sense-by-sense approach that has dominated research on the senses and sensations to date. More on the topic of synesthesia presently.

The *Handbook of Multisensory Processes* (now in its second edition) is a landmark text. But even though it is "revolutionary science" (Kuhn) as regards neuroscience, it remains "normal science" from a sensory studies perspective due to its failure to grapple with deep historical facts and its imperviousness to cross-cultural understandings of the sensorium. As regards the history of the senses, there is but one line in the *Handbook* that alludes to the complex history of sensation we have been tracing. The editors observe that "it is interesting to note that with the specialization of modern research and the tendency to focus on the functional properties of individual senses, an early perspective was set aside, namely, that perception is fundamentally a multisensory phenomenon" (Calvert, Spence, and Stein 2004, xi). They do not elaborate further. As regards the anthropology of the senses, there is again but one line (one line in 915 pages!): it is noted that the McGurk effect is significantly weaker in Japanese test subjects than in U.S. test subjects (Bernstein, Auer, and Moore 2004). Such restricted allusion to the senses in the expanded field (i.e., the senses in history and across cultures, rather than the laboratory) point to a serious lacuna in the presumed universality of the account of human perceptual processes presented in the *Handbook*.

At least one of the editors of the first edition was, however, sensitive to this issue – namely, Charles Spence, the director of the Crossmodal Research Laboratory at Oxford University. With characteristic verve, he joined a team of researchers and travelled to Northern Namibia to investigate the question of cultural variations in crossmodal interactions. This team found that the Bouba-Kiki (shape-sound symbolism) effect held among the Himba of Namibia – that is, the Himba mapped a rounded shape (resembling a sack of potatoes) to the sound "bouba" and an angular shape (an irregular, pointy star-like figure) to the sound "kiki," similarly to Europeans. This finding might be taken to suggest that this effect represents a perceptual universal. However, the team also found that

> in contrast to Westerners, the Himba did not map carbonation (in a sample of sparkling water) onto an angular (as opposed to rounded) shape. Furthermore, they also tended to match less bitter (i.e. milk) chocolate samples to angular rather than rounded shapes; the opposite mapping to that shown by Westerners. (Bremner et al. 2013, 165)

This experiment is noteworthy for its "double-crossing" protocol: crossing cultures and crossing modalities, and for its demonstration that "cultural-environmental as well as phylogenetic factors play a central role in shaping our repertoire of crossmodal correspondences."[9]

CROSSMODAL OVERTURES

To pick up on the other aspect of the lacuna at the heart of the *Handbook* – namely, the short shrift given to the long history of reflection on the *interrelation* of the senses – the preceding discussion has gone a considerable way toward correcting this occlusion. It is now time to turn our attention to the work of some more contemporary students of the senses. Consider "The Unity of the Senses" (1927) by the early twentieth-century musicologist Erich M. von Hornbostel. This essay is remarkable not only for its assertions that "there is a sensuous that is not limited to any single sense" (i.e., not a "private property of any one sense") and that there are "super-sensuous sense-perceptions" (which point to a common sense in the archaic sense of the term) but also for the way Hornbostel canvassed and cited various cross-cultural evidence (limited though it was) in support of his claims. This essay recuperates the philosopher Aristotle's notion of the common sense, but with an empirical twist.

Another early example of a crossmodal approach to the study of perceptual processes is presented by psychologist Paul Rozin in "'Taste-Smell Confusions' and the Duality of the Olfactory Sense" (1982). Rozin makes the point that flavour perception is contingent on the blending of the senses of smell and taste and whether an olfactory stimulation is referred to the body (mouth) or the external world. This phenomenon is sometimes called "odour-taste synaesthesia" and is actually the topic of one of the studies in the *Handbook* as well. In their chapter, Richard Stevenson and Robert Boakes (2004) begin by noting that, perhaps because it is such a common effect, this variety of synaesthesia has failed to attract much popular attention or scientific documentation. Yet the evidence is clear: "the majority of people appear to experience odor-taste synaesthesia. First, *sweet* is one of the most common descriptors applied to odors ... [Furthermore,] when smelling an odor, most people can more easily recognize a taste-like quality such as sweetness than more specific qualities such as strawberry- or banana-likeness" (2004, 69). This finding raises the question: When we speak of the odour of vanilla or strawberry as "sweet" are we speaking in metaphor rather than reporting an actual olfactory sensation? Stevenson and Boakes answer this question in the negative– that is, they reject the "metaphor-explanation," as is typical of psychological researchers, in contrast to geographical researchers, such as Yi-Fu Tuan and anthropological researchers, such as Silvia Casini. The central argument of their chapter is physiological, namely,

> that, as a result of eating and drinking, patterns of retronasal odor stimulation co-occur with oral stimulation, notably of the taste receptors, so that a unitary percept is produced by a process of either within-event associative learning or by a simple encoding as one event. Eating sweet vanilla-flavor ice cream will ensure that the retronasal odor of vanilla becomes associated with sweetness; on some

later occasion the smell of vanilla will seem sweet, even if no conscious recollec-
tion of eating ice cream comes to mind. (Stevenson and Boakes 2004, 81)

Stevenson and Boakes (2004, 73) further assert that "Odors display taste
properties but do not elicit auditory or visual sensations." Here, however, in
rejecting the possibility of audio-olfactory or visuo-olfactory synaesthesia
out of hand, the authors overreach their discipline, for this assertion can be
questioned from an anthropological perspective. Counterexamples include the
"golden smell" of ancient Egyptian lore (Goldsmith, personal communication)
and the "green smell" known to certain Indigenous peoples of Australia (Young
2005). Furthermore, it is common in various African languages to speak of
"hearing a smell." Among the Dogon of Mali, for example, speech is understood
to have "material properties that ... are more than just sound ... [It] has an
'odour'; sound and odour having vibration as their common origin, are so near
to one another that the Dogon speak of 'hearing a smell'" and classify words
as smelling either "sweet" or "rotten" accordingly (Calame-Griaule 1986, 320).
This association between smell and sound is reflected in the way the Dogon
will operate on the nose of a young person (e.g., through piercing) in order to
discipline and correct both their hearing and their speech. Hence, the Dogon
practise audio-olfactory synaesthesia despite the fact that there is no basis for
this in human physiology, at least not according to Stevenson and Boakes.

This écart between the (presumed) certainties of neuroscience and the
wealth of counterfactuals anthropology brings to the table illustrates a point
made by Sander Gilman (1988, 1–2) in *Goethe's Touch*: "Our fantasies about the
senses are in no way limited by the biological realities of the senses ... We can
(and do) attribute and associate with any given sense much that is beyond the
innate capacity of that sense." Where we differ from Gilman (who, being a literary scholar, is more attuned to fictional accounts of the senses) is in questioning
whether the "innate capacity" of a sense can be specified independently of the
cultural context of its usage, and in our focus on sensory *practice*, or *ways* of
sensing. Sensory practices may seem fictional, but the fact that they have a performative dimension makes them actual. This goes equally for the "findings" of
Stevenson and Boakes in their psychology laboratory.

Charles Spence, based at Oxford University, is the foremost theorist of the
"sensory interaction" paradigm, which has been revolutionizing the psychology
and neuroscience of perception. Intimations of his approach can be discerned
in the work of other scholars, such as Hornbostel, but no psychologist has theorized the multisensory integration of the brain in as comprehensive a fashion as
Spence. He has also explored a wide range of sensory combinations and upset
many deep-set assumptions about the exclusivity of different sensory faculties
in the process. "Crossmodal Correspondences" (2018a), originally published
in 2011, and revised and updated for inclusion in *Senses and Sensation* III,

addresses the "crossmodal binding problem." This problem has to do with how the brain "knows" which stimuli to bind out of the myriad different unisensory signals that bombard our senses at any given time. Conventional explanations have focussed on the role that temporal and spatial factors play in modulating multisensory integration. Spence elevates the discussion to a whole new plane by documenting how crossmodal *correspondences* between diverse unisensory features play a key role in the binding process that generates unified percepts.

Spence's latest book is entitled *Sensehacking: How to Use the Power of Your Senses for Happier, Healthier Living* (2021). It condenses the insights of his vast academic output (he is the author or co-author of more than one thousand peer-reviewed journal articles and numerous books) into an easily digestible self-help book or user's guide to the senses. In *Sensehacking*, he theorizes many phenomena of everyday life from the standpoint of sensory multiplicity and interactionism. Topics range from safe driving to the sensory design of hospitals, and from how to lay a table to "the natural ideal" or "biophilia hypothesis" (e.g., our love for indoor plants, or a walk in the forest). As regards the natural ideal, for example, he writes: "the key point to remember is that we experience nature through *all* of our senses, and so ensuring as balanced a diet of multisensory stimulation as possible is probably one of the best things any of us can do to promote the health and well-being of both ourselves and those we care most about" (63). While those moments in his writing where Spence defers to evolutionary psychology are problematic,[10] his overarching message is sound: "getting the sensory balance right" and mixing up the senses is crucial to our physical, emotional, mental, and social well-being.

Summing up, the point of Spence's sensory interactionist paradigm is that two (or more) senses are typically better than one – and, more to the point, the senses are "relationally produced" (Dawkins and Loftus 2013) – that is, they are not the silos that mainstream psychological accounts of "sensory processing" make them out to be; rather, they are interactive, and interstitial (see further DeSalle 2018). Indeed, one can hear echoes in Spence's work of the Aristotelian understanding of the common sense. Following Spence's lead, we should all get "hacking," particularly since, if we do not, the consumer engineers and marketing gurus will hack our senses for us.[11]

II. Probes

The conversation that follows continues the discussion in the corresponding sections of the previous two chapters. Its focus is on what the Spencerian sensory interaction paradigm and like-minded approaches of other sensory studies scholars can bring to the discussion of such key concepts as *materiality* and *affect*, and such key domains as *gustation* and *cosmology/ecology*, beginning with the latter. The reader is reminded that while they are welcome to read the following probes longitudinally (i.e., sequentially), a better strategy would be to read them latitudinally (i.e., across the chapters of this part) in keeping with the "mosaical" (non-lineal) manner in which they were composed.

1 *Ontology*. Rupert Sheldrake trained in biology and biochemistry at Cambridge University in the early 1960s and developed the theory of "morphic resonance and morphic fields" to explain what could not be explained about plant development by reference to genes and gene products alone. Morphogenesis also depends on "organizing fields" and "formative caustation," which, he alleges, operate above and beyond the genetic. Sheldrake subsequently extended his theory to animal behaviour and human culture (Sheldrake 2011, 2009). In a nutshell, his theory puts forward "'the idea of mysterious telepathy-type *interconnections* between organisms and of *collective* memories within species' and accounts for phantom limbs, how dogs know when their [human companions] are coming home, and how people know when someone is staring at them" (Shermer 2005) – all seemingly very paranormal.

  Sheldrake could be said to fit the model of the "abnormal scientist" (in Kuhn's sense) or, to put it bluntly, the heretic; indeed, the editor of *Nature* declared Sheldrake's *A New Science of Life* (1981) "the best candidate for burning there has been for many years" (Maddox, quoted in Horgan 2014). What is so disturbing to "normal scientists" is that Sheldrake's theories revivify a kind of Lamarckism, although his theories actually extend far beyond Lamarck's discredited theory of the transmission of acquired characteristics because they are ostensibly cosmological and sociological, not merely genetical or even epigenetical, in scope. For example, Sheldrake (n.d.) holds that "memory is inherent in nature": it is not confined to the hidden recesses of the brain, or the genome of a species. How can there be memory in the absence of a nervous system? the normal scientist scoffs. Enter Sheldrake's theory of "non-local resonance" or "similarity reinforcement" across space and time, which purportedly explains how similar behaviours come to be manifested in separated groups. The overarching implication of Sheldrake's research is that we are all creatures of habit. Citing Francis Huxley, he observes that Darwin's most famous book could more appropriately have been entitled "The Origin of Habits."

2 *Emplacement*. Preoccupied as it is with mental processes, psychology does not engage with concepts of emplacement. Even the idea of the "embodied mind" that comes out of cognitive neuroscience is oblivious to the *genius loci*, the sense of place, in geography (Tuan 1974) and anthropology (Feld 2005).

3 *Materiality*. The popular science literature of today is brimming with accounts of the "remarkable convergence" of body and machine, biology

and technology. Humans are expanding their sensory powers through technological extensions, while machines are being equipped with human perceptual capacities. Designing sensors that can take over the functions of the human sensory system, such as electronic tongues and noses (Geary 2002; Rodriguez Mendez and Preedy 2016), and developing sensory prostheses (or even neuroprostheses) for use by injured combat veterans (Gay 2015) has become big business, and it keeps intellectual property lawyers busy patenting all the new discoveries. This area of research could be called sensory extensionism, and it is all very exciting. However, rarely does this literature problematize the social context of the production and instrumentalization of such knowledges. There is a need for more critical culturally and sensorially *grounded* analyses of these prostheses, such as Ingemar Pettersson's analysis in "Mechanical Tasting: Sensory Science and the Flavorization of Food Production" (2017).

Pettersson, a historian of science and technology in the Department of Economic History at Uppsala University, discusses the development at MIT in the late 1950s of a device designed to enhance and substitute for human sensory abilities to evaluate food texture. It was known as the "Strain gage denture tenderometer," and it consisted of a mechanical dental apparatus that could measure, with extreme precision, the "chewing resistance" or tenderness of foodstuffs. The tenderometer (which is really quite eerie in appearance, more like a Halloween decoration than an instrument of science) is a paragon example of the drive to scientize subjectivity or "make the subjective objective" (see Shapin 2016). Pettersson brings out well how the pursuit of objectivity and standardized knowledge coevolved with the rise of mass production and the emergence of the so-called sensory sciences in the twentieth century.

Pettersson's path-breaking research is complemented by the collection of studies in the anthropology of the food science (or "sensory evaluation") laboratory assembled by Jacob Lahne and Christy Spackman in "Accounting for Taste" (2018). The research they and their contributors report on "show the reliance of the food sciences on reducing the body to model a molecular interface ... a reduction that locates sensory experiences squarely in physical objects that can be measured or quantified" (2018, 4). But they do not stop there. By employing critical Science and Technology Studies (STS) approaches they are able to expose the sociality of sensation that undergirds the pursuit of objective sensory knowledge in the food science laboratory. This in turn leads them to propose "a reframing of sensation not as an out-there object but as embodied and contextualized labor" (4). This move, which shifts the onus from physiology (back) to practice, has major implications for the sensory and sociopolitical reformation of food design and production.

4 *Memory*. We may think of memory (and memories) as consisting mainly of thoughts of the past. The neurologist Antonio Damasio, however, in such works as *The Feeling of What Happens* (1999), theorizes that what we remember at any given time is *recreated* in the brain through "chemical and neural changes and adjustments that formed part of a perception and persist to some extent as part of the memory" (Callard and Papoulias 2010, 258). Memories, therefore, do not just call up "images of an event or object but [also] images of our interactions with that event or object" (258). These images have as much to do with predicting the future as with retrieving the past, and by so doing enable us to navigate the world successfully.

In "Consciousness as 'Feeling in the Body'" (2005) Kathryn Linn Geurts subjects Damasio's neurobiological theory of memory and cognition generally to a cultural critique. She analyses how the highly visual language Damasio uses to express his discoveries (e.g., screen-based metaphors), and in particular his postulate of a unified self, reflects the lifeworld and ideological presuppositions of contemporary Western culture, which is rooted in the political philosophy of possessive individualism. She then expounds on the tenets of a West African theory of the embodiment of consciousness – namely, that of the Anlo-Ewe of Ghana, which is significantly more aural, proprioceptive, and interpersonal in orientation. According to Anlo-Ewe sensuous epistemology, two people can share the same sensation: empathy runs deep. The neuroscientist would attribute this to the stimulation of "mirror neurons," but that would be to smuggle in a visual or spectral epistemology, whereas the Anlo-Ewe sensorium is constructed around the notion of *seslelame* ("feel-feel at flesh inside"). By placing the two accounts (neurobiological and anthropological) on a par, and reflecting on their points of agreement and disagreement, Geurts lays the foundation for a truly cross-cultural theory of embodied cognition.

Memories are the stuff of dreams, and dreams are typically saturated with sensory imagery. However, in one of the most influential theories of dream interpretation – namely, Freudian theory – the richness of this imagery is largely ignored, dismissed as "manifest content" whereas the trick (according to Freud) is to dig deeper and get at the "latent content" of the dream. "On Listening to a Dream: The Sensory Dimensions" (1985) by psychiatrist Alfred Margulies was first published in *Psychiatry* in 1985, and it languished there, unnoticed, until we sought to underscore its importance by flagging it as a "critical and primary source" and reprinting it in *Senses and Sensation* III. Margulies calls Freud and his followers to their senses and details how much can be learned from listening to the sensory processes of dreaming *in themselves*, processes such as synaesthesia, kinaesthesias of standing (or falling), and so forth. Margulies' wake-up call brings a much-needed emphasis on embodiment and sensory process to the interpretation of dreams. It is as radical in its approach to the interpretation of dream symbolism as either Freudian or Jungian psychology, and it doesn't even require recourse to some hypothetical notion of an "unconscious" to be effective. It just requires the analyst to listen to the dream narratives of a patient with their senses in mind.

In "Synesthetic Gestures: Making the Imaginary Perceptible" (2021), the folklorist Katharine Young approaches the interpretation of dreams from the standpoint of somatic psychology. In this approach, the therapist attends as closely to the gestures of the patient as to the verbal content of the dream narrative and also encourages the patient to express their thoughts with gestures (something any of us do; we just don't think about it). In this way, the "tactile-kinaesthetic body" of the patient is engaged, and the imaginary is rendered perceptible for patient and therapist alike. The gestural is not confined to physical motions, however, nor is it confined to "visual communication," for other senses may be activated "synesthetically," according to Young. She recounts a session that centred on a female patient imagining a "dream baby" (which tragically turned out to be a "lost baby," in the final analysis) in the company of her therapist, who asks her what her baby smells like (sweet), tastes like (seawater), sounds like (flocks of gulls), feels like (cushions of silk), all the while carefully observing the gestures she makes to "metaphorize" the imaginary object – the baby (e.g., the lifting of the chest, the slow in-breath, the closed eyes, the outfolded hands as she says "sweet"). As Young (2021, 96) observes, "gestures solicit the real by materializing the airy nothings of thought as palpable somethings."

Young's approach harks back to the archaic notion of the imagination as a sensory faculty (not a cognitive faculty), one of the "inner senses," and hence extensible in space (contrary to the Cartesian *esprit*). In dreams, perception has no object, at least not in the external world, but through the performativity of gesture it does. This brings us back to the point that psychoanalytic approaches could be significantly enriched, if only psychoanalysts were to stop searching for the "latent content" in some hypothetical unconscious and start focussing on the "manifest content" of dream imagery (Margulies) and on the extension of the sensorium through "synaesthetic gesture" (Young; see further Abrahamson 2020).

5 *Alterity.* Blind persons are commonly attributed a special sensitivity to the auditory (e.g., the iconic figure of the blind musician). This "gift" is believed to "compensate" for their visual impairment. Should "compensation" be added to the list of intersensory relations, such as additive, superadditive, etc., discussed earlier? In "An Auditory World: Music and Blindness" (2007), Oliver Sacks considers the "neural correlates" for the precocious musicality of certain blind people. He begins by noting that there are social forces behind this channelling (which have to do with the blind being excluded from many other occupations), but argues that there must be internal forces at work too, since blind children who have never

been subject to any formal musical training also often display a penchant for musicality. Part of the explanation for this, according to Sacks, may lie in the phenomenon of "cross-modal plasticity" – that is, in the "reallocation" of the (otherwise dormant) visual cortex to the processing of auditory input. Like Charles Spence, Sacks consistently directs our attention to the analysis of intersensory relations.

"The Menagerie of the Senses" (2006) by Cambridge literature and cultural studies scholar Steven Connor was the first article in the first issue of *The Senses and Society*. In this piece, Connor explores "our relationship to our senses" – not sensory experience in itself, but our *relations* with our senses. He observes that there are two traditions to the way we "care for" (or manage) our senses: limitation and intensification. Limitation "stresses the dangers of surrendering to or being inundated by sensuality, and consequently emphasizes the need for the discipline or regulation of the senses" (2006, 10). The other tradition, intensification, "emphasizes the need to educate the senses, to refine them, or extend their powers, sometimes by a removal of all restrictions, as in Rimbaud's efforts at a 'dérèglement de tous les sens,' sometimes by refinement and selective intensification" (11).

"Both regulation and intensification require an active, productive, self-conscious care and management of the senses," Connor (2006, 11) writes. He retrieves and employs the word menagerie to compare the management and training of diverse human senses to European practices of collecting and exhibiting diverse "exotic" animals. Connor then goes on to speculate that animals "play an indispensable, though often ignored, part in our care of the senses. While our senses mediate the world to us, animals mediate our senses to us; animals are thus the mediators of the mediation" (12). He provides the historical example of medieval bestiaries and considers how "the imaginative recruitment of animals" (with their special or "super" senses) to categorize and transform human powers continues in such present-day representations as the "bat-like" sense of radar and the "spidery" sense of the World Wide Web. He states that these "new forms of sensitivity to our world continue to implicate and improvise upon the animal, changing its meaning and ours in the process" (24).

In the twenty-first century such "new forms of sensitivity to our world" must, I submit, encompass a new sensitivity to the non-human animals who are our fellow inhabitants of Earth. We must, therefore, move beyond the medieval focus on the use-value of animals – whether this value be material or symbolic – to consider the lives and experiences, the needs and desires, of animals themselves. From this perspective, the animal menagerie can be recognized as a place of intensive deprivation and suffering, and not simply a stimulus for the human imagination to elaborate models of sensory and social organization (see Senior 2004; Plumb 2015).

6 *Mediation*. Visualization and the visual display of information have received the lion's share of attention to date in studies of sensory communication, stimulated initially by Edward R. Tufte's landmark work, *The Visual Display of Quantitative Information* ([1983] 2001). The principles as well as best practices for visual communication within a contemporary Western context are now pretty well settled. Sonification and the auditory display of information have been attracting increasing attention of late (see Pink and Bijsterveld 2012, section 3) but remain undertheorized. Florian Grond and Thomas Hermann, both researchers in the field of Human-Computer Interaction (HCI), seek to correct this oversight in "Interactive Sonification for Data Exploration" (2014). They note that auditory display has a number of advantages relative to visual display, such as being "eyes-free," having a high temporal resolution, and not always requiring a directed focus and orientation. So far, however, the focus in auditory display research has been on the design of the auditory object or signal (i.e., on sound-making), with insufficient attention being paid to processes of reception (i.e., sound-listening), or to the potential role of sound in multimodal display and communication. To overcome this blindspot, they offer a taxonomy of "listening modes," or "techniques of hearing," and show how these can be adapted to achieve different purposes (e.g., normative, descriptive, etc.). They also draw on sound art and "musicianly listening" to introduce an aesthetic dimension to the scientific applications of sonification. The result is an integrated theory of modes of listening that might be fruitfully extrapolated to other ways of sensing, such as smelling or touching (on olfactory display, see Bembibre and Strlič 2017; on haptic display, see Parisi 2018).

7 *Affect*. The philosopher Brian Massumi is a prominent theorist of the affective turn. Affect theory is distinguished by its emphasis on the immediacy of experience in place of the constructedness of experience, and intensity in place of ideology (White 2017). The argument he presents in *What Animals Teach Us about Politics* (2014) represents something of a departure from affect theory, though, by virtue of its engagement with the anthropologist Gregory Bateson's theory of the pragmatics of animal (including human) communication as opposed to Massumi's normal focus on direct, unmediated perception. Massumi hails Bateson's "A Theory of Play and Fantasy" (1972) for the way it draws attention to the element of "metacommunication" in the playful encounter between, say, two wolf cubs. When one cub gives the other a nip, the nip enacts a paradox: it carries the meaning "this is not a bite" and thereby transforms the definition of the situation from one of combat to one of play (bite : nip :: combat : play). The nip violates the logic of stimulus-response and the logic of the excluded middle at once. It also sets the stage for what Massumi calls "transindividual mutual inclusion,"

which takes us straight back to the familiar (to him) terrain of affect theory. Massumi celebrates the creativity and surplus of vivacity in "playing animality," and urges philosophers (especially political philosophers) to ponder what animals can teach us about politics as the art of the possible.[12]

8 *Movement.* Greg Downey is an anthropologist of sport and one of the leading scholars of the field known as neuroanthropology (Lende and Downey 2012). During his fieldwork in Brazil, he apprenticed himself to a master practitioner of *capoeira*. This Brazilian martial art is known for its virtuosic displays of balancing while off-balance and lightning-quick strikes that defy standard Western assumptions about what the body is capable of. In addition to its unique kinaesthesiology, *capoeira* involves a unique visuality. Success at fending off attacks depends on cultivating what is known as the "sideways glance" – that is, on the practitioner dispersing their attention over the entire visual field and suppressing the reflex tendency to visually track moving objects or actions. This is a fascinating example of how "culture tunes our neurons," or in other words, how cultural practice can overwrite the way the brain is supposed to be wired (see Howes 2015a). The astounding "corpophysics" (Downey) of *capoeira* provide further evidence of the astonishing variety of sensory *techniques* across cultures.

9 *Representation.* In recent years, linguistic anthropologist Asifa Majid has been systematically troubling the received wisdom concerning the representation of the senses in language. In a special issue of *The Senses and Society* (Majid and Levinson 2011), she and her colleagues at the Max Planck Institute for Psycholinguistics extended the comparative study of sensory vocabularies from its traditional, monomodal focus on colour lexicons to other fields of sense. Her rigorously multimodal approach upset the evolutionist theory of Paul Berlin and Brent Kay in *Basic Color Terms* (1969) by showing that cultures which were low on Berlin and Kay's evolutionary scale with respect to the linguistic discrimination of colours far outshine and outperform English speakers in regards to other sensory terminologies. Another debate stirred up by Majid has to do with the vocabulary of smell. The neuroscientists Jonas Olofsson and Jay Gottfried (2015) have argued that olfactory naming is "difficult" because of the way the brain is organized. It is true that the English language has but two or three dedicated smell words, which is the basis of Oloffson and Gotfried's claim about the brain, but it turns out that English is not representative of language in general (Luhrmann 2014). Indeed, Olofsson and Gottfried's position is flatly contradicted by the olfactory vocabulary of the Maniq, a hunter-gatherer people of Malaysia studied by Majid, as the Maniq have fifteen dedicated terms for smell. Majid concludes her debate with Olofsson and Gottfried with the assertion that only by "taking culture seriously," and not foreclosing discussion by insisting on

supposedly universal patterns of neural circuitry, can we arrive at an account that reflects "the variability of odor lexicons and odor-naming abilities in the human population as a whole" (2015, 630; see further Majid 2021).

10 *Gustation.* "Good food" is nutritious food according to health experts, while in high-end restaurants goodness has to do with the authenticity of the ingredients. However, we miss a lot about the sensory experience of food in thinking this way. What interests Charles Spence (2018b) and Spence and his coauthor Betina Piqueras-Fiszman (2014) is not the honest meal but "the perfect meal," as evoked by M.F.K. Fisher in "The Pale Yellow Glove" (1937, 83):

> Once at least in the lifetime of every human, whether he be brute or trembling daffodil, comes a moment of complete gastronomic satisfaction. It is, I am sure, as much a matter of spirit as of body. Everything is right, nothing jars. There is a kind of harmony, with every sensation and emotion melted into one chord of well-being.

The perfect meal, then, has less to do with taste, the stimulation of the fungiform papillae on the tongue, and more to do with the mode of presentation, or "total experience" of a meal, ranging from the company we keep at table to the music playing in the background to the weight of the cutlery: the heavier the cutlery the better the food tastes (and the more one is willing to pay for it). The implication of Spence's research is that rather than concentrating on the ingredients, the focus should be on the interplay of the senses and the enveloping atmosphere. Consider "airline food" and beverages. In one study, it was found that more than a quarter of the passengers chose tomato juice when flying, even for breakfast, and even though they never or rarely drank it on ordinary occasions. Why? The answer has partly to do with the proteinaceous taste of umami (which is integral to tomato juice and Worcestershire sauce) but more to the point, this experiment found, is that the blaring sound of the airplane's engines augments the perception of umami flavour while interfering with our ability to taste sweetness. The choice is obvious, though the reasons are not, since we do not normally think of hearing as having any role to play in tasting.

On the contrary, hearing has very much to do with tasting, as Spence's famous "sonic chip" experiment exposed: the crunchier the sound of the potato chip when bitten into (with the sound being delivered via headphones), the crunchier and fresher the taste – by as much as 15 per cent. Intrigued by news of this discovery, the renegade restaurateur Heston Blumenthal enlisted Spence as a collaborator in the experimental design of the dishes on offer at his restaurant on the outskirts of London, the Fat Duck. One of their culinary creations is "The Sound of the Sea," which involves diners being given headphones and a conch shell containing an iPod Shuffle, which plays a marine soundtrack that has the effect of heightening their perception of the dish they are served. Spence has also teamed up with chef Jozef Youssef of Kitchen Theory to create gustatory extravaganzas that incorporate image projections, mist, and carefully curated soundtracks to complement and accentuate the savours on offer (Youssef and Spence 2021).

Mixing the senses is at the heart of Spence's experiments in research-creation. Other factors he has delimited as impacting the flavour of a meal (as measured by the amount patrons are willing to pay for it, for example) include the colour and form of the plate (avoid red, bowls are best) and, of course, the aroma. It is better to make customers wait to be served, while wafting the smell of food cooking in the kitchen throughout the dining establishment so as to whet the appetite: the anticipation of a meal should be played up as much, if not more, than the actual consumption of it. Of course, many chefs know this intuitively, but Spence provides the science to back it.

While restaurateurs have taken note of Spence's "new science of eating," which he calls "gastrophysics," and applied it, the so-called sensory professionals of the food science industry have not, for the most part, and their "creations," which are our common fare, accordingly reek of artificiality (Classen et al. 1994, 197–200; Lahne and Spackman 2018). Within the confines of the sensory evaluation laboratory (white, sterile, well lit, air conditioned, divided into individual cubicles), panelists are plied with one sensation at a time (this is facilitated by using blindfolds, ear defenders, etc.) and instructed to "evaluate" it. The results are then summed to arrive at the the ideal (read: normal) profile for the food or beverage under scrutiny. To inject even a smidgen of multi- or intersensoriality into the research design would be to risk losing control of the "variable" to be tested, and so is left out (Howes 2015c; see also Teil 2019). Nothing could be further from the meal as a total sensory and social phenomenon, which may explain why so many of us find it perfectly normal to dine alone from some plastic tray of food that has been microwaved.

The next step, from a sensory studies perspective, is to consider the social, political, and environmental elements of the production of food and the experience of eating. Sidney Mintz's (1985) classic study of the history of sugar production and consumption, with its ties to the ruthless exploitation of slaves in the plantation economy on the one hand, and the subhuman sustenance of the industrial worker on the other, remains one of the finest examples of this approach. Anna Tsing's *The Mushroom at the End of the World* (2015) complements Mintz's study, exploring the social and environmental consequences of a commodity chain of extraordinary complexity centring on the matsutake mushroom, and the ongoing possibility of life amidst capitalist ruination.

11 *Synaesthesia.* As discussed in the corresponding subsection of chapter 1, neuropsychologists like V.S. Ramachandran (Ramachandran, Hubbard, and

Butcher 2004) are dismissive of the "metaphor explanation" of synaesthesia and have sought to localize synaesthesia in the brain. Neuropsychologists have also devised tests to screen out pretenders (Baron-Cohen and Harrison 1997). Sceptics persist, however, and argue that synaesthesia is "merely metaphorical" with the same passion that neuroscientists display when they insist it is "purely physiological," or not at all. The question arises: why relegate? Why assimilate synaesthesia exclusively either to metaphor (i.e., figurative speech) or to the abnormal (i.e., the hyperconnected brain)? Why not proceed on both fronts at once? This is the breakthrough signalled by Yale psychologist Lawrence E. Marks and Catherine M. Mulvenna's ecumenical approach to the phenomenon in "Synesthesia on Our Mind" (2013). They treat synaesthesia *relationally,* comparing how crossmodal metaphors in language on the one hand and synaesthesia in perception on the other differ in certain respects and overlap in others. This focus on the relations *between* metaphor and synaesthesia leads to the discovery that synaesthetic experience and metaphorical cognitions often display "a common set of cross-domain relations," and should therefore be theorized as expressions of "creative cognition," or what we call *intersensoriality*. Marks and Mulvenna's hybrid theory of synaesthesia as "perceptual metaphor" represents a significant advance over Ramachandran's reductionist, exclusionary definition of synaesthesia, and lines up nicely with Charles Spence's empirical investigation of crossmodal correspondences, Yi-Fu Tuan's model of synaesthesia as a two-way street, and Silvia Casini's "pedagogy of the image."

In the final chapter of *Ways of Sensing* (2014), which is entitled "Unravelling Synaesthesia," Constance Classen and I shifted the grounds of discussion by championing Lawrence Sullivan's theory of "cultural synaesthesia" as a counterpoint to the "congenital" (neuropsychological) theory of synaesthesia. In his theory, Sullivan, a scholar of comparative religion at Harvard, foregrounds the cosmological dimension of the unity of the senses and the practical effect on cognition of the ways in which the senses are mobilized in ritual and utilized in everyday life. He argues that when crossmodal relations are enacted in ritual or concretized by technologies (whether instructional, mechanical, or chemical – as with the use of the hallucinogenic *Banisteriposis caapi* plant by the Desana), they acquire a social life that exceeds their mental life and become "actual." The question of whether the cross-sense linkages are metaphorical or physiological is beside the point from a performative perspective. We also advanced a social theory of synaesthesia, among other things. This theory posits that when social interdependence or mixity is embraced, then sensory interdependence is also likely to be celebrated or treated as normal; when social "purity" matters most, however (Nazi Germany being an extreme example), then synaesthesia tends to be excoriated and suppressed. These tendencies, which are relative to each other and therefore admit of many degrees, may help explain why synaesthesia has flitted in and out of focus as a topic of scientific and popular interest, as a reflection of the prevailing structure of social relations.

Concluding Note

"Neuromania" is the term coined by physician and philosopher Raymond Tallis (2011) to describe the manner in which the rise of neuroscience has resulted in a drastic restriction in our understanding of human consciousness. According to neuroscience, the external world is filtered by the properties of the receptor systems and the way the brain is wired, such that what passes for reality is "all in our heads" and "down to our DNA" (Hollingham 2004). However, as we have seen, this mediation is itself mediated by the "loops" between brain and body, society or culture and the environment (following Kirmayer), and the senses also modulate each other.

Attending to the loops and modulations should lead us to be sceptical of the "extended mind hypothesis" that comes out of cognitive neuroscience and philosophy (for an accessible account, see *Supersizing the Mind* [A. Clark 2008]). This "hypothesis" is a rather peculiar way of compensating for the privatization of sensation when analysed from a psychophysical perspective as well as the collateral notion that perception or meaning-making goes on "in some grotto in our heads" (Geertz 1986). With its idea of the "leaky" brain, or "essential interpenetrability or commingling of mind and world" (Ingold 2011, 236), the extended mind hypothesis only intensifies the already exaggerated mentalism of the cognitivist paradigm. What is needed is rather a socially nuanced theory of the *extended sensorium*, such as Francois Laplantine offers in *The Life of the Senses* (2015). The latter theory recognizes the senses as intelligencers in their own right, rather than devices for information pickup in an environment (*pace* Ingold 2000 following Gibson 1979), and as having a life, a social life to be exact, as well.

In this chapter, we have explored some of the many different ways in which the sensorium is constructed and the senses are lived in history and across cultures. This investigation has underscored the need to supplement the conventional focus on sense receptors and neurological processes with attending to practices of perception, techniques of the senses, ways of sensing, and expanding the "scientific" purview to include the contributions of historical and Indigenous "local biologies" (Niewöhner and Lock 2018), psychologies (Heelas and Lock 1981), and neurologies (Reichel-Dolmatoff 1981) to our understanding of the life of the senses, including the life of the mind.

How many senses are there? The tendency in recent years has been to defer to the neurosciences for the answer to this question, and to count on physiology. Approached from a sensory studies perspective, however, the response is that "the senses are infinite and innumerable" (Hamilakis 2014) since the answer depends on how they are used, on how perception is practised.

PART TWO

Case Studies

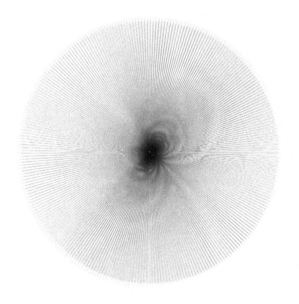

Collideroscope series (2022) © Erik Adigard, M-A-D

CHAPTER FOUR

The Modern Sensorium: A Case Study in Sensory History, 1920–2001

The Cold War and hot jazz, the Roaring Twenties and the Swinging Sixties, the silent screen and virtual reality – these were among the dominant sensations of the twentieth century. They resulted from a mix of technological developments and social and aesthetic change. Such developments and changes occurred rapidly during the period from 1920 to 2000 (the focus of this chapter) and transformed the sensory world so dramatically that it seemed almost a brand-new creation. Indeed, "Make it new!" was the cry of art as of commerce (Armstrong 2005, ch. 5; Pells 2011).

The twentieth-century world was one in which age-old social distinctions were dissolving, in which the faces seen and the voices heard took on an unprecedented diversity in terms of ethnicity, gender, and class. It was also a world of impossibly tall buildings and incredibly fast vehicles, of soaring aircraft, of moving and talking pictures, of alluring processed foods and of endlessly malleable synthetic materials. Little wonder that commentators on twentieth-century culture often make prominent reference to Disneyland. For people of previous centuries, the twentieth-century industrial world might have seemed a kind of "Disneyland": fantastical and thrilling, but also, as has often been noted, strangely soulless, a world in which the dominant value seemed to be the pursuit of money in order to achieve a chimeric happiness through the acquisition of material goods. In previous eras sensory indulgence was often conceptualized as a hindrance to spiritual development. However, in the twentieth century the path to personal fulfilment was increasingly presented as passing through the pleasures of the senses.

In this chapter, characteristic twentieth-century phenomena are coupled in pairs in order to bring out the interplay of different elements of the sensory and social order of the time. The epilogue draws out the implications of what "doing sensory history" can do for our understanding of social change.

The Automobile and the Airplane

The twentieth century was quickly identified as an age of speed by Modernist writers and artists, and at the centre of this whirlwind age was the automobile. The writer F.T. Marinetti declared in the *Manifesto of Futurism* that, due to the automobile, "we believe that this wonderful world has been further enriched by a new beauty, the beauty of speed" (2006, ch. 2). The sensory impact of the automobile was not limited to the exhilarating sensation of velocity it offered, however, but included a full range of perceptions. As the Dadaist Guillermo de Torre exclaimed in his poem "Al volante" (At the steering wheel), "the car is a convex bow that shoots insatiable trajectories ... the windshield multiplies our eyes ... and the wind liquefies sounds" (cited by Giucci 2012, 129–30).

The very smell of the automobile symbolized power and freedom for many, as noted by Proust, who found the odour of petrol "delicious" in its evocation of "the joy of speeding over [the countryside]" and "of being on one's way to a longed-for destination" (1984, 48). Automotive odours might also represent progress and success. When the founder of the Honda Motor Company, Soichiro Honda, saw his first car – a Ford Model T – in his Japanese hometown, he knelt to smell its dripping oil and dreamt of one day manufacturing automobiles himself (Ingrassia and White 1994, 236)

A number of Modernist artists noted that car windows framed the world as a series of pictures. Henri Matisse brought out this aspect of automobile travel in his painting *The Windshield*, which depicts a car interior with the picturesque nature of the view from the windshield implied by a sketch pad lying on the dashboard (see Danius 2002, 136). The speed of the automobile, however, blurred and scattered the scenes it presented. The perception that the objects seen through car windows were themselves moving was described by Proust in "Impressions de route en automobile." He imaginatively declared that during his drive houses "came rushing towards us, clasping to their bosoms vine or rose-bush" while trees "ran in every direction to escape from us" (cited in Danius 2002, 140).

It was not only the view *from* the car, but also the view *of* the car that transformed perception. As a prestige object and a technological wonder, a shiny new automobile attracted admiring looks and desiring touches. The sight of cars hurtling along a road enhanced the impression of living in a whirlwind age. The Futurist Giacomo Balla captured some of this feeling in a series of drawings and paintings that employed abstract representations of spinning wheels, rushing wind, scattered light, and roaring engines to approximate the "thrilling onrush of visual, tactile, and aural sensations" experienced by viewers at an automobile racetrack (Poggi 2008, 29).

At the same time as it dominated the exterior landscape, however, the car isolated its passengers from the environment. This created a sense of alienation from the external world, which, viewed through a windshield, might appear to be little more than a movie projected onto a screen. This tactile isolation was deemed to be a definite advantage by those who decried the indiscriminate contact that might occur among passengers taking public transportation. One early twentieth-century commentator, for example, denounced how, due to the crowding of bodies in Los Angeles trams, "a bishop embraced a stout grandmother" and "a tender girl touched limbs with a city sport" (cited by Bottles 1987, 22). The automobile avoided such blurring of physical and social boundaries by providing each (middle-class) individual and family with a protective and private mode of travel. As a protected and private space, however, the car would also come to function as a central site for intimate encounters and courtship.

The automobile, in fact, not only transformed twentieth-century perceptions, but it also fostered new ways of life and new material worlds. With the increase in car ownership, city streets often became more places of passage for automobiles than paths for pedestrians. Highways cut through or bypassed old towns and neighbourhoods, spawning their own network of gas stations, diners, motels, and strip malls. Suburbs sprang up in locations once deemed too distant for commuting to urban centres but now seen as only a short drive away. Attached or underground garages enabled drivers to move from car interior to house or building interior without ever stepping outside. As a result, the outdoor world became increasingly foreign to city dwellers – either something one avoided by being in a car or a place one went to for a change of scene by travelling in a car.

Customs changed, and people preferred "driving in the country in the afternoon" to "sitting stiffly in the parlor" (cited by Kihlstedt 1983, 162). Pastors and priests warned that the new practice of the Sunday family car trip was threatening church attendance (Heitmann 2009, 88). Rushing around in an automobile was said to create a condition of nervousness, a state in which slowing down or stopping were intolerable because they interfered with the pressing impulse to speed ahead. Everything was now required to be speedy and streamlined, including food, work, music, and language itself, which was compressed in both its verbal and literary forms (see, for example, Tichi 1987, 220).

Coupled with the automobile as a marvel of modern transportation, the airplane also transformed people's ways of sensing. Its direct sensory and social impact was not as widespread as that of the automobile. Very few people had private airplanes and, until the latter part of the century, the high cost of flying made it an elite mode of transportation, the prerogative of businessmen, government officials, and the vagabond socialites who came to be known as "the jet set." However, the airplane's impact on the imagination was enormous. "Of all the agencies ... that made the average man of 1925 intellectually different from [one] of 1900, by far the greatest was the sight of a human being in an airplane," wrote the American journalist Mark Sullivan in 1935 (cited in Bilstein 2003, 16).

Seemingly supernatural in its ability to transport people across the skies, the airplane symbolized the human transcendence of ordinary physical limitations. Numerous people recorded experiencing a sense of spiritual elevation when travelling in or simply watching a plane flying above the earth. In the purity of the sky there was "no ugliness ... no grasping" and no "mean streets and bickering" (cited in Bilstein 2003, 21).

The airplane freed the human sensorium from earthbound sensations. Blue became the dominant colour, the coldness of high altitude the dominant feeling, and the roar of the engine the dominant sound (the onomatopoeic word "zoom" was coined to express the sound and speed of an airplane as it soared into the sky). Flight provided astounding bird's-eye or God's-eye views of the world. The Argentine art critic Julio Payró noted in the 1930s that, in contrast to the automobile, with its blurred views and focus on the road, the airplane gave "a cartographic, futurist idea of the landscape" (cited in Giucci 2012, 135). Looking down on earth from a plane made the geographic borders dividing countries seem insignificant – there were no borders in the sky. It was, indeed, hoped by many that "with the new aerial age will come a new internationalism" as people flew from one country to another dissolving physical and cultural barriers (cited in Bilstein 2003, 20).

Like the automobile, the airplane separated people from the environment; however, in the case of the latter this detachment was total. "Oh! I have slipped the surly bonds of earth," declared aviator John Gillespie Magee in his oft-cited poem "High Flight" (Roberts and Briand 1957, 171). In a very mechanical form of apotheosis, the airplane carried its passengers up into heaven. This pseudo-religious view of air travel was expressed by Apollinaire in his poem "Zone," in which an airplane is likened to Christ and depicted rising into the sky accompanied by angels (1971, 118–19). New spiritual senses replaced the old earthly ones. Flying in the "untrespassed sanctity of space," the aviator was able to "put out [his] hand, and touch the face of God" (in Roberts and Briand 1957, 171; see further Corn 1983). That there were, in mundane reality, no gods to be touched and no angels to be seen on the "angel-side of clouds" (Kipling), no "heaven" to be found in the heavens, was discomfiting to many, even though modern science had already put paid to traditional notions of a geographical heaven and hell. The premodern cosmos had been filled with good and evil forces and their sensory manifestations (Classen 2012, 28). The twentieth-century cosmos seemed chillingly empty. When humans landed on the moon in 1969, the event aroused a similar range of emotions – awe at what seemed a supernatural feat, and disappointment that, after millennia of myths and stories, that's all there was to the moon.

It was not only the ability of planes and rockets to leave the earth that riveted the twentieth-century imagination, but also their ability to drop things on earth – in particular, explosives. Many parts of the world experienced the devastation produced by aerial bombing during the twentieth century. The atomic bomb, developed in the United States during the Second World War and "harnessing the basic power of the universe," as President Truman put it (cited by Hein and Selden 1997, 4), vastly intensified the destructive power of aerial bombing. The sudden transformation of the city of Hiroshima into a pile of formless rubble after an atomic bomb had been dropped on it by one single airplane made it clear that the god-like power of modern technology could destroy life as well as enhance it. The picture of the giant mushroom cloud produced by the detonation of an atomic bomb became one of the most powerful and disturbing images of the latter part of the century. The purely visual nature of the picture made it all the eerier because its silence seemed to convey a silencing of voices and an annihilation of listeners.

The wartime use of the airplane tarnished its image as an agent for spiritual and social transformation. The final blow to the notion of the airplane elevating its passengers above worldly cares and conflicts came not in the twentieth century, however, but in 2001, when four American passenger planes were hijacked by terrorists and used as weapons of mass destruction. The era of the airplane as otherworldly was over.

The Skyscraper and the Bungalow

The desire to rise above the ground that produced the airplane manifested itself architecturally in the skyscraper. Made possible by advances in engineering and the invention of the elevator, skyscrapers were erected in major cities around the world from the 1930s on. In city centres where land was limited and expensive, it made sense to build upwards rather than outwards, to house people in the sky rather than on the ground. However, skyscrapers were not only monuments to efficiency, they were also emblems of corporate and urban might and even sublimity, for their great height aroused the feelings of awe evoked in previous centuries by soaring cathedral spires. The majesty of the skyscraper did not point to the power of God, however, but rather to human ingenuity.

... Who made the skyscrapers?
Man made 'em, the little, two-legged joker, Man.
Out of his head, out of his dreaming, scheming skypiece ...

(Sandburg 1976, 320)

Standing up straight and tall like giants, skyscrapers were themselves figurative men, proudly displaying themselves as conquerors of the landscape.

The sensory impact of skyscrapers was experienced corporeally through their looming presence on city streets and the upward movement of their elevators, but it was their visual effects, the views of and from skyscrapers, that were most often remarked. Seen from a distance, a skyline of skyscrapers presented the city as a site of power and wonder. And while "close up there are things that are not very comforting: littered streets, corner drug deals, broken down tenements" (G. Douglas 1996, 2), by keeping eyes looking upwards skyscrapers diverted the senses from the often far less attractive scenario of the ground environment. The view *from* the skyscraper, in turn, minimized the significance of the sensory experiences of life on the ground as it maximized the power of sight to encompass and survey.

It was not just its height that gave the skyscraper its particular visual potency, but also its lack of ornamentation. The sleek, often reflective facade of the skyscraper seemed to transform the building into pure presence. Making no allusions, affording no distractions, it was simply, mammothly there. The smooth, clean surfaces of the skyscraper matched the smoothness and cleanliness of pavement, and the smoothness of automobile travel, to offer an illusion of urban life as similarly smooth and clean – ordered and controlled by modern technology.

The skyscraper's lack of ornamentation also suggested that the work undertaken in such a building would be highly functional, and even ruthless, with no deviations from the prescribed course. The main use of the skyscraper was as a corporate office building and therefore its design mimicked the supposedly no-nonsense office work that took place inside, and which ideally resulted in a commercial dominance equivalent to the architectural dominance of the building. Furthermore, just as the skyscraper's facade lacked distinguishing features, so did the lives of workers toiling inside: each individual simply contributed to the monumental effect of the whole. As skyscrapers were the most prominent buildings in the big city, the big city itself became a symbol of faceless corporate power and functionalism.

The aesthetic and symbolic values of the skyscraper were mirrored in many of the artistic productions of the century. While the prosaic, commercial functions of the skyscraper might not appeal to the artistic imagination, its clean, functional lines, soaring height, and display of technological mastery did. Depicting a skyscraper in a painting became a sign of an artist who was confronting the realities of modern life. Painters such as Joseph Stella (*Skyscrapers*) and Georgia O'Keefe (*Manhattan*, 1932), depicted the buildings as stark geometrical patterns of light and dark rising into the sky. The Brazilian composer Hector Villa-Lobos traced a picture of the New York City skyline onto a musical staff and used it as the basis for an orchestral suite. The term "Skyscraper moderne" was coined to refer to furniture and housewares inspired by the forms of skyscrapers. In 1934 Malcolm Cowley proclaimed that "the writers of our generation ... had one privilege: to write a poem in which all was but order and beauty, a poem rising like a clean tower" (cited in Tichi 1987, 289).

The counterpart to the urban skyscraper was the suburban bungalow. Imported from India and redesigned by the British early in the century, the low-profile, open-layout bungalow went on to gain popularity in cities around the world (King 1984). That its airy design was particularly suited for hot climates made no difference, as modern heating systems could take care of any chilling effects of open spaces and large windows in colder climates.

The growth of bungalow-filled suburbs was made possible by the spread of the family automobile. In the nineteenth century the suburbs had often been regarded as undesirable places to live. Most people who could afford it wished to live within convenient walking distance of work and amenities. The urban outskirts were frequently considered unhealthy, poor, and criminal, emitting a "great variety of fetid and disgusting smells" (Bottles 1987, 6). In the twentieth century, the greater mobility provided by the automobile transforned the outskirts of cities into places of respite from the "concrete jungle" of the city centre – places where inexpensive housing, green spaces, and fresh air abounded.

The bungalow captured the spirit of the time by offering a more informal space for family living that was suggestive of the easier-going social relations of the new century. The low profile and large windows of the bungalow and its mid-twentieth-century variation, the ranch house, allowed it to be filled with the sunshine that was absent from downtown streets perpetually shaded by office towers. The lawn that stretched out in front of the house and the roomy yard behind added a relaxing, natural aspect, and the possibility of outdoor cooking – even swimming in a pool if the budget allowed – which contributed to the bungalow's "vacation home" atmosphere and its cultural value as an antidote to the pressures and formalities of city life (Howes 2010).

For many, making the switch from renting an urban apartment to owning a suburban bungalow – however humble and undistinguished – was also an important step up the social ladder. In England bungalow ownership was even said to be accompanied by a new style of speech to go along with the new social status it conferred: the so-called bay window accent (McKibbin 1998, 79).

However, some viewed the expanding tracts of bungalows with dismay. The social historian Lewis Mumford condemned such suburbs as

a multitude of uniform, unidentifiable houses, lined up inflexibly, at uniform distances, on uniform roads, in a treeless communal waste, inhabited by people of the same class, the same income, the same age group, witnessing the same television programs, eating the same tasteless pre-fabricated foods, from the same freezers, conforming in every outward and inward respect to a common mould. (cited in C. Clark 1986, 227)

Bestselling books, such as *The Organization Man* by William H. White, *The Man in the Gray Flannel Suit* by Sloan Wilson, and *The Crack in the Picture Window* (1957) by John Keats, warned that the suburbs united with the corporate world in offering stifling monotony and imposing mindless conformity.

In a song called "Little Boxes" (written and composed by Malvina Reynolds in 1962 and transformed into a hit by her friend Pete Seeger when he made a cover of it in 1963), there is reference to bungalows as "little boxes made of ticky tacky ... little boxes all the same," which produced families "all the same." If people escaped to the suburbs hoping to find more scope for individuality and more sensory diversity than in their downtown office buildings, it seems they were out of luck (see Creadick 2010; Baxandall and Ewen 2000).

The reputed dullness of the suburbs, in fact, gave a new prominence to the city centre as a hub of activity. This was particularly the case at night when the suburbs lay dark and silent and the city scintillated with light and movement. In her catchy hit song of 1964, "Downtown," Petula Clark urged people to go downtown and "listen to the music of the traffic in the city," look at the "pretty" neon lights, and dance the night away. During the day the city centre might be a cold and hard-edged arena for business transactions, but at night it became a fantasy land of sensuous pleasures. However, such pleasures were assumed to be for the most part off-limits to the family men and women who inhabited the suburbs.

As the century progressed, women, in their role as housewives, especially came to be seen as the "victims" of suburban monotony. While suburban men drove off every weekday to their jobs in the city, women remained ensconced in the family bungalow. Indeed, the bungalow itself – low profile, close to "nature," and the centre of family life – conveyed notions of femininity in contrast to the masculine associations of the vertical, business-centred skyscraper. New labour-saving devices such as vacuum cleaners and washing machines meant that the women left at home had more free time, but, stuck in the suburbs as they were, limited possibilities for creative action or mental stimulation. In 1963 Betty Friedan's *The Feminine Mystique* detailed the plight of the "trapped" housewife in terms of her supposedly drab sensory life:

> Each suburban wife struggled with her [dissatisfaction] alone. As she made the beds, shopped for groceries, made slipcover material, ate peanut butter sandwiches with her children, chauffeured Cub Scouts and Brownies, lay beside her husband at night – she was afraid to ask even of herself the silent question – "Is this all?" (1963, 15)

The bungalow, which had once represented freedom, now seemed to be a prison. The time, it seemed, had come for women's liberation.

By the last decades of the century the bungalow had lost much of its appeal. Rather than appearing fresh and stimulating it looked tired and boring. In 1946, the authors of *Tomorrow's House* had claimed that "even a poor architect has a hard time making a spreading, one-story house unattractive" (C. Clark 1986: 177). In the 1980s the generation that had grown up in such houses appeared to think just the opposite, that even a *good* architect would have a hard time making a spreading, one-story house attractive.

The desire for home comforts that the bungalow awakened, however, had not disappeared; the "dream house" had simply taken another, and grander, form. It had two stories instead of one, two (if not more) bathrooms and two garages – for the liberated woman of the house needed her own car now. If anything, the home was regarded as even more of an oasis from the stress of city living than before, due to innovations in home media technologies and the trend towards "cocooning" or retreating into the home. Nor had the drive for conformity epitomized by the uniformity of suburbia disappeared. Instead it had become masked by the seeming diversity of options offered by such things as customized interior fittings, cable television, multiple flavours of ice cream, and assorted varieties of toothpaste. These might all simply be choices from a limited menu (Archer 2005, 337); however, they provided a pleasant sense of individuality while ensuring that life in the little (though increasingly bigger) boxes of suburbia carried on.

The Camera and the Screen

The twentieth century was marked by an increasing proliferation of visual imagery. Photography, once the domain of professionals, became a hobby that almost anyone could practise with the aid of an inexpensive compact camera and a photo developing service. Every middle-class family could have albums filled with snapshots (first black and white and then colour) of family celebrations and vacations. As a key means of embodying personal history, the family photo album transformed the past into a series of visual images. If Proust had lived a few decades later, perhaps it might have been a photo album, and not a madeleine dipped in tea, that awakened his recollections of the past.

Home photography supplemented the multiplicity of photographs in magazines, newspapers, and books. The realistic quality of these images added to their impact. Unlike illustrations, they appeared to offer unmediated visual access to the people and scenes they represented and thus transform their viewers into eyewitnesses. Susan Sontag observed that photographs "have virtually unlimited authority in a modern society" due to the fact that they are not perceived merely as representations of reality, but as "something directly stencilled off the real," a skimming, as it were, of actual visual surfaces (1973, 154). By the end of the century, the photograph had in some ways become more "real" than the real thing, as photographs and films posted on the Internet began to acquire a life and value of their own (see Howes and Classen 2014, 89–92).

The relatively effortless process of taking a photograph, compared to drawing a picture, placed the sensory emphasis on the visual end result, rather than on the manual craft. As Walter Benjamin wrote in 1936, "photography freed the hand of the most important artistic functions which henceforth devolved only upon the eye looking into a lens" (1973, 20). The photograph itself, by eliminating all sensory information but the visual, gave an added value to visual appearance. If the visual was all that this wondrous new technology of reproduction could depict, then it was essential to make the most of visuality. This emphasis on "looking good" in contemporary culture was enhanced by pervasive advertising imagery that promoted products and the people pictured with them in terms of their visual appeal (Ewen 1988).

The function of the camera in modern society, however, was not only to record significant people and places, to capture "slice-of-life" moments, or to showcase desirable merchandise. It was also to surveil. Already in the First World War cameras, carried aloft on airplanes, were put to the service of military reconnaissance. Over the course of the century the camera became essential to peacetime surveillance as well. Introduced in the 1970s, video surveillance of public spaces as a form of social control was widespread by the century's close: "Today, the ubiquitous video 'security' camera stares blankly at us in apartment buildings, department and convenience stores, gas stations, libraries, parking garages, automated banking outlets, buses, and elevators. No matter where you live you are likely to encounter cameras; some places simply bristle with them" (Staples 2000, 59). Even in the sky, cameras mounted on satellites circled the Earth, capturing images that were viewed down on the ground. The world had never been so watched. "Has the camera replaced the eye of God?" asked John Berger in 1978 ([1980] 1991, 57).

This constant monitoring elicited less public concern than one might have expected. Perhaps its social benefits seemed greater than its intrusiveness. Perhaps the visualism of twentieth-century culture had accustomed people to being looked at. However, it did raise questions about the loss of privacy in contemporary society and spawn a thriving academic sub-field called surveillance studies (see Lyon 2007).

Turning from the camera to the screen, cinema, the most popular form of entertainment in the first half of the century, further contributed to the optical orientation of the age. Viewing a film was not an exclusively visual experience, of course. After sound came to the "silent screen" in the late 1920s, movies engaged the ears as well as the eyes. Even the early cinematic experience could, in fact, be quite synaesthetic. The more elaborate cinemas showcased sumptuous architectural fittings, featured a live orchestra, and had elegant cafés (Richards 2009). The movie theatre also served as a site for familial or romantic hand holding and cuddling. Nonetheless, it was the visual effects of the films shown there that drew the most attention.

Cinema seemingly magnified the power of sight by presenting larger-than-life images. At the same time, techniques of filming and editing – close-ups, slow motion, camera angles, abrupt changes of scene – trained movie audiences in radically new ways of seeing and gave a whole new interest to being a spectator. The fact that movies were shown in a dark theatre – or "picture palace" – in which people sat motionless and (ideally) silent, enhanced their sensorial power. While the fantasy fare of cinema provided an "escape" from the tedium and restrictions of everyday life, it also taught people to seek release only though their eyes, ears, and imaginations, while not moving an inch. The cinema audience seemed like a collection of eyes all fixed on one point.

With the invention of television in the mid-twentieth century, however, a new form of leisure viewing emerged. Television shows had many of the same traits as the movies shown at the cinema, but they appeared on a small screen and were intended for private viewing in the home. Watching television was not something one went out to do, but something one stayed in to do. In 1938 the British novelist Elizabeth Bowen gave as one of her reasons for enjoying the cinema, "I like sitting in a packed crowd in the dark, among hundreds riveted on the same thing" (cited by Richards 2010, 23). Millions of television viewers might all be "riveted on the same thing," but they were no longer sitting together in a packed crowd. Twentieth-century spectatorship changed from being communal to being largely familial or individualist.

As watching a television show was as easy as pressing a button and setting the channel, and as there was no need to leave one's home to do it, television also vastly increased the amount of time people spent passively viewing a screen. Instead of being a once-a-week activity, as cinema was in its heyday, television became a daily activity. A good part of peoples' lives in the second half of the century, therefore, was spent passively watching images flickering on a screen.

The declining cost of television ownership resulted in it becoming a fixture in virtually all homes in the developed world. In his dystopic novel of 1956 about life in the suburbs, *The Crack in the Picture Window*, John Keats described the sensory uniformity created by mass television viewing in the days when there were few channels:

> Every house ... was dark ... but within every shuttered living room there gleamed a feeble phosphorescence, a tiny picture flickering in that glow. Over the bewitched community there swelled a common sound. Sometimes it was the fanfare, introducing a commercial. Sometimes it was the thin, jubilant cry of the studio audience in New York ... Sometimes it was the dumb-de-dumb-dumb musical signature of a period crime piece. But whatever the sound, it was a common sound, rising above the darkened houses, for everyone watched the same shows. (1957, 79)

Watching shows at home did allow viewers to participate in a variety of activities not possible in a movie theatre, such as eating a meal. However, it also significantly shaped activities within the home. For example, many families began eating meals in front of a television set instead of around a table. This new custom of clustering around the television led to its being considered the modern successor to the hearth (Spigel 1992). Whereas sitting around a hearth had left people free to converse and look at each other, however, the television interfered with familial interaction through its demands for visual and auditory attention. At the same time, the mass diffusion of television programs and advertising created a widely shared visual and sonic pool of information and tropes that helped to dissolve differences of class, gender, and ethnicity.

This emphasis on seeing at the expense of other, more traditional forms of sensory engagement was disturbing to many. Parents worried that their children were spending too much time watching television and not enough playing outside. Social critics feared that the twentieth century's obsession with visual surfaces signalled an ailing and alienated society. American educator Neil Postman warned that we were "amusing ourselves to death" with the facile "visual delight" of television (1985). "From television to newspapers, from advertising to all sorts of mercantile epiphanies, our society is characterized by a cancerous growth of vision, measuring everything by its ability to show or be shown, and transmuting communication into a visual journey," proclaimed the French philosopher Michel de Certeau (1983b, 18). And then came the personal computer and the Internet, which turned even greater numbers of people into "hypervisualists," constantly scanning images and texts on a screen. However, the fact that images and texts could be created and transmitted, as well as viewed on the Internet, meant that the new medium of the computer did not simply continue the sensory trajectory of the cinema and television, but rather fostered a new sensory dynamic that would await the next century to disclose its social effects (i.e., "social media").

Plastic and Pollution

The substance that characterized the physical world of the twentieth century and provided a material base for much of its cultural expression was plastic. The term "plastic," in fact, covers a variety of synthetic or semi-synthetic substances, from the celluloid used in film and cheap jewellery to the vinyls employed in records, raincoats, and exterior siding. However, plastic became the umbrella term for all these creations of the chemical industry. Technical advances resulted in plastics that were amazingly durable as well as low cost. "Plastic is forever," touted one industry pioneer, "and a lot cheaper than diamonds" (cited in Miekle 1995, 9).

Over the course of the century the material became a familiar component of ordinary life. A family celebrating Christmas in the United States in the 1970s, for example, might have a plastic Christmas tree decorated with plastic ornaments and featuring plastic Barbie dolls and Lego blocks as presents. In a famous line from the 1967 movie *The Graduate*, a recent college graduate who is uncertain about his future is told by a businessman friend of his father, "I just want to say one word to you. Just one word ... Plastics ... There's a great future in plastics. Think about it" (cited in Miekle 1995, 3).

Like its material uses, the sensory properties of plastic were multiple. Easy to shape, colour, and texture, plastic might approximate anything. It could be made to look like wood or it could be made to look like glass, it could resemble flowers or it could mimic gemstones. Nonetheless, on close inspection, it always retained something "plasticky" in its look and feel. Plastic itself had no imitators, for who would imitate such a cheap and indeterminate substance?

Due to its mutability, plastic engendered a notion of the malleability of the material world. The French philosopher Roland Barthes wrote of plastic in the 1950s that it embodied "the very idea of ... infinite transformation" (1972, 79). Plastic's mutability coincided with twentieth-century desires to reshape not only the physical environment but also society and even the human body through cosmetic and surgical procedures (i.e., "plastic surgery"). Limits set by nature or by custom no longer seemed to hold in a plastic world. Anything could take on a new form.

While plastic was embraced by the twentieth century for its malleability and low cost, it was also despised (at least by the educated classes) for its "inauthenticity." Over the course of the century, in fact, the word "plastic" came to be a synonym for "fake." Social critics saw plastic as sign and symptom of a society in which simulations had a greater appeal than reality. When the businessman in *The Graduate* affirms that there is a great future in plastics, the line is not intended to serve as an indicator of commercial acumen, but as an indictment of the superficiality and materialism of Western culture.

It was not only the look and feel of the twentieth-century industrialized world that breathed artificiality, however, but also the taste. Convenience foods – from the quick meals served up by fast food restaurants to the prepared foods stocked at the supermarket (such as the frozen "TV dinners" made to be warmed and eaten while watching television) – became increasingly popular during the century. The new processed foods also had new artificial flavours and colours, many of them derived from petrochemicals just like most plastics (see Classen, Howes, and Synnott 1994, 187–200). In their song of 1972, "Plastic Man," the Kinks sung disparagingly of a "plastic man" who "eats plastic food with a plastic knife and fork." Many processed foods, of course, were packaged in plastic, if not canned or boxed. The contents of the supermarket thus seemed, from one perspective, to represent one more triumph of modern technology, and, from another, one more of the shams of contemporary life.

Within the context of a material culture that seemed increasingly artificial, the natural world acquired a new value as a place and source of authenticity, where one could experience the "real" thing. The sights and sounds and scents of nature were extolled as both physically and spiritually refreshing. This desire

for natural experiences was bolstered by the dramatic growth in urban populations during the century. Trips to the countryside and camping became popular
ways for urbanites to replenish their senses and spirits through immersion in
natural settings, especially after workers won the right to paid vacation time in
many countries (Aron 1999).

At the same time as the pure air and green vistas of the wilderness were
acquiring a new value for city dwellers, however, an awareness developed of
how the natural world was being depleted and polluted by industrialization
and technological development (Barr 1970; Parr 2010). The lumber industry
was devastating forests, factory smoke and automobile exhaust were poisoning
the air, chemical waste was contaminating rivers, nuclear power created radi-
oactive by-products, and mass production was resulting in mass garbage. All
the wondrous inventions and sensations of modernity, it seemed, had negative
counterparts in environmental degradation and sensory malaise. In return for
the thrill of speeding in an automobile one breathed air tainted with smog.
One "paid" for the spectacle of electric light by giving up the view of the night
sky. That plastic lasted "forever" no longer seemed such a good thing when
that plastic was piling up in landfills and creating vast "garbage patches" in the
ocean.

Discussing the "sensory shock" occasioned by this new awareness of environmental pollution, Constance Classen wrote:

> Even the clean look of the modern city with its subterranean sewers, its electrical
> energy, its sleek buildings, its shiny cars and its synthetic products has turned out
> to simply be a mask for immense waste. We are dismayed to learn that, in the end,
> dirt is "cleaner" than plastic. (2009, 177)

Nor was the issue only a matter of aesthetics: human health and the well-
being of the whole ecological system were adversely affected. Rachel Carson
began her pioneering work on environmentalism, *Silent Spring* (1962), by contrasting the sensory experience of a country town before and after intensive
use of pesticides. The "before" description spoke of "green fields" and "white
clouds of bloom," of "barking foxes" and "clear, cold streams." In the "after"
description animals and children have sickened and died, the apple trees bear
no fruit, the vegetation is brown and withered, and "on the mornings that had
once throbbed with the dawn chorus of robins, catbirds, doves, jays, wrens, and
scores of other bird voices there was now no sound; only silence lay over the
fields and woods and marsh" (1962, 1–2).

In Carson's account aesthetic blight accompanies and testifies to environmental blight. Even pleasant sensations, however, might warn of environmental
disaster. A late twentieth-century counterpart to Carson's book, for example,
might have been titled "Warm Winter" and detailed how, due to the effects of

global warming, an unusually warm winter could no longer be regarded as a pleasant break from the customary cold weather of the season, but rather now served as one more ominous sensory sign of an ailing world.

The natural world had once been conceptualized as immensely powerful with limitless resources, but by the last decades of the century this view was seriously challenged. It was not only accounts and experiences of the proliferation of garbage, smog, oil spills, and deforestation that led to a change in attitude, however. The view from above provided by airplanes and, more dramatically, spaceships contributed greatly to the perception of the Earth as bounded and frail. Astronaut Russell Schweickhart, who spent ten days in orbit in 1969, observed that from space the Earth appeared "so small and so fragile and such a precious little spot in the universe" (cited in White 1998, 38). These words captured the sentiments of many who saw, or saw a picture of, the Earth looking like a lone, blue balloon floating in a vast dark sky. The new conceptualization of the natural world as vulnerable and requiring human protection, therefore, was partly grounded in an actual view of the world.

The Counterculture and Rock Music

The environmental movement that flourished in the second half of the twentieth century was part of a larger complex of social and political developments that challenged conventional modes of thinking about and interacting with the world. These included decolonization, feminism, civil rights movements, and anti-war protests. For the older generation, born in the early decades of the century, it often seemed as though society was being turned on its head, with those who were previously "invisible," "silent," and subordinate now insisting on being seen and heard and treated as equals (see, e.g., Thomas 2012).

One notable instance of this change was the massive 1963 March on Washington for Jobs and Freedom, highlighted by Martin Luther King Jr.'s "I Have a Dream" speech, which focussed public attention on the disadvantaged position of African Americans within society. Describing the effect the march had on the senses of both participants and observers, one young woman said,

> I saw people laughing and listening and standing very close to one another, almost in an embrace ... White people [were] staring in wonder. Their eyes were open, they were *listening*. (Euchner 2010, part 2)

The fact that the event, and others like it, was widely broadcast on television increased its social and sensory impact.

Social reformers often aimed to encourage empathy for oppressed peoples by enabling others to see the world through their eyes. A classic example of this approach is the non-fiction book *Black Like Me*, published in 1961, which conveyed the experiences of a white man passing as Black in the Southern United States (Griffin 2004). The author, John Howard Griffin, described how, though nothing of his identity had changed but his skin colour, he began to receive what he called the "hate stare" from whites and found his applications for work rejected.

The book not only helped bring a skin colour that was supposed to be socially invisible to the fore of mainstream consciousness, but also a voice meant to be socially unheard – for "I" could never be "Black" according to the rules of the dominant culture. And, of course, the catch in the title was that the writer was not, in fact, Black. As a white man he *did* have the "right" to speak, but the fact that he was using his voice to tell of his experiences as a "Black" man confounded social distinctions based on race and positioned skin colour as a superficial sensory trait with enormous and unjust cultural ramifications. The "Black is Beautiful" and "Black Power" movements of the 1960s and '70s attempted to reverse traditional stereotypes and exclusionary practices concerning African Americans by associating positive qualities with a dark skin colour (Ogbar 2004; Thomas 2012).

"Counterculture" was the term often used to refer to the broad, youth-centred movement in the 1960s and 1970s that supported new social values, while at the same time rejecting the conventional, middle-class way of life, summarized by one activist, Robert Alter (writing in 1971), as "a fresh-frozen life in some prepackaged suburb, Howard Johnson's on Sundays, Disneyland vacations, the cut-rate American dream of happiness out of an aerosol can" (cited in Belasco 2007, 62). In opposition to this "synthetic substitute for reality," people were urged to "reach out to each other with noises/gestures/visions to create a new and common reality," as a flier distributed by one countercultural group put it (cited by Kramer 2013, lix).

The sensory manifestations of this quest for an alternative way of life were numerous. One of the most visible everyday signs of countercultural trends concerned changes in hairstyles and dress. Long, loose hair, T-shirts, jeans, miniskirts, and bright "psychedelic" colours all signalled a rebellion against the more controlled and formal modes of self-presentation of previous decades and, more broadly, a rejection of conventional social roles and values. Bare feet, in turn, expressed a desire for a greater closeness with nature.

"Unisex" clothing and hairstyles were often taken by the mainstream to represent an unsettling loss of gender distinctions: women apparently wanted to look and act "like men," and men apparently wanted to look and act "like women." This last was also said to manifest itself in the pacifist tendencies of the counterculture, which led to long-haired young men defying brush-cut, gun-wielding soldiers with flowers, opposing "war" with "love" and hardness with softness.

This brings us to the issue of tactile values. The counterculture asserted that the social role of the police and the military was not only to protect and defend, but also to coerce and suppress. "Police brutality" became a widely discussed public issue. The pacifist approach adopted by many social reformers and widely associated with the counterculture, by contrast, implied an unwillingness to employ aggressive forms of touch to dominate others. One popular form of social protest of the time, the sit-in, involved the physical occupation of a site. This tactic would result in the protests' opponents taking on the role of aggressors when they resorted to tactile force to clear the site. The sit-in also had the attraction of simplicity – to protest, all one needed to do was to sit.

Non-violent actions such as sit-ins and marches were not the only form in which the desire for social change found expression, however. In the United States the 1960s were marked by race riots in major cities. Mass riots by protesting students and workers, notably the 1968 riots in France, shook many other countries. A number of countercultural groups began with non-violent protests, but, inspired by Marxist ideology and fired by youthful energy and idealism, ended up espousing armed revolution as the only means of overthrowing the political, business, and military alliances that maintained the status quo. The social turmoil of the time, and its extensive media reporting, hence, brought the politics of touch to the fore of public consciousness.

The counterculture's questioning of the social institutions of marriage and the nuclear family and its experimentation with communal living and "free love" (facilitated by the invention of the birth control pill) brought touch to the fore of public consciousness in another way. At the time, such practices were often seen as evidence of the moral and corporeal laxity of contemporary youth. Blame was frequently placed on the mid-century shift in childrearing practices that had replaced the strict, no-cuddling techniques advocated in the early decades of the century with an approach mandating tender, hands-on care. The childrearing "bible" by Benjamin Spock, *Baby and Child Care* ([1946] 1998), had helped revolutionize childrearing by urging parents to hug their children, feed them when they were hungry, and refrain from corporal punishment (see Synnott 2005). The result, some said, was a generation of soft, self-indulgent "flower children" who could not be counted on to discipline their bodies, uphold social values, or defend their country. The debate over tough or tender touch in childrearing continued to the end of the century. However, generally the tender approach won out, with the age-old tradition of corporal punishment in schools, for example, being banned in many countries in the last decades of the century. And while communal living did not catch on, the "sexual revolution" supported by the counterculture ultimately led to widespread changes in public attitudes towards sexuality.

Turning to the sense of taste, this was primarily affected by the counterculture's desire for a more "spiritual," "natural," "environmentally sound," and "ethical" diet. Synthetic, industrially produced foods were rejected (at least in theory) in favour of natural or organic foods, which were touted as both healthier and more flavourful. Perhaps the defining taste of the movement was that of granola, a mixture of oats, nuts, and dried fruit, which made for a nutritious and "natural" snack.

During this period vegetarianism, which challenged the values of the "establishment" at the basic level of food production and consumption, emerged as a popular countercultural diet. Francis Moore Lappé's *Diet for a Small Planet* (1971) argued convincingly that meat-eating supported a wasteful use of natural resources. Others saw clear parallels between the exploitation of women and workers and the exploitation of animals for food. Feminist vegetarian groups were founded. Struck by the miserable conditions of farm animals, the prominent advocate for farmworkers rights, Cesar Chavez, became a vegetarian. In a few decades vegetarianism went from being regarded as a bizarre fad or cult practice with dangerous health consequences to being tenuously accepted as a healthy and morally defensible alternative to a meat-based diet. Tellingly, when the 1998 edition of *Baby and Child Care* advocated a vegan diet for children, it raised some eyebrows but did not cause much of a stir (Spock and Parker 1998).

The sensory heart of the counterculture was music. The song "We Shall Overcome" was sung by civil rights marchers, anti-war protesters, and striking farm workers, with the line "We'll walk hand in hand" expressing the sense of solidarity experienced by agitators for reform. While protest songs and folk music played an important role in giving a musical voice to the counterculture, however, it was rock music that had the most impact. This was not only, or even primarily, because many rock musicians addressed social issues or made countercultural statements in their songs. It was, rather, the music itself that in multifold ways appeared to subvert conventional social mores. Its strong beat gave momentum to desires for social change or, at least, for excitement. Its loudness provided an immersive environment and also expressed the demand of dissatisfied youth to be heard. The simple structure of most pieces, their frequent authorship by members of the band performing them, and the fact that many performers were not trained musicians or singers gave rock music the aura of authenticity that the counterculture demanded. Rock musicians were no slick, "synthetic," crooners performing cover songs. And although rock musicians were overwhelmingly white, by fusing elements from African American and European musical traditions, their music served as a model for a racially integrated society. The free-form dance styles that accompanied rock music, in turn, physically conveyed the contemporary craving to be freed from conventional social strictures.

Rock musicians themselves played an essential role in promulgating the styles and values of the counterculture through their own appearance and lifestyles. The radio became the essential medium for transmitting this musical tidal wave. However, the crowds that gathered for live rock concerts, memorably the 400,000 at the Woodstock Rock Festival in 1969, could feel in their numbers the power of a movement whose time had come.

Critics denounced rock music for its seeming power to subvert, mobilize, and disorder. Its so-called African rhythms were said to incite deviations from "civilized" behaviour as well as encourage white youth to mix with "coloureds." The "sensuous gyrations" performed by certain singers (notably Elvis Presley) and their dancing fans were said to arouse sexual passions, and again called up comparisons with "savage" sensorialities – one reviewer compared them to "an aboriginal mating dance" (Martin and Seagrave 1988, 62). The fact that rock concerts sometimes ended in brawls seemed to confirm the music's destabilizing effects. While these criticisms convinced some to forswear rock music, however, others saw them as evidence of its liberating potential.

One aspect of the counterculture frequently associated with rock music was the use of drugs. Along with patchouli oil, the odour of burning marijuana was the defining scent of the movement. Drug use was a form of social bonding, a means of experiencing alternate realities and, in the era of popular psychology, a fast route to the development of "human potentiality." Its promise of non-linguistic revelations had a strong appeal due to the countercultural emphasis on corporeal and spiritual fulfilment (as evidenced, for example, by Aldous Huxley's call for a "non-verbal humanities" in *The Doors of Perception* (1954).

Hallucinogenic drugs such as LSD transformed the user's sensory perceptions, inducing sensations of vibrating colours and shifting shapes, and deepening the experience of music. Such visionary sensations helped inspire the psychedelic artwork popular at the time and contributed to the synaesthetic tendencies of the counterculture, which, in its search for holism, saw rock music as part of a sensory and social totality. Perhaps this synaesthetic tendency was expressed most strongly by Pete Townshend, a member of the rock band the Who, when he spoke of wishing to "translate a person into music" by "feed[ing] information – height, weight, astrological details, beliefs and behaviour – about that person into the synthesizer" (cited in Wilkerson 2006, 176). It was as though the multisensory fantasies of the nineteenth-century Symbolists were being brought to life (see Classen 1998, ch. 5).

Drugs (like rock music itself), however, were also associated with escapism and anarchism, and regarded as purveyors of mindless pleasures and instigators of gratuitous violence, with the synaesthetic revelations they promised dissolving into sensory excess. The addictive nature and often-harmful physical effects of a number of popular drugs, in turn, alarmed many people both inside and outside the movement,

Another way in which the counterculture sought to access alternative realities was by turning to the East, and particularly India. India seemed an almost magical land of both spiritual and sensory plenitude. As such it provided a rich range of styles and practices to be reinterpreted in Western settings. The bright colours and swirling patterns of Indian aesthetics made a good match with psychedelic designs. Indian melodies and instruments added "exotic" notes to rock music. "Yoga" and "meditation" provided engaging spiritual and corporeal practices. Fashionable young men sported Nehru jackets and Western followers of Krishna dressed in orange robes and chanted Hindu prayers. More substantially, the non-violent protests popularized by Gandhi in India's struggle for independence helped inspire the marches and sit-ins of Western protest movements. Indian traditions of vegetarianism and showing compassion for animals, in turn, were enlisted to support the vegetarian movement in the West. These Western forays into Eastern cultures exoticized the East at the same time as they glorified it; however, they also indicated a growing openness towards other cultures that helped pave the way for the late twentieth-century rise of multiculturalism in the West.

Eventually, in the 1980s, the counterculture lost momentum. On the one hand, mainstream society eventually incorporated many of the changes advocated by the movement (particularly as the youth of the 1960s and '70s grew older and acquired positions of authority). On the other hand, most supporters of the counterculture turned out to be not all that radical in their aspirations. Some of the sensory signs and practices of the counterculture, such as psychedelic art, walking barefoot, and the scent of patchouli, became dated. Others, such as meditation and alternative medicines – crystal therapy, therapeutic touch, aromatherapy – became part of the "New Age" movement. Yet others, such as yoga and vegetarianism, acquired increasing mainstream recognition.

Rock music continued to be popular to the end of the century; however, the ways in which it was experienced changed. Music television transformed it into a media spectacle, with a new emphasis on accompanying visuals. At the same time, radio declined in popularity. (Significantly, the first music video to be aired on the U.S. MTV music video channel was "Video Killed the Radio Star" by the Buggles.) The Walkman, a portable audio cassette player with headphones, privatized the experience of music, with users listening to their personal favourites rather than tuning in to the mass broadcasts of a radio station (see Bull 2000).

Unlike the popular music of the 1960s and '70s, furthermore, which was closely associated with dance, the new music, heard through a portable Walkman, accompanied ordinary, everyday movement – walking, shopping, riding a bus. Dance itself declined as a recreational activity and mode of self-expression in the 1990s. In the early '70s Susan Sontag wrote that photography had become almost as popular a pastime as dancing (1973, 8). With the spread of digital cameras and the salience of Internet imagery, by the end of the twentieth century it had become far more popular. Collective culture itself was in the process of becoming digital, as computer networks made new, long-distance, and disembodied modes of connectedness possible. As for the senses, their ultimate destination, a destination for which they had been prepared by the century's succession of technological "wonders," seemed to be the glowing virtual reality of cyberspace.

The Senses in Space

Space itself – outer space, that is – had also been breached. NASA put humans on the moon in 1969 and images of Neil Armstrong and Edwin "Buzz" Aldrin bouncing about on the lunar surface were beamed into households and schoolrooms via television. Apart from the experience of weightlessness, what other sensations awaited the astronaut? Does space smell? Apparently it does. It smells like "wet ashes in a fireplace" (Armstrong) or has "a pungent, metallic smell, something like … the smell in the air after a firecracker has gone off" (Aldrin).[1]

At the same time that humans pondered the sensations of outer space, might there be extraterrestrials interested in the sensations of Earth? Scientists at NASA decided it might be the case, so they put together a committee, chaired by the astronomer Carl Sagan, to determine what information should be transmitted about life on Earth. Previously, in the early 1970s, two etched plaques with information about the location of the Earth, and the form of the human body, had been included on space probes. Now, in 1977, the committee put together a playlist and launched the resulting "Golden Record" (along with instructions on how to play it) into orbit aboard the twin Voyager space probes in 1977. Much deliberation went into the composition of this playlist. It included spoken greetings in fifty-five languages and diverse sounds of Earth (volcanoes, crickets) as well as musical selections, such as the pianist Glenn Gould playing the Prelude and Fugue in C Major from J.S. Bach's *The Well-Tempered Clavier*. Other selections included some Mozart, Chuck Berry's rendition of *Johnny B. Goode*, and the Mali musicians of Benin performing "Cengunmé," a percussive polyrhythmic instrumental. Since making a good impression was the whole point of this exercise, it is interesting to speculate on which piece of music would impress the extraterrestrial addressees the most: the melodious fugue or the polyrhythmic drumming?

Space, "the final frontier," as it was styled in the opening sequence to the popular television series *Star Trek* (1966–9), held out the promise of starting afresh and making peace with alien civilizations by not "interfering" (in a marked departure from the conventional colonization script). This was aided by the multi-ethnic composition of the crew of the starship USS *Enterprise*, which included Lieutenant Nyota Uhura (Nichelle Nichols) and Lieutenant Hikaru Sulu (George Takei) alongside the genial commander Captain James Kirk (William Shatner), and the hyperrational alien Commander Spock (Leonard Nimoy). However, the exploration of space also entailed collaborating with computer technologies, or artificial intelligences. The potential perils of such a collaboration would be elaborated in Stanley Kubrick's 1968 film masterpiece *2001: A Space Odyssey*, in the confrontation between HAL (for Heuristically programmed ALgorithmic computer) 9000 and astronaut David Bowman.

Advances in computer technology over the next decades would accentuate the uneasiness of humanity's increasing collaboration with and dependence on the powers of computation.

Concluding Note

This chapter has given historical shape to the theoretical reflections of the chapters in part 1 by engaging in what Michael Herzfeld (2001) calls "theoretical practice" – or, in the instant case, "doing sensory history." It has shown how doing sensory history involves sensing between the lines of written sources where more conventional historians at best succeed at reading between the lines. Second, it has involved investigating the material culture of the modern age by sensing how the automobile and the airplane, the skyscraper and the bungalow, and processes of plastification and pollution have shaped the life of the senses in late modernity. Third, it has shown the importance of attending to various countercurrents, such as the counterculture of the 1960s, and in this way arrive at an understanding of the politics of perception, or "intracultural variation" (Classen 1997), in the constitution of the sensorium. The twentieth century made considerable progress vis-à-vis drawing attention to diverse social and sensory inequalities, but there is still much work to be done as regards rectifying such inequalities.[2]

CHAPTER FIVE

Melanesian Sensory Formations: A Comparative Case Study in Sensory Ethnography

Papua New Guinea (PNG) presented a melange of sensations to me when I travelled there in 1990 to carry out field research for my doctoral thesis in anthropology. I was attentive to these sensations because, a year earlier, I had invited Paul Stoller, author of *The Taste of Ethnographic Things: The Senses in Anthropology* (1989), to give a lecture in Montreal. Entitled "In Sorcery's Shadow," he spoke about his apprenticeship as a sorcerer among the Songhay of Niger, about experiences beyond the pale of reason, and about the senses, which he argued had been given short shrift in conventional ethnographic writing. The hall was packed. One could sense that anthropology was at a turning point. A revolution was at hand – the "sensorial revolution."[1] Stoller was calling us to our senses.

The sensations that first struck me in PNG were those of the palate. They included

- partaking of grubs (they taste much like peanut butter)
- eating sago jelly (not a pleasant consistency and a rather sour flavour)
- masticating ginger (not for its taste, but to "hot up" one's breath)
- making coconut soup (a male specialty in the region)
- people asking me "What do they feed you in Canada?" while admiring my girth (even though I was quite slim by North American standards)
- I especially remember the euphoric kick from getting the proportions of a betel chew (betel leaf, areca nut, slaked lime) just right, but not knowing how to expectorate the bright red juice properly (i.e., as a jet, not a spray) and so being a liability to those who partook of a chew together with me.

During my sojourn in the Massim region, Milne Bay Province, some of the more salient sensations included:

- the inhabitants of Budoya on Fergusson Island being summoned to a church service by the peel of a bell (if they belonged to the local

Protestant denomination) or the sound of a slit gong (if they were Roman Catholic)

- the thatched cottage where Maria von Trapp of *The Sound of Music* fame and two of her siblings lived during their sojourn at Budoya as lay missionaries in the 1950s[2]
- the setting sun bathing the still surface of the ocean in a uniquely South Sea kind of gloaming; or, on another occasion, pitching and rolling on the waves in a boat that plies the route between Alotau and Dobu (in mortal fear for my life)
- the reverberations of a thunderstorm rolling across the ocean
- the turbulent boiling and sulphurous stench of the hotspring at Dei'dei[3]
- a senior man with a halo of frizzy white hair and gleaming skin, whom people called "the Computer," sorting out how the kula valuables in the possession of a man who recently died should be reintroduced into the "Kula Ring" (famously described by Malinowski in *Argonauts of the Western Pacific* ([1922] 1961) and still a going concern)

In the Washkuk Hills (halfway up the Sepik River), East Sepik Province:

- gazing at the ceiling of the council chamber in Ambunti (modelled on a men's house), every inch covered with bark paintings of the spirits, and the workshops where men churned out painted wood sculptures of their culture heroes and other spirits in anticipation of the arrival of a boatload of tourists on the *Melanesian Explorer*[4]
- a bone-jarring ride in the back of a pickup truck being baked by the sun, which seemed to concentrate all its energy on a patch of my right hand as I clung to the rollbar: I can still feel the pain when I think about it (I was subsequently instructed to smear my skin with clay, the only effective sunscreen, when exposed in this way)
- trudging through a swamp, sinking up to my calves in the mud with each step (and that was on a path), and tormented by the swarms of mosquitos
- a Kwoma man whose cicatrized back looked like the skin of a crocodile telling me that if anyone backstabbed him with a knife in a brawl he "wouldn't feel a thing!"

In Port Moresby (the national capital):

- big, burly men from the Highlands strolling around town, their fingers entwined (one never saw cross-sex couples walk this way)
- the posters on the tradestores advertising TRUkai rice (with an image of a muscle man wearing a tribal mask) and Pepsi-Cola (never Coca-Cola), and Kool (mentholated) and Winston cigarettes.
- the Port Moresby Show: at this annual festival, there is a dance competition at which troupes of dancers from every corner of the country come to put

on a show. The biggest crowd-pleaser appeared to be the troupe of Trobriand youths strutting about the grounds in their colourful grass skirts and loincloths, sprigs of herbs attached to their knees and elbows, their bodies glistening with coconut oil, tossing areca nuts to the on-lookers, who hooted at the sexual precocity of the youths' ribald pelvic thrusts. Other groups included a troupe from Oskapmin, deep in the interior, bedecked with layers of possum furs and trinkets, stomping and jangling in place, and a female troupe from the northern coast, in their beautiful barkcloth vestments, swooping and swaying like the frigate bird in flight.

How was it possible for the panel of judges to evaluate the performances at the Port Moresby Show, I wondered, when the dance styles were so disparate, so incommensurable? How might I arrive at an emic appreciation of this rich sensory panoply?

It was only much latter, when I was working with Jamie Furniss on translating François Laplantine's *Le social et le sensible* (2005) into English, that I finally came upon the words to describe this approach, which I have taken to calling "participant sensation." As Laplantine (2015, 2) writes in *The Life of the Senses*, "The experience of [ethnographic] fieldwork is an experience of sharing in the sensible [*partage du sensible*]. We observe, we listen, we speak with others, we partake of their cuisine, we try to feel along with them what they experience." As this quote suggests, it is not actually an emic perspective the anthropologist arrives at, but rather a "sharing of the sensible." Granted such a partition is more intimate than participant observation (the conventional method of anthropology), it still involves feeling *along with*, not feeling *per se*. Another way of putting this is to say that participant sensation involves cultivating the capacity to *be of two sensoria* (one's own and that of the culture studied) and, therefore, *of more than one mind* about things (Howes 1990a and 2003, 10–14).

While partly inspired by Stoller's work, the question I really wanted to address in going to PNG was this: Are people in oral societies more "ear-minded" than people in literate societies, assuming that the latter must be more "eye-minded," since for them words are reduced to "quiescent marks on paper" (Ong 1982)? This question had been planted in my brain a decade earlier, when I attended a talk by Marshall McLuhan in the Senior Common Room at Trinity College, Toronto. In his talk, McLuhan expounded on the "laws of media" (posthumously published as McLuhan and McLuhan 1992). I was fascinated by his account of the mediated sensorium, and the differential "effects" of media on the life of mind and society.

I credit my early exposure to McLuhan's thought with having shielded me from being seduced into believing in the "prereflective unity of the senses" by reading Merleau-Ponty (most graduate students in anthropology read his *Phenomenology of Perception* [1962] in those days). Unlike the philosopher, the (sensorially minded) ethnographer is as attentive to the discrimination and conflict of the senses as in how they coalesce. As Eric McLuhan (n.d.) wrote in a biography of his father, McLuhan was fascinated by the implications of a device used in the dentistry of his day known as the "audiac," which involved the use of headphones to "bombard the patient with enough noise to block pain from the dentist's drill" and, by way of illustration of his notion of the ever-shifting "ratio" of the senses, McLuhan noted how "in Hollywood the addition of sound to silent pictures impoverished and gradually eliminated the role of mime, with its emphasis on the sense of touch."

While McLuhan's thesis informed the questions I asked, the answers I came away with led me to question the technological determinism of his position. It dawned on me that there are as many differences to the orchestration of the senses *among* so-called oral societies as there are *between* oral societies and literate societies. Hence, each culture must be approached on its own sensory terms.

In the epilogue to *The Varieties of Sensory Experience* (1991), entitled "Sounding Sensory Profiles," Constance Classen and I set out a framework for the sensory analysis of one's own and other cultures. It involves investigating the sensory dimensions of the natural and built environment, body decoration, art, ritual, mythology, and "intracultural variation" (the divisions of gender, class, ethnicity, and dis/ability) in an effort to model the sensory profile of a culture – that is, its "ways of sensing" the world (Howes and Classen 1991; Howes and Classen 2014). In what follows, I shall use those categories to order my account of the life of the senses in, on the one hand, the Massim world (the island societies of Fergusson, Dobu, and the Trobriands – all of which participate in the Kula Ring) and, on the other, the Middle Sepik world (centring on the Kwoma, who inhabit the Washkuk Hills in the vicinity of Ambunti). The comparative dimension to this ethnographic study is important, for I would argue that it is only by comparing (i.e., noting the contrast effects) of two or more sensory regimes that one can arrive at an understanding of their inner workings.

I should add that many great ethnographers had preceded me to these two regions – Bronislaw Malinowski, Reo Fortune, Géza Róheim, Annette Weiner, and Nancy Munn in the case of the Massim, and John Whiting and Stephen Reed, Ross Bowden and Margaret Williamson in the case of the Kwoma of the Washkuk Hills. I had immersed myself in this literature, to prime my senses, before going to PNG myself. I should also note that the "ethnographic present" in the following account extends from the 1910s (when Maliniowski carried out his fieldwork in the Trobriands) to 1990.

Sensuous Geography

As Yi-Fu Tuan (1977, 6) observed in *Space and Place*, "What begins as undifferentiated space becomes place as we get to know it better [through our senses] and endow it with value." How, then, is space known and valued in the

Figure 3. A kula canoe on the island of Dobu, Massim region, Milne Bay Province, festooned with decorations in preparation for a kula expedition. Photo courtesy of the author.

Massim world? The villages of Fergusson and Dobu are built on sandy beaches and consist of thatched huts on posts. The villages are all oriented toward the sea. Men go out on the sea in fleets of dugout canoes to neighbouring islands to visit and receive kula valuables from their kula partners or, conversely, welcome and give kula valuables to their partners when the latter come calling (see figure 3). There are two main classes of valuables: necklaces (*bagi*), which circulate clockwise, and armshells (*mwali*), which circulate counterclockwise around the Ring. Women do not go on these expeditions,[5] nor do men who are sick. They are said to be "heavy" in contrast to the buoyant bodies of the "Argonauts" (as Malinowski dubbed them) of the region. The buoyancy of being at sea is valued over the heaviness of being on land.

The Kwoma took the Washkuk Hills by force some generations back. Their name means "mountain people." The nine traditional villages of the Kwoma are situated on hilly outcrops. They consist of thatched huts scattered along the ridge, and a clearing with a Haus Tambaran (distinguished by its soaring architecture) at its centre – the exclusive preserve of the men. The men go out in the hills to hunt, and it is also their responsibility to plant the yam gardens on the hillsides, which the women then tend. Women otherwise go down into the swamps each day, to fish in the steams and to process sago. Being on the ridges, where the ground is firm, is valued over going down into the morass – the oozing, infirm terrain – of the swamps. As we shall see further below, the sensory orders of these cultures are ones that very much privilege men.

Body Decoration

In the Massim world, having smooth, gleaming skin is paramount. This is achieved by scraping the skin with the edge of a shell to remove the "hiding darkness" and then rubbing it with coconut oil so it glistens. There are spells to help make one's face glow "as the full moon" or "as a bud of the white lily" (Malinowski 1929, 365–6). Colourful (dyed) grass skirts are worn on ceremonial occasions and fragrant pigments are used to embellish the skin with delicate tattoos. Massim culture is a culture of kinetic (or mobile), smooth, radiant, and redolent sensations. This effect is produced or enhanced by not eating, for certain foods are reputed to dull one's appearance. Not eating also makes one feel more buoyant, less heavy. There are special substances – certain mushrooms, for example – that are used to suppress hunger. Generally speaking, it is considered better for a man to give food (e.g., yams) to his brother-in-law, or present food to a kula partner, than for him and his family to consume it themselves. This is one way to acquire *butu*, a term meaning "noise" and also "fame."

Among the Kwoma, food *is* valued. It is good to look and feel stolid. (I was admired for my girth, for example.) Sago "fits" the stomach, I was told, and is therefore valued, however sour the taste, though not as much as yam. Men take their food "hot" (or warm anyway) in the men's house. It is prepared by women and brought to them by the children. Contact between the sexes is minimal, because women's "coldness" is inimical to men's "heat." It is particularly important for men to keep their distance from women in the lead-up to planting yams, or carving and painting a wood sculpture, or going on a raid. Odour is also important in this connection. It is said that if a man has the smell of a woman about him, he will be a target for the enemy's spears, as if spears had noses (Bowden 1983, 103).

Scarification (which is absent from the Massim) is common among the Kwoma. Both men and women have their skin cicatrized as a sign of endurance or fortitude and of beauty. I was struck by how the ridges of a cicatrized skin resembled the ridges of the landscape, both equally valued. The culture of the Kwoma is a culture of loud, stolid, hard, ridge-like sensations and of standing one's ground. The emphasis is on fortifying bodily boundaries, unlike in the Massim where the accent is on extending the body in space. The Kwoma also decorate their bodies on ceremonial occasions, with scented herbs and paint, but the ideal colour is black. Only senior men are permitted to paint their skins and faces black, though, as a sign of the number of homicides they have committed.

Artefacts as Quali-signs of Value

In the Massim world, the most valued articles are the kula armshells and necklaces. The armshells are fashioned from white conus shells while the necklaces are strung from tiny red or salmon-coloured shell beads. Much polishing goes into the fabrication of these valuables, so that they glow, an effect enhanced by rubbing them with coconut oil. They are also decorated with trinkets called *bwibwi* – cowrie shells, bits of tin and plastic, and beads attached to a frame (see Howes 2003, fig. 2). The trinkets and frame *extend* the body of the shell both in visual grandeur and by virtue of the motility of the *bwibwi* as well as the tinkling sound they give off when the shell is hoisted. As Nancy Munn (1986, 114) observes, "shell décor extends the body [of the shell] in space and the mobile décor makes a sound that ramifies the space – as if putting it into motion – so that what may be out of sight may nevertheless be heard."

The bigger, more important (and profusely decorated) shells each have names, and as they make their way, slowly, around the Ring they also become storied – vested with the names of all the big men through whose hands they have passed. One of the *mwali*, a magnificent specimen, I was shown on Dobu, which had just been introduced into the kula, had the name "Telephone," appropriately enough. The legions of smaller shells, with a few token decorations, have no name and circulate among "nothing" men.

Big men, or "men of influence" as they are known, have multiple kula partners, and when the latter come to visit there is always much speculation regarding who will go away with which shell. Success at the kula depends on mastering kula talk (knowledge of the "paths" of different shells, and the flattering speech that will induce a partner to "throw" one valuables) and on presenting a fine appearance. This is achieved by stopping at a beach just short of one's destination to bathe,[6] take care to scrape one's skin clean, and oil and decorate it – especially the face – with paint. This has the effect of "intensifying visibility and presence" (Munn 1986) with the result that the kula partner "looks at us, sees our faces are beautiful; he throws the *vaygu'a* [valuables] at us" (Malinowski

[1923] 1961, 336). I remember how one quite prominent man on Dobu literally swooned in the presence of his handsomely adorned, much younger kula
partner.

It bears noting that no self-respecting man of the kula ever barters for a
kula valuable (e.g., by offering money or other goods in order to obtain the
object of their longing). That would be bad form. Rather, by "playing" (on the
analogy of playing cards) an armshell of particular renown on one occasion a
man may position himself to receive an equally precious necklace on another
occasion (when it comes his turn to visit). Much calculation goes into each
such exchange. Sometimes expectations are fulfilled, but they can equally well
be dashed. Big men pride themselves on the fact that there are distant islands
where people have "never seen my face, but they know my name" (Munn 1986,
106; Weiner 1988, 143). Renown – that is, *butu* (noise, fame) – is eagerly sought
out. This is the underlying motivation for kula exchange, not "the love of give-
and-take for its own sake," as Malinowski surmised (Weiner 1988, 9). Acquiring *butu* involves coming to have one's name circulate independently of one's
body. This effect is amplified by the songs that celebrate the men's exploits that
are composed and sung by the women upon the men's return home.

If being in the world is above all a matter of sound in the (male) Massim world,
in the Middle Sepik it is above all a matter of sight. The annual yam harvest festival
is the high point of the sensory and social calendar. In preparation for the festival,
men produce reams of bark paintings of the spirits, which are affixed to the ceiling of the men's house (where they "watch over" the village). They also carve and
paint wood sculptures of the spirits, such as the fearsome *yena* heads (see Howes
2003, fig. 6), which are arranged in an altar, along with other paraphernalia, inside
the men's house (see figure 4). The men also bring the large bamboo flutes and
other noisemakers (e.g., bullroarers, stompers) out of storage, taking care that the
women do not spy on them. A screen is constructed around the men's house for
the climactic event of the festival, when the senior men make the spirits heard: that
is, the senior (initiated) men take up their position inside the men's house while
the women and junior (non-initiated) men remain outside, on the other side of the
screen, and the senior men proceed to generate a great noise by means of the instruments, while the women and non-initiated men cower in fear without, having
been led to believe that the din is the voice of the all-powerful spirits.

Unlike in the Massim world, where sound (having one's name voiced) is *the*
index of social status, among the Kwoma, being a painter or carver and being
able to see the spirits for what they are – rather than being fooled by what one
hears – is *the* mark of distinction. This represents an inversion of the "theory of
oral mentality" (see Howes 2003, 113–21), according to which sound should be
privileged over sight in societies that lack writing. But from the standpoint of
the anthropology of the senses, this inversion is just another reminder that each
society must be approached on its own sensory terms.

Figure 4. Approaching the men's house in the village of Tongwinjamb, Washkuk Hills, East Sepik Province. Photo courtesy of the author.

Mythologizing the Senses

The Kwoma have many mythological cycles, but the myth that most stood out to me – as foundational to the Kwoma sensory and social order – is the myth of "The Origin of the Flutes." According to this myth, it was Kwoma women who first discovered the flutes while they were out fishing in the swamp. They secretly smuggled the instruments to a tree house, where they entertained themselves by playing them continuously. In an inversion of the contemporary division of labour, the women commanded the men to prepare food and deposit it at the base of their lofty treetop dwelling. They also treated the men cruelly. Upset by this, the men teamed up with a borer beetle, which ate through the base of the tree and toppled it. The men seized the flutes and so became the masters of the aural means of communication with the spirits (in addition to the visual means of communication – e.g., bark paintings, sculptures – which they already possessed), and now it is they who command the women to make the food that they eat within the confines of the men's house.

It is interesting that male superiority should be portrayed as the result of an act of treachery and tied to which sex controls the means of communication with the spirits. This is a decidedly non-essentialist way of explaining gender relations. It has nothing to do with physical prowess or rationality (versus emotionality) or any other such specious marker of gender difference. Rather, it all depends on who does the seeing and sounding.

There are many mythological cycles in the Massim world. There is a Trobriand myth that has attracted considerable attention for the way it intersects with one of the hallowed myths of Western culture, especially to those of a psychoanalytic persuasion: namely, the Oedipal myth. The Oedipus myth or "complex" (in Freudian terms) derives from the story of a man who fell in love with his mother and murdered his father. In *The Sexual Life of Savages*, Malinowski famously declared that there is no Oedipus complex in the Trobriands. This is due to the matrilineal organization of the society (in contrast to the patriarchate, under matriliny it is the mother's brother who is the authority figure, while the father is a familiar, caring figure). Malinowski also pointed to the absence of the motif of mother-son incest in contrast to the salience of the motif of sister-brother incest in the corpus of Trobriand mythology. He was referring to the Sulumwoya myth, the myth of the origin of desire. We shall come to it in a moment.

Malinowski was badgered into recanting his heretical theory by the psychoanalytic establishment of his day (he shouldn't have, as we shall see presently), and, latterly, Melford Spiro (1982) took it upon himself to analye Malinowski's corpus of writings to prove, once and for all, that the Trobrianders were not immune to the Oedipus complex. Spiro's analysis overrode or ignored certain sensorial facts, however, which, had he attended to them, would surely have caused him to be more cautious about legislating for all humanity on the basis of the assumptions of Western psychology and kinship relations. One of these facts has to do with how marriage is consummated. Premarital sex is condoned and expected in the Trobriands, but what a courting couple must never do is sit down to a meal together. Marriage is solemnized by the couple sharing a meal in public. The second fact has to do with desire. In the Trobriands, as elsewhere in the Massim world, desire is magical, not instinctual. As Reo Fortune (1963, 235) notes, "Without a love charm to arouse and create desire, desire does not exist according to native theory."

The most effective way to ensnare the affections of another is by the Sulumwoya spell. This spell is uttered over a concoction that consists of the sweet-scented mint (*sulumwoya*) and *kwayawaga* plants boiled in coconut oil. The agent then secretly sprinkles the potion on the person of the love interest. Here is how Spiro summarizes the Sulumwoya myth in *Oedipus in the Trobriands*:

According to the relevant aspects of this myth, a boy prepared a concoction of love magic in his hut. Later, his sister entered the hut and accidentally brushed against the vessel containing the concoction, causing some of it to fall on her. As a result she was consumed with lust for her brother and, despite his repeated attempts to elude her, she relentlessly pursued him until, finally, he capitulated to her desire and they committed incest. (1982, 27)

While Spiro's summary is admirably succinct, it leaves out the two *most* relevant aspects of the myth, both of which centre on what could be called the entrainment of the senses: namely, what happened to the sister-brother couple *after* they committed incest, and what the specific ingredients of the concoction were in the first place. For this we must turn to Malinowski:

ashamed and remorseful, but with the fire of their love not quenched, they went to the grotto at Bokaraywata where they remained *without food, without drink*, and without sleep. There also they died, clasped in one another's arms, and through their linked bodies there grew the sweet-smelling plant of the native mint (*sulumwoya*). (Malinowski [1923] 1960, 127–8, emphasis added)

A man from the isle of Iwa went and discovered the plant growing out of the lovers' bodies following a vision he had in a dream, and he passed the plant, and the spell that activates its power, on to his kin. They continue to receive royalties for its use.

Spiro (1982, 7) bruskly dismisses Malinowski's interpretation of the myth: "rather than reflecting the special power of the libidinal attraction of the boy for his sister [as Malinowski claimed], the myth shows the special power of this type of love magic to overcome inhibitions arising even from the incest taboo." Spiro is correct, of course, to insist that the myth does not expose any specific attraction between siblings. Where he errs is in supposing that desire is instinctual, for we know from the ethnographic record that it is actually *magical* in that lust does not exist prior to the culturally coded signals that evoke or create and channel it, only in their wake. Spiro also errs by ascribing prime importance to the act of sex, as though it were the telos of all amorous encounters, and ignoring the importance attached to sharing a meal together in public to solemnize a union. In other words, he gets the entrainment of the senses backwards. The myth is actually perfectly consistent with Trobriand courting and marriage etiquette: the accidental spilling of the scented oil leads to an act of smelling, and this leads to an act of copulating, but the young couple are barred from ever committing the act of marriage (i.e., eating together).

According to the Freudian theory of the "erotogenic zones" of the body and "the phases of psychosexual development" (oral, anal, genital, in that order), the search for "oral gratification" is "pregenital." Trobriander theory holds the reverse: genital gratification is "preoral," as it were. Thus, it was not because the young couple were too obsessed with making love that they went without sleep and eventually died, but because they knew that they could never indulge their gustatory impulses in concert, never share a meal in public. Their last thoughts would thus have been of food: the "impossible object" of their desire was a marriage feast.

So much for Freudian theory, and so much for the "prereflective unity of the senses" (Merleau-Ponty 1962), I would add. It is the *entrainment* of the senses – the specific sequence in which they are evoked – that matters foremost. Hence, in the face of his Freudian detractors, Malinowski should have gone on insisting on the primacy of social organization (here, matriliny over patriarchy) and the cultural preformation of the senses – and desire.

On the Sociality of Sensation

In my doctoral dissertation, which was subsequently published as *Sensual Relations: Engaging the Senses in Culture and Social Theory* (2003), I argued that social relations are sensual relations, and vice versa, building on Georg Simmel's observation: "that we get involved in [social] interactions at all depends on the fact that we have a sensory effect upon one another" (Simmel 1997, 110). This idea of the indissociability of the social and the sensible (Laplantine 2015) is one of the cardinal principles of the anthropology of the senses, and sensory studies generally. As a corollary to this, each culture must be approached on its own sensory terms.

The senses are entrained differently in different societies. In the Massim world, as we have seen, the proper (culturally sanctioned) use of the senses involves suppressing hunger and not eating, so the body becomes light and buoyant (not heavy) and one has more food to give away to others (not eat oneself), which is one driver of *butu*. Second, it involves cultivating a radiant appearance by rubbing the skin with coconut oil and painting it with fragrant pigments. This has the effect of intensifying presence. Ideally, this radiant presence will make one's kula partner swoon and "throw" valuables at one.

But the ultimate goal is beyond vision: it is to grow out of sight and into sound by having one's name circulate apart from one's face and body through being attached to a named kula valuable as it slowly makes its way around the Ring, never resting for long in any one man's hands. In this social system, exchange takes precedence over accumulation, for gift giving is the source of renown (*butu*) and is considered more enduring than possessing things. The kula valuable, with its motility, magnitude (augmented by *bwibwi*), smoothness, luminousness, and above all its name and the chiming sound it gives off is endowed with all the same "quali-signs of value," to use Nancy Munn's (1986) language, as its (temporary) possessor. The valuable holds up a polysensory mirror to its holder.

A word about that tinkling sound. The sound of the *bwibwi* chiming is the first "ramification" (Munn) of success in the kula exchange. Say the recipient were from Dobu and the gifting took place on Kilavila in the Trobriands, then the news would be relayed by various creatures, including the monitor lizard who trumpets on the island of Tewara (near Dobu), and the women, "staying at home [on Dobu] hear the sound and send round word that their men folk have secured valuables" (Fortune 1963, 221). It is much the same in the Trobriands: returning home from Dobu, the kula voyagers' waiting kin "profess to hear thunder roar and feel the ground shake – nature's witness to the success of the voyage and the spreading fame of the men" (Weiner 1988, 139). This is what it means to attain "thunderdom," the most vaunted state of being in the Massim world (Howes 2003, 77–81).

If in the Massim world the accent is on the extension of the perimeters of the body through olfactory, visual, and above all acoustic media, in the Middle Sepik world the accent is on the fortification of the body and standing one's ground. Fortification takes the form of eating "hot" food if one is a man: the carbohydrates augment one's stolidity and the "heat" one's generative power as a progenitor of children, planter of yams, painter, sculptor, and victor in battle. Fortification also takes the form of cicatrizing the skin so it becomes hard and the lines of bumps resemble the hilly ridges, which give the Kwoma their name, "mountain people." Thus, the skinscape is isomorphic to the landscape of the Middle Sepik – the hills, that is, not the swamps.

This entrainment of the senses is nicely exemplified by the stance a Kwoma big man will take in a debate: his face blackened, he shouts down his opponents, and in the climactic moment, thrusts his upper body forward and sticks out his tongue. The Kwoma do not value listening, they value shouting, and above all they value seeing. The highest knowledge is visual: it consists in seeing/knowing that the terrible voice of the spirits is "what men do" (Tuzin 1980). This is a terrible secret to have to bear.

Kwoma culture is a culture of secrecy in which occupation (occupying the Washkuk Hills, occupying the men's house) takes precedence over exchange. But no society can exist without some form of exchange, starting with matrimonial exchange (i.e., marrying out). Among the Kwoma, due to the rule of clan (village) exogamy and virilocal residence, women go to live with their husband in the latter's village upon marriage. The women are never incorporated into their husband's clan, however. They remain aliens, and their allegiance to their patriclan (i.e., their brothers) is a constant source of friction and suspicion. Brothers "look after" their sisters, and should the latter be subject to mistreatment by their husbands, the brothers will ensorcel them (using materials supplied by the sister). Hence, any illness or misfortune in the husband's village is blamed on the treachery of the wife's brothers. Significantly, when Bowden (1983, 481) asked "What do you call your brother-in-law?" in an effort to elicit Kwoma kinship terminology, they responded, "Enemy."

If Kwoma men are the masters of the visual and aural universe (they make the bark paintings and sculptures of the spirits, and they are the voice of the spirits since they control the flutes, etc.), then what is women's role in the sexual and sensory division of labour? Significantly, they weave net bags, which come in many sizes, and the pendants that serve as mementos of events. This observation led me to realize that while Kwoma men may be the masters of the audiovisual universe, Kwoma women are the mistresses of tactility. The net bags they weave are used to transport the products of their labour (sago, yams, and also infant children), and the special miniature net bags (rather like purses) they will give to a lover. Net bags also figure among the paraphernalia of the altar at the yam harvest ceremony, so female power is present even though the women are absent physically. And by marrying out into one of the other eight villages, they weave the Kwoma people together, despite the fractiousness of the men, who are committed to defending the patrilineal order of society and to upholding the divisions of the visual and aural universe.

I have a pendant that was given to me by the woman of the house in Ambunti at which I stayed as a souvenir of my visit. It is crocodile-like in form (with its oblong shape), though it has six appendages (not four), and the snout is indistinguishable from the tail. What really makes it crocodile-like is its texture, the weave of the fibre and the rows of tiny kina shells sewn on its back. This memento is thus isomorphic to the skinscape and the landscape in the same way that, in the Massim region, kula valuables resonate with the same kinetic, visual, and acoustic qualities as the bodies of the men and of the ocean when a thunderstorm comes rolling in.

To sum up, social relations are sensual relations in the Middle Sepik as in the Massim world; only the arrangement of the senses is different. The answer to the question with which I started (the question McLuhan planted in my brain) is that people in oral societies are not necessarily more "ear-minded" than their counterparts in ("eye-minded") literate societies. Rather they are polysensorially minded. This polysensoriality gives the lie to the assumption of the "prereflective unity of the senses" (Merleau-Ponty 1962) as well as any presumptions regarding the "interchangeability" of the senses (e.g., Ingold 2000). The senses and sensations are hierarchized differently in different societies, and in different contexts within the same society, whence the multiple heterarchies to the varieties of sensory experience across cultures.

Conclusion

This chapter has sought to demonstrate what "doing sensory ethnography" involves in practice. The sensory anthropologist starts with a collection of ethnographic fragments, a jumble of impressions, and gradually, by seeking to sense and make sense together with others, begins to grasp what could be called "the unity-in-multiplicity of sensible qualities" (see the next chapter). Patterns of sensing emerge out of the initial chaos of impressions, and the anthropologist, if they are percipient enough, succeeds at discerning and weaving a tapestry of the senses and sensations, anchored in their analysis of local techniques of perception and action. Even the weave of a humble net bag can speak volumes. Through continuously tacking between their personal perceptual style and the textures, scents, sounds, and sight of the Indigenous life world, the anthropologist (ideally) manages to become "of two sensoria," and hence of more than one mind about things.

Sensory ethnography involves "leading with the senses" in mind and leaving no sense unturned in the process. It starts with the "dérèglement" (Rimbaud) of one's own senses and then gradually learning how the senses are *entrained*, both in the sense of enskilled (Ingold 2000) and in the sense of sequenced, in the culture under study. Failing to get the entrainment right may result in the anthropologist looking where they ought to be listening (and vice versa), or missing how sensations in one modality are "transduced" (Helmreich 2015) into those of another. For example, as regards men in the Massim world, not eating engenders brilliance of body decor, which helps induce a kula partner to bestow the finest valuables on the man, and this transmutes into his name circulating apart from his physical being; conversely, for masculine subjects in the Middle Sepik universe, eating engenders stolidity and "heat" – essential for procreating, planting yams, and perpetrating homicides – which is in turn reflected in how much of a man's body he is allowed to paint black on ceremonial occasions. By contrast, among Middle Sepik women tactile acts of weaving are transformed into social bonds, while Massim women engage in a form of exchange parallel to the Kula Ring, centring on banana-leaf bundles (Weiner 1976). The senses, then, are "produced relationally" in the practices of everyday life (Dawkins and Loftus 2013), and periodically reset in the context of ritual. The senses are both crafted and crafting (Harris 2016) and, thanks to this, generate "worlds of sense" (Classen 1993b) that in turn inform the sense of self.

PART THREE

Multisensory Aesthetics

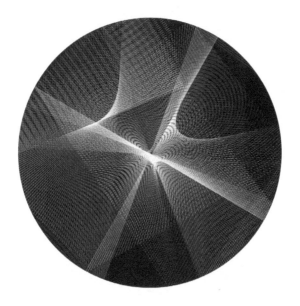

Collideroscope series (2022) © Erik Adigard, M-A-D

CHAPTER SIX

"A New Age of Aesthetics": Sensory Art and Design

This chapter offers a hidden history of the senses in art that belies the ideology of medium specificity – that is, of painting as for eyesight alone, and of music as only for the ears – by bringing out the *interplay* of the senses in the constitution of painting, music, and other fields of artistic endeavour, and how this widespread (but under-recognized and under-theorized) *intersensoriality* chimes with the original (mid-eighteenth-century) definition of the term "aesthetic." As regards design, this chapter explores the marriage between art and commerce that gave rise to the design professions in the 1920s and the progressive aestheticization of everyday life that has ensued. According to Virginia Postrel, in *The Substance of Style*, we live in "a new age of aesthetics" – an age in which "design is everywhere, and everywhere is now designed" (2003, 24). Indeed, it is impossible to miss the burgeoning emphasis on the "sense appeal" of commodities and retail establishments. Attractive design is no longer a luxury: "We, [as] customers, demand it," Postrel (2003, 5) claims. However, to comprehend how aestheticization has taken command of the everyday, we need to step back and consider the origins of the aesthetic itself.

Part I. Laying The Foundations

Overtures

In "Aesthetics and Anaesthetics," intellectual historian Susan Buck-Morss provides a helpful introduction to the prehistory of "aesthetics" as a discursive category.

> *Aisthitikos* is the ancient Greek word for that which is "perceptive by feeling." *Aisthisis* is the sensory experience of perception. The original field of aesthetics is ... reality – corporeal, material nature ... It is a form of cognition, achieved through taste, touch, hearing, seeing, smell – the whole corporeal sensorium. The

terminae of all of these – nose, eyes, ears, mouth, some of the most sensitive areas of the skin – are located at the surface of the body, the mediating boundary between inner and outer. This physical-cognitive apparatus ... is "out front" of the mind, encountering the world pre-linguistically, hence prior not only to logic but to meaning as well. (1992, 7)

However, Buck-Morss continues, the term "aesthetic" has undergone a reversal of meaning in the modern era: now it is "applied first and foremost to art – to cultural forms rather than sensible experience, to the imaginary rather than the empirical, to the illusory rather than the real" (1992. 7).

The origin of this mutation in meaning can be traced to the work of the eighteenth-century German philosopher Alexander von Baumgarten (see Howes 2011). He took over the term *aisthēsis* from the Greek and applied it to his new "science of sense cognition," which was to occupy an intermediary rung, as a "science of the lower cognitive power" (*gnoseologia inferioris*, sense perception) in contradistinction to "the higher cognitive power" (reason). By limiting aesthetics to the perception of the "unity-in-multiplicity of sensible qualities," Baumgarten sought to insulate it from being reduced to "arid" intellectual knowledge. He held that the intellect was "the poorer" for the fact that it trafficks exclusively in "distinct ideas," as opposed to the "confused and indistinct ideas" generated by the senses (to use the language of his day). For Baumgarten, therefore, the disposition to sense acutely meant attending to the nature of sensory experience in itself, rather than trying to rationalize perception (Gregor 1983, 364–5; Pérez-Gómez 2016, 72–3), and he departed from the canonical discussions of beauty in Western philosophy by proposing that aesthetics had foremost to do with the perfection of perception rather than with the perception of perfection, or beauty. The essence of aesthetics, for him, involved (to repeat) perceiving the "unity-in-multiplicity of sensible qualities" – a decidedly corporeal capacity (Eagleton 1990).

Baumgarten's new "science" was quickly appropriated and just as quickly subverted by his contemporaries. They replaced his emphasis on the sensuous disposition of the artist with a taxonomy of "the five arts" (architecture, sculpture, painting, music, and poetry). The scope and criteria of the various arts were delimited in terms of the dualism of vision (epitomized by painting) and hearing (epitomized by either music or poetry). The "dark" or "lower" senses of smell, taste, and touch were deemed too base to hold any significance for the fine arts. Theatre and dance were also excluded on account of their hybrid character, since they played to vision and hearing or movement at once (see Rée 2000).

Baumgarten's worst fears concerning the rationalization of aesthetic perception were realized in Immanuel Kant's *Critique of Judgment* (1790). Kant attempted to transcend the dualism of vision and hearing and replace it with a fundamental division between "the arts of space" (e.g., painting) and "the arts of time" (e.g., music), accessible to "outer intuition" and "inner intuition," respectively (Rée 2000, 58–60). It could be said that Kant rarefied aesthetics by divorcing it from perception and substituting intuition. After Kant, aesthetic judgment would be properly neutral, passionless, and disinterested (see Turner 1994; Eagleton 1990). This definition of aesthetics may have resulted in a drastic curtailment of human sensuousness (see Vercelloni 2016), but at least it guaranteed the autonomy of the enclave now known as "art."

In "Sensory Separation and the Founding of Art History," the lead chapter of her *Art, Museums and Touch* (2010), Fiona Candlin explores the fallout of the Kantian revolution. She presents a sensory analysis of the works of Alois Riegel, Heinrich Wölfflin, and Erwin Panofsky, who are commonly regarded, in retrospect, as the founders of the discipline of art history. All three posit trajectories of increasing "perceptual sophistication" as unfolding since antiquity (Riegel takes Egyptian art as his starting point), in which tactile perception is the precursor to optical perception and the progression of artistic styles culminates in the modern use of linear perspective and naturalistic representation. On this account, "accomplished art," which is to say European art (according to the prevailing conceit), depends on the banishment of the physical sense of touch and the achievement of a disembodied, abstracted system of visual representation. Even in the doctrine of "tactile values" elaborated by Bernard Berenson, it is the illusion of touch (i.e., the way a painting appeals to the "tactile imagination"), not the materiality of touch, that is extolled. Candlin goes on to show how the "sensory demarcation" of art history persists in visual culture studies, despite certain protestations to the contrary (e.g., Mitchell 1992). The history of art proper thus depends on the separation of vision from touch and the delegitimation of any sort of haptic engagement with art objects.[1]

In *The Museum of the Senses* (2017), Constance Classen also addresses this issue of the separation and exaltation of vision over touch:

> prior to the modern era no firm divide separated the fine arts from the decorative arts ... Renowned sculptors also designed salt cellars and candlesticks. Eminent painters decorated furniture. The evident manual uses of such craft work seemed to naturally bring artistic productions within the realm of touch. (2017, 41)

"However, in the view of the anti-touch brigade," she continues, referring to Hegel and Kant (who prepared the ground for Riegel, Wölfflin, and Panofsky),

> touch was primitive and vulgar and therefore not an apt medium for experiencing the lofty values of art ... It was this view which came to dominate modern aesthetic theory [citing Candlin]. Influential philosophers such as Hegel and Kant agreed that art requires pure "visual" contemplation. Touch, it was claimed, kept one tied to the base material world and thus could never experience beauty as a spiritual

value. The "fondling of the voluptuous parts of marble statues of female goddesses has nothing to do with the contemplation of art," Hegel quipped, dismissing with one jibe any possibility of touch having aesthetic value … As a result of such attacks, both painting and sculpture were cut off from tactile experience. Only craft work remained within the realm of touch, its manual characteristics seemingly preventing it from achieving the visionary qualities of "true" art. (2017, 41–2)

In *Consumer Culture and Postmodernism* (1991), sociologist Mike Featherstone reflects on the derivation of the phrase "the aestheticization of everyday life." "If we examine definitions of postmodernism," he writes, "we find an emphasis upon the effacement of the boundary between art and everyday life, the collapse of the distinction between high art and mass/popular culture, a general stylistic promiscuity and mixing of codes" (1991, 65). Featherstone proceeds to disclose "the *genealogy* of *postmodernité*" (or what Postrel [2003] would call "the aesthetic age") and bring out its linkages with modernity. In one of its senses "the aestheticization of everyday life can refer to the project of turning life into a work of art" (Featherstone 1991, 66). Featherstone cites the example of the artistic countercultures that sprang up in mid- to late-nineteenth-century European urban centres, such as Berlin and Paris – the preserve of Baudelaire and company. In its most salient sense for us now, however, "the aestheticization of everyday life refers to the rapid flow of signs and images which saturates the fabric of everyday life in contemporary society" (1991, 67). As Postrel (2003, 4) suggests, "Aesthetics has become too important to be left in the hands of the aesthetes," whence the growth of the so-called culture industries, "with painting moving into advertising, architecture into technical engineering, [and] handicrafts and sculpture into the industrial arts, to produce a mass culture" (Featherstone 1991, 73). The burgeoning importance and salience of "design" spells both an extension of art into the everyday, and the end of art's autonomy, or perhaps even "the end of art" and "the end of reality" at once (following Baudrillard 1983), as images and reproductions proliferate endlessly, and "culture" is everywhere.

In *All-Consuming Images* (1988), communications and sociology professor Stuart Ewen documents how, in the early decades of the twentieth century (that is, rather earlier than Featherstone would allow), giant industrial corporations, such as AEG, began to develop multipurpose styling divisions. An industrial aesthetic was born, with a view to bringing coherence to the perceived "disorder" of the marketplace and consolidating corporate identities by creating a certain corporate look. This development tipped the scales of capitalism, as consumption came to drive production and attractiveness came to override considerations of functionality or efficiency in the manufacture and marketing of products (see Howes 2005c). Advertising companies sprang up and brought a new level of artistry to everyday life. A premium was attached to "eye-appeal," but the so-called creatives of the day also turned their attention on the "lower" senses, most notably touch, which were seen as having been repressed by civilization, and sought to capitalize on their appeal as well. (This was the beginning of the "checklist" approach to sensory marketing, though it would not come to full fruition until the turn of the twenty-first century.) If "art for art's sake" was the banner cry of the artists, "art for control's sake" was the goal of the thoroughly modern designers and advertisers, or "consumer engineers" (Sheldon and Arens 1932).

By way of example of the recuperation of touch by design professionals, consider the following words of advice from Sheldon and Arens in *Consumer Engineering*:

> Almost anything that is bought is handled. After the eye, the hand is the first censor to pass upon acceptance, and if the hand's judgment is unfavourable, the most attractive object will not gain the popularity it deserves. On the other hand, merchandise designed to be pleasing to the hand wins an approval that may never register in the mind, but which will determine additional purchases ... Manufacturing an object that delights this sense is something you do but don't talk about. (Sheldon and Arens 1932, 98–102)

Already in 1932 these brave new consumer engineers had imagined "subliminal seduction" – not as involving the projection of images ("Eat popcorn!" or "Drink Coke!") on a movie screen that go by too fast for the conscious mind to register (that technique was only invented later (see Key 1974), but by making commodities "snuggle in the palm," and so tap into the haptic subconscious.

Disciplining the Senses in the History of Art and Design

Standard histories of art and music since the beginning of the twentieth century are keyed to the succession of styles: from Cubism to Abstract Expressionism and Pop Art, for example, or from the atonal compositions of Schoenberg and Webern to the polyrhythms of jazz and the experimental work of John Cage. They do not deign to treat non-Western art, nor the industrial arts discussed above. In his overview of the artistic trends of the twentieth century in the introduction to *Sensory Arts and Design* (2017), sociologist Ian Heywood disturbs these unilinear, monosensory narratives by bringing out the extent to which multisensory experimentation also figured in this history, animating the artistic work of such avant-garde movements as Dadaism and Fluxus, and the design work and education program of the Bauhaus school. Heywood also surveys the contributions of critical philosophers, like Theodor Adorno on the "commodification of listening," Martin Jay on "ocularcentrism," and Gilles Deleuze on the "logic of sense." In doing so, he resituates the recent history of art, music, and design within the larger context of transformations in the meaning and uses of the senses over the course of the twentieth century.

In "Disciplining the Senses: Beethoven as Synaesthetic Paradigm" (2010), art historian Simon Shaw-Miller (who is also the author of *Eye hEar: The Visual in Music*) begins by reflecting on the disciplinary and institutional divisions that gave rise to art and music as distinct fields of knowledge and endeavour (for example, music as to be performed in the concert hall, not the drawing room or pub), and the division between the faculties of seeing and hearing that are supposed to hold art and music apart. His overarching argument is that these divisions are "historically contingent," and that much can be learned from focussing on the "interconnections" and referrals that the disciplining of the arts and the disciplining of the senses both occluded and stimulated. Shaw-Miller's starting point is the moment around 1800 when music was reconstituted as "absolute." Shorn of words and no longer bound to depicting scenes, instrumental music, as exemplified by Beethoven's symphonies, became "pure" and "dematerialized" (i.e., unearthly, otherworldly), and, in short order *by that same token*, "the condition to which all arts [including painting] aspire," in the nineteenth-century English essayist and art critic Walter Pater's famous phrase.

On Shaw-Miller's account, absolute music and synaesthesia (the unison of the arts and senses) are different sides of the same coin and must be studied conjointly. He illustrates his thesis through a close reading of the Prussian Romantic writer E.T.A. Hoffmann's *Kreisleriana* papers (1810–13). In *Kreisleriana*, Hoffman reviewed the work of a variety of Romantic composers (Haydn, Mozart) but gave special treatment to Beethoven's Fifth Symphony. In his review of the Fifth, Hoffmann alternates between formal analysis of the harmonic, melodic, and rhythmic structure of the symphony, on the one hand, and intensely imagistic and polysensory or "synaesthetic" language on the other. Shaw-Miller observes that Hoffmann celebrated Beethoven's Fifth both for its "high level of rational control" and for it being

> the true music of the night, that romantically sublime site where it is hard to see, but easy to imagine. This condition corresponds to that of absolute music itself, which, in attempting to sever its connections to other arts and senses, to close its eyes to all but sound, provided instead a rich site for all types of imagery and the liberation of the inner eye. (2010b, xxii)

We can see here another prime example of what Candlin calls "sensory demarcation." In Hoffman we can also see the prototype of the contemporary sensory studies scholar, like Shaw-Miller himself. Shaw-Miller is a historian of art who takes music as his object, and thus focusses on the interface, the crossing of sensory boundaries in the arts, instead of treating them severally (see further Shaw-Miller 2013; Halliday 2013).

Hendrik N.J. Schifferstein is a professor of design at the Delft University of Technology. In collaboration with Charles Spence (e.g., Schifferstein and Spence 2008) and others, such as Lisa Wastiels, the co-author of "Sensing Materials" (2014), he has excavated the psychological foundations of multisensory product experience and theorized the emergent field of multisensory design. There are two broad trends that drive contemporary research in multisensory design. One is the sensory checklist or additive approach. This is supposed (ideally) to yield products with the right look, the right sound, the right scent, etc., following extensive laboratory testing of the sort reported on in the articles in the *Journal of Sensory Studies*. Incidentally, the title of this journal has nothing to do with the academic field of sensory studies as presented here. It is addressed to chemists and other so-called sensory professionals with their one-sense, one-sensation-at-a-time approach to the evaluation and development of consumer products, most notably food and beverages. The sensory professional toils away in the secretive sensory evaluation laboratories of the flavour companies that, for instance, line the New Jersey Turnpike, a.k.a. the Flavor Corridor. (For a peek inside these laboratories, see "Accounting for Taste" (Lahne and Spackman 2018); and for a critique, see Howes 2005c and 2015c).

The other is the superadditive approach, Schifferstein's specialty, which focusses on the interaction of product attributes or "how the senses work together in creating experiences." The latter approach pays careful attention to, for example, correspondences between stimulation in different modalities, the congruence of sensory messages but also the advantages of introducing discrepancies (i.e., an element of surprise), the sequencing of sensations, and patterns of sensory dominance in material perception. Throughout, the emphasis is on *interaction* – interaction between the senses, and interaction between user and product. As will be recalled from our discussion in chapter 1, the geographer Paul Rodaway presented a broadly similar range of intersensory relations as crucial to the practice of sensuous geographies.

For all its emphasis on interaction and sensory diversity (i.e., product differentiation through the selection and incorporation of multiple sensory attributes) and on "enriching" the experience of the consumer, there are some potentially troubling consequences of multisensory design. One of these has to do with the usurpation of the role formerly played by craftspeople in the production of material culture (Sennett 2009; Classen 2014a). Another has to do with privatization, or the trademarking of sensations. Whereas formerly companies were only permitted to trademark names and logos, now they compete to register the colour, shape, sound, scent, and feel of their goods. To take the case of smell, British Airways has used "a signature scent of 'Meadow Grass' in their executive airport lounges ... UK consumers can now buy darts arrows that have been impregnated with the smell of beer, while consumers in the Netherlands can buy tennis balls impregnated with the smell of green grass as part of a registered brand" (Schifferstein and Spence 2008, 156). Some commentators see this as an encroachment on the sensory commons as the range of scents, the divisions of the colour spectrum, and the array of sounds, etc., fall under private control (Elliott 2012, 2019; Howes and Classen 2014, 114–18). This development gives new meaning to the phrase "monopoly capitalism" – the monopolization of the senses in the interests of moving merchandise.

II. Probes

The discussion in this section circles back and picks up on the conversation in the corresponding section of the chapters that make up part 1 of this Manifesto, with particular emphasis on what sensory studies scholars working in the fields of art history, architecture, film, dance, design, and literature have contributed to the investigation of these topics. The reader is welcome to read these probes longitudinally, but for maximum effect and comprehension, they may wish to read them latitudinally (i.e., across chapters 1, 2, and 3).

1 *Ontology*. In *Beautiful Data: A History of Vision and Reason since 1945*, in the chapter called "Visualizing" (2014), Orit Halpern, a professor of interactive design and theory, documents the birth of an "algorithmic optic" in the post-war years (1945 on) as concretized through the work of the prominent designer and artist Gyorgy Kepes based at MIT, the equally prominent designer-pedagogues Charles Eames and George Nelson based at UCLA, and the influential urban planner-policymaker Kevin Lynch, author of *The Image of the City* (1960). In post-war design practice, she writes, "Vision and cognition were rendered equivalent, a 'process,'" and envisioned as part of "a single computational channel that could be algorithmically represented, materialized as technology, and circulated autonomously, separate from content" (Halpern 2014, 81). The emphasis throughout this work was on seeking the "pattern" that organized perception. This involved reducing sense to "data," and discovering (or postulating) the connections between data in different media or modalities without regard for the latter's specificity (due to the prior folding or collapse of perception and cognition into vision). All this was with a view to giving people "a feeling about relationships." The superordinate "faith in vision" that informed mid-twentieth-century design practice laid the foundation for the world of ubiquitous computing we inhabit now, wherein computation has taken the place of sensation (see further on this point Nudds 2014). It is instructive to compare the designer vision of the new "interface" described by Halpern with the multisensory cosmologies of Hildegard of Bingen, Boehme, and Fourier discussed by Classen in *The Color of Angels* (1998) and consider the corresponding diminution of the sensory imaginary.

2 *Emplacement.* In the book *Alien Agency* in the chapter entitled "Resonances: Experimental Encounters with Sound Art in the Making" (2015)
design professor Chris Salter presents an "autoethnography" of his encounters, over a span of more than twenty years, with sound artists Sam Auinger
and Bruce Odland, collectively known as O+A. O+A's oeuvre includes
many highly acclaimed art installations in which they bring what they call
a "hearing perspective" to bear on diverse urban environments. In contrast
to R. Murray Schafer's acoustic ecology, with its denunciation of urban
noise and privileging of "hi-fi environments" or downright silence (Kelman
2015), O+A practice a kind of *intersensory ecology*, which aims to rebalance
the optic and the sonic. In other words, they embrace the clamour but also
seek to harmonize it, as in *Sonic Vista*, an installation on the bridge over
the Main River in Frankfurt am Main, Germany. Their *modus operandi* involves, first, recording and analysing the ambient sounds of a given locale,
and then using specially designed speaker systems to remix, harmonize,
and play back the discordant sounds of the city, thereby enabling urban
denizens to perceive their environment anew. Salter's chapter contains
many key insights into the agency, materiality, and aesthetic potential of
sound (including noise), which extend to all aspects of sound studies.

   In the concluding section of his chapter, Salter takes up the question, "Can
architecture hear?" The idea of architecture as sentient will strike many as
odd and unfounded, or even as "animistic." However, it is actually very well
grounded, first, in the understanding of perception as a two-way street that
follows from the interactive conceptualization of how the senses function that
is integral to the sensory studies approach and, second, from the realization
that "We live, work and play in gigantic complexes of sound – their distribution is what we call architecture. Far from neutral shells, the shapes, textures,
and materials applied to surfaces produce the invisible, dynamic forces we
label acoustic phenomena" (Salter 2015, 62). The point here is that sounds
cannot exist apart from the spaces that they move in and through, and the
resonances given off by, for example, the parabolically shaped spaces of many
traditional forms of architecture, like the ancient Pueblo site of Chaco Can-
yon, New Mexico, are very different from those generated by the interaction
of sound waves with the rectilinear surfaces of the (poured concrete, brutalist)
"Euclidean geometries of boxes and cubes" characteristic of the modern Western city. Salter concludes with a plea for "hearing architecture" and evokes the
multiple benefits to our sense life that would accrue if only more architects
and urban planners were to adopt a "hearing view" after the example of O+A.

   In their introduction to *Elements of Architecture: Assembling Archaeology, Atmosphere and the Performance of Building Spaces* (2016), anthropologists Mikkel Bille and Tim Flohr Sørensen articulate an emergent
approach within architecture and archaeology that seeks to balance the

tangible and the intangible by deflecting attention from the solidity and stability of built spaces to their "atmosphere" and processual dynamics. Resisting the "ontological fixation" of conventional architectural studies, they argue that architecture is always "more than tangibility, merging instead with anticipation, sensation, time and impermanence" – that is, with "reality" (or "the ontological") as always in the process of becoming, rather than "what is" (Bille and Sørensen 2016, 143). Their approach is resolutely *relational*: "atmosphere" (a markedly sensuous notion) is defined as "the co-presence of subject and object" (following Gernot Böhme 2016), while buildings are defined as "assemblages of elements" (elements in the sense of fragments such as door frames and windows but also *the* elements of water, air, etc.). Their work reminds us that the study of material culture must make space for the agency of the senses in rendering the built environment sensible. For example, atmosphere is something you can feel but never quite put your finger on. It is an emergent, intersensorial quality of space.

In *Attunement: Architectural Meaning after the Crisis of Modern Science* (2016), McGill architectural historian Alberto Pérez-Gómez presents a hidden history of Western architecture that is in tune with the approach advocated by Bille and Sørensen, and also extends beyond it. *Attunement* is an essay in retrieval that draws out the sense (or "meaning") of such constructs as "temperance" or "character" and analogies to music and poetry or even mathematics (not in the sense of computation, though, but rather the proportionalities of Pythagoras' number harmony). Prior to the Enlightenment, the construction of buildings was all about creating moods deemed to be salubrious, and "producing appropriate atmospheres to the activities they housed" (Pérez-Gómez 2016, 82). It was "mimetic of a traditional cosmos" (74) and, while rooted in place, the *genius loci*, architecture was not for all that static, but more a form of "gestural speech" (171). Not all these archaic constructs were erased by the censure of sensuousness under the influence of Descartes, and again in the Age of Reason. Indeed, Pérez-Gómez highlights diverse counterreactions, such as the Romantic cult of *Stimmung*. Nevertheless, the die was cast, algebraization and instrumentalization took command, and this paved the way for the emergence of the idea of the architectural form as a "machine for living" and as "following function" in High Modernism. This was in place of architecture as "physiognomic lifeworld" (170).

The point of departure for Pérez-Gómez's sensorial archaeology of architecture is Merleau-Ponty's phenomenology of perception with its accent on "the primacy of experience and perceptual synaesthesia (the integrated sensory modalities)" (1962, 65) and the notion of the embodied mind and idea of perception as "enaction" that comes out of contemporary cognitive neuroscience. By pouring this new wine into the old bottles – the age-old constructs – of architecture, Pérez-Gómez enables us to savour the old constructs anew. His archaeology of architectural perception also positions him to mount a spirited attack on modern architecture, whose "meaning" has come to depend "upon nothing more than an efficient, mechanical understanding of structure and a cost-effective use of materials, expressed automatically through the buildings' forms" (2016, 127). He is particularly vituperative in his critique of computer-assisted design (CAD): "The fact that computers can solve mathematical problems doesn't justify imagining them as a model for human reasoning; we are neither metal and plastic nor digital" (157). What gets lost as a result of the triumph of CAD is "the qualitative perception of *places*, the so-called genius loci" (83). We must insist that our architects rekindle the sense of place for us.

3 *Materiality*. Mark Miodownik is a leading scholar of materials science, based at University College London. His book *Stuff Matters* (2013) stands out for the extent to which it is no less attuned to the sensible qualities than to the atomic properties and structures of all the "stuff" that surrounds us.[2] "The central idea behind materials science is that changes at invisibly small scales impact a material's behaviour at the human scale" (Miodownik 2013, 5). Take the case of glass. Glass is interesting because it is also invisible at the human scale. Miodownik makes the point that glass does not symbolize invisibility or transparency, it *is* transparent, and this sensory attribute is what accounts for its profound impact on the order of things in Western culture, from the shape of the modern city (glass-encased skyscrapers) to envisioning and manipulating the insensible (via the miscroscope or nanotechnology). It might be wondered: if glass has had such an impact, then why is it not more precious? Its minimal affective charge is to be explained in terms of its sensible qualities, too, according to Miodownik (2013, 157): "in its purest form, it is a featureless material: smooth, transparent, and cold. These are not human qualities."

Miodownik's material-sensorial analysis of glass is complemented by Chad Randl's article entitled "Sensuality and Shag Carpeting: A Design Review of a Postwar Floor Covering" in *The Senses and Society* 5 (2010). Shag fibre is a markedly sensual material, by way of contrast to glass. It is a product of the synthetic revolution. According to Randl, shag fit the postwar cultural preference for casual living, as exemplified by the practice of lounging on the floor watching TV or listening to LPs, instead of sitting on chairs or a sofa, and the new atmosphere of sexual permissiveness and experimentation: shag carpeting, as an "extension" (McLuhan) of body hair, with all the same connotations, was especially popular in bachelor pads, but also used to line bathrooms. Soft, plush, "natural" (fur-like, grass-like), shag fibres ushered in a new style of human sensuousness. Randl brings out well how this transformation in sensuality was directed by the style divisions of firms such as Dupont Chemical, with their legions of "consumer engineers" who are actively (re)shaping our *Umwelts*.

4 *Memory*. In *The Skin of the Film* (2000), film studies scholar Laura U. Marks introduces the term "intercultural cinema" to refer to the experimental videos produced by Third World filmmakers living in diaspora, and other marginal collectives. Their histories are uniformly silenced and rendered invisible by the official institutions of the state and mainstream media. As a result, Marks argues, the only material such artists have to work with is unofficial, personal, sensual (i.e., un-mediated) memory. Marks' argument is that these subaltern filmmakers use the medium of film in unique ways to represent the unrepresentable. Their armoury of techniques includes the black screen with voice-over, extreme close-ups, grainy images, and montage. (Grainy film footage, for example, is framed by Marks as speaking to the touch more than to the eye, accentuating ambiguity and intensifying the participation of the audience in deciphering meanings by complicating the sense-making process.) These techniques are deliberately deployed to disrupt the prevailing visual order and mobilize intimate memories, which are typically of a tactile, olfactory, or gustatory nature. Marks coined the term "haptic visuality" (in contradistinction to the optical visuality of Hollywood) to refer to the intersensorial, intercultural representational tactics used by these filmmakers to render the personal political as well as accessible to a wider audience.[3]

   It is an interesting question whether the medium of film can function in the synaesthetic manner Marks suggests. One could argue that film screens out the non-audiovisual senses, but Marks finds support for her thesis in the post-representational film theory of Gilles Deleuze, and Henri Bergson's doctrine of sense memory: "Perception is never a mere contact of the mind with the object present," Bergson ([1908] 1991, 103) wrote, "it is impregnated with memory-images which complete it as they interpret it," with the implication that film can activate touch-memory, smell-memory, etc. (see further Sobchak 1991). It is essential to keep in mind, however, that many artists around the world continue to work with multisensory materials to encode their memories and aspirations.

5 *Alterity*. Fiona Candlin introduced us to the othering of touch in her chapter entitled "Sensory Separation and the Founding of Art History," as discussed above. The devaluation of touch is manifest not only in the rarefied realm of academic art history, but also in the institutional realm where objects are sorted into "fine art" or "visual art," on the one hand, and handicrafts, on the other – and relegated to very different collections accordingly: art museum vs. craft gallery (see Classen 2014a). Research in the anthropology of art can help trouble this dichotomy, and also direct our attention to the aesthetic potential of

the so-called lower senses.[4] Take Australian Aboriginal art, for example. Such art, particularly the "dot paintings" with their extraordinary vibrancy, have attracted an international audience (and market). But alongside this High Aboriginal art, as it were, there are other less well known "experimental traditions" that have surfaced in the community art centres that dot the Central and Western Desert. Animated films that feature characters fashioned from clay (i.e., "earth belong country") represent one such "tradition." The fibrework of the Tjanpi Desert Weavers women's art collective constitute another. This emergent tradition is examined by Jennifer Biddle in *Remote Avant-Garde* (2016). According to Biddle, these soft sculptures give expression to a "vital materialism." It is art made "in and from country," a sentient countryside (indwelt by ancestors). The artists profess that they have "strong feelings toward our grasses" and weave them into forms that capture the full panoply of objects and creatures that cohabit the landscape, from birds and trees to Toyotas, teapots, and movie cameras. This is 3D printing with a human touch and a "hypertexture" that radically outstrips the sensuousness of the little plastic figurines of 3D printing. Moreover, this art delivers a visceral hit: it is art "you can smell."

The fibrework of the Tjanpi Desert Weavers embodies a very different trajectory for art history from the one laid down by Riegel, Wölfflin, and Panofsky. In contrast to the separation of the senses and of cultures, and the evolutionary typology they used to order the history of art, the art of the remote avant garde scrambles history and makes a point of mixing modalities. As Biddle (2016) notes, the experimental art forms that have emerged in the Central and Western Desert are "flagrantly intercultural" but at the same time rooted in aboriginal tradition – a tradition which centres on "marking" and thereby caring for or "enlivening" country. It is also decidedly intermodal or "multiplatform." For example, Rhonda Unurupa Dick's art practice involves taking digital photographs of country, retouching them with inscriptions that trace the paths of the Ancestors in the Dreaming, and also overwriting them with words in Indigenous languages that call out to be spoken, and so reiterate the deep connection of Aboriginal people to their territories.

Richard Schechner is a leading theorist of performance studies and an accomplished dramaturge as well. In "Rasaesthetics" (2001) he begins by asking, "Where in the body is theatricality located?" For the Greeks, and all the European types of theatre derived from the Greek, this would have been the eyes. (The term *theatre* derives from a Greek root word meaning "a sight" and "to view.") For the Indian author of the *Natyasastra* (an ancient Sanskrit manual of performance and performance theory), however, this would have been the palate, and, according to Schechner, the belly and bowels. In India, one goes to "taste" a performance, not to "see" it. The operative term here is *rasa*, which refers to the sap or juice of plants (hence flavour), the non-material essence of a thing, and a state of heightened emotion (Goswamy 2005; Pinard 1991) The flavourful (as opposed to spectacular) theory of how to produce and appreciate a dramatic performance is condensed in the following excerpt from the *Natyasastra*, where the analogy is drawn to the experience of a meal:

> Persons who eat prepared food mixed with different condiments and sauces, if they are sensitive, enjoy the different tastes and then feel pleasure; likewise, sensitive spectators, after enjoying the various emotions expressed by the actors through words, gestures, and feelings feel pleasure. This feeling by the spectators is here explained as the *rasas* of *natya*. (quoted in Schechner 2001, 29)

This is the starting point for Schechner's theory of rasaesthetics and the rasaboxes movement exercise (developed in collaboration with his colleagues at East Coast Artists). The rasaboxes movement exercise described in "Rasaesthetics" is for training actors, but not just actors. Rasaesthetics is open to anyone to try out and expand their cultural, sensorial, and emotional horizons through movement. It is a form of cross-cultural, multimodal aesthetic (Howes 2011), and it is very rich. Schechner even folds certain (then) breaking neurobiological findings on the enteric nervous system or "brain in the belly" into his theory, and elevates the whole field of neurobiology in the process, though it is an open question whether the author of the *Natyasastra* would ever sanction this incorporation. Cross-cultural translation is difficult. Schechner's invention of rasaesthetics is more in the nature of a creolization or syncretic blending. It is, at the same time, a potent cross-cultural intervention in the expanding field of the senses in performance (Banes and Lepecki 2007).

6 *Mediation*. In 2006, art historian Caroline A. Jones curated an exhibition at the MIT List Visual Arts Center called *Sensorium: Embodied Experience, Technology and Contemporary Art*. In "The Mediated Sensorium," the introduction to the catalogue (Jones 2006b) that accompanied the show, Jones contextualizes the work of the new media artists featured in the exhibition, artists such as Mathieu Brand, who "translates the body heat of his spectators into the visible spectrum," and Janet Cardiff, who "simulates the whisper of subconscious thought" in her sound art installations (Jones 2006a, 11). Jones does much more than merely contextualize the artworks, however. In "The Mediated Sensorium," she prefaces her discussion of the art with an account of the "segmentation," "bureaucratization," and commodification/instrumentalization of the senses in the culture at large and in the writings of the highly influential mid-twentieth century New York art critic Clement Greenberg. The latter's work, with its high formalism and repeated warnings against "genre confusion," raised the "sensory demarcation" of art (Candlin) to an extreme level.

But the age of the ideal modern viewer, as of the hi-fi auditor, has been eclipsed in the ensuing decades as more and more artists, driven by a "desire to escape sense for sensation," and attracted by the idea of "sensory miscegenation" (in place of purity), have used digital technology to create art that is intersensory. This convergence/disruption is nicely encapsulated by *Sensorium* artist Natascha Sadr Haghighian's installation, which channelled sound through a miscroscope (a "singing microscope"). Thus, according to Jones (2006a, 33), art viewers in the twenty-first century are increasingly met with "dramatically synaesthetic and kinaesthetic scenarios," and it has come to pass that "our experience of mediation itself is where art happens" (the mediation of the senses by technology and society, and the mediation of one sense by another). To put it otherwise, there are no more *objets d'art*, only experiences. Art has come off the wall, and the (ideally) sensorially neutral space of the white cube (the paragon space of Modernist art) has come to be suffused with a profusion of sensations – critical sensations, Jones (2006a, 44) would add: "*Sensorium* dreams that we can come to feel the body pulsing in tandem with its prosthetic extensions and microscopic addenda, that we can learn to partner our proliferating technologies in increasingly coordinated, supple, and critically conscious ways." Madeline Schwartzman's comprehensive survey of technological sensory extensionism in contemporary performance art in *Seeing Yourself Sensing: Redefining Human Perception* (2011) also attests to the groundswell of sensory reflexivity and critical sentience in the creative arts.

7 *Affect.* In "Sound Studies without Auditory Culture" (2015), Yale musicologist Brian Kane presents a critique of the "ontological turn" in sound studies, as represented in the work of a triumvirate of sound studies scholars (Steve Goodman, Christoph Cox, and Greg Hainge). The latter treat sound as material, affective "force." This "force" is held to "impact" the subject in the "split second" prior to perception (i.e., hearing as such) and the intervention of cognition. Kane brings some much-needed clarity to a rancorous debate. As he observes, the ontological turn, which dovetails with the affective turn, "directly challenges the relevance of research into auditory culture, audile techniques, and the technological mediation of sound in favour of universals concerning the nature of sound, the body, and media" (Kane 2015, 3). It does so in the name of "a philosophical naturalism with respect to sound" inspired by the work of Gilles Deleuze. Kane exposes how this naturalism in fact smuggles in a particular metaphysics – that is, a "metaphysics of the virtual and the actual" – and perpetuates an outmoded dualism between perception or cognition and the body. Kane's point is that sound studies divorced from "auditory culture" (i.e., the study of the "modes of listening" particular to a given culture or historical period) has no purchase. It is an abstraction of listening that ignores the manner in which the sonic, even when conceived as operating at the level of "vibrational force," is always conditioned or mediated by

"hearing cultures" (Erlmann 2004). The proponents of what Kane calls "ontography" (i.e., the triumvirate of Goodman, Cox, and Hainge) think of their work as going beyond or delving beneath "representation" and "signification," but end up trapped in their own (metaphysical) representations. There can be no sound studies without auditory culture, no affect without sense, Kane holds. "Ontography" (the brainchild of Goodman) is fundamentally unsound. Kane's article was published in the inaugural volume of the journal of *Sound Studies*, edited by Michael Bull and Veit Erlmann. It will be interesting to see whether his call is heeded.

8 *Movement.* In "Sense, Meaning and Perception in Three Dance Cultures" (1997), dance anthropologist Cynthia Jean Cohen Bull (formerly Cynthia Novack) presents a sensory ethnography of dance. She begins with a phenomenological account of the interplay of the senses in her own experience as a dancer, but then nuances her analysis through paying close attention to the cultural context of the dance event. Importantly, she views the senses "not as fixed biological or psychological mechanisms but as dynamic processes shaped by and through culture" (1997, 264). This orientation led her to discern and describe a series of "unique associations" in the dance forms she examines, between the sense of sight and ballet, between the haptic and contact improvisation, and between the sense of hearing and Ghanaian dance:

> Comparing the role of the senses in these dance forms evokes both the similarities and the differences of emphasis in how sensation and intelligibility are shaped within each form. Conversely, juxtaposing three kinds of dancing in a discussion of their relationship to the realm of the senses points to the embeddedness of social and political meanings in behaviors and practices. (1997, 271)

Cohen Bull's comparative cultural and intersensorial study of the three dance forms, as differing incarnations of "meaning in motion," places dance anthropology on a radically new and illuminating footing. It is a deep pity that she died at such a young age, but one can see her sensorially savvy approach living on in, for example, the work of Tomie Hahn in *Sensational Knowledge* (2007).

9 *Representation.* Ralf Hertel is professor of English at the University of Trier. In his contribution to *A Cultural History of the Senses in the Modern Age, 1920–2000* (Howes 2014a), Hertel (2014) presents a close reading of the representation of the senses in the English (mainly British) literature of the twentieth century. Hertel approaches literature as a site for the "negotiation of perception" due to the way it reflects and tries to make sense of the impact of technological and social forces on the ways in which we sense the world. Technology has the effect of both extending and refining

the senses (e.g., the X-ray) and supplanting or numbing them as we become increasingly reliant on diverse prostheses and are bombarded by the stimuli of mass culture. The scene in Thomas Mann's novel *The High Mountain* where the character of Castrop contemplates an X-ray of his own hand exemplifies the first of these two effects, while Kathy Acker's novel *Empire of the Senseless* gives expression to the second.

Hertel distinguishes three periods: the Modernist period (1920–45) characterized by a "preoccupation with sensation," as exemplified by the attempt to capture the immediacy of sense experience in the novels of Virginia Woolf; the post-war years (1945–1970s) when there is a focus on the traumatized body in pain, as typified by the panoply of damaged bodies in the plays of Samuel Beckett; and, the postcolonial period (1980s on), which continues the focus on the pain of existence and also introduces characters with exceptional and often stereotypical sensory abilities that disturb the conventional Western ordering of the senses, such as the gargantuan, hypersensitive nose of the main protagonist in Salman Rushdie's *Midnight's Children*. As Hertel observes, these are all differing takes on the embodiment of mind and the mediatory role of the senses in the production of experience. In the final part of his chapter, Hertel investigates the impact of virtual reality (VR) as "a world in which one is freed of the body and the biological facts apparently determining our identity in off-line reality" (2014, 312). But there is a twist to Hertel's account. He concludes by noting that literature has always been implicated in recalibrating our perception by virtue of the fictional worlds it creates, which are no different in principle from the virtual worlds of VR.

In "Towards a Multisensory Aesthetic: Jean Giono's Non-Visual Sensorium" (2018), literary scholar Hannah Thompson brings a critical disability studies perspective to bear on the representation of the senses and sensation in literature. Her work is of interest for the way it brings out how writing need not be as beholden to sight as is commonly supposed. It is possible to adopt various non-visual strategies and enlist other than visual modalities in the inscription of experience, as exemplified in her analysis of the use of sensory imagery in a novel by Jean Giono:

> Night. The river was shouldering its way through the forest, Antonio went as far as the tip of the island. On one side was deep water, as supple as a cat's fur, on the other the whinnying of the ford. Antonio touched the oak. He listened with his hand to the quivering tree. (Giono quoted and discussed in Thompson 2018, 315)

In her work, Thompson forges an alliance between sensory studies and critical disability studies, This nexus has emerged as a highly productive focus for research in recent years (Friedner and Helmreich 2015; Levent, Kleege, and Muyskens Pursley 2013).

10 *Gustation*. Barbara Kirshenblatt-Gimblett is another leading theorist of performance. Like her colleague at the Tisch School, Richard Schechner (both now retired), she too has brought a concern with savour to the centre of performance studies. Her article "Playing to the Senses: Food as a Performance Medium" (1999) is a landmark, and it serves as the point of departure for art historian Mark Clintberg's synoptic article on "Alimentary Art" (2017). There are still those who would turn up their noses at the thought of food as a medium of art (as Vercelloni [2016] notes, Kantian snobbery runs deep), but food has become one of the most explosive fora for aesthetic experimentation since the implosion of the high formalism of the mid-twentieth century (Jones 2006c). Interest in the aesthetic potential of foodstuffs actually dates back to the Futurists, as Clintberg documents, before going on to present a masterful overview or smorgasbord of both historic and breaking contemporary "gustemologies" (Sutton 2010), including his own experience mixing multisensory cocktails. Food is a sensory field, however, that particularly demands that attention be paid to its social, environmental, and ethical implications as well as to its aesthetic potential.

11 *Synaesthesia*. "Art and the Senses: From the Romantics to the Futurists" by Constance Classen (2014a) is emblematic of the new *multisensory, crossmodal art history*, an approach that is also exemplified by the work of Fiona Candlin, Simon Shaw-Miller, and Caroline A. Jones – all of whom we have encountered previously – and others such as Doug Kahn (1999), François Quiviger (2010), Francesca Bacci and David Melcher (2011), Madeline Schwartzman (2011), and Bruce R. Smith (2009), to mention only the leading lights.

Classen's chapter, which first appeared in *A Cultural History of the Senses in the Age of Empire*, centres on the demarcation, differential valuation, and experimental crossing or fusing of the senses and the arts in the nineteenth century and the first two decades of the twentieth century. It is a hidden history of art, before the veil of genre purity descended on writing about art in the mid-twentieth century, thanks to the influential New York art critic Clement Greenberg. Of particular note is Classen's attention to the sensory politics of art. "By rethinking the conventional ordering of the senses," she writes, the Romantic, Symbolist, Futurist, and Arts and Crafts movements (all of which she treats)

> not only challenged the conventional ordering of the senses ... [as of] the arts, but also the ordering of society – for ... the different senses were associated with particular social groups. Raising the so-called lower senses to the realm of art suggested an allied cultural elevation of the so-called lower races, classes and sex. (Classen 2014a, 209)

Of course, this elevation was not without a considerable degree of cultural and gender stereotyping, and also precipitated significant blowback. For example, the German physician Max Nordau, writing in 1893, branded the avant-garde artists of his day as a horde of "sensory degenerates." (His book *Degeneration* would later be trumpeted by the Nazis, who abhorred all forms of racial as of sensory "miscegenation.") But this is precisely Classen's point: it is imperative to be attentive to the intimate connection between sensory ordering and social ordering, sensual relations and social relations.

In "Art and the Senses," Classen also points to the recycling of past sensoria. For example, the Symbolist predilection for evoking cross-sensory correspondences was inspired by medieval models of the senses and cosmos, which she treated in "On the Color of Angels" (1998). While thus derivative, the art of this period was also highly original and experimental in the numerous different ways it sought to cross or combine the senses, whether it be the Symbolist drive to create a symphony of the senses or the Futurist preoccupation with producing a clash of the senses through discordant sensations. In this respect, the various movements (particularly the Futurists) anticipated many of the "multiplatform" experiments of contemporary art (a point also noted by Jones 2006a). *Plus ça change, plus c'est la même chose*, one might say, were it not for the fact that the sensory infrastructure of art and society has kept shifting, sometimes subtly, sometimes radically, in the intervening years. The sensorium is like a kaleidoscope, or "collideroscope" in McLuhan's phrase.[5]

As observed earlier, in our discussion of Orit Halpern's chapter entitled "Visualizing" in *Beautiful Data* (2014), design art took leave of the senses (save for vision) in the mid-twentieth century and came to centre on computation, the "algorithmic optic." While certainly true in some key respects, Halpern's account of the abstraction of the senses in design does not give us the whole picture. In "Sensing Things: Merleau-Ponty, Synaesthesia and Human-Centredness" (2018), Nigel Power, a professor of design based in Bangkok, refreshingly recounts how design has, in fact, repeatedly "rediscovered the senses." For example, the perceptual psychologist J.J. Gibson's notion of "affordances" has been explored and applied to various aspects of design. Power is wary of that particular manifestation of the sensory turn in design, however, precisely because it is rooted in perceptual psychology. He prefers the philosopher Maurice Merleau-Ponty's account of perception as fundamentally "synaesthetic." Instead of canalizing the senses, Merleau-Ponty urges us to recognize how "our senses interact by implying and invoking each other" (quoted in Power 2018, 363). Power sees this phenomenologically inspired approach, which has been dubbed "design synaesthesia," as holding great promise for the growing, "human-centred" movement in design because of its focus on "lived-experience," the interpenetration (as opposed to separation) of the senses, and the "shared corporeality" of designer and audience. Power's design manifesto foregrounds "sensorial intelligence" as a counterpoint to the "disembodied computational brain," and bodies forth an approach to design that resonates strongly with the transformation in the understanding of "sensory processing" that emerged out of the sensorial revolution in the human sciences, as documented in the chapters of part 1.

Concluding Notes

This chapter has tracked some of the groundbreaking sense-based research that has transpired within the disciplines of art history, literature, film theory, dance, music, and the visual arts, architecture, and design. It has shown how the ideal of "genre purity" that took hold in the mid-twentieth century has come undone as a result of artists and designers taking to experimenting with diverse multi- and intermodal techniques and media platforms. This shift can be seen as recuperating the original meaning of the term "aesthetic" as the perception of "the unity-in-multiplicity of sensible qualities" (Baumgarten).

The chapter has been particularly concerned with enucleating the "marriage between art and commerce" (Ewen 1988) in the burgeoning field of sensory design and the "debureaucratization" (Jones) of the senses in late modern art. It has brought out how the currents of sensory demarcation vs. cross-pollination in the creative arts were entangled with the rise and demise of social ideologies, such as Naziism, which abhorred "miscegenation" and denounced the confusion of the senses in the avant-garde art of the period. Indeed, the poster boy of Nazi art criticism, Max Nordau, attributed the synaesthetic tendencies in this art to "'diseased and debilitated brain-activity'; for what healthy mind would want to relinquish 'the advantages of the differentiated perceptions of phenomena' and regress to the confused sensory world of 'the mollusc'?" (Nordau in Classen 1998, 118–21). By contrast, avant-garde and new media artists (according to Caroline A. Jones) as well as Third World filmmakers living in diaspora (according to Laura U. Marks) have sought to break down social barriers and create a framework for a more open society by mixing the senses.

It is an open question, however, whether these avant-garde art experiments or, if we turn to design, the aestheticization of everyday life under the aegis of twentieth-century consumer capitalism is generative of a more open society, or just another ploy to monopolize the senses in the interests of moving merchandise. There is no question that the "new age of aesthetics" (Postrel 2003), with its surfeit of sensations, has brought on a democratization of luxury, which is one of the hallmarks of liberalism. However, the "race to embrace the senses" on the part of designers, marketers, and other "consumer engineers" (Sheldon and Arens) so as to give us consumers "what we demand" (Postrel 2003) has arisen in conjunction with an equally intense drive to privatize the sensory commons through "advances" in trademark law (Howes and Classen 2014, ch. 5). The emancipation of the senses, which one might have thought to be imminent in light of these developments, has been postponed.

CHAPTER SEVEN

Sensory Museology: Bringing the Senses to Museum Visitors

In the chapters of part 1, we saw how the sensory revolution in the human sciences, beginning in the 1990s, led to the emergence of a range of new academic fields and approaches, including sensory anthropology, the history of the senses, and sensuous geographies. One of the latest and most striking instances of this expansion has been in the field of museum studies. In 2014, *The Senses and Society* devoted a special issue to reviewing breaking developments in this dynamic new area of inquiry. This special issue, which I had the pleasure of editing, was called "Sensory Museology" (Howes 2014b). In what follows, an account is given of the transformation of the museum from its earliest incarnation in the seventeenth and eighteenth centuries as a site of intimate encounter between persons and things into a site for "single sense epiphanies" in the nineteenth century (Kirshenblatt-Gimblett 1998, 58) and then how, in recent decades, the museum is being reimagined as a site of engagement for all the senses.

The first section of this chapter presents an introduction to sensory museology, highlighting the ways in which the contributions to the special issue rethink the museum along other than visual lines, with particular reference to the rehabilitation of the haptic. The next two sections delve into the thorny issue of overcoming presentism or historicizing perception – that is, of bringing sensory pasts back to life and also imagining alternative sensory futures. It surveys some of the many ingenious display strategies that curators now use to bring the senses to museum visitors (and vice versa) so they can immerse themselves in the sensory worlds of other times and places, appreciate art within stimulating multisensory environments, make sense of modern urban landscapes, and develop a sense of the future of sensory design. In the last two sections of this chapter, the focus shifts from research to research creation. The *Tate Sensorium* show at Tate Britain in 2015 and *The Senses: Design Beyond Vision* exhibition at the Cooper-Hewitt, Smithsonian Design Museum in 2018 both added an experimental dimension to the experience of the exhibition, the former by distributing wristbands to the visitors which recorded their affective response to the paintings that were showcased, and the latter by taking the idea of interactive display to a whole new level. Both exhibitions also represented significant departures from "sensory demarcation" (Candlin 2010) and instituted sensory interaction in its place, to sensational effect.

From "Don't Touch" to "Please Touch": The Rehabilitation of the Haptic

Perhaps the most salient trend in the new museology has been the rehabilitation of touch. The importance currently being given to the sense of touch in museum studies is evidenced by the number of recent publications dealing with the subject. These include *The Engaging Museum* (Black 2005), *The Power of Touch: Handling Objects in Museums and Heritage Contexts* (Pye 2007), *Touch in Museums* (Chatterjee 2008), *Art, Museums and Touch* (Candlin 2010), and *Museum Materialities* (Dudley 2009). Indeed, some museum scholars now assert that "touch and object handling should be built into the gallery as a normal element of the display" (Black 2005, 265). The rehabilitation of touch has in turn created a more receptive environment for the (re)introduction of other senses traditionally classified as "lower" – in contrast to the "higher," "aesthetic," more "intellectual" senses of sight and hearing – such that smell and taste are now being actively solicited instead of censored.[1]

Until comparatively recently, however, scholars, curators and especially museum directors typically thought of the museum as a site of pure spectatorship, with objects in glass cases and visitors warned to keep their hands off. While this situation was generally true of twentieth-century museums, and largely remains the case today, research into the sensory history of early museums has uncovered a different scenario. The first museums of the seventeenth and eighteenth centuries, such as the Ashmolean in Oxford, were hands-on sites in which visitors expected and were permitted to handle artefacts (e.g., Ovenell 1986, 147; Classen and Howes 2006). Analysis of visitor and curatorial accounts of handling that date from this period reveals four major reasons for this tactile engagement (following Classen 2005a, ch. 24, 2012, ch. 6). The first reason for handling artefacts was to learn more about these intriguing objects than was accessible to vision alone. The use of touch as a means of learning was fundamental to contemporary notions of scientific investigation as well as popular practice. The natural philosopher and curator of experiments of the Royal Society, Robert Hooke, for example, writing in 1662, stated that the ocular inspection of objects under study needed to be accompanied by the "manual handling ... of the very things themselves" (Hooke 1971, 335).

The second reason for handling artefacts was for aesthetic appreciation. Touch was widely believed to enhance one's enjoyment of art objects. It was also declared by aesthetic philosophers such as Johann Gottfried Herder to allow access to forms of beauty unavailable to the eye (Norton 1990). The third reason for employing touch was in order to experience a sensation of intimacy with the original creators of the objects on display. The fourth reason, and the one which probably seems most alien to museumgoers today, was for purposes of healing. Rare and precious, exotic or of great antiquity, museum objects were often treated as charms. In a practice with origins in the touching of relics, visitors sometimes handled museum artefacts with the hope that some of their reputed power would rub off on themselves and give them a cure for some ailment or misfortune, or at least an increased sense of well-being (Classen 2017, ch. 1).

By the mid-nineteenth century, such hands-on practices were increasingly rare in museums (Candlin 2010), and by the later nineteenth century – an important period for the foundation of public museums around the world and the entrenchment of "the exhibitionary complex" (Bennett 1995) – it was generally assumed that collections were to be seen and *not* handled by the public. It would appear that this was not only because such handling was thought of as too damaging. It was also because the motivations that had earlier made the sense of touch such an important medium in the museum were no longer believed to be valid. Aesthetic appreciation, it was now understood, could not come through handling, and touching museum artefacts was no longer believed to possess any therapeutic value.

The demotion of touch was otherwise precipitated through the progressive inculcation, via "prestigious imitation," of new ways of walking, looking, sitting, and speaking. As Helen Rees Leahy documents in *Museum Bodies* (2012), learning how to stand at the "correct" distance from an artwork, walking at a pace that is neither too fast nor too slow, and knowing what to "feel" (without touching, of course) are corporeal techniques that must be mastered if a museum visitor is to display the requisite degree of cultural competence. The normative practices of attentive viewing and self-restrained comportment, which were the corollary of "the *institution* of the artwork as an object of contemplation" (Leahy 2012), resulted in the interposition of more and more distance between the average museum visitor and the work of art or exotic artefact, whether there were physical barriers (a glass case, a rope) or not. Only curators and connoisseurs were permitted to handle objects on account of their expert knowledge, and only curators possessed the authority to interpret objects (Candlin 2010; Krmpotich and Peers 2013, 35–43).

While the transformation of museumgoers from handlers into spectators, and of curiosities into object lessons in the "progress of civilization," proceeded apace, there were also certain holdouts. A case in point is the enduring fascination with mummies discussed by Constance Classen in "Touching the Deep Past: The Lure of Ancient Bodies in Nineteenth-Century Museums and Culture" (2014d). As she shows, older styles of tactile and indeed multisensory investigation survived in the case of the mummy through the Victorian period.

Her careful reconstruction of how the senses and affects were mobilized in the context of the sourcing or acquisition, exhibition, and public unwrapping of the "long dead" gives new depth to such theoretical constructs as "the archaeology of perception" and "the social life of things."

In "Incorporating the Period Eye" (2014), Helen Rees Leahy elaborates on her analysis in *Museum Bodies* and adds more layers to our understanding of the sensorial subconscious by exploring the recent trend towards staging "exhibitions of exhibitions." These displays seek to reproduce past conventions of spectatorship and in so doing sensitize contemporary visitors to shifts in the corporeality and performativity of "going to the museum." Historically outmoded ways of sensing spring back to life at these redos, giving the museum experience a reflexive edge – at least to the extent that the safety and hygiene standards of the contemporary museum allow.

Sandra Dudley (2014) continues the exploration of how visuality is structured by comportment and movement in her article on surprise and proprioceptivity in the Pitt Rivers Museum in Oxford. She analyses how the action of stooping to open one of the storage drawers under the display cabinets in the Pitt Rivers transforms sight from a distance sense into a proximity sense. The manual action of opening and shutting the drawers results in a form of visuality closely allied with touch, quite different from the typical surveying gaze of the strolling museumgoer. This action has the potential to draw the visitor into a more intimate and dynamic engagement with museum objects, even though they remain ensconced under glass. The museum drawer can hence be seen as the prototype of the interactive display.

The first public museums to reverse the hands-off trend and include handling as part of their program were children's museums and science museums, established for the most part in the twentieth century as counterparts to traditional museums. However, these museums rarely allowed for any tactile contact with objects deemed to be collectables – the classic display items of museums. It was not until the late twentieth century that handling sessions began to form part of the standard offerings at mainstream museums, such as the British Museum with its "hands on desks."[2] At 4:00 pm each day in the Enlightenment Gallery at the British Museum, a docent will lay out a series of objects on a desktop. The handling collection on one of the days I visited the museum included a tiny bronze statue of Ganesh (the Hindu elephant god), a carved wooden pig from Melanesia (used as a token of exchange), and a little, much worn piece of cloth from the wrapping of an Egyptian mummy (by far the most popular of the exhibits). It also included a stone axe, which fit comfortably in the palm of one's hand: it was delightful to have the chance to heft it. The axe prompted a conversation about what its equivalent might be in the material culture of today. One fellow visitor suggested that it was the equivalent of a cellphone. This interesting observation was as anachronistic as it was peculiarly apposite.

The invention of hands-on desks or tactile tables forms part of a general trend to make museums more "interactive" and engaging for contemporary visitors (Anderson 2004; Hooper-Greenhill 1994, 1995). It was also influenced to some degree by the efforts of organizations for the visually impaired to gain full access (physical *and* intellectual) to museum collections (Candlin 2010). This trend is tracked by Mark Clintberg (2014) in his essay on the "Stimulating the Senses" program at the National Gallery of Canada. This program is primarily aimed at visitors with low vision but also allows sighted visitors to participate. As Clintberg relates in his autoethnography of a touch tour wearing a blindfold, encountering the sculpture that was the focus of the tour without the interposition of sight, and then being invited to model his impressions using clay, deepened his enjoyment and understanding of the piece in a host of ways. It also sensitized him to the underdevelopment of his own sense of touch as a mode of understanding and representing the material world. Handling objects had formed no part of his training as an art historian.

The contemporary revalorization of touch in the museum has otherwise derived an important impetus from requests by Indigenous communities to either regain possession of or have hands-on access to ancestral artefacts "owned" by museums (Peers and Brown 2003; Krmpotich and Peers 2013). Marie-Pierre Gadoua's essay "Making Sense through Touch" (2014) pertains to this trend. She describes a project in "collaborative archaeology" that she ran at the Mc-Cord Museum of Canadian History in Montreal. It involved inviting Inuit elders to share their knowledge about their traditional material culture through participating in handling sessions of objects in the McCord collection. In this exercise, it was the objects (e.g., hunting implements, a model kayak, and some items that had no known use) that posed the questions. The sessions were lively occasions, particularly once the gloves came off, both for the participants (on account of the social relations and storytelling the objects prompted) and for the objects, which were temporarily "brought back to life" through being handled. The workshops led to the recovery and occasional discovery of "affordances" that the professional archaeologists and the curators present had never suspected, and the realization that, in the final analysis, the meaning of an object is in its use. Videoclips of the workshops were to be integrated in the McCord Museum's exhibitions and website, thereby constituting an "archive of the immaterial" (Leahy 2014) alongside the collection itself.

In her remarks on the emotional benefits of the workshops (e.g., evoking cultural pride, alleviating stress – especially for those Inuit who were in Montreal on medical visits), Gadoua alludes to another growing area of research in sensory museology. It has to do with the renewal of interest in the healing value of museum artefacts. In 2007, researchers at University College London were awarded a £300,000 grant by the Arts and Humanities Research Council to study the therapeutic benefits of handling museum pieces. Recent studies undertaken in this area suggest that "handling museum objects can have a positive impact on patient wellbeing" (Chaterjee, Vreeland, and Noble, 2009, 175). This points to a possible major new development for the use of touch in twenty-first-century museums, and one which harks back to the healing role of object handling in early museums.

The final essay in "Sensory Museology," by Julia T.S. Binter, entitled "Unruly Voices in the Museum: Multisensory Engagement with Disquieting Histories" (2014) analyses the display strategy of "versioning" as employed by the curator Anette Hoffman in *What We See*. This exhibition, which was shown in Cape Town, South Africa, and Vienna, Austria, was designed to trouble visitors' visual perception of a collection of life casts of Namibian people made by a German artist and self-proclaimed anthropologist in the 1930s. It did so by conjoining the sight of the casts with the voices of the Namibians (originally recorded on wax cylinders, then "forgotten," but thanks to Hoffman's diligence, tracked down, digitized, and now susceptible of playback). The casts were also set off by some very lively portraits of the speakers by contemporary South African artists. The resurrected voices spoke to the sensory deprivation and alienation of the colonial encounter (including the experience of being cast) in ways that had both an unsettling and profoundly conscientizing effect on the visitors.[3]

The reintroduction of touch to the museum has been further facilitated by the use of haptic interfaces employing digital technology. By combining a three-dimensional image of a virtual artefact with simulated sensations of touch produced by a desktop device that provides force feedback to the user's fingertip, the digital technology known as haptics allows museum visitors to "feel" three-dimensional works of art without physically touching them (McLaughin et al. 2002; Paterson 2007).

To sum up, in the museum of the twenty-first century, the senses are making a comeback, especially touch. Didactic instruction has increasingly come to be supplemented by multimodal approaches to learning, disinterested contemplation has been offset by affective participation, and the authority to interpret objects has been redistributed as in the case of Gadoua's experiment in collaborative archaeology at the McCord. In place of being a site/sight for "single sense epiphanies" (Kirshenblatt-Gimblett 1998, 58) the museum is becoming a kind of sensory gymnasium. While at times the new emphasis on experiencing the properties of things might remain at the level of "sensationalism," it also has the potential to recreate the museum as an exciting place of historical, cross-cultural, and aesthetic discovery and inspiration.

Historicizing the Senses in the Museum

But can the sense (and senses) of the past ever truly be recovered? It is in the nature of sensations that they are ephemeral and fleeting, gone in the same instant that they register. There is nothing enduring about them. This is a thorny issue, and one which the historian Mark M. Smith grapples with head on in a brief section called "On Method" in *Sensing the Past* (2007b). Smith asks, What does it mean for an author or the curator of an exhibition (including "living history" exhibitions or historical reenactments) to claim that their offering enables the reader or visitor to "experience the world as they did" – with the "they" here referring to the people of, say, colonial Williamsburg, or nineteenth-century Amsterdam?

The first problem is the problem of multiple constituencies. To focus on the museum experience to start with, while it may be presumed that visitors come to the exhibition with much the same sensory apparatus (physically speaking) as the creators of the artefacts on display, representing the period sensorium is not a straightforward matter at all. There would have been cleavages to that sensorium along gender, racial, or ethnic and class as well as other lines, such as disability. And just as there is no uniform "they," there is no uniform "we" or "us," since the contemporary sensorium is no less internally divided or fractured than its predecessors.

The second is the problem of multiple senses. We know that the hierarchy of the senses has shifted over time (Ong [1967] 1991; Classen 2014b), so that striking the right balance of the senses entails paying careful attention to how the senses were weighted or valued differently in different periods, and recreating that balance in the present. The third problem is that of historical authenticity, since many of the artefacts of the past, not to mention the physical ambience, may be degraded, or no longer extant. Fortunately, in the case of sound, for example, as Dutch sensory historian Karin Bijsterveld brings out in "Ears-On Exhibitions: Sound in the History Museum" (2015), it is now possible to simulate the aural contours of the past thanks to advances in technology, such as the Virtual Soundscapes Builder©. Another recent breakthrough involves the use of liquid gas chromatography to analyse and synthesize historical odours combined with the use of odour wheels (on the analogy of the colour wheels used in the wine industry) to train the visitor's senses to pick up on diverse nuances of, say, an old library (Bembibre and Strlič 2017). These devices are already shifting the focus from the *what* to the *how* of perceiving, which is where the idea of "ways of sensing" or "techniques of perception" comes in (Howes and Classen 2014). As Phillip Vannini (Vannini, Walkul, and Gottschalk 2012) observes, as we sense we also make sense – that is, we find meaning *in* sensation. (Recall that the word "sense" already bridges this duality, since "sense" encompasses both sensation *and* signification, feeling *and* meaning as in the "sense" of a word.) Hence the importance, according to Bijsterveld (2015), of catering to the senses of the visitor through such techniques as "framing" an exhibition, using first-person narratives (in order to promote identification), sensory instruction, and "involving the body." In this way museum curators can (potentially) give visitors access to the historical meaning of the senses – the "sense of the senses," as it were. Furthermore, as Bijsterveld and Smith both suggest, historical texts can have an important role to play in this process through the "contextualization" they provide – so long as due attention is paid to sensing *between* the lines of the written sources in an effort to help the visitor *apperceive* the habitus of historical subjects.

War museums have become another key site for tapping into or reactivating the historical sensory subconscious. For all that war is "senseless," "unrepresentable," and even "unthinkable," it leaves a material and sensory legacy, and it behooves us to strive to comprehend this legacy lest we forget the terrible toll that war takes on life – including the life of the senses. The challenge of facilitating such comprehension within a museological context falls to the "conflict curator." Paul Cornish (2017) of the Imperial War Museum (IWM) in London has related the considerations that informed the design of the acclaimed multisensory First World War galleries at the IWM, which opened in 2014. Alys Cundy, in "War, Memory and the Senses in the Imperial War Museum" (2017), presents a fine-grained sensory analysis of the *visitor* experience of the IWM from the creation of its first semi-permanent public display in 1920 down to 2014. Cundy highlights the role of the imagination in conjuring the sensescapes of the battlefields both for the veteran whose personal sensory memory is engaged by the displays of war matériel and for the visitor with no direct experience of the conflict, but whose "cultural memory" is mobilized by the "generated sensory experiences" created by the curators with the help of multisensory display techniques. Cundy goes on to challenge the assumed polarity between artifice and artificiality that has dogged discussion of heritage representation of conflict on account of the way this distinction, in her opinion, trivializes the creative role of the visitor's imagination. Her analysis of the "sensory display potential" of material culture is a major contribution to the emerging field of sensory museology and will be of interest to the many curators in other types of museums (art, ethnology, craft) who are now actively enlisting the senses as means of engaging the general public.

One of the most successful and acclaimed recent interventions in sensory museology is the exhibition *A Feast for the Senses: Art and Experience in Medieval Europe*, curated by Martina Bagnoli,[4] which opened at the Walters Art Museum in Baltimore in the fall of 2016. Bagnoli kindly shared with us the proposal she submitted on behalf of the Walters to the National Endowment for the Humanities in order to secure funding. This proposal, or "Project Narrative" as it is called, gives us a behind-the-scenes glimpse into all the theoretical contextualization, logistical challenges, and sheer imagination that goes into mounting an exhibition that is explicitly designed to stimulate and engage the senses of the museum visitor and thereby expand their mental and emotional as well as sensorial horizons.

In the proposal, Bagnoli (2018) begins by situating her project in relation to the wider field of sensory studies, and she brings out the interdisciplinary relevance of her project to the advancement of knowledge in such far-flung fields as history of science (including Science and Technology Studies), history of religion, and theatre. *A Feast for the Senses* is not just another art exhibition: it is a sense-switching game changer. It extends an invitation to the museum visitor to exercise their senses (instead of having to check them at the entrance, along with their umbrella) and contemplate the multisensory dimensions of such classic medieval sites as the garden, the church, and the royal court. As Bagnoli further brings out, in medieval Europe, objects were fashioned to *perform* in specific environments, appearances *mattered* (and not just visual appearances: saintly relics smelled of roses, sinners were attributed a reek of decay), and there was a keen interest in *materiality* (a sensuous and spiritually active materiality, not the materialism of contemporary Western culture).

In the project narrative, Bagnoli (2018) not only sets the theoretical stage for the *Feast for the Senses* exhibition, she also summarizes the careful planning involved in negotiating loans and transporting objects, the considerations that went into the construction of sound stations, smell stations, and objects one can feel (e.g., prayer beads) to enhance comprehension, and also lays out an ambitious outreach and communications strategy in which no platform is left unturned, just as no sense is left unturned in the exhibition itself. *A Feast for the Senses* truly set a new bar. It banished any thought of the supposedly primitive nature of Gothic art and gave the visitor access to some of the (more agreeable) sensations of the late Middle Ages. Huizinga, with his notion of "historical *ekstasis*" (Ankersmit 2005), would have approved.

Designs and Designers on the Senses

Since its inception in 2006, *The Senses and Society* journal has featured a sensory design review section in each issue. In this section there can be found reviews of architecture and objects ranging from Millennium Park, Chicago (Vodvarka, Irish, and Malnar 2006), to virtual environments (Kapralos, Collins, and Urube-Quevedo 2017) and from the Apple iPod (Bull 2006) to Whole Foods Markets (Mack 2012). These reviews evidence the extent to which aestheticization has taken command of the sensescape of everyday life. The journal also has a section devoted to exhibition reviews. These reviews document the high degree of sensory experimentation that has come to inform contemporary installation art and museum display.

Two exhibition reviews from the annals of *The Senses and Society* offer key insights into the emerging fields of sensory urbanism and sensory design, respectively. In their article, Alan Nash and Michael Carroll ([2006] 2018) review the *Sensations urbaines/Sense of the City* exhibition (2005–6) at the Canadian

Centre for Architecture (CCA) in Montreal. This exhibition was curated by then director of the CCA, Mirko Zardini. Zardini exemplified precisely the "critical engagement" with the senses that the design theorist Nigel Power (2018) calls for in his "Sensing Things" manifesto. Rather than use "the five senses" as a framework, Zardini structured the exhibition thematically: the first room was called "Nocturnal city," the second "Seasonal city," followed by "Sounds of the city," "Surface of the city" and "Air of the city."

One approached the *Sense of the City* exhibit via a darkened corridor, which echoed with diverse pre-recorded sounds of the city – "a kind of visual palette cleanser for what lies ahead," as one reviewer puts it (Nash and Carroll 2018, 379). The corridor opened on a welcome hall, the walls of which were lined with interesting facts (like 15 January 1957 being the coldest day in recorded history in Montreal) and giant silhouettes of animals whose sensory capacities dwarf those of human beings. This montage of animal modes of sensing sensitized the visitor to the contingency of the human *Umwelt*. The rooms themselves made a point of juxtaposing sensations. In "Nocturnal city": darkness and light, and visual and tactile (Braille-like) maps. In "Seasonal city": videos of snowclearing (a massive logistical operation) and images of ice palaces – the former denying, the latter embracing the seasonal cycle. In "Air of the city": a diatribe on the homogenizing effects of air conditioning next to a living wall of plants as well as a series of laboratory beakers containing synthesized scents of fresh-baked bread, garbage, etc. "Surface of the city" focused on "the second skin of the earth" – namely, asphalt, both plain and patterned (including a chunk of bitumen one could touch) juxtaposed with images of cobblestone streets with their attendant clatter and dust. The room dedicated to "Sound of the city," designed by R. Murray Schafer, was dotted with pods on which one could recline and put on headphones that enabled one to sample the soundscapes of New York, Vancouver, and other global cities. The message regarding the relativity of perception in the welcome hall, coupled with the clash of sensations in each of the rooms that followed, stimulated visitors to think twice about the great deodorization, illumination, and mobilization (or "pave paradise") drives of modernity, and to contemplate a range of more ecological and aesthetic alternatives. There were many prominent architects and urban planners among the record crowds who took in the exhibition. The "sensorial intelligence" (Nigel Power) of Mirko Zardini's "alternative approach to urbanism" in *Sense of the City* (2005) helped spark the lively discussion at the "Sensing the City" lecture series that accompanied the exhibition, and subsequent developments in the field of sensorial urbanism

Stefan Szczelkun and Bill Arning's (2006) reviewed *Touch Me: Design and Sensation*, a Wellcome Trust Exhibition designed by Graphic Thought Facility which ran at the Victoria & Albert Museum in the summer of 2005. The exhibition celebrated various advances in the development of haptic interfaces, such as a virtual keyboard that could be projected onto any surface, and some quite comic devices, like "Suck and Smile" teething rings with exaggerated facial expressions, and a hanging spherical alarm clock radio (which would rise a few more inches off the bed with each smack of the snooze button). Significantly, both reviewers of the exhibition for *The Senses and Society*, while amused, felt that the exhibition did not live up to its title. They comment on the degree to which hygiene considerations appeared to have limited the initial selection of objects and access to those that were included (e.g., there was nothing for the palate). They also felt short-changed by the number of devices that were no longer functioning due to overzealous fingering. One of the reviewers also expressed alarm at the idea underlying one of the exhibits: a futurist dress fitted with tubes that dispensed healing fragrances. The fragrances were supposed to modulate the wearer's moods, but the reviewer found it "horrendous" to contemplate the implicit assumption that the world of the future would be suffused with "a stench so unpleasant that one would need continuous replenishment with nice smells and could never inhale outside a perfumed bubble" (Szczelkun and Arning 2006, 152). While both reviewers lauded the curators for attempting to imagine the future of sensorial design and report back, they also expressed a certain ambivalence about some of the exhibits.

Design Beyond Vision

While *Touch Me: Design and Sensation* sought to inspire visitors with visions of the future of sensory design, *The Senses: Design Beyond Vision*, which brought together some forty objects and over sixty-five design projects and ran at the Cooper Hewitt, Smithsonian Design Museum in New York City from April to October 2018, set its sights squarely on the present. With this show, billed as an "inclusive celebration of the sensory richness of design," and the accompanying catalogue, with its "call to action for a multisensory design practice," the former curated and the latter edited by the team of Ellen Lupton and Andrea Lipps, sensory design came of age. In place of futurity, the focus of *The Senses* show was firmly on accessibility, and it testified to the great strides that have been made in inclusive design during the intervening decade. *The Senses* was also noteworthy for its emphasis on the multiplicity and interactivity of the senses both in the objects and projects on display and in the design of the exhibition experience as a whole.

Cooper Hewitt Director Caroline Baumann aptly enucleated the groundbreaking sensibility that informed the exhibition in a statement to the press:

> Across all industries and disciplines, designers are avidly seeking ways to stimulate our sensory responses to solve problems of access and enrich our interactions with the world. *The Senses* shares their discoveries and invites personal revelation of the

extraordinary capacity of the senses to inform and delight. Within the inclusive environment created for the exhibition ... [multiple measures have been taken] to ensure the exhibition will be welcoming to visitors of all abilities, an important step forward in our ongoing commitment to making Cooper Hewitt accessible to everyone.[5]

Thus, the show included many objects and experiences that were specifically designed for a "diverse and differently-abled audience" on the principle that two (or more) senses are always better than one. Out of consideration for visually impaired visitors, there were maps that could be seen, felt, and heard; out of consideration for hearing-impaired visitors, there was audio that could be felt through the skin and a themed section on architecture informed by DeafSpace principles; and, taking into account some of the needs of dementia sufferers, there was a display of coloured tableware to facilitate discrimination (e.g., food/dish) and a scent player that released smells (e.g., grapefruit, curry, or chocolate) to stimulate the appetite at mealtimes. These accommodations were augmented by Braille labelling, twice-weekly descriptive tours led by Lupton, and an Accessible Exhibition App.

Novel sensory conjugations abounded, such as "Tactile Orchestra," an interactive installation consisting of an undulating wall covered in black synthetic fur embedded with sensors: when one person stroked it, a recording of a single string instrument would play, and when multiple persons touched it one could hear the full composition. Other installations included: scratch-and-sniff wallpaper, the "Ostrichpillow" (a portable sensory isolation contraption), and a film animation that translated bird songs into bursts of colour and motion entitled "Visual Sounds of the Amazon." The catalogue is especially rich in pointers that highlight the distinctive features of each sense and how they interact, such as "Sound is material," "Flavor is smell," "Color amplifies the sensation of taste and flavor": each slogan is accompanied by a paragraph that bristles with factual observations and reflections on how mingling the senses can inform and delight us at once.

Not all of the sensations on offer were pleasing. A few were quite jarring. Some installations purposely provoked cognitive dissonance in the viewer, such as a video called "For Approval": this video included a scene in which what looked like eggs drop on a ceramic plate but bounce instead of smash (their shells being made of soft rubber). Another installation, called "A Seated Catalogue of Feelings," involved sitting on a chair (or one could clutch a pillow to one's chest), putting on headphones, and listening as a voice intoned a message (with the same message projected on the floor), such as "an avalanche of frozen peas," "falling backwards into a tub of Jello," or "the last nail in your coffin." The seat would then begin to rumble with a pre-recorded pattern of corresponding tactile sensations. The translation – or rather, transduction – of sentences into vibrations was highly evocative.

With eleven main themes, ranging from "The Sensory Table" to "Shaping Sound," and from "Tactile Library" to "Sensory Materials," staging a coherent experience or "narrative" for the exhibition posed a real challenge. To this end, Lupton and Lipps commissioned the New York–based design agency Studio Joseph. As Monica Coghlan of Studio Joseph observed, "One of the things that was very clear from the beginning was that the premise was how the senses influence each other, not as separate experiences"; and as Wendy Evans Joseph stated, "We were determined to create a complementary embrace that gave each piece its 'day in the sun' and demonstrated its relationship to other objects." The problem of allowing for sound and sensory isolation of one display from another so as to avoid cacophony while at the same time creating the conditions for a symphony of sensations and encouraging fluidity of movement was solved by the careful positioning of objects and installing a screen system consisting of vinyl strips of varying hues and transparency (rather like a bead curtain) that shimmered and could easily be parted by visitors to allow them freedom of movement in their "journey of discovery." In this manner, the "what" of saying or *message* (i.e., the narrative of multi- and intersensoriality) was seamlessly integrated with the "way" of saying or medium.

Ellen Lupton created a graphic for the poster announcing her plenary address at "Uncommon Senses III: Back to the Future of the Senses,"[6] which provides the perfect finishing touch to this exposition (see figure 5).

The Senses exhibition stimulated my senses in numerous creative ways. Nevertheless, I did have reservations about it. One had to do with the relative lack of cultural diversity. It is true that *The Senses* boasted a star-studded roster of designers of international renown. However, with all due respect, it must be said that many designers tend to rely on their own intuitions even when they engage in co-design with a give target population. As an anthropologist, I am an advocate for the practice of ethnography as an essential first step or prelude to imagining "design solutions." Doing ethnography involves getting out of the studio and out of one's own head and immersing oneself in the analysis of the practices of everyday life among diverse populations. I was also somewhat perturbed by the technological dependency of the vast majority of the "design solutions" on display. For, apart from all the cutting-edge technologies of perception that can be used to dazzle us, there are the *techniques* of perception or *ways* of sensing, rooted in particular traditions the world over, that also deserve our attention. Studying these practices, which continue to flourish on the outskirts of the technological dynamo of modernity (and even within it) can provide insights into alternative orchestrations of the senses which lie beyond the ken of the professional designer.[7] This cross- and intercultural grassroots approach to designing objects and environments will be the subject of the next chapter.

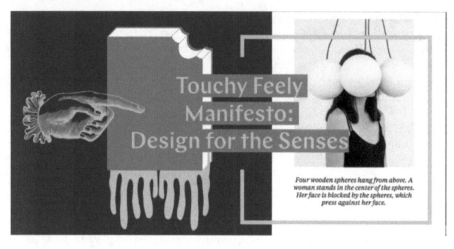

Four wooden spheres hang from above. A woman stands in the center of the spheres. Her face is blocked by the spheres, which press against her face.

Figure 5. Graphic for Ellen Lupton's plenary address at the Uncommon Senses III conference. *Tactile Headset*. Design: Alessandro Perini, executed by Rossella Siani, VAHA (Naples, Italy). Materials: Wooden spheres, metal chains, vibration speakers, ceiling mount, 2018. Photo by Michela Benaglia. Used with permission of Ellen Lupton and Michela Benaglia.

The Work of Art in the Age of Virtual Augmentation

Flying Object is a creative agency, co-founded by Peter Law and Tom Pursey, based in London. Their proposal for an exhibition entitled *Tate Sensorium*, which centred on three artworks from Tate Britain's collection, won the 2015 IK Prize for using technology to "connect the world with art from the Tate collection." With the £70,000 prize commission in hand, they set about creating a show that introduced cutting-edge technologies from the field of virtual reality (VR) to address the following questions and objectives (to quote from the original submission):

> Imagine walking up to an artwork in a gallery and hearing the scene depicted; feeling the textures carved out of stone; smelling the dense atmosphere. How would this affect your experience of the artwork? Would the stimulation of different senses begin a deeper emotional engagement with the work? ...
>
> For each [work] we intend to sensitively develop themes in the artwork to enhance – and not obscure – the core visual perception of the work. We'll develop an auditory experience, and layer on a tactile, gustatory or olfactory experience as appropriate ...

On top of that, we'll involve visitors in the experiment, by [giving them] … the latest in wearable physiological measurement technology to let them track how their bodies respond to a multisensory experience of art. (Flying Object and Chatfield 2018, 375)

This experiment in "multisensory immersive design" integrating art and science shattered the sensory sterility and "pure opticality" of the Modernist art gallery (or white cube), and attracted record crowds (four thousand visitors, 100 per cent capacity). It is important to emphasize, however, that Flying Object had no intention of distracting from the "core visual perception" of the works, only to supplement and thereby enhance this perception by introducing diverse non-visual stimuli generated by a battery of VR devices designed by the experts (or "sensory specialists") they recruited to join them in creating this highly memorable multi- and intersensory aesthetic experience.

The devices included the Vortex Midi, a timed scent-release machine; binaural audio, a form of audio production that "allows the designer to place sounds all around a headphone-wearing visitor with extraordinary psychological realism"; and ultrahaptics, "a device which creates moving, tactile sensations in mid-air, creating a feeling like 'dry rain.' No gloves or attachments; the feeling is projected onto your bare hands using ultrasound" (Flying Object and Chatfield 2018, 376).

The four artworks that Flying Object eventually chose to focus on were different from the three works presented in their initial submission. For example, they dropped John Martin's *The Great Day of His Wrath* (1851–3), which, had they included it, would have entailed conjuring the dread a Victorian public would have experienced when confronted with Martin's awesome depiction of the end of the world. Instead, the four paintings they settled on were all works of contemporary British art: Richard Hamilton's *Interior II* (1964), which uses a mix of collage and oil paint to depict a room of jumbled up planes, dominated by a screenprint portrait of the lead actress in the 1949 film *Shockproof*; John Latham's *Full Stop* (1961), a towering painting displaying a (spray-painted) black circle on an unprimed canvas; David Bomberg's *In the Hold* (ca. 1913–14), which uses an abstract geometric framework with a range of colours (from dull browns to lighter blues filling each of the triangles) to depict the uploading of a cargo ship; and Francis Bacon's *Figure in a Landscape* (1945), which portrays a man in a woollen suit sitting on a metal chair in a landscape modelled on Hyde Park interspersed with elements of an African landscape: the head of the figure is overpainted with black, and appears to be speaking into a microphone.

In the darkened room at Tate Britain given over to *Tate Sensorium*, each of the paintings were presented in visual isolation – spotlit so they loomed out of the enveloping darkness – and surrounded by a multisensory installation designed to bring out the painting's content, process, and contemporary history. The experience of the painting was "led" by one sensory stimulus and supported by others, all designed to direct the visitor's attention to different aspects of the work. For example, the content and process of Latham's painting, which made use of spray-paint, were duplicated by using ultrasound to pepper the viewer's hand with individual dots when they reached toward the painting. In the case of *Figure in a Landscape*, scent diffusers emitted an equine smell (reflecting the fact that in 1945 Hyde Park still had a bridle path), the audio evoked the ambient sounds of the park and the metallic sound of the bench,[8] and the pièce de résistance was a chocolate truffle. As Pursey explains,

> The painting has been found to contain dust from Bacon's studio, apparently thrown or smeared into the canvas. Here we led with something to eat: on the face of it, a "taste" experience, although what was offered was also designed to have significant haptic stimuli. A dark chocolate ball contained a "dust" (mirroring the art historical fact) made of cacao nibs, salt, burnt orange (reflecting the presence of orange flowers in the background), lapsang souchong tea (a smokey tea – the smokiness a reference to the artwork's WW2 timeframe), and charcoal (to reflect the black). When the chocolate ball was bitten into, the "dust" filled the mouth with a surprising and unpleasant dryness, before the chocolate ball then melted and the sweetness came through. (Pursey and Lomas 2018, 359)

The interactive or participatory component of the installation was transformed into digital data by equipping each visitor with a biometric device (the E4 Empatica wristband). The wristband was used to "capture each user's Skin Conductance Response (SCR) and heartrate over the course of the experience, and output this at the end, as a neatly designed and easy to interpret printout" (Flying Object and Chatfield 2018, 376). Visitors were invited to contemplate these printouts while relaxing in the Evaluation Room adjacent to the exit and were also provided with a list of suggestions for other works in the Tate collection they might wish to peruse, based on an analysis of their arousal levels as recorded by the app. Thoughtfully, Flying Object also made this data available to researchers.

Tate Sensorium was acclaimed but not without controversy. Shouldn't it be faulted for leaving nothing to the imagination – that is, for filling up or saturating the imagination with extraneous sensory data? What of the detachment that is supposed to be the hallmark of the aesthetic experience after Kant (who famously dismissed the senses of taste and smell as having any aesthetic vocation whatsoever)? Did it not "Disneyfy" art by aligning with the hyperaesthetic "experience economy" of late consumer capitalism? These are among the questions raised by David Lomas, professor of art history at the University of Manchester. For all his qualms about the application of technologies derived from VR in the art museum, and *Tate Sensorium*'s embrace of late capitalist hedonism, Lomas still found merit (and a modicum of art-historical truth) in the sensory surfeit on account of the way it activated diverse cross-modal associations and transpositions. "We should not forget," he writes "that the pioneers of abstract art often appealed to correspondences with the other arts, notably music" (Pursey and Lomas 2018, 363). For example, one of Bacon's early mentors, the Australian abstract painter Roy de Maistre, experimented with creating colour charts on the analogy of musical notes, and it is conceivable that the "flat areas of vibrant, often jarring colors" that are a hallmark of Bacon's style were inspired by de Maistre's colour-music theories. Significantly, the audio that accompanied *Figure in a Landscape* is described as "referencing the color palette and the painting's visual texture" – that is, "it is predicated on analogies in exactly the same manner as early abstract art" (363).

At the same time, being a purist, Lomas remained conflicted. He allows that "to have succeeded in luring youthful audiences to the gallery and introducing them to some great art – something that would not have occurred without all the paraphernalia and the extra buzz of an experiment … is enough to justify it," yet he could not unburden himself of the thought that the application of VR technologies "tends inescapably to promote a virtual experience at the expense of a more genuine one constituted by myself standing in front of a painting that actually exists in my space" (Pursey and Lomas 2018, 365). This speaks to the "aura" of the artwork, its "presence," as theorized by Walter Benjamin in "The Work of Art in the Age of Mechanical Reproduction" (1973),[9] although Benjamin's paradigm is not entirely apposite, since in the case of *Tate Sensorium* the original, not some copy, remains at the centre of the viewing experience, and the technology of mechanical reproduction has actually been superseded by the technology of virtual augmentation in the wake of the digital revolution. The VR devices augmented the presence of the work by activating the non-visual senses, making it more "real" (or hyperreal). But this sensory plenitude could be seen as problematic when the artwork is actually about lack, as with Bacon's painting:

> Bacon described how *Figure in a Landscape* "started from a straightforward photo, then this black spread across the canvas." Situated at the heart of the composition, this gaping void … becomes in a sense the real subject of the work … To add to a void, does not that take away from it, by making of it less of Nothing and more of something? (Pursey and Lomas 2018, 364)

Paradoxically, and also "happily," Lomas goes on to aver, "this hypothetical objection turns out not to have been borne out in practice. Tom Pursey reports that: 'What people told us was that [the addition of the chocolate] really made the black almost throb'" (364–5). In other words, the visual perception of the black hole or void was heightened by the gustatory sensation of biting

into the truffle. This in turn speaks to the original mid-eighteenth-century definition of the essence of aesthetics as involving, if we follow Baumgarten, the
perfection of perception (rather than the perception of perfection, or beauty)
through enabling the viewing subject to grasp "the unity-in-multiplicity of sensible qualities" (see *supra* pp. 143–4). Digging yet deeper, what *Tate Sensorium*
accomplished was to (re)create the conditions for the experience of art as "synesthesis" – "the simultaneity of sensations" (not to be confused with synaesthesia) as in medieval Byzantium (Pentcheva 2006).[10] This *virage* indexes an even
deeper art historical truth: it is not the degree to which a painting corresponds
to reality (virtual or otherwise) that matters, but the correspondence of the
senses it engenders.

From the perspective of the anthropology of the senses, however, a further step needs to be taken in the case of such multisensory evocations of art;
namely, to create *mindful sensations* – that is, sensations that link the social
modes of sensory production with those of sensory consumption. For example,
in the case of Bacon's *Figure in A Landscape*, the African associations of the
landscape and of the chocolate could have been linked to the extremely harsh
working conditions on many African cocoa farms. These kinds of sensory and
social insights are needed to make the multisensory experience of art not only
aesthetically stimulating, but also socially enlightening.

CHAPTER EIGHT

Performative Sensory Environments: Alternative Orchestrations of the Senses in Contemporary Intermedia Art

In this chapter, I begin by reporting some of the teaching techniques used by R. Murray Schafer while he was Composer in residence at Concordia University during the fall term of 2005. I will also discuss the end-of-term production he facilitated, entitled *The Theatre of the Senses*. Schafer and his students' production may be regarded as a prototype for the widespread experimentation with the creation of "intermedia art" in the contemporary art world. In these experiments, art is dematerialized in the sense that it comes off the wall, off the pedestal, etc., and instead suffuses the space of the installation with a symphony of sensations by engaging multiple modalities via diverse media, whence its "intermediality." It may otherwise take the form of a scent, which is totally immaterial, or a performance, where the parts played by actors and audience intertwine, dissolving the so-called fourth wall.

Chris Salter, who holds the Concordia University Research Chair in New Media, Technology and the Senses, is one of the prime movers of the sensorial revolution in the creative arts. In section 2, I present a sensory ethnography of my experience working with Salter and others, with a specific focus on the design strategies they deploy – namely, sensory restriction, multisensory integration, and sensory decolonization – to create a form of intermedia art called "performative sensory environment" (Howes and Salter 2015, 2019; Salter 2015). The performative sensory environment is like a museum display, only instead of presenting objects it elicits and mixes up the senses, and audience members are transformed from passive spectators into active participants in the co-production of "experiences." In some countries, these sorts of creative endeavour go under the name of "arts-based research," while in others, most notably Canada, they are framed as exercises in "research-creation."[1] Research-creation involves uniting artistic expression, scholarly investigation, and material experimentation to generate new ways of being and knowing. As such these performance/installation artworks occupy a space "between art and science" (Born and Barry 2010; Galison and Jones 2014; Sormani, Carbone, and Gisler 2018) or "between art and anthropology" (Schneider and Wright 2010, 2013; Cox, Irving, and Wright 2016) and therefore produce and communicate knowledges in ways that conventional academic or artistic specialties cannot touch. New ways of being and knowing are generated within the performative sensory environment, which the visitor gets to try out. The proof is in the experience.

I. Prototype

R. Murray Schafer and The Theatre of the Senses

During his tenure as Composer in Residence, Schafer led a Master Class in the Senses for seventy-five students from Concordia University's departments of Music, Theatre, Film and Dance. Transforming the classroom into a sensory gymnasium, Schafer had his students exercise each of their sensory faculties by, among other things, composing "smellodies," tasting apples, going on barefoot walks around the grassy Loyola campus of the university, and foregoing speech for a period so as to heighten their receptiveness to the world around them. He also lectured on some of his past works, such as *The Palace of the Cinnabar Prince* (Part 8 of the Patria Cycle),[2] which was set around a wilderness lake, and *Ko Wo Kiku* (Listen to the Incense), which was commissioned by the Kyoto Symphony Orchestra.

The objective of the course was for the students, in groups of ten or twelve (with each group representing a cross-section of the disciplines), to mount a performance entitled *The Theatre of the Senses*. The students were thus called upon to negotiate disciplinary as well as sensory boundaries in conceptualizing the twelve pieces or "rooms" that would make up the show that was to be held at an undisclosed location on 5 December 2005. Due to Schafer's own preferences and interest in exploring the communicative and emotive potential of the non-audiovisual senses, the students were also banned from using virtually any of the communications technologies that have become such a ubiquitous feature of contemporary performance and installation art. This ban provoked some consternation on account of the students being so accustomed to relying on electronic media to achieve effects. But they rose to the challenge in an exemplary fashion, as we shall see.

On the night of 5 December, the audience congregated in the foyer of the Hall Building, on Concordia's downtown campus, and we were bussed at twenty-minute intervals in groups of thirty to the performance space, blindfolded. This space turned out to be a cool, multipurpose building in the industrial district of Montreal. The Parisian Laundry, as it is known, consists of two wide-open hardwood floors, supported by metal pillars, and a concrete cellar. The space was partitioned into chambers by means of curtains. The prevailing hue was burnt orange, and the lighting was for the most part subdued, bordering on the crepuscular.

After converting our blindfolds into face masks, we climbed the metal stairs to the second floor. There we were entreated (wordlessly, by means of gestures) to divest ourselves of our coats, our boots, and our stockings by sinuously clad attendants, who then invited us to follow a path of fabrics taped to the floor, applauding our every step. Underneath the fabrics were foam core, hangers, willow branches, plastic bags, bubble wrap, popcorn kernels, occasionally overlaid with onions, mint leaves, raw pasta, evergreen branches, tea, and white bread. Treading the path had the effect of transforming the soles of our feet from lowly means of locomotion into exquisite organs of perception. At the end of the path our feet were attentively washed in warm water and dried by another chorus of attendants.

We then crouched down to crawl through an opening in the curtains into the next room and were summoned to compose ourselves on some straw. There was a grainy black-and-white projection on one wall, and countless apples (resembling planets) suspended on strings from the ceiling. Two performers in leotards crawled over and around us and started the apples spinning. At the trill of a flute, four ten-foot-tall columns of linen (encasing dancers), lit from within by candles, glided slowly and eerily towards us, chanting, and stopping just short of our prone bodies.

Ushered into the next room, we processed (slowly, wordlessly) around an altar of candles on the floor, past a meditating officiant, and then knelt down in a circle. Behind a backlit screen, tea was being served. In time, we were each presented with a bowl of tea, which we duly imbibed, but only after having been shown how to waft its aroma to our noses with a wave of the hand, and bidden to cup our hand to our ear to listen to its essence.

In the next chamber, we were greeted by a dancer who bowled and tossed clementines at us, then joined in a chant that seemed to emanate from the very core of our being led by a silver-haired woman dressed in orange who said, "Hum with me." Various facts about the nutritive, curative, and sensory qualities of citrus fruits were posted on the walls. We were encouraged to read and contemplate these facts to the accompaniment of a duet of xylophone and guitar. There were also various stalls dedicated to recycling the clementine peels. At one, the peels were fashioned into jewellery. At another, they were ironed flat and exuded a delightful hot orange scent as we rubbed them on our skin.

We then descended the metal stairs to the ground level, which proved torturous to our naked feet, and came upon another shadow play. This one involved a hooded figure on the other side of a window, behind a thick sheet of milky white plastic, who plastered the sheet with some substance that looked like frost when it dried. A few audience members tried to mirror the movements of the hooded dancer and touch her hands, but they were frustrated due to the opacity of the medium. Then we had the chance to dip our hands in "paint" made of icing sugar and engage in digital painting of our own. Another exuberant chorus of attendants applauded us (leading us to wonder who was doing the acting) and then washed and towelled dry our hands.

A "dinner party" awaited us in the next room, where we were each presented with a glass of water and straw and then took our seats at a table strewn with dry pasta, plates of carrots, French bread, and microphones. Our hosts invited us to experiment with the acoustics of the spread by blowing bubbles in the water, spilling the pasta onto our plates, and using the cutlery as drumsticks, while passing around the mikes. This dinner party was a feast for the ears.

In the ensuing space we sat on chairs in groups of ten and were handed slips of paper assigning us an animal identity (chicken, pig, goat). The papers instructed us to respond from the perspective of the animal we had drawn to the questions asked of us by a pseudo-psychiatrist with a clipboard. "Do you know where you are?" "Are you worried about your coat and boots?" This set presented us with the opportunity to articulate our experience of the performance thus far, but it was complicated by the fact that we had no common language. Wanting to remain "in character," I did not think it proper to resort to English, and so was confined to uttering "brock!" (in chickenspeak). I was saved from my predicament by a young man who invited me to come and take a deep breath with him, and then ushered me through a curtain into a room that was bathed in the flickering light and soothing scent of aromatic candles arranged in a huge iron chandelier shaped like an arrowhead. On a barren white wall there were cut-out letters in white cardboard spelling "LISTEN." But listen to what? To our inner selves? To the walls and radiators? To the sounds of other groups making their way through other chambers of the exhibition? Most of us focussed on this last. The bleeding of sounds emanating from different rooms was curiously decentring. I felt myself going out through my ears in a powerful reversal of the customary way in which we "receive" sense impressions.

Then came the descent into the underground (the cellar), stepping gingerly down the treads of a back stairwell, past clouds of fluff, feathers suspended on strings, and more sinuously swaying performers in glittery party masks. At the base of the stairs, our masks were converted back into blindfolds and our hands were guided to a rope, which would lead us, stumbling, up on our feet and down on our knees, through a labyrinth of textures including crepe paper, cold steel, rough timber, bubble wrap, and a clothing bag with a living person in it. Profoundly disoriented, I shall always remember the cool touch of the hands that took hold of my wrists and delivered me from this dungeon of sensations.

The furnace room came next, with its exposed beams and pipes, where it was impossible to stand upright. We beat on the pipes and grated our fingernails on other surfaces, all ingeniously amplified, so as to produce an industrial din of hugely discordant proportions. The following room had spotlit jars with labels proclaiming SMELL ME. These alchemical vessels contained blends of aromatic oils as well as bits of plastic dolls and sprigs of herbs. I wished I could know the ingredients of these elixirs so as to experience them again. Three small spotlit picture frames also lined the walls, training our gaze on the crumbling concrete. I wanted to reach through them, but suppressed the impulse, using my eyes like fingers instead. Around the corner was a standing set of drums and cymbals and some old manual typewriters where one could join in the jam session or tap out one's impressions of the exhibition. A plant stood in a corner with a flashlight suspended over it, which one could set in motion to produce fantastic whirling shadows.

Then came the ascent, up more torturous stairs (under which there sat a musician in a bear suit playing a guitar). A door opened, releasing us into the winter night. We crossed a courtyard with light snow falling, and then climbed up another flight of stairs to the room where our sensory odyssey had begun two hours earlier. Feeling both dazed and relieved, we retrieved our coats and boots, and then boarded the bus that took us back to the Hall Building.

The Theatre of the Senses provided members of the audience with a chance to step out of our selves (due to the dimness of the lighting and the depersonalizing effect of the masks) and into our senses. Thanks to the ministrations of the actors, and the phenomenal properties of the props and settings, we came to experience our senses in new and unexpected ways. Alternately lulled and bombarded by sensations of differing intensities, we came away with the feeling of having had each of our senses cleansed.

The tingling sensation in the soles of our feet (which lasted for hours afterwards) was the most potent reminder of the experience. How revelatory it was to have our soles liberated in this way and become organs of perception in their own right! Equally memorable were all the ways in which we had had our senses crossed, such as feasting with our ears, touching with our eyes, smelling sounds, tasting paint (icing sugar). Our senses were untracked and retracked in all sorts of novel combinations that exposed the limitations of the dominant ways in which "information" is tracked in our audiovisual civilization.

The Theatre of the Senses was in some respects a throwback to a "1960s Happening" (see Higgins 2014) as some audience members noted, but it was a creative (rather than derivative) anachronism. *The Theatre of the Senses* could also be linked to the nineteenth-century tradition of the "total work of art" or *Gesamtkunstwerk*, which Schafer has done so much to expand by situating his pieces in wilderness settings (so that all of nature becomes a stage). It was a truly collaborative project, in which all the senses, like all the arts, conspired and were transmuted into each other, just as the conventional line separating actors from audience was effaced, liberating us from our respective roles, and permitting us to experience each other's presence in surprising new ways.

II. A Threefold Typology Of Experimentation In Contemporary Intermedia Art

For the past decade, I have had the privilege of participating as a co-researcher in the design and evaluation of a series of "intermedia" artworks or installations under the creative direction of my colleague, Chris Salter. Our collaboration has centred on theorizing, constructing, and evaluating what we call "performative sensory environments" (Howes and Salter 2015, 2019; Salter 2015). My role has been to nourish the team with general ideas for how to arrange the senses differently by writing briefs. These general ideas would then be mixed with other ideas from the electronic arts, synthesized and transmuted into the installation artworks conceptualized by Salter in association with various artistic collaborators, most notably TeZ (Maurizio Martinucci). My role has also involved participating in the debriefing sessions after visitors have had the chance to experience the installation, with a view to tabulating their responses. The method used during these sessions is a specially tailored form of sensory ethnography, which we call "participant sensation" (Howes 2019a).

Salter has designed many performative sensory environments over the years, including *Displace*, which was shown at the 2011 meeting of the American Anthropological Association in Montreal, TodaysArt in the Hague, and *Haptic Field*, which was shown at Chronus Art Center in Shanghai in 2017, and at Martin Gropius Bau, Berlin, and in Bandung, Indonesia, in 2018. Let us begin with the latter.

Sensory Restriction: The Haptic Field *Project*

My brief for the *Haptic Field* project made note of the fact that when we turn to explore the significance of the skin across cultures, we find that it is not always regarded as that which sets oneself off from others (i.e., it is not an envelope, the way it is presumed to be in the West), but rather something one shares with others. Consider the term *ngalki*, "skin" in the language of the Yanyuwa of northern Australia. Ngalki is used to refer to a person's group in the kinship system (or "skin group"), to the voice of a person, and to the sweat of their armpits, in addition to their literal epidermis (Kirton and Timothy 1977). The term "skinship" has been coined by anthropologists to evoke this distributed or relational understanding of the skin as encompassing the various members of one's kin group (Gregory 2011).

Elsewhere in Australia, and among the San of South Africa, it is supposed that a person can foretell the approach of a relative from the feeling of "tappings" on their skin. These twitches correspond to known points on the relative's body, such as an old wound, or the pressure from a carrying strap. To quote a San informant: "When a woman who had gone away is returning to the house, the man who is sitting there feels on his shoulders the thong with which the woman's child is slung over her shoulders; he feels the sensation there," and knows she will soon appear (Bleek and Lloyd 2009). Evidently, among the San, touch is not a proximity sense. It can operate at a distance.

Beyond these examples of skinship, we find that, in numerous cultures, the surface of the body, or "skinscape" (Howes 2005d), is continuous with the surface of the earth, or landscape. In Aboriginal Australia, the landscape *is* a skinscape – composed of the material traces of the bodies of the ancestral beings who roamed across and shaped it during the primordial period referred to as the Dreaming (Biddle 2003). A chief of the Wet'suwet'en First Nation of British Columbia, testifying at a land claim hearing, expressed this notion of the skinscape this way: "If you know the territory well, it is like your own skin. Sometimes you can feel the animals moving on your body as they are on the land, the fish swimming in your bloodstream … If you know the territory well enough, you can feel the animals" (quoted in Howes and Salter 2015).

The Cashinahua of Peru call this sort of awareness "skin knowledge" (Howes 2005d). It is what enables a man to find his way in the jungle and locate prey. He uses "hand knowledge" to shoot the prey. In addition to the skin and hand, the Cashinahua recognize four other sense organs: the ear (which receives and stores social knowledge), the liver (emotional knowledge), the genitals (seat of the life force), and the "eye-spirit." Interestingly, the latter, visual sense is only deemed to be active when under the influence of hallucinogens. It enables a person to see the spritual "insides" of other people and things (a kind of X-ray vision). The Cashinahua sensorium thus has a very different configuration from that of the "normal" Western subject (Keifenheim 1999; Kensinger 1995). Cashinahua "feel" with their skin and hands what an English-speaker, for example, would say they "see."

We also read and reflected on Valentine Daniel's classic essay "The Pulse as an Icon in Siddha Medicine" (1991). In Siddha medicine (a humoral medical tradition of South India), the physician, when examining a patient, begins by determining the patient's pulse, moves on to sensing his own pulse in contradistinction to that of the patient (or contrapuntal phase), and then attempts to synchronize his pulse with the patient's pulse: in this way the physician arrives at first-hand knowledge of the patient's symptoms. This is another example of exterodermality, or the fusion of haptic horizons across bodily boundaries, like among the San. It rubs against common sense (as common sense is constituted in the modern West).

What these cross-cultural facts point toward is an understanding of skin as social instead of individual, as interface instead of envelope, and as knowledgeable or sentient in its own right instead of subservient to cognition and the brain (or the eye). In modern Western culture, Didier Anzieu (the controversial anti-Lacanian psychoanalyst) elaborated an in-depth understanding of the skin as a porous medium. This understanding of the skin is also the awareness that the skin studies scholar strives to arrive at. As Marc Lafrance observes in the Introduction to "Skin Matters" (a special issue of *Body & Society*): the skin is seen as "open, processual, relational, and sentient; it is human and non-human, material and immaterial, indeterminate and multiple" (Lafrance 2018, 4).

Haptic Field took the understanding of the skin as open, processual, and relational and used that as the basis for a multimedia evocation of haptic sensations. The iteration that was shown at the Martin Gropius Bau, as part of the Berliner Festspiele in 2018, consisted of four darkened rooms of varying dimensions with different lighting arrays. The light sources consist of small LEDs sheathed in acrylic tubes suspended on wires from the ceiling or (in one of the rooms) affixed to the walls, all at different heights and different concentrations. The LEDs change in intensity, brightness, and colour in sync with the sinusoidal sound waves of varying frequencies diffused by two- and four-speaker setups in two of the four rooms to create various (preprogrammed) "audiovisual states." These design elements, which create a symphony of sound and light, are familiar from other immersive environments created by Salter and TeZ such as *Displace* (see below). What sets *Haptic Field* apart from the many other works of intermedia art Salter has created is the costume, or second skin, donned by participants.

This supplementary skin consists of a garment with seven custom-designed wireless haptic actuators (or what Salter and developer Ian Hattwick call "Vibropixels") that produce variegated levels of tactile intensity (or "haptic tracks") across the body, albeit concentrated in the upper arms, chest, and thighs. The Vibropixels also emit light, which is synchronized to the haptic track so that each visitor can see and feel the luminous-vibrational pattern that they – along with the other visitors (there are up to eighteen visitors at a time) – emit. But they do so only through a glass darkly, as it were, because the crowning piece of the suit is a pair of frosted safety goggles. They give the light sources an auratic, halo effect and the atmosphere a gauzy hue. Other visitors lack definition and seem almost like spectres, except for the Vibropixels attached to their body, which pulsate, in unison with one's own. The eighteen random individuals become a skingroup for the duration of their visit since all come to share the same feeling, all pulsate as one. Most visitors groped their way through the rooms, but one couple – sensing themselves to be free from the censorial gaze of the other – batted the dangling LED lights about and danced wildly. "The room made you dance," they explained afterwards.[3]

It might be wondered: What does all this have to do with sensory restriction? Salter explained the thinking that went into the design of the installation in an interview with Renée Dunk:

> The *Haptic Field* experience helps people see with their eyes taken away ... The exhibition uses the "smart" technology of wearable devices – something that we now take for granted – in a non-visual way to create a sensory experience ... With

a reduced depth of field, *Haptic Field* is like moving through an alien landscape; it's like existing in a world that is actually invisible. Past participants have said it's like "living on the moon." ... When you're perceptionally disoriented, you have to rely on other senses to tell you about the world. (quoted in Dunk 2017)

In previous installation artworks, such as *Atmosphere* and *Displace*, Salter had experimented with fog machines (see Salter 2015, ch. 3). *Haptic Field* was different. The frosted goggles used in *Haptic Field* altered everything by instigating a derangement and rearrangement of the senses.

Haptic Field is situated "between art and anthropology," in Schneider and Wright's (2010) apt phrase; that is, it is an exercise in research-creation that fuses aesthetic and social scientific methodologies and generates knowledge of a profoundly sensuous – and sensible – nature (see further Born and Barry 2010; Galison and Jones 2014; Sormani, Carbone, and Gisler 2018). This is in contrast to the purely verbal or "logocentric" character of print publications, such as the ethnographic monograph, or the mainly visual (ocularcentric) character of cinematic productions, such as ethnographic film, as will be discussed further below.

Here is a sample of some of the reflections that were shared with us by audience members who participated in the *Haptic Field* research-creation experiment when it was shown in Berlin. They were elicited during the sensory ethnographic interviews (employing the methodology of participant sensation) that were held immediately after their tours:

"I was really in another world. I was gone. I was in a trance and then I thought, this is really how I'm moving through the stages of my life. I can't see ... I'm not sure where I'm going ... I sense someone else ... what is the next step ... and then I thought, this is how I move through my life."

"I felt like connected to everyone ... not caring about who he or she is ... beyond gender, beyond everything ... just connected with everything because we have the same lights and are feeling the same vibrations at the moment ... like insect species in the night ... like fireflies."

"It's like in Alice in Wonderland. Drink this and you'll get inside the ballroom."

So, did we succeed in attuning visitors to the possibility of redistributing the tangible – that is, of shared touch? Some comments hinted at this, as when one visitor remarked that "there was no boundary between my body and the space," but that was rather coarse (i.e., lacking in specificity). Did we succeed at "opening a crack" in the conventional Western sensorium (our announced intention)? Yes, judging by the response of the first visitor quoted above, who plunged deep within her soul and came back with a new grasp on her life, but then the report of the second visitor quoted above far exceeded our intentions: he articulated his experience as one of crossing species (not just cultural) boundaries and coming to perceive his fellow visitors as akin to fireflies. This excess of identification was due to the absence of any script or narrative that could have focussed his attention (but that was part of our plan). The third visitor quoted above had a transcendental experience: this impression was also voiced by others, the experience being "like a religion we do not know" in the words of one visitor, "an opportunity to get lost" suggested another (this in the age of Google maps, hence a welcome release).

Of course, there were those who resisted being drawn in: strolling the exhibition space arm-in-arm, their goggles pushed up on their foreheads, chatting. Most visitors, however, wanted to be drawn in and abjured talking so as to concentrate on trying to decode the meaning of the flashing pulses (for more reactions see Howes and Salter 2019).

Multisensory Integration: IFF's Avant-Garden Project

Immersive media art of the sort pioneered by Salter has been theorized by Isabelle Choinière, Enrico Pitozzi, and Andrea Davidson in *Through the Prism of the Senses: Mediation and New Realities of the Body in Contemporary Performance. Technology, Cognition and Emergent Research-creation Methodologies* (2020). As they state in the introduction, one of their book's main goals is "to demonstrate that immersive media art does not simply consist of a combination of various media (music and images, for example)"; rather, its essence "articulates and creates meaning in an open space of interaction between different forces staged within extended sensorial and perceptual environments" (Choinière, Pitozzi, and Davidson 2020, 17–18). In other words, intermediality – or better, intersensoriality – is one of the defining features of this genre of artwork.

In addition to highlighting the interaction of media in immersive media art, Choinière, Pitozzi, and Davidson (2020, 18) see some type of conversion or transformation produced in the audience as another essential element: "the environment becomes tactile," they write, it "produces vibrations on the surface of the spectator's skin, inducing sensations that can intervene radically on perception. In other words, a principle of transformation is called into play and *one will neither be able to perceive nor recognize this transformation until it has completed its process.*"

The emphasis in the above passage is squarely on tactility. In what follows, I would like to make a case for volatility, specifically, the volatility of smell. Smells are immersive, profoundly immersive, and the olfactory experience can be deeply transformative, but smell's potential is rarely exploited in new media art. The anosmia of the contemporary art scene has been challenged of late, for example, by "Belle Haleine: The Scent of Art" exhibition at the Tinguely

Museum in Basel, Switzerland (Howes 2015b; see also Enríquez 2018). The research-creation exercise and exhibition I describe below, called *Avant-Garden*, takes that challenge to a new level.

The objective of the project, sponsored by International Flavors and Fragrances Inc, was to create ten new olfactory sensations using a curated selection of more than forty synthetic molecules, such as Operanide and Starfleur, that had been created at IFF over the previous half century.[4] Synthetic molecules have no counterpart in nature, unlike natural or natural-identical molecules containing extracts from rose or jasmine, for example. To highlight the experimental aspect of this exercise, the project was called "Avant-Garden." It provided an opportunity for the ten Fine Fragrance perfumers – eight from New York, one from Paris, and one from São Paulo – at IFF headquarters in New York City, who were tasked with developing these new scents to think "outside the box." This was both on account of the novelty of the materials they were instructed to compose with, such as Operanide and Starfleur, and on account of the interdisciplinary composition of the working groups to which they were assigned.

Each perfumer was paired with a "scientist" whose expertise was definitely not in chemistry, but rather in linguistics (Asifa Majid) or anthropology (myself), architecture (Juhanni Palasmaa) or meteorites (Denton Ebel), sound art (Florian Hecker) or psychiatry (Mazda Adli), etc. These pairings were born of the conviction that true innovation requires "uncommon partnerships."[5] Each working group also involved the active participation of the members of the world-renowned Dutch experience design studio Polymorf, most notably Frederik Duerinck and Marcel van Brakel (see https://www.polymorf.nl/about). The deliberations of the working groups, which were quite animated and wide ranging, were orchestrated or "conducted," if you will, by the head of Creative Marketing for North America at IFF, Anahita Mekanik, herself an accomplished artist with a highly refined aesthetic sense.

Each working group met three or four times via Skype to discuss the topic they had chosen to explore. Then, based on the conversation, the perfumer was tasked with creating a new scent or series of scents using the synthetic and other molecules, and the Polymorf team was charged with fleshing out the scent – that is, creating an installation in which it could be inserted for display purposes. All ten scents were displayed at the *Avant-Garden* exhibition, which was housed in a temporary gallery on the eighth floor of IFF headquarters in New York (see figure 6). I had the opportunity to visit *Avant-Garden* in July 2018, just before it closed.

The temporary gallery was what you could call an immersive space. It was shrouded in black curtains, which swished as you brushed past them, and the light was dim. The *Avant-Garden* logo figured prominently on the signage in the entrance, and variations on it appeared on the plaques next to each of the ten

AVANT-GARDEN

by **IFF**

Figure 6. André Lenz, *Xerography*: cover illustration of the IFF Avant-Garden catalogue, 2018. Used with permission of André Lenz.

installations, some in alcoves, others in their own curtained room. There was a futuristic quality to many of the installations. This was in accordance with the creative blueprint for the initiative, which asked the participants to imagine what role scent would play in our everyday lives five or fifty years hence. By way of example, "Mood Cloud" consisted of an app designed to measure stress levels in the city and display these graphically on a monitor, while two drone-activated dirigibles floated about the room dispensing "well-feeling" scents to the stressed out.

Another particularly compelling installation, entitled "Dialect for a New Era" (the brainchild of anthropological linguist Asifa Majid and IFF perfumer

Laurent Le Guernec in conversation with Polymorf), consisted of sixteen il-
luminated pedestals. One bent over to read the words inscribed on the top of
each pedestal and pushed a button to release a blast of scent. The inscriptions,
all very eclectic and poetic, included "Being perfectly entangled with another,"
"Acting righteous because of feeling fragile in a world changing too fast," and
"The disposability of once precious goods." Of course, none of these states can
be captured in a single word, and that was the point: the scents were to be used
in place of words in this ingenious dialect for a new era. No more complaining
about the poverty of the English language when it comes to words for smell: the
scents would constitute a language of their own! A couple of ingenious (and
amusing) aroma-dispensing devices for injecting scents into a conversation
were laid out on a sideboard for visitors to play with.

The working group I was involved in was called "Sacred Now." It included
the perfumer Yves Cassar and Frederik Duerinck, Marcel van Brakel, and Peter
Boonstra of Polymorf as well as Anahita Mekanik. Early in our conversation,
the topic of the widespread yearning for "spiritual" or transcendent experiences
arose, and the discussion turned to the importance of giving people a sense of
purification and elevation. Scent, whether in the form of fragrance or smoke,
commends itself to the spiritual imagination on account of its volatility and
ephemerality, not to mention its galvanizing effect on the memory and emotions. As Michel de Montaigne put it in his *Essays*,

> I have often noticed that [scents] cause changes in me, and act on my spirits ac-
> cording to their qualities; which make me agree with the theory that the introduc-
> tion of incense and perfume into churches, so ancient and widespread a practice
> among all nations and religions, was for the purpose of raising our spirits, and of
> exciting and purifying our senses, the better to fit us for contemplation. (Mon-
> taigne, *Essays*, 1580)

How might a sense of the sacred be kindled through modern technology for
a contemporary audience, however? Here, the biggest challenge, I suggested, is
that we live in a universe of contingency and chance, where there is no overarching order. The four (sometimes five) elements of ancient Greek and medieval
cosmology – Earth, Air, Fire, Water (and Aether) – for example, used to provide
such a framework for contemplating the whole, but it had been dissolved into
the 118 elements of the Periodic Table of Elements as proposed by Mendeleev
(though he counted only sixty-three). On this account, the phenomenal world
of the senses is epiphenomenal, a world of "secondary qualities" (dependent on
the human perceptual apparatus) in contrast to the "primary qualities" of matter, such as solidity, extension, motion, and number. In *Science and the Modern
World*, Alfred North Whitehead ([1925] 1987, 99) characterized the atomic universe of modern physics as "a dull affair, soundless, scentless, colourless; merely

the hurrying of material, endlessly, meaninglessly." Coupled with this dissolution is the fact that we moderns live in an accelerated culture, a culture of speed, of velocity (Virilio 1986), which is not conducive to contemplation, only distraction.

I suggested that to meet the challenge of evoking the sacred in the context of an advanced secular society we should take the motif of the fivefold, or *quinta essentia*, as our starting point, and elaborate a system of crossmodal correspondences for the modern age. Yves Cassar composed an accord – a master scent or "engine" – in accordance with the numerological principles we had agreed on. He used five iconic IFF synthetic molecules to do so: Musk Z4, Operanide, Ambertonic, Coolwood, and Saffiano. I can attest that the harmony of this accord is so perfect that the five are experienced as one. Meanwhile, Frederik and Marcel composed a series of three moving image sequences (videoclips) and accompanying soundtracks.

There were some major logistical challenges to staging the *Sacred Now* installation, or "interface," in the language of the *Avant-Garden* exhibition catalogue (IFF 2017). The installation took the form of three fluted wooden pillars in a row, each one topped with a spinning cube. Each cube showed one of the moving image sequences, projected on its sides from within. Upon first entering the alcove with these three "totems," as Anahita called them, the cubes would be spinning too fast or too slow for one to be able to discern the images clearly. However, the pillars were equipped with sensors that charted the visitor's movements, and this data fed into a program that in turn modulated the cubes' speed of rotation. This meant that by displacing oneself this way or that, one could influence the speed at which the cube rotated atop its pedestal, and the image on its four surfaces would resolve into one continuous image. The automated scent dispenser and the soundtrack were also activated by the viewer discovering the "sweet spot" in front of the pedestal. In the words of the catalogue, "Only at a specific position in space will the viewer be able to witness the alignment of sound, scent, and sight. In that moment, perfumery finds its higher purpose by connecting with the preciousness of the ephemeral" (IFF 2017).

There was a "principle of transformation" at work in the *Sacred Now* installation, as Choinière, Pitozzi, and Davidson would be quick to note, and true to their definition of that principle, it is not possible to "perceive and recognize this transformation until its process has been completed" (2020, 18). In the instant case, completion of the process depended on the viewer activating the intersensorial algorithm that animated this multisensorial installation, which in turn precipitated a quintessential revelation of an ordered cosmos at the phenomenal level. The catalogue is not quite so transcendental in its evocation of the sublime endpoint of this process. It speaks instead of how "In a complex secular world, to capture the sublime is to find simple meaningful moments of bliss hidden in day to day reality" (IFF 2018). Either way, the installation was well suited to "fit us for contemplation," as Montaigne would say.

Sensory Decolonization: The "Sensory Entanglements" Project

The final design strategy to be discussed here could be called "sensory decolonization." It is at the heart of the "Sensory Entanglements" project, also directed by Chris Salter. This project is grounded in the collaboration of Indigenous and non-Indigenous artists and scholars from Canada (Cheryl L'Hirondelle, David Garneau, and the present writer) and Australia (Brenda Cross, r e a Saunders, Jennifer Biddle). As Salter writes,

> the team is attempting to explore the productive tension in how the "newness" of emerging technologies (despite their colonial origins and structures) might enable an "Indigenizing" of sensorial artistic experiences that disrupts historical boundaries, challenges entrenched borders, creates potential forms of culturally specific empathy, and potentially may de-colonize the representation of otherness. (2018, 89)

Cheryl L'Hirondelle is an interdisciplinary artist of mixed Cree/Métis, German/Polish ancestry, and one of the original members of the "Sensory Entanglements" research team. In December 2016, in collaboration with Plains/Woodland Cree elder Joseph Naytowhow, her artistic partner, she staged *Yahkâskwan Mîkiwahp* (or "light tipi").[6] The materials for this performance piece consisted of bundles of prairie sage and high-powered handheld flashlights. Participants were invited to convene at an open space near downtown Toronto in the falling dark. There they took up positions in a large circle, clutching their smouldering sage bundles, and were instructed to hold their flashlights up in the air in the form of the poles of a tipi. The ghostly image of a tipi took shape against the backdrop of the Toronto skyline with the CN Tower. The non-Indigenous participants in this smudging ceremony were enveloped in the clouds of smoke and interpellated in an Indigenous architectural form. This created a rupture both in the conventional ordering of the senses and of space in the dominant society, and set the stage for a sharing circle, in which Cheryl engaged the audience by sharing stories, song, and Indigenous teachings and language in a bid to connect the participants with the earth and waters, and open their hearts and minds. This performance, then, uses the media of sound, light, smoke, and scent as well as proprioception to "fit" the audience for contemplation of a more inclusive society. It implicated them in the pressing work of *conciliation* between Indigenous and non-Indigenous peoples (Robinson 2016; Garneau 2016).

Another founding member of the "Sensory Entanglements" research team is the Métis scholar, artist, and art critic David Garneau, who is an associate professor of visual art at the University of Regina, Regina, Saskatchewan. With the assistance of Garnet Willis, a technical wizard and student in the Individualized (INDI) PhD program at Concordia, David created an installation entitled *Heart Band* (see figure 7). It is an interactive sound installation

Figure 7. David Garneau and Garnet Willis, *Heart Band.* Interactive sound installation: ten painted hand drums mounted on an array and activated by sensors and electromagnetic drivers; 150 cm high, 270 cm long, 90 cm wide. 2019. Photo courtesy of Agustina Isidori.

that consists of ten hand drums featuring paintings in a Métis beaded style, arranged in a figure-eight pattern that conforms to the infinity symbol of the Métis flag. While this installation displays Métis culture, it is also "flagrantly intercultural" (Biddle 2016) due to the fact that drums are common to many musical traditions and that, in the instant case, their skins are of plastic (rather than hide) and electrified. As Garneau declares in his artist statement, this may be taken to suggest that "beneath this [Métis surface] is a bond among peoples at the level of bodies, heart, music, relations with each other and with special things" (nd).

Heart Band was to be shown at a conference at Concordia University entitled "Uncommon Senses III: The Future of the Senses" and at the "Why Sentience?" conference sponsored by the International Symposium on the Electronic Arts (ISEA). Both conferences were scheduled to take place in Montreal in May 2020. The onslaught of the COVID-19 pandemic in March 2020 resulted in both conferences having to be postponed, ISEA2020 until October 2020, and

"Uncommon Senses III" until May 2021. The ISEA2020 organizers also elected to migrate their conference online. Virtualizing the event was the only option, given the ongoing restrictions on in-person gatherings. The artists were accordingly asked to make three-minute videos of their works.

This request could have sounded the death knell for the aesthetic of *Heart Band*, since an interactive installation depends on the active corporeal presence of an audience for its completion. But it did not. Ingeniously, David saw the virtualization of his installation as an opportunity rather than an obstacle: he resolved to invite a renowned African dancer, Zab Maboungou, who lives in Montreal, to "dance the drums" and film her performance. I was fortunate to be able to attend the shoot at Zab's dance academy, the Cercle d'Expression Artistique Nyata Nyata, on "the Main" – that is, St. Lawrence Boulevard – in August 2021.

Before describing Zab's performance, let me say a few words about the objects and soundscape of the installation. David's original plan was to commission handmade drums from Métis elders in his home province, but he decided against this plan (see Garneau 2016 for an account of some of the considerations that weighed on him in making this decision). The instruments had the appearance of Métis drums – their faces painted with colourful designs in the Métis beaded style by David (see figure 8) – however, their skins were actually made of plastic and their innards were wired with sensors to detect the ambient movements of the intended audience. The sensors in turn triggered soundclips of heartbeats –David's own heartbeats, in fact. The clips were pre-recorded by Garnett Willis, using an ingenious device. First, Garnett recorded David's resting heartbeat (63 bpm) Then, David performed a series of calisthenics exercises, including jumping jacks and burpees (74 bpm). Finally, David ran up five flights of stairs and back (hitting 96 bpm). The various tracks were then looped to form sequences, and which sequence sounded, as well as the transition between them, would be determined by the closeness/distance of the members of the audience as they milled about as well as the cadence at which they moved.

Two things stand out about how the drums were wired for sound. First, unlike conventional musical instruments, which only produce sound when the musician strikes them, or blows through them, or draws a bow across their strings, the drums are contactless, rather like the theremin. Second, the drums could be seen as sentient beings: they were designed to sense movements and produce sounds all on their own. In other words, they appeared to be animated. This allusion to the so-called animistic world views of Indigenous peoples was deliberate, but it was not the case that the drums were "alive" or attributed "agency" by their human maker, as in the conventional anthropological account of animism (see Matthews and Roulette 2018 for a critique of this account). The drums were not "animate things," but rather embodiments

Figure 8. David Garneau and Garnet Willis, *Heart Band* (details). Photos by Barbara Willis Sweete, used courtesy of Garnet Willis.

of a "relational ontology." The latter view eschews essentialism and objectification at once:

> instead of seeing all entities as having a preexisting essence … [it] asserts that entities only emerge when they are in relation with other entities … This means [apprehending or] studying persons and things not in terms of who or what they *are* (i.e., their essence), but what they do in terms of their capacity to act and affect. (Mopas and Huybregts 2020, 37)

The projected interaction of human and other-than-human "actants" at the heart of David's installation, with its emphasis on relationality and technologically distributed sensing, gives powerful expression both to Indigenous understandings and to the emergent notion of "the more-than-human sensorium" (Lupton and Maslen 2018).

Next, consider all of the cultural and intercultural layers to *Heart Band*, especially when it came to be performed by Zab. First, there is the fact of the artist's identity as Métis. Second, there are the drums, which in this work are both symbols of traditional Métis culture and symbols of the electronic arts (hence of the wider electronic culture of the "sensor society") due to being wired with sensors that play back electrified cadences. Third, as the crowning touch, there is Zab's performance of the installation. This was due to happenstance, admittedly, but it could equally be seen from the perspective of Choinière, Pitozzi, and Davidson (2020, 18) as the "completion" of the artwork, as when they write "a principle of transformation is set up; and one cannot perceive and recognize this transformation until its process has been completed."

It bears underlining that while Zab was engaged as a stand-in for the (absent) intended audience, her role extended far beyond that. She was the prime mover, the prime mediator. Of Franco-Congolese origin, she brought her African ancestry to the activation of the installation. This resulted in a triangulation of the artwork: David's artwork – Zab's enactment of the artwork – the audience's experience of the artwork via video. This triangulation transcended (and also extended) the bounds of the "Sensory Entanglements" project, which, as will be recalled, was centred on the coming together of Indigenous and non-Indigenous artists and scholars from Canada and Australia. Zab's intervention gave an even more radical intercultural dimension to the project, reconstituting it as a tri-continental research-creation collaboratory. The interplay of the senses was keyed to the interplay of cultures, and vice versa, a point we shall come back to presently.

Turning now to Zab's performance on 11 August, during the rehearsal, which lasted about twenty minutes, Zab familiarized herself with the drums, trying out various gestures and dance movements. During the performance, which also lasted about twenty minutes, she began by addressing the drums:

three steps forward, three steps back, sometimes shaking her dangling right
arm, bending forward and backward from the abdomen, her eyes fixed on
some distant plane, her concentration total. She always approached the drums
orthogonally, never straight on. Then, she started introducing a twirl into her
movements (see figure 9) as she pivoted from one drum to the next while circling the platform. In the next sequence, she would take up a position *between*
two drums (two pairs of drums in particular) and play them with different
parts of her body – gyrating her pelvis, flapping her chest, etc. This had the
effect of transmuting the heartbeats into distinct musical phrases, discernible
rhythms before she moved on and the cacophony of heartbeats resumed, or the
drums she was dancing went silent.

A couple of times, Zab placed her right hand on the drum with a handprint
design, but this was to commune with it, not to strike it (see figure 10). At the
climactic moment of the performance, she balanced on her left leg and leaned
well back, her right leg pointed toward a drum, and the sole of her right foot almost touching it. She held this gravity-defying pose for close to thirty seconds.
The graceful tension of her body was palpable. (I know because I was seated
right under and just to the side of the arch she formed with her back.) And then
she broke into a whirling dance, pirouetting around the platform in a frenzied
(but controlled) pace until she arrived at a spot where she stood stock-still, and
the drums went silent.[7]

Zab and I spoke afterwards, together with David (via video link), and Florencia Marchetti (who coordinated the event), and one of Zab's former students, Diane Roberts, who (like Florencia) is enrolled in the research-creation
stream of the Interdisciplinary Humanities PhD Program at Concordia. Zab
expounded on her philosophy of dance, both verbally and corporeally. Our
conversation put me in mind of François Laplantine's (2020) recent article on
choreography as a methodology for sensory ethnography. I noted that in my
practice of (non-filmic) sensory ethnography, I am compelled to "linguify"
meaning. She responded that "movement is meaning," and related the following incident: Michael Crabb, dance critic for the *Toronto Star*, had gone to see
her dance and the next evening attended a lecture she was giving. Afterwards,
Crabb confided to Zab, "You talk just like you dance." It is rare to be so fluent in
language and the body at once.

We also talked about how African dance differs from Western ballet. (I know
dance anthropologist Cynthia Jean Cohen Bull would have smiled on this discussion [see *supra* p. 158].) Zab noted that ballet was invented in the court of
Louis XIV, the "Sun King," whose authority derived directly from God (ges-
turing straight up). This verticality is reflected in the straight back of the ballet
dancer. "No protuberances," Zab said, thrusting her rump out and her chest
forward, to evoke the contrast with African dance. African dance is also distinguished by its earthiness (feet stomping firmly on the ground), with none

Figure 9. Zab Maboungou completing *Heart Band* by dancing the drums. Photo courtesy of Florencia Marchetti.

of the emphasis on weightlessness and airiness of ballet. Zab calls her academy Cercle d'Expression Aristique Nyata Nyata (meaning Earth Earth) accordingly.

In a particularly telling move, Zab crouched, with her legs apart, and made a scooping movement with her pelvis. This motion could be perceived as sexy, were it not so fecund. It is "from the loins that the world is *enfantée* [peopled]," she explained. Zab implied that there was a sacral element to her pelvic gestures: an opening of the body to the gods. Perhaps it was significant that the angle of this gesture was parallel to the earth rather than directed upward (like when we were discussing Louis XIV).

Our conversation ranged over many other topics, each one more revelatory of cultural and sensorial difference. "Sound is space and space is sound," she said, which nicely encapsulated the ambience of the performative sensory environment she had just enacted. Or, again: "Space is not empty, it has all kinds of presences, such as ancestors. Our ancestors are not 'departed,' they live on in us,

Figure 10. Zab Maboungou hand-to-hand with one of the drums. Photo courtesy of Agustina Isidori

and around us." These remarks were accompanied by a sweeping gesture with her arms, which took in the surrounding space horizontally – again, unlike when we were discussing the heaven-derived authority of the Sun King.[8]

We intended to show *Heart Band* live at "Uncommon Senses III" in May 2021. The idea was to invite the audience to interact with the installation while we recorded their movements, then invite them to watch the video of Zab's performance, and then have them tour the installation anew, tracking how their movements were altered (or not). This triangulation would augment the intercultural dimension of the audience's experience of the installation and open another crack in the Western sensorium. Unfortunately, the COVID-19 pandemic made it impossible for us to carry out this plan, as the Uncommon Senses III conference had to be held online, so the day of reckoning for our research-creation experiment has been postponed.

Conclusion: Intermediality Is the Message

This chapter has presented an autoethnographic account of experimentation with three design strategies for the creation of immersive intermedia art: sensory restriction, multisensory integration, and sensory decolonization as exemplified by Salter's *Haptic Field* installation; Schafer's *Theatre of the Senses* and the *Avant-Garden* exhibition at IFF; and the "Sensory Entanglements" research project. The preceding analysis has shown that one of the defining features of the performative sensory environment is that it is multimodal by design, or what Bissera Pentcheva (2006) would call a "synesthesis." This interactive integration of the senses evokes a sense of the whole, which challenges entrenched borders, both between the senses and between bodies, and thereby creates the conditions for a more inclusive perception of society and the cosmos.

Marshall McLuhan is famous for the suggestion that "the medium is the message" (McLuhan and Fiore 1967).[9] What is the message of the performative sensory environment? It is that "intermediality is the message," and with intermediality comes intersensoriality, and with intersensoriality (of the kind imagined by Salter and company) there comes the possibility of enhanced intercultural empathy and communication.

By way of closing, let me cite one last example of an installation that gives expression to the intersensorial and intercultural dimensions of cross-cultural intermedia art. Jeneen Frei Njootli is a Gwich'in interdisciplinary artist, originally from Whitehorse, who is known for her intense performance pieces, many of which centre on the caribou. A piece called *Herd* evokes the threat to the caribou (and her peoples') continued existence due to the opening up of oil and gas development in the caribou breeding grounds along the Yukon border with Alaska. "In *Herd*, she grinds a set of caribou antlers with power tools, then amplifies and distorts the screech. The audience is given ear plugs and respiratory masks — bone dust and the smell of burning antler fill the air" (Ngao 2018). Frei Njootli's "noise performances" have a profoundly visceral impact. This sensory assault is intended to jar the audience into recognition of the advanced state of environmental (and cultural) degradation under late capitalism. "Our elders say that if there are no caribou, we'll all cease to exist … The caribou and we are intertwined" (quoted in Ngao 2018).

The message of Frei Njootli's piece is intercultural: a critique of the depredations of capitalism from an Indigenous perspective. Its power stems from its intermediality. Its message is also ecological: humanity's fate is "intertwined" with the fate of the caribou. As such, Frei Nootjli's work raises the notion of "the more-than-human sensorium" a level, through incorporating an *interspecies* perspective into the mix.

The sensations and sentiments mobilized by *Herd* are decidedly discordant. At the same time, by underscoring the discord the work gestures toward the possibility of a concord or "synesthesis" by inspiring us to contemplate the revolutionary potential of striving for an *ecology of the senses*.[10] Our lives as humans, like the lives of the caribou, are in the balance – that is, in the "*ratio* of the senses" (McLuhan 1962).

Notes

Prologue: Coming to Our Senses

1 For an excellent introduction to Serres' take on human sensuousness, see "Michel Serres' Five Senses" (Connor 2005).

2 On the linguistic turn, see Surkis 2012; on the pictorial turn, see Mitchell [1992] 1994.

3 For the derivation of this phrase (which comes from Marx 1987), see Dawkins and Loftus 2013. As will become apparent, however, we mean rather more by it.

4 This is in contrast to the philosopher Merleau-Ponty's doctrine of "the prereflective unity of the senses" in the *Phenomenology of Perception* (1962).

5 Influential statements regarding the relationship between language and perception include *Language, Thought and Reality* (Whorff 1956) and *The Tractatus Logico-Philosophicus* (Wittgenstein [1922] 2020).

6 This quotation is from "Introducing Sensory Studies" (Bull et al. 2006, 5) in the inaugural issue of *The Senses and Society*. The anthropologist Clifford Geertz puts this point well in the following passage, where he contests the psychologization of meaning, and vouches for

> The perception that meaning, in the form of interpretable signs – sounds, images, feelings, artefacts, gestures – comes to exist only within ... ways of worldmaking; that it arises within the frame of concrete social interaction in which something is a something for a you and a me, and not in some secret grotto in the head. (Geertz 1986, 112–13)

7 This quote comes from *Archaeology and the Senses* by Yannis Hamilakis. Hamilakis proposes a bold new multisensory vision for a "sensorial archaeology" that has many points in common with the present Manifesto for Sensory Studies. The full quote reads:

> the field of archaeology, having primary access to the materiality of the world, is in a privileged position to explore the sensuous arenas and to contribute immensely to the broader discussion on sensorial experience and its *social-power effects* ... [by] deriving a new understanding (which will also engender a

new practice) of the entanglement between materiality and human sensory and sensuous action and experience … The senses are infinite and innumerable, and an archeology of sensoriality can in fact contribute to the exploration of hitherto unrecognized sensory modalities. (Hamilakis 2014, 5, 9)

8   This quote is also from "Introducing Sensory Studies" (Bull et al. 2006, 5).

9   We think here, for example, of Charles Fourier's political economy of the senses and critique of the sensory ills of the civilization of his day, and of Margaret Cavendish's feminist epistemology of the senses and vision of a woman-centred community. The critical sensory philosophies and politics of Fourier and Cavendish are discussed by Constance Classen in *The Color of Angels* (1998).

10   On sensory ethnography, see Laplantine 2015 and Howes 2019a; on sensory history, see Classen 2001 and Corbin 2005; on research-creation, see Schneider and Wright 2010, Galison and Jones 2014, and Salter 2015.

11   This Manifesto is keyed to works published or translated into English, but the interdiscipline of sensory studies, as articulated in "Introducing Sensory Studies" (Bull et al. 2006), has actually become thoroughly multilingual and international in the intervening years. Notable contributors include Danièle Dubois, Marie-Luce Gélard, Christine Guillebaud, David Le Breton, and Jean-Paul Thibaud; Olga Sabido Ramos, Rosario Caballero, and Javier E. Díaz Vera; Bettina Beer and Holger Schulze; Mikkel Bille and Tim Flohr Sørensen; Mirko Zardini and Vincent Battesti; Helmi Järviluoma and Rajko Muršič; Keizo Miyasaka and Dong Shaoxin.

12   Many of the 101 chapters in *Senses and Sensation* were published in non-mainstream journals or obscure (and occasionally out-of-print) books, or were never previously published (e.g., conference papers, exhibition project narratives). Some of the other chapters in the compendium were edited by the present writer or rewritten by the contributor. This reference work can serve as a handy companion to the present Manifesto, but it is not essential, for I have endeavoured to extract the essence of each of the chapters assembled there and elaborate on their key points in what follows.

13   This definition of research-creation comes from a grant application written by Chris Salter entitled "RE-CREATE: Research Creation as Culture and Practice."

14   On stillness, see Vinge 1975; on the spectatorial, see Rorty [1979] 2017; on locomotion, see Ingold 2004 and Sheets-Johnstone 1999; and, on perception as enaction, not representation, see Noë 2006.

15   The "more-than-human sensorium" encompasses, for example, plant-sensing (Myers 2015) and machine intelligence (Salter 2022), the "liveliness" of materials (Ingold 2011) or "vibrancy" of matter (Bennett 2010), the datafication of life (Lupton and Maslen 2018), and much, much else.

1 On the Geography and Anthropology of the Senses

1   Rodaway (1994) insists that "interest in sensuous geographies is not new." His framing of it certainly was, though, and there really is no comparison between the

approach he launched and the "perception geography" of the 1960s and 1970s. The latter was behavioural in orientation whereas the orientation of sensuous geography is decidedly cultural.

2 Ambiance also figures in the name of a network, the International Ambiances Network, which emerged out of the Centre de recherche sur l'espace sonore et l'environnement urbain (CRESSON), under the direction of Jean-Paul Thibaud of the Graduate School of Architecture of Grenoble, France. The derivation of the Ambiances Network from CRESSON is analogous to the derivation of "multimodal anthropologies" from visual anthropology: many out of one.

3 A third is the geography of tourism (see Crang 1999; Edensor 2002; Obrador-Pons 2007; Lynch n.d.). On the anthropology of displacement see Yoshimizu 2022.

4 Seeger (1975) was as influenced by the media theory of Marshall McLuhan as the structuralist theory of Claude Lévi-Strauss. This influence can be seen in the way he treats Suyà body decorations as infratechnological "extensions of the senses" and the Suyà sensorium as a combinatory.

5 The following sources provide additional insight into the origin and development of the anthropology of the senses: Howes 1991; Seremetakis 1994b, 2019; Classen 1997; Herzfeld 2001, ch. 11; Bendix and Brenneis 2005; Robben and Slukka 2007; Hsu 2008; Pink 2009; Porcello et al. 2010; Pink and Howes 2010; Ingold and Howes 2011; Howes 2015a; Cox, Irving, and Wright 2016; Elliott and Culhane 2017; Howes 2019a.

6 Representative ethnographies include Feld [1982] 1990; Desjarlais 1992, 2003; Roseman 1993; Sutton 2001; Geurts 2002; Farquhar 2002; Howes 2003; Pink 2004; Downey 2005; Hahn 2007; Hirschkind 2009; Throop 2010; Barcan 2011; Irving 2016. See further Hamilakis 2014, and Skeate and Day 2020 for an account of the sensorial turn in archaeology.

7 There is an obvious tie-in here to the "more-than-representational" tendency in the new cultural geography (see Lorimer 2005).

8 There are currently multiple ethnographers and philosophers who engage with dance. See, for example, Davida 2011; Dankworth and David 2014; and Manning 2009.

9 The medium of film has also been hailed within geography as the most affective way to evoke the "more-than-human" (see J. Lorimer 2010).

2 On the History and Sociology of the Senses

1 On Huizinga's founding contribution to cultural history, see Ankersmit 2005 and Midgley 2012. On Febvre's role in the establishment of the Annales School, see Burguiere 2009.

2 I invited Alain Corbin to write "Histoire et anthropologie sensorielle" (1990). It was first published in a special issue of *Anthropologie et Sociétés* on the theme of "Les cinq sens" (Howes 1990b). I remain deeply indebted to him for accepting my invitation and instigating what has proved to be such a productive cross-disciplinary dialogue.

3 Mark Smith is also the editor of the Studies in Sensory History series from University of Illinois Press (recently transferred to Penn State University Press and rebaptised Perspectives on Sensory History). Importantly, the series is concerned "not simply with the way people thought about the senses but also the full social and cultural *contexts* of [sensory] experiences," to quote from the series description (emphasis added).

4 Berlin was "the twentieth century's paradigmatic space" (Bornemann, quoted in Brill 2010), the argument goes, in the same way Paris figured as the cultural capital of the nineteenth century.

5 Benjamin was the author of many aphorisms that have inspired other cultural critics (e.g., Taussig 1993) but have had a somewhat pernicious impact on sensory historiography because they are aphorisms, not historical points. Brill is to be lauded for enucleating these aphorisms. For example, she points out that when Benjamin discusses "tactility" he is not referring to the haptic per se, but to a mode of perception (or way of sensing) that represents a unique conjugation of the senses. Richard Cavell (2002) and Norm Friesen ([2011] 2018) have performed a similar service for McLuhan's writings, which are also replete with aphorisms or what are often now called "sound bites."

6 Other areas of sociology in which a sensory studies approach has made significant inroads include the sociology of work (Fine 1996, 1998), the sociology of "multiculture" (Rhys-Taylor 2017), and the sociology of everyday life (Kalekin-Fishman and Low 2010; Vannini et al. 2012; Highmore 2011). The emphasis throughout this literature is on understanding "the senses as interaction" (Vannini, Waskul, and Gottschalk 2012), or, to put this another way, how the senses are "relationally produced" in everday life (Dawkins and Loftus 2013).

7 Van Campen (2007) had already written an important book on synaesthesia – the "hidden sense," he called it – before tackling Proust.

8 The novelty of Harris analysis should not distract us from its antiquity; basically, she (re)discovered the Aristotelian common sense. Her analysis also invites comparison with pulse-taking in Siddha (Ayurvedic) medicine, as will be discussed in chapter 8.

3 On the Psychology and Neurobiology of the Senses in Historical and Cross-Cultural Perspective

1 I owe the kaleidoscope analogy to McLuhan ([1964] 1994) and the figure of a fugue of the five senses to Lévi-Strauss ([1969] 1979, 147–64).

2 Classen elaborates on the reasoning behind classifying speech as a sense:

> The thought of speech as a sense seems odd to us moderns. This is partly because we conceive of the senses as passive recipients of data, whereas speech is an active externalization of data. It is also because we think of the senses as natural faculties and speech as a learned acquirement. The ancients, however, had different ideas on the matter. They were apt to think of the senses more as

media of communication than as passive recipients of data. The eyes, for example, were believed to perceive by issuing rays which touched and mingled with the objects to which they were directed. (Classen 1993b, 2, emphasis added)

3 I am indebted to Richard Newhauser for bringing these references to my attention.

4 Where does the psi faculty come from? "The symbol Ψ (psi) has long been used to represent the 'general psychical world' ... in contradistinction to the 'general physical world' represented by Φ [phi]" (Schoch and Yonavjak 2008, 9). Hence the term "psi faculty." The extreme mentalism of parapsychology is otherwise reflected in the term "anomalous cognition," which is the latest term for ESP.

5 By way of example of the revolution (not evolution) of the sensorium, consider Walter Ong's (1982) periodization of the phases to the technologization of the word: "primary orality" (referring to the dominant form of communication in oral societies), "chirographic," "typographic" (referring to successive forms of literate society), and "secondary orality" (referring to the instantaneity and face-to-device-to-face quality of electronic communication in the wired society of today). The successive phases, then, actually form a loop. See further Howes 1991, 170–5 and 2003, 113–21; Classen 1993b, ch. 6.

6 This phrase deliberately echoes the Saussurian notion that language consists of "differences without positive terms" (Saussure 1959). That said, there are problems with using a linguistic model to conceptualize how the senses function (see Howes 2003, ch. 1).

7 Actually, McLuhan was more a Thomist (than an Aristotelian) at heart, and he also had an ear for Joyce (see Cavell 2002).

8 Regarding the revelation of the molecular world beneath the five senses, see Locke (1975), whose thoughts on perception were very much influenced by advances in microscopy.

9 For an early example of cross-cultural, cross-modal experimental design, see Wober 1991.

10 For example, I cannot see how the fact that "most of us" in the urban West set our home thermostats "to a fairly uniform 17–23°C (63–73°F)" has anything to do with the ambient temperature of life on the African Savvanah, the birthplace of humanity (Spence 2021, 29–30). There are far too many cultural (and technological and commercial) forces that have impinged on the definition of comfort (see, e.g., Crowley 2005) – or "the comfort zone" in modern parlance – during the intervening eons for it to be possible to trace unilineal descent. The idea that our reliance on air conditioning and/or central heating is "selected" by evolution is rather a stretch, particularly when there are so many other "solutions" to hand: if it's too cold, for example, one can put on more clothing.

11 Spence has, in fact, consulted for numerous major corporations ("from Johnson & Johnson to Unilver, from Asahi to the VF corporation, and from Dulux to Durex," to mention but a few, so his research on crossmodal correspondences has become embedded in the design of many commodities and technomediated "experiences."

12 As a contribution to affect theory, Massumi's essay bristles with newness, but in other respects it is old hat. In the 1960s and 1970s Bateson and his circle already extended their theory of interaction patterns and pathologies from animal communication to marriage counselling to international relations (see Watzlawick, Bavelas, and Jackson 1981). Thus, when Massumi imports Bateson's model of animal communication into his discussion of politics, he is actually leading us down a path that has been thoroughly charted before. Furthermore, the problem with Massumi's affectively charged theory of transindividual "forces" is that it lacks an adequate theory of perception (Kane 2015).

4 The Modern Sensorium: A Case Study in Sensory History, 1920–2001

1 See the "Taste and Smell" episode of the documentary *Human+: The Future of Our Senses*, directed by Vincent Bathélémy, produced by Bonne Pioche/Idéacom International. Interestingly, astronomers now report that the gas clouds of the Milky Way taste like raspberry and smell like rum. This discovery is due to the development of astrochemistry, which, together with acoustic astronomy, means that astrophysicists are no longer confined to gazing upon the stars and planets through the lens of a telescope. The seventeenth-century German philosopher and mystic Jakob Boehme, with his celestial alchemy of the senses, might see confirmation for his sensory cosmology in this discovery (see Classen 1998, ch. 1).
2 For example, regarding inequalities arising from the racialization of the senses, see Le Breton (2017), Stoever (2016), Sekimoto and Brown (2020), and Hsu (2020); see further Howes (2019b) on the need to "trouble law's sensorium."

5 Melanesian Sensory Formations: A Comparative Case Study in Sensory Ethnography

1 This term "sensorial revolution" would not be used until 2006 (Howes 2006). At the time of Stoller's lecture in Montreal (i.e., 1989), anthropology was in the grip of the "secondary textual revolution" – that is, the "writing culture" (Clifford and Marcus 1986) movement. (The "primary textual revolution" had been instigated by Clifford Geertz, with his idea of "reading culture" or cultures "as texts" [see Howes 1990a and 2003, 17–23 but also Howes, Geertz, and Lambert 2018].) Stoller's work straddled this divide: it was an "experiment in ethnographic writing" that invoked/ evoked the senses as its distinguishing feature.
2 I went in search of an oral society and what did I find? Ironically, at Budoya I met people who fondly remembered Maria von Trapp (portrayed as Louisa in *The Sound of Music*) and recalled her time with them as a golden age of orality. For example, thanks to her coaching, the Budoya choir won all the local singing competitions, even against choirs coached by Tongan missionaries (who were reputed to have the best voices in the Pacific). This tradition continues. Making my way

back to my lodgings at the Roman Catholic mission station each night, I could hear voices joined in song, as people practised for the upcoming opening of a new hospital on neighbouring Goodenough Island. While the night air was (still) alive with the songs Maria taught them (see Chandler 2017), people lamented the fact that their incantations no longer had the same force as in the days of their ancestors. My female companion on a hike to the hotsprings at Deïdei was disappointed and apologized for the fact that the spells she uttered failed to cause the spirit of the water to "awake" (i.e., shoot up).

3 The spectacular hotsprings at Deïdei were captured on film by the oceanographer Jacques Cousteau in one of his many documentaries (though not the smell, of course).

4 The voyage of the *Melanesian Explorer* is the subject of a documentary film by Dennis O'Rourke called *Cannibal Tours*.

5 On Dobu, I heard tell of some matriarchs who participated in the Kula ring on the same footing as the men. In the Trobriands, women have their own parallel system of exchange, centring on the transfer of banana-leaf bundles (see Weiner 1976).

6 Significantly, when I went with two companions by motorboat from Ambunti to Tongwinjamb to attend a marriage feast, we also stopped at a beach, just short of our destination, and there (in marked contrast to Massim custom), my companions bid me to join in a meal. "But we are going to a feast!" I protested. Better to eat up now, they responded, to be safe (i.e., not risk consuming food that has been ensorcelled by strangers). It was awkward not to eat any of the food that was offered to me at the marriage feast, and I relented, but not without some trepidation.

6 "A New Age of Aesthetics": Sensory Art and Design

1 Candlin's larger point is that this theoretical othering of touch is belied by numerous actual practices, such as the tactile intimacy between art object and connoisseur, and that it is possible to contemplate an aesthetics of touch that is not beholden to vision (Candlin 2010; see further Classen 1998, ch. 6; Rée 2000)

2 Miodownik (2013, xviii) states that "there is a scientific discipline especially dedicated to systematically investigating our sensual interaction with materials" (2013, xviii) – namely, psychophysics. However, it must be said that the methodology of psychophysics has come in for serious critique in recent years, and is steadily being supplanted by sensory studies methodologies (Howes 2015b; Lahne and Spackman 2018)

3 The point of departure for Laura Marks' theory of haptic visuality is a series of distinctions originally introduced by Alois Riegl (see Marks 2000, 162). It is to be wondered whether Marks' recuperation of Riegl's art history does not inject a perverse (neo)orientalism (see Candlin 2010) into the contemporary discourse on the senses in cinema.

4 The anthropology of the senses as applied to art is exploding many Western aesthetic canons: see Schneider and Wright 2010; Cox, Irving, and Wright 2016; Edwards, Gosden, and Phillips 2006; Classen and Howes 2006; Howes and Classen 2014, ch. 2).

5 Classen also makes the point that synaesthesia is but one of many forms of intersensoriality employed by the artists of this period – an important corrective to Ramachandran's position, as discussed in chapter 1.

7 Sensory Museology: Bringing the Senses to Museum Visitors

1 In addition to smell and taste now figuring as suitable topics for investigation and exhibition (e.g., *The Art of Scent 1889–2012* show at the Museum of Art and Design, New York, in 2013; *Belle Haleine: The Scent of Art* at the Museum Tinguely, Basel, in 2015), there is a growing emphasis on the multisensoriality of museum objects and on the importance of enabling visitors to experience "the properties of things" directly instead of only via labels or being told what to look for (Edwards, Gosden, and Phillips 2006; Dudley 2009, 2012; Enriquez 2018). This stress on the experiential is one of the hallmarks of sensory museology. For a useful overview of these developments, see *The Multisensory Museum: Cross-Disciplinary Perspectives on Touch, Sound, Smell, Memory, and Space* (2014), edited by Nina Levent, formerly the executive director of Art Beyond Sight, and Alvaro Pascual-Leone, professor of neurology at Harvard Medical School.

2 At first, hands-on offerings at mainstream museums tended to be child-oriented, in keeping with the modern notion of touch as an "infantile" or "primitive" means of comprehending the world (see Classen 2001, 2012). Adults, it was assumed, would better relate to museum exhibits through the more "mature" and "intellectual" medium of sight. At the turn of the twenty-first century, however, curators recognized that visiting children were accompanied by adults and, in fact, often provided a motivation for adults to visit a museum. Hands-on activities involving the whole family were therefore increasingly made available. As one scholar of museum display practices has written, "Today the value of touch for every museum visitor is widely recognized" (Pearson 1991, 122).

3 Martina Bagnoli had already curated a number of highly acclaimed, sensational exhibitions at the Walters, including *Treasures of Heaven* (Bagnoli et al. 2010; see further Classen 2017). She belongs to the avant-garde of the sensory turn in museology.

4 The press release can be found here: https://www.cooperhewitt.org/2018/02/27/cooper-hewitt-smithsonian-design-museum-to-present-the-senses-design-beyond-vision/.

5 The abstract for Lupton's talk at Uncommon Senses III reads as follows:
   This crunchy, slurpy, brainy talk explores how designers can engage the human body. "Ocularcentrism" is the dominance of vision over all other senses in modern society. The empire of the eye excludes people who touch, hear,

or smell but do not see. Inclusive design practices range from eyes-free interaction design and audio description to typographies and topographies of touch. Opening up to all our other senses not only includes more people but reveals new possibilities for visual design as well.

6 We think here of what Jennifer Biddle (2016) calls the "remote avant-garde" – that is, the work of the Aboriginal artists of the community art centres of the Australian Outback whose aesthetic experiments often outflank those of the cosmopolitan avant garde through their ingenious combinations of local materials and technology, such as claymation films that employ substances that "belong country" (e.g., clay, ochre, etc.) and "mark" or "enliven" the local in the process (see *supra* p. 155). Likewise, as regards technological breakthroughs like, for example, the cochlear implant, it has been shown that the effectiveness of such devices depends heavily on the home language environment and diverse other social, economic, political, and intimate factors (Lloyd and Tremblay 2021). Finally, there are the many inspiring examples of everyday pursuits and practices, such as knitting or making your own cyanometer as presented by Anna Harris in *A Sensory Education* (2021), which do not require a studio or museum setting to be valorized.

7 The conjugation of sight and hearing was elaborated further at the contemporaneous *Soundscapes* exhibition at the National Gallery in London. Six musicians and sound artists were each invited to choose a painting from the collection and compose a soundtrack. In this way visitors were enabled to "hear the painting" and also "see the music." The soundtracks were not mere literal renditions of the depicted scenes, though. Rather, they were contrapuntal, interweaving the audio and the visual to create a kind of fugue of the senses, or "synesthesis" (Pentcheva 2006).

8 It is an interesting question whether Baumgarten would have approved of Flying Object's technologization of the aesthetic, and whether Benjamin would have seen it as a distraction, or something more

9 Reference could likewise be made here to the poetry of Baudelaire or the paintings of Gustave Moreau – or, even better, to the canvases of the Spanish Surrealist painter Remedios Varo (see Classen 1998, 109–22, 131–4). Ultimately, what all these manifestations of cross-modality in art gesture towards, if we follow Bateson (1973), is that "Art is about relationships."

10 For my part, though I never witnessed the show, courtesy of Tom Pursey, I did have a chance to sample the chocolate that was used to "lead" the experience of Bacon's painting. Biting it set off a dust storm in my mouth, which still lingers in the palate of my imagination. This tasting was at the Oxford meeting of the Aesthetic Network in September 2017, where Pursey gave a presentation on *Tate Sensorium*, commented on by Charles Spence and David Lomas. The Aesthetic Network (2015–18) was dedicated to evaluating methods of aesthetic inquiry across disciplines. For a sample of the Aesthetic Network's research output, see the special issue of *The Senses and Society* edited by Dee Reynolds and Boris Wiseman (2018).

8 Performative Sensory Environments: Alternative Orchestrations of the Senses in Contemporary Intermedia Art

1 Other names for this modality-splicing genre (i.e., research-creation) within anthropology include art-ethnography (Schneider and Wright 2013), multimodal anthropologies (Collins, Durington, and Gill 2017), imaginative ethnography (Elliott and Culhane 2017; Kazubowski-Houston and Auslander 2021), and transmissions or "the tactical combination of making and communicating" as framed by the contributors to *Transmissions* (Jungnickel 2020).
2 See Kirk McKenzie's (2006) entry on the Patria Cycle for the *Canadian Encyclopedia*.
3 There is a short video of *Haptic Field* available at https://vimeo.com/240738010 (accessed 15 August 2020).
4 Operanide is described as "ultra-amber, intense, balanced"; Starfleur is character- ized as "crystaline, luminous, crisp." The thirty synthetic molecules have been plot- ted on a graph with four cardinal points: Water, Life, Energy, and Transformation (IFF 2017).
5 Like four of the other nine scientists, I was referred to IFF by the Norwegian olfac- tory artist Sissel Tolaas, who was the advisor to the Scientific Committee for the Avant-Garden project. Like them (full disclosure), I received an honorarium for my role in the project.
6 There is a short video of *Yahkâskwan Mîkiwahp* (or "light tipi") available at https://www.youtube.com/watch?v=dZmcbEA1Q9Y (accessed 15 August 2020).
7 There is a short video of Heart Band at https://sensoryentanglements.org/All-Art- works (accessed 15 November 2020).
8 To pursue this discussion further, see Zab's book *Heya ... Danse! Historique, poé- tique et didactique de la danse africaine* (Maboungou 2005).
9 Or "the medium is the massage" in the original title of McLuhan's book with Fiore. This title was due to a typo, which McLuhan decided to keep, on account of the multiple readings of the book's main point it permitted: Message, Mess Age, Massage, Mass Age, all of which are accurate. See https://en.wikipedia.org/wiki/ The_Medium_Is_the_Massage (accessed 15 August 2020).
10 Jeneen Frei Njootli's installation, like Cheryl L'Hirondelle's performance piece, stands for an interculturally inspired social ecology of the senses. There is nothing quite like it in the anthropological or psychological literature to date: neither J.J. Gibson's (1979) conception of an "ecological psychology" of perception nor even Bateson's (1973) idea of an "ecology of mind" come close. The sociality of the Njootli and L'Hirondelle pieces also set them apart from other artistic interven- tions, like the Ice Watch installation by the Icelandic eco-artist Olafur Eliasson and Danish geologist Minik Rosing (Chaberski 2019).

References

Abrahamson, D. 2020. "Strawberry Feel Forever: Understanding Metaphor as Sensorimotor Dynamics." *The Senses and Society* 15 (2): 216–38. https://doi.org /10.1080/17458927.2020.1764742.

Alpers, S. 1983. *The Art of Describing: Dutch Art in the Seventeenth Century.* Chicago: University of Chicago Press.

Amato, J. 2001. *Dust: A History of the Small and the Invisible.* Berkeley, CA: University of California Press.

Anderson, B. 1983. *Imagined Communities.* London: Verso.

Anderson, G. 2004. *Reinventing the Museum: Historical and Contemporary Perspectives on the Paradigm Shift.* Walnut Creek, CA: Altamira Press.

Anderson, S.R., and D.W. Lightfoot. 2002. *The Language Organ: Linguistics as Cognitive Physiology* Cambridge: Cambridge University Press.

Ankersmit, F. 2005. *Sublime Historical Experience.* Stanford, CA: Stanford University Press.

Aporta, C. 2005. "Satellite Culture: Global Positioning Systems, Inuit Wayfinding, and the Need for a New Account of Technology." *Current Anthropology* 46 (5): 729–46.

– 2006. *Anijaarniq: Introducing Inuit Landskills and Wayfinding.* Nunavut: Nunavut Research Institute. CD-ROM.

Appadurai, A., ed. 1983. *The Social Life of Things.* Cambridge: Cambridge University Press.

Archer, J. 2005. *Architecture and Suburbia: From English Villa to American Dream House, 1690–2000.* Minneapolis: University of Minnesota Press.

Armstrong, T. 2005. "The Senses and the Self." In *Modernism: A Cultural History.* Cambridge: Polity Press.

Arnheim, R. 1969. *Visual Thinking.* Berkeley: University of California Press.

Aron, C.S. 1999. *Working at Play: A History of Vacations in the United States.* Oxford: Oxford University Press.

Astor-Aguilera, M., and G. Harvey, eds. 2018. *Rethinking Relations and Animism: Personhood and Materiality.* London: Routledge.

Atkins, P.W. 1997. *The Periodic Kingdom of the Elements*. New York: Basic Books.

Bacci, F., and D. Melcher, eds. 2011. *Art and the Senses*. Oxford: Oxford University Press.

Bagnoli, M., ed. 2010. *Treasures of Heaven: Saints, Relics and Devotion in Medieval Europe*. London: British Musueum Press.

– 2018. "*A Feast for the Senses* at The Walters Art Museum (Exhibition Project Narrative)." In *Senses and Sensation IV*, edited by D. Howes, 389–406. Abingdon: Routledge.

Banes, S., and A. Lepecki, eds. 2007. *The Senses in Performance*. London and New York: Routledge.

Barasch, M. 2001. *Blindness: The History of a Mental Image in Western Thought*. London: Routledge.

Barcan, R. 2011. *Complementary and Alternative Medicine: Bodies, Senses, Therapies*. Abingdon: Routledge.

Barker-Benfield, G.J. 1992. *The Culture of Sensibility: Sex and Society in Eighteenth Century Britain*. Chicago: University of Chicago Press.

Barnes, D.S. 2006. *The Great Stink of Paris and the Nineteenth-Century Struggle against Filth and Germs*. Baltimore: Johns Hopkins University Press.

Baron-Cohen, S., and J. Harrison, eds. 1997. *Synaesthesia: Classic and Contemporary Readings*. Oxford: Blackwell.

Barr, J. 1970. *The Assaults on Our Senses*. London: Methuen and Co. Ltd.

Barthes, R. 1972. *Mythologies*. Translated by A. Lavers. London: Paladin.

Bateson, G. 1973. *Steps to an Ecology of Mind*. St. Alban's: Granada.

Baudelaire, C. 1978. *The Painter of Modern Life and Other Essays*. New York: Garland.

Baudrillard, J. 1983. *Simulations*. New York: Semiotext(e).

Bauman, Z. 1988. "Is There a Postmodern Sociology?" In *Postmodernism*, edited by M. Featherstone. London: Sage.

Baxandall, M. 1972. *Painting and Experience in Fifteenth Century Italy*. Oxford: Oxford University Press.

Baxandall, R., and E. Ewen. 2000. *Picture Windows: How the Suburbs Happened*. New York: Basic Books.

Bégin, C. 2016. *Taste of the Nation: The New Deal Search for America's Food*. Champaign: University of Illinois Press.

Belasco, W.J. 2007. *Appetite for Change: How the Counterculture Took on the Food Industry*. Ithaca, NY: Cornell University Press.

Bembibre, C., and M. Strlič. 2017. "Smell of Heritage: A Framework for the Identification, Analysis and Archival of Historic Odours." *Heritage Science* 5 (2). https://doi.org/10.1186/s40494-016-0114-1.

Bendix, R. 2005. "Time of the Senses?" *Current Anthropology* 45 (4): 688–90.

Bendix, R., and D. Brenneis, eds. 2005. Special issue, "The Senses." *Etnofoor* 18 (1).

Benjamin, W. (1936) 1973. "The Work of Art in the Age of Mechanical Reproduction." In *Illuminations*. Harmondsworth: Penguin Books.

Bennett, J. 2010. *Vibrant Matter: A Political Ecology of Things*. Durham, NC: Duke University Press.

Bennett, T. 1995. *The Birth of the Museum: History, Theory, Politics*. London: Routledge.

Benthien, C. 2002. *Skin: On the Cultural Border between Self and the World*. New York: Columbia University Press.

Bently, L., and L. Flynn, eds. 1996. *Law and the Senses: Sensational Jurisprudence*. London: Pluto Press.

Berger, J. 1972. *Ways of Seeing*. Harmondsworth: Penguin Books.

– 1991. *About Looking*. Toronto: Random House.

Berger, P., and T. Luckmann. 1966. *The Social Construction of Reality: A Treatise in the Sociology of Knowledge*. Garden City, NY: Doubleday.

Bergson, H. (1908) 1991. *Matter and Memory*. New York: Zone.

Berlin, P., and B. Kay. 1969. *Basic Color Terms: Their Universality and Evolution*. Berkeley: University of California Press.

Bernstein, L.E., E. Auer, and J.K. Moore. 2004. "Audiovisual Speech Binding." In *The Handbook of Multisensory Processes*, edited by G. Calvert, C. Spence, and B.E. Stein. Cambridge, MA: MIT Press.

Betts, E., ed. 2017. *Senses of the Empire: Multisensory Approaches to Roman Culture*. Abingdon: Routledge.

Biddle, J. 2003. *Breasts, Bodies, Canvas: Central Desert Art as Experience*. Sydney: UNSW Press.

Biddle, J. 2016. *Remote Avant-Garde: Aboriginal Art under Occupation*. Durham, NC: Duke University Press.

Bijsterveld, K. 2015. "Ears-On Exhibitions: Sound in the History Museum." *Public Historian* 37 (4): 73–90. https://doi.org/10.1525/tph.2015.37.4.73.

Bille, M., and T.F. Sørensen. 2016. "Into the Fog of Architecture." In *Elements of Architecture: Assembling Archaeology, Atmosphere and the Performance of Building Spaces*, edited by M. Bille and T.F. Sørensen, 1–23. London: Routledge.

Bilstein, R. 2003. "The Airplane and the American Experience." In *The Airplane in American Culture*, edited by D. Pisano. Ann Arbor: University of Michigan Press.

Binter, J. 2014. "Unruly Voices in the Museum: Multisensory Engagement with Disquieting Histories." *The Senses and Society* 9 (3): 342–60. https://doi.org/10.2752/174589314X14023847039674.

Black, G. 2005. *The Engaging Museum: Developing Museums for Visitor Involvement*. Oxford: Routledge.

Blackman, L. 2012. *Immaterial Bodies: Affect, Embodiment, Mediation*, London: Sage.

Bleek, W., and L.C. Lloyd. 2009. *Bushman Presentiments*. In *The Sixth Sense Reader*, edited by D. Howes, 93–6. Abingdon: Routledge.

Blesser, B., and L.R. Salter. 2009. *Spaces Speak: Are You Listening? Experiencing Aural Architecture*. Cambridge, MA: MIT Press.

Böhme, G. 2016. *The Aesthetics of Atmospheres*. Edited by J.-P. Thibaud. London: Routledge.

Borges, J. 1962 "Pierre Menard, Author of the Quixote." In *Labyrinths: Selected Stories and Other Writings*. New York: New Directions.

Born, G., and A. Barry. 2010. "Art-science: From Public Understanding to Public Experiment." *Journal of Cultural Economy* 3 (1): 103–19. https://doi.org/10.1080/17530351003617610.

Bossomaier, T.R.J. 2012. *Introduction to the Senses: From Biology to Computer Science*. Cambridge: Cambridge University Press.

Bottles, S.L. 1987. *Los Angeles and the Automobile: The Making of the Modern City*. Berkeley: University of California Press.

Bourdieu, P. (1979) 1984. *Distinction: A Social Critique of the Judgment of Taste*. Cambridge, MA: Harvard University Press.

Bowden, R. 1983. *Yena: Art and Ceremony in a Sepik Society*. Oxford: Pitt Rivers Museum.

Bremner, A.J., S. Caparo, J. Davidoff, J.W. de Fockert, K. Linnell, and C. Spence. 2013. "'Bouba' and 'Kiki' in Namibia? A Remote Culture Make Similar Shape-Sound Matches, but Different Shape–Taste Matches to Westerners." *Cognition* 126: 165–72. https://doi.org/10.1016/j.cognition.2012.09.007.

Brill, D. 2010. *Shock and the Senseless in Dada and Fluxus*. Hanover, NH: University Press of New England.

Broadie, A. 2003. *The Cambridge Companion to the Scottish Enlightenment*. Cambridge: Cambridge University Press.

Broglio, R. 2008. *Technologies of the Picturesque: British Art, Poetry and Instruments, 1750–1830*. Lewisburg, PA: Bucknell University Press.

Buck-Morss, S. 1992. "Aesthetics and Anaesthetics: Walter Benjamin's Artwork Essay Reconsidered." *October* 62: 3–41. https://doi.org/10.2307/778700.

Bull, C.J.C. 1997. "Sense, Meaning and Perception in Three Dance Cultures" In *Meaning in Motion: New Cultural Studies in Dance*, edited by J. Desmond, 269–88. Durham, NC: Duke University Press.

Bull, M. 2000. *Sounding Out the City: Personal Stereos and the Management of Everyday Life*. Abingdon: Routledge.

– 2006. "Iconic Designs: The Apple iPod." *The Senses and Society* 1 (1): 105–8.

– ed. 2018. *The Routledge Companion to Sound Studies*. London: Routledge.

Bull, M., and L. Back, eds. (2003) 2016. *The Auditory Culture Reader*. Abingdon: Routledge.

Bull, M., P. Gilroy, D. Howes, and D. Kahn. 2006. "Introducing Sensory Studies." *The Senses and Society* 1 (1): 5–7. https://doi.org/10.2752/174589206778055655.

Bunkše, E.V. 2007. "Feeling is Believing, or Landscape as a Way of Being in the World." *Geografiska Annaler: Series B, Human Geography* 89 (3): 219–31. https://doi.org/10.1111/j.1468-0467.2007.00250.x.

Burguiere, A. 2009. *The Annales School: An Intellectual History*. Translated by. J.M. Todd. Ithaca, NY: Cornell University Press.

Burnett, C., M. Fend, and P. Gouk, eds. 1991. *The Second Sense: Studies in Hearing and Musical Judgment from Antiquity to the Seventeenth Century*. London: Warburg Institute.

Burr, C. 2002. *The Emperor of Scent: A True Story of Perfume and Obsession*. New York: Random House.

Butler, S., and A. Purves, eds. 2013. *Synaesthesia and the Ancient Senses*. London: Routledge.

Buttimer, A. 2010. "Humboldt, Granö and Geo-poetics of the Altai." *Fennia* 188 (1): 11–36.

Bynum, W.F., and R. Porter, eds. 1993 *Medicine and the Five Senses*. Cambridge: Cambridge University Press.

Cahill, P.A. 2009. "Take Five: Renaissance Literature and the Five Senses." *Literature Compass* 6 (5): 1014–30. https://doi.org/10.1111/j.1741-4113.2009.00656.x.

Calame-Griaule, G. 1986. *Words and the Dogon World*. Translated by D. La Pin. Philadelphia, PA: Institute for Human Values.

Callard, F., and C. Papoulias. 2010. "Affect and Embodiment." In *Memory: Histories, Theories, Debates*, edited by S. Radstone and B. Schwarz. New York: Fordham University Press.

Calvert, G., C. Spence, and B. Stein, eds. 2004. *The Handbook of Multisensory Processes*. Cambridge, MA: MIT Press.

Calvino, I. 2005. "Under the Jaguar Sun." In *Empire of the Senses*, edited by D. Howes, 304–17. Abingdon: Routledge.

Candlin, F. 2010. "Sensory Separation and the Founding of Art History." In *Art, Museums and Touch*, 9–27. Manchester: Manchester University Press.

Cardeña, E., S.J. Lynn, and S. Krippner, eds. 2000. *Varieties of Anomalous Experience: Examining the Scientific Evidence*. Washington, DC: American Psychological Association.

Carpenter, E. 1973. *Eskimo Realities*. Toronto: Holt, Rinehart and Winston.

Carson, R. 1962. *Silent Spring*. New York: Houghton Mifflin.

Casini, S. 2017. "Synesthesia, Transformation and Synthesis: Toward a Multi-sensory Pedagogy of the Image." *The Senses and Society* 12 (1): 1–17. https://doi.org/10.1080/17458927.2017.1268811.

Cavell, R. 2002. *McLuhan in Space: A Cultural Geography*. Toronto: University of Toronto Press.

Çelik, Z. 2006. "Kinaesthesia." In *Sensorium: Embodied Experience, Technology and Contemporary Art*, edited by C.A. Jones, 159–62. Cambridge, MA: MIT List Visual Arts Center and MIT Press.

Chaberski, M. 2019 "Resensing the Anthropocene: Ambividual Experiences in Contemporary Performative Arts." In *Emerging Affinities: Possible Futures of Performative Arts*, edited by M. Borowski, M. Chaberski, and M. Sugiera, 149–74. Berlin: transcript Verlag.

Chandler, J. 2017. "How *The Sound of Music*'s Von Trapp Family Ended up Teaching Music in PNG." https://www.abc.net.au/news/2017-02-06/trapp-family-singers-missionary-legacy-lives-on-in-png-choir/8211156. Accessed 15 August 2020.

Chatterjee, H. 2008. *Touch in Museums: Policy and Practice in Object Handling*. Oxford: Berg.

Chatterjee, H., S. Vreeland, and G. Noble. 2009. "Museopathy: Exploring the Healing Potential of Handling Museum Objects." *Museum and Society* 7 (3): 164–77.

Chenhall, R., T. Kohn, and C.S. Stevens. 2021. *Sounding Out Japan: A Sensory Ethnographic Tour.* Abingdon: Routledge.

Choinière, I., E. Pitozzi, and A. Davidson. 2020. *Through the Prism of the Senses: Mediation and New Realities of the Body in Contemporary Performance. Technology, Cognition and Emergent Research-creation Methodologies.* Bristol: Intellect Books.

Clark, A. 2008. *Supersizing the Mind: Embodiment, Action, and Cognitive Extension.* Oxford: Oxford University Press.

Clark, C.E. 1986. *The American Family Home: 1800–1960.* Durham, NC: University of North Carolina Press.

Classen, C. 1991. "Literacy as Anti-Culture: The Andean Experience of the Written Word." *History of Religions* 30 (4): 404–21.

– 1993a. *Inca Cosmology and the Human Body.* Salt Lake City: University of Utah Press.

– 1993b. *Worlds of Sense: Exploring the Senses in History and Across Cultures.* London and New York: Routledge.

– 1997. "Foundations for an Anthropology of the Senses." *International Social Science Journal* 49 (153): 401–12. https://doi.org/10.1111/j.1468-2451.1997.tb00032.x.

– 1998. *The Color of Angels: Cosmology, Gender and the Aesthetic Imagination.* London: Routledge.

– 2001. "The Senses." In *Encyclopedia of European Social History*, vol. 4, edited by P. Stearns. New York: Charles Scribner's Sons.

– ed. 2005a. *The Book of Touch.* Abingdon: Routledge.

– 2005b. "McLuhan in the Rainforest: The Sensory Worlds of Oral Cultures." In *Empire of the Senses*, edited by D. Howes, 147–63. Abingdon: Routledge.

– 2009. "Green Pleasures: Sustainable Cities and the Senses." *Harvard Design Magazine* 31.

– 2012. *The Deepest Sense: A Cultural History of Touch*, Champaign: University of Illinois Press.

– 2014a. "Art and the Senses: From the Romantics to the Futurists." In *A Cultural History of the Senses in the Age of Empire, 1800–1920*, edited by C. Classen, 185–210. London: Bloomsbury.

– ed. 2014b. *A Cultural History of the Senses.* 6 vols. London: Bloomsbury.

– ed. 2014c. *A Cultural History of the Senses in the Age of Empire, 1800–1920,* London: Bloomsbury.

– 2014d. "Touching the Deep Past: The Lure of Ancient Bodies in Nineteenth-Century Museums and Culture." *The Senses and Society* 9 (3): 268–83. https://doi.org/10.2752/174589314X14023847039872.

– 2017. *The Museum of the Senses: Experiencing Art and Collections.* London and New York: Bloomsbury.

– 2019. "The Senses at the National Gallery." *The Senses and Society* 15 (1): 85–97. https://doi.org/10.1080/17458927.2020.1719744.

Classen, C., and D. Howes. 2006. "The Museum as Sensescape: Western Sensibilities and Indigenous Artefacts." In *Sensible Objects: Colonialism, Museums and Material Culture*, edited by E. Edwards, C. Gosden, and R.V. Phillips, 199–222. Abingdon: Routledge.

Classen, C., D. Howes, and A. Synnott. 1994. *Aroma: The Cultural History of Smell*. London: Routledge.

Clifford, J., and G. Marcus, eds. 1986. *Writing Culture: The Politics and Poetics of Ethnography*. Berkeley: University of California Press.

Clintberg, M. 2014. "Where Publics May Touch: Stimulating Sensory Access at the National Gallery of Canada." *The Senses and Society* 9 (3): 310–22. https://doi.org/10.2752/174589314X14023847039755.

Clintberg, M. 2017. "'My enlightenment is born and propagated through my guts': Alimentary Art, 1917–2017." *The Senses and Society* 12 (3): 267–81. https://doi.org/10.1080/17458927.2017.1367486.

Cobussen, M., V. Meelberg, and B. Truax, eds. 2017. *The Routledge Companion to Sound Art*. London: Routledge.

Cohen, M. 1994. "The Art of Profane Illumination." *Visual Anthropology Review* 10: 44–9. https://doi.org/10.1525/var.1994.10.1.44.

Cohn, S.A. 1999. "A Historical Review of Second Sight: The Collectors, Their Accounts and Ideas." *Scottish Studies* 33: 146–85.

Collins, S.G., M. Durington, and H. Gill. 2017. "Multimodality: An Invitation." *American Anthropologist* 119 (1): 142–6.

Condillac, E.B. de. (1754) 2002. *Treatise on the Sensations*. Manchester: Clinamen Press.

Connerton, P. 1989. *How Societies Remember*. Cambridge: Cambridge University Press.

Connor, S. 1997. *Postmodernist Culture*. Oxford: Blackwell.

– 2004. "Edison's Teeth: Touching Hearing." In *Hearing Cultures: Essays on Sound, Listening and Modernity*, edited by V. Erlmann, 153–72. Abingdon: Routledge.

Connor, S. 2005. "Michel Serres' Five Senses." In *Empire of the Senses*, edited by D. Howes, 318–34. Abingdon: Routledge.

– 2006. "The Menagerie of the Senses." *The Senses and Society* 1 (1): 9–26.

Corbin, A. (1982) 1986. *The Foul and the Fragrant: Odor and the French Social Imagination*. Translated by M.L. Kochan, R. Porter, and C. Prendergast. Cambridge, MA: Harvard University Press.

– 2005. "Charting the Cultural History of the Senses." In *Empire of the Senses*, edited by D. Howes, 128–42. Abingdon: Routledge.

– 1990. "Histoire et anthropologie sensorielle." *Anthropologie et sociétés* 14 (2): 13–24.

– (1994) 1998. *Village Bells: Sound and Meaning in the 19th-century French Countryside*. New York: Columbia University Press.

Corbin, A., and G. Heuré. 2000. *Alain Corbin. Historien du sensible. Entretiens avec Gilles Heuré*. Paris: Editions la Découverte.

Corbin, A. 2018. *A History of Silence: From the Renaissance to the Present Day*. Cambridge: Polity.

Corn, J.J. 1983. *The Winged Gospel: America's Romance with Aviation*. Oxford: Oxford University Press.

Cornish, P. 2017. "Sensing War: Concept and Space in the Imperial War Museum's First World War Galleries." In *Modern Conflict and the Senses*, edited by N. Saunders and P. Cornish, 13–28. London: Routledge.

Cosgrove, D. (1984) 1998. *Social Formation and Symbolic Landscape*. Madison: Wisconsin University Press.

Counihan, C., and S. Høglund, eds. 2018. *Making Taste Public*. London: Bloomsbury.

Cox, R., A. Irving, and C. Wright, eds. 2016. *Beyond Text? Critical Practices and Sensory Anthropology*. Manchester: Manchester University Press.

Crang, M. 1999. "Knowing, Tourism and Practices of Vision." In *Leisure/Tourism Geographies: Practices and Geographical Knowledge*, edited by D. Crouch. London: Routledge.

Creadick, A.G. 2010. *Perfectly Average: The Pursuit of Normality in Postwar America*. Amherst: University of Massachusetts Press.

Crowley, J. 2005. "Homely Pleasures: The Pursuit of Comfort in the Eighteenth Century." In *The Book of Touch*, edited by C. Classen, 82–91. Abingdon: Routledge.

Csordas, T. 1990. "Embodiment as a Paradigm for Anthropology." *Ethos* 18 (1): 5–47. https://doi.org/10.1525/eth.1990.18.1.02a00010.

– ed. 1994. *Embodiment and Experience: The Existential Ground of Culture and Self.* Cambridge: Cambridge University Press.

Cundy, A. 2017. "War, Memory and the Senses in the Imperial War Museum, 1920–2014." In *Modern Conflict and the Senses*, edited by N. Sauders and P. Cornish, 361–74. London: Routledge.

Curtis, N. 2010. *The Pictorial Turn*. London: Routledge.

Daniel, V. 1991. "The Pulse as an Icon in Siddha Medicine." In *The Varieties of Sensory Experience*, edited by D. Howes, 100–10. Toronto: University of Toronto Press.

Danius, S. 2002. *The Senses of Modernism: Technology, Perception and Aesthetics*. Ithaca, NY: Cornell University Press.

Dankworth, L., and A. David, eds. 2014. *Dance Ethnography and Global Perspectives: Identity, Embodiment, and Culture*. London: Palgrave Macmillan.

Dant, T. 1999. *Material Culture in the Social World*. London: Open University Press.

– 2005. *Materiality and Society*. New York: McGraw-Hill.

Davida, D., ed. 2011. *Fields in Motion: Ethnography in the Worlds of Dance*. Waterloo: Wilfrid Laurier University Press.

Dawkins, A., and A. Loftus. 2013. "The Senses as Direct Theoreticians in Practice." *Transactions of the Institute of British Geographers* 38: 665–77.

de Boer, W. 2013. "The Counter-Reformation of the Senses." In *The Ashgate Research Companion to the Counter-Reformation*, edited by A. Bamji, G.H. Janssen, and M. Laven. Farnham, Surrey: Ashgate.

de Certeau, M. 1983a. "The Madness of Vision." *Enclitic* 7 (1).

– 1983b. *The Practice of Everyday Life*. Berkeley: University of California Press.

Degen, M. 2008. *Sensing Cities: Regenerating Public Life in Barcelona and Manchester.* London: Routledge.

– 2014. "The Everyday City of the Senses." In *Cities and Social Change: Encounters with Contemporary Urbanism*, edited by R. Paddison and E. McCann, 92–112. London: Sage.

Degen, M., and G. Rose. 2012. "Experiencing Designed Urban Environments: The Senses, Walking and Perceptual Memory." *Urban Studies* 49 (15): 3271–87.

DeSalle, R. 2018. *Our Senses: An Immersive Experience.* New Haven, CT: Yale University Press.

Descola, P. 2013. *Beyond Nature and Culture.* Chicago: University of Chicago Press.

Desjarlais, R. 1992. *Body and Emotion*, Philadelphia: University of Pennsylvania Press.

– 2003. *Sensory Biographies.* Berkeley: University of California Press.

Dias, N. 2004. *La mesure des sens. Les anthropologues et le corps humain au XIXe siècle.* Paris: Aubier.

Douglas, G.H. 1996. *Skyscrapers: A Social History of the Very Tall Building in America.* Jefferson, NC: McFarland & Company.

Douglas, M. 1973. *Natural Symbols.* London: Routledge.

– 1982. *In the Active Voice.* London: Routledge.

Downey, G. 2005. *Learning Capoeira*, Oxford: Oxford University Press.

– 2007. "Seeing with a 'Sideways Glance': Visuomotor 'Knowing' and the Plasticity of Perception." In *Ways of Knowing: New Approaches in the Anthropology of Experience and Learning*, edited by M. Harris, 222–41. Oxford: Berghahn Books.

Drewal, H.T. 2012. "Creating Mami Wata: An Interactive, Sensory Exhibition." *Museum Anthropology* 35 (1): 49–57. https://doi.org/10.1111/j.1548-1379.2012.01121.x.

Drobnick, J., ed. 2006. *The Smell Culture Reader.* Abingdon: Routledge.

Dudley, S., ed. 2009. *Museum Materialities: Objects, Engagements, Interpretations.* London: Routledge.

– ed. 2012. *Museum Objects: Experiencing the Properties of Things.* London: Routledge.

– 2014. "What's in the Drawer? Surprise and Proprioceptivity in the Pitt Rivers Museum." *The Senses and Society* 9 (3): 296–309.

Dugan, H. 2011. *The Ephemeral History of Perfume: Scent and Sense in Early Modern England.* Baltimore, MD: Johns Hopkins University Press.

Dundas, J. 1985. "'To See Feelingly': The Language of the Senses and the Language of the Heart." *Comparative Drama* 19 (1): 49–57.

Dundes, A. 1980. *Interpreting Folklore.* Bloomington: Indiana University Press.

Dunk, R. 2017. "Christopher Salter's Haptic Field: 'Its like living on the moon.'" https://www.concordia.ca/cunews/main/stories/2017/06/26/christopher-salters-haptic-field-its-like-walking-on-the-moon.html. Accessed 15 August 2020.

Durie, B. 2005. "Doors of Perception." *New Scientist*, 29 January 2005, 185 (2484): 34–6.

Eagleton, T. 1990. *The Ideology of the Aesthetic.* Oxford: Blackwell.

Eck, D. 1998. *Darsan: Seeing the Divine Image in India.* 3rd ed. New York: Columbia University Press.

Edensor, T. 2002. *Tourists at the Taj: Performance and Meaning at a Symbolic Site.* London: Routledge.

Edensor, T. 2007. "Sensing the Ruin." *The Senses and Society* 2 (2): 217–32. https://doi .org/10.2752/174589307X203100.

– ed. 2010. *Geographies of Rhythm.* Farnham, Surrey: Ashgate.

– 2012. "The Rhythm of Tourism." In *Real Tourism: Practice, Care and Politics in Contemporary Travel Culture*, edited by C. Minca and T. Oakes. London: Routledge.

Edensor, T., and S. Sumartojo. 2015. "Designing Atmospheres: Introduction to Special Issue." *Visual Communication* 14 (3): 251–65. https://doi.org/10.1177 /1470357215582305.

Edwards, E., and K. Bhaumik, eds. 2008. *Visual Sense: A Cultural Reader.* Oxford: Berg.

Edwards, E., C. Gosden, and R. Phillips, eds. 2006. *Sensible Objects: Colonialism, Museums and Material Culture.* Abingdon: Routledge.

Eidsheim, S. 2015. *Sensing Sound: Singing and Listening as Vibrational Practice.* Durham, NC: Duke University Press.

Elliott, C. 2012. "Taste^{TM}: Interrogating Food, Law and Color." *The Senses and Society* 7 (3): 276–88.

– 2019. "Sensorium®: The Splash of Sensory Trademarks." *Canadian Journal of Law and Society* 34 (2): 243–59. DOI: https://doi.org/10.1017/cls.2019.13.

Elliott, D., and D. Culhane, eds. 2017. *A Different Kind of Ethnography: Imaginative Practices and Creative Methodologies.* Toronto: University of Toronto Press.

Enríquez, L.E. 2018. "Perfume: A Sensory Journey through Contemporary Scent." *The Senses and Society* 13 (1): 126–30.

Erlmann, V., ed. 2004. *Hearing Cultures: Essays on Sound, Listening, and Modernity.* Oxford: Berg.

Euchner, C. 1963. *Nobody Turn Me Around: A People's History of the 1963 March on Washington.* Boston: Beacon Press.

Evans, J., and S. Hall, eds. 1999. *Visual Culture: The Reader.* London: Sage.

Ewen, S. 1988. *All-Consuming Images: The Politics of Style in Contemporary Culture.* Boston: Basic Books.

Fabian, J. 1983. *Time and the Other: How Anthropology Makes Its Object.* New York: Columbia University Press.

Farquhar, J. 2002. *Appetites: Food and Sex in Post-Socialist China.* Durham, NC: Duke University Press.

Featherstone, M. 1991. *Consumer Culture and Postmodernism.* London: Sage.

Febvre, L. (1942) 1982. *The Problem of Unbelief in the Sixteenth Century: The Religion of Rabelais.* Translated by B. Gottlieb. Cambridge, MA: Harvard University Press.

Feibel, J. 2000. "Highland Histories: Jacobitism and Second Sight." *Clio* 30 (1): 51–77.

Feld, S. (1982) 1990. *Sound and Sentiment: Birds, Weeping, Poetics and Song in Kaluli Expression.* 2nd ed. Philadelphia: University of Pennsylvania Press.

– 1991. "Sound as a Symbolic System: The Kaluli Drum." In *The Varieties of Sensory Experience*, edited by D. Howes, 79–99. Toronto: University of Toronto Press.

– 1996. "Waterfalls of Song." In *Senses of Place*, edited by S. Feld and K. Basso, 91–135. Santa Fe, NM: School of American Research Press.

– 2005. "Places Sensed, Senses Placed: Toward a Sensuous Epistemology of Environments." In *Empire of the Senses*, edited by D. Howes, 179–91. Abingdon: Routledge.

Feld, S., and D. Brenneis. 2004. "Doing Anthropology in Sound." *American Anthropologist* 31 (4): 461–74.

Findlay, V. 2002. *Colour: Travels through the Paintbox*. London: Hodder and Stoughton.

Fine, G.A. 1996. *Kitchens: The Culture of Restaurant Work*. Berkeley: University of California Press.

– 1998. *Morel Tales: The Culture of Mushrooming*. Cambridge, MA: Harvard University Press.

Fingarette, H. 1972. *Confucius – The Secular as Sacred*. Longworth, IL: Waveland Press.

Finnegan, R. 2002. *Communicating: The Multiple Modes of Human Interconnection*. London: Routledge.

Fisher, M.F.K. "The Pale Yellow Jacket." In *Serve It Forth*. New York: Macmillan.

Flying Object and T. Chatfield. 2018. "Tate Sensorium (Exhibition Project Narrative)." In *Senses and Sensation*, vol. 3, edited by D. Howes, 375–84. Abingdon: Routledge.

Fortune, R. 1963. *Sorcerers of Dobu*. New York: E.P. Dutton.

Foucault, Michel. 1973. *The Birth of the Clinic: An Archaeology of Medical Perception*. Translated by A.M. Sheridan Smith. New York: Random House.

– 1979. *Discipline and Punish: The Birth of the Prison*. Translated by A.M. Sheridan Smith. New York: Vintage Books.

Friedan, B. 1963. *The Feminine Mystique*. New York: Norton.

Friedman, A.M. 2016. "Perceptual Construction: Rereading *The Social Construction of Reality* through the Sociology of the Senses." *Cultural Sociology* 10 (1): 77–92. https://doi.org/10.1177%2F1749975515615149.

– 2016. "'There Are Two People at Work That I'm Fairly Certain Are Black': Uncertainty and Deliberative Thinking in Blind Race Attribution." *Sociological Quarterly* 57 (3): 437–61. https://doi.org/10.1111/tsq.12140.

Friedner, M., and S. Helmreich. 2015. "Sound Studies Meets Deaf Studies." *The Senses and Society* 7 (1): 72–86. https://doi.org/10.2752/174589312X13173255802120.

Friesen, N. (2011) 2018. "Vision and the Training of Perception: McLuhan's Medienpädagogik." *Enculturation: A Journal Of Rhetoric, Writing And Culture* 12.

Fuller, S. 2000. *Thomas Kuhn: A Philosophical History for Our Times*. Chicago: University of Chicago Press.

Gabaccia, D.R. 2000. *We Are What We Eat: Ethnic Food and the Making of Americans*. Cambridge, MA: Harvard University Press.

Gadoua, M.-P. 2014. "Making Sense through Touch: Handling Collections with Inuit Elders at the McCord Museum." *The Senses and Society* 9 (3): 323–41. https://doi.org/10.2752/174589314X14023847039719.

Galison, P., and C.A. Jones, eds. 2014. *Picturing Science, Producing Art*. London: Routledge.

Garneau, D. 2016. "Imaginary Spaces of Conciliation and Reconciliation: Art, Curation, and Healing." In *Arts of Engagement: Taking Aesthetic Action In and Beyond the Truth and Reconciliation Commission of Canada*, edited by D. Robinson and K. Martin, 21–41. Waterloo: Wilfrid Laurier University Press.

Gavrilyuk, P.E., and S. Coakley, eds. 2011. *The Spiritual Senses: Perceiving God in Western Christianity*. Cambridge: Cambridge University Press.

Gay, M. 2015. *The Electric Brain: The Dramatic High-Tech Race to Merge Minds and Machines*. New York: Farrar, Straus and Giroux.

Gearin, A.K., and O.C. Sáez. 2021. "Altered Vision: Ayahuasca Shamanism and Sensory Individualism." *Current Anthropology* 62 (2): 138–63.

Geary, J. 2002. *The Body Electric: An Anatomy of the New Bionic Senses*. London: Weidenfeld and Nicolson.

Geertz, C. 1957. "Ethos, World-View and the Analysis of Sacred Symbols." *Antioch Review* 14 (4): 421–37. https://doi.org/10.2307/4609997.

– 1973. *The Interpretation of Cultures*. Boston: Basic Books.

– 1986. "The Uses of Diversity." *Michigan Quarterly Review* 25 (1): 105–23.

– 2000. "Common Sense as a Cultural System." In *Local Knowledge*, 164–78. Boston: Basic Books.

Gélard, M.-L., ed. 2016. "Contemporary French Sensory Ethnography." Special issue, *The Senses and Society* 11 (3).

Geurts, K.L. 2002. *Culture and the Senses: Bodily Ways of Knowing in an African Community*. Berkeley: University of California Press.

– 2005. "Consciousness as 'Feeling in the Body': A West African Theory of Embodiment, Emotion and the Making of Mind." In *Empire of the Senses*, edited by D. Howes, 164–78. Abingdon: Routledge.

Geurts, K.L., and E.G. Adikah. 2006. "Enduring and Endearing Feelings and the Transformation of Material Culture in West Africa." In *Sensible Objects: Colonialism, Museums and Material Culture*, edited by E. Edwards, C. Gosden, and R.B. Phillips, 35–60. Abingdon: Routledge.

Gibson, J.J. (1966) 1983. *The Senses Considered as Perceptual Systems*. New York: Praeger.

– 1979. *The Ecological Approach to Visual Perception*. Boston: Houghton Mifflin.

Gilman, S. 1988. *Goethe's Touch: Touching, Seeing and Sexuality*. New Orleans: Graduate School of Tulane University.

Giucci, G. 2012. *The Cultural Life of the Automobile: Roads to Modernity*. Translated by A. Mayagoitia and D. Nagao. Austin: University of Texas Press.

Goldstein, E.B. 2002. *Sensation and Perception*. 6th ed. Pacific Grove, CA: Wadsworth.

Goodwin, C. 1994. "Professional Vision." *American Anthropologist* 96 (3): 606–33.

Goswamy, B.N. 2005. "Rasa: Delight of the Reason." In *The Taste Culture Reader*, edited by C. Korsmeyer, 215–25. London: Bloomsbury.

Grace, J. 2020. *Multiple Multisensory Rooms: Myth Busting the Magic*. Abingdon: Routledge.

Graif, P. 2018. *Being and Hearing: Making Intelligible Worlds in Deaf Kathmandu.* Chicago: HAU Books.

Granö, J.G. 1925. *Atlas of Finland.* Finland: Helsinki.

– (1929) 1997. *Pure Geography.* Edited by O. Granö and A. Paasi. Translated by M. Hicks. Baltimore and London: Johns Hopkins University Press.

Granö, O., and A. Paasi. 1997. "Preamble: The Intellectual and Social Contexts of J.G. Granö's *Pure Geography.*" In *Pure Geography*, by J.G. Granö, xiv–xxvii. Baltimore and London: Johns Hopkins University Press.

Grasseni, C., ed. 2007. *Skilled Visions: Between Apprenticeship and Standards.* Oxford: Berghahn Books.

Gregor, M.J. 1983. "Baumgarten's Aesthetica." *Review of Metaphysics* 37: 357–85.

Gregory, C. 2011. "Skinship: Touchability as a Virtue in East-Central India." *HAU: Journal of Ethnographic Theory* 1 (1): 179–209.

Griffin, J.H. 2004. *Black Like Me.* San Antonio, TX: Wings Press.

Grimshaw, A. 2001. *The Ethnographer's Eye: Ways of Seeing in Modern Anthropology.* Cambridge: Cambridge University Press.

Grond, F., and T. Hermann. 2014. "Interactive Sonification for Data Exploration." *Organized Sound* 19: 41–51. https://doi.org/10.1017/S1355771813000393.

Hahn, T. 2007 *Sensational Knowledge: Embodying Culture through Japanese Dance.* Middletown, CT: Wesleyan University Press.

Halliday, S. 2013. *Sonic Modernity: Representing Sound in Literature, Culture and the Arts.* Edinburgh: Edinburgh University Press.

Halpern, O. 2014. *Beautiful Data: A History of Vision and Reason since 1945.* Durham, NC: Duke University Press.

Hamilakis, Y. 2014. *Archeology and the Senses: Human Experience, Memory and Affect.* Cambridge: Cambridge University Press.

Hammer, G. 2019. *Blindness through the Looking Glass: The Performance of Blindness, Gender, and the Sensory Body.* Ann Arbor: University of Michigan Press.

Harris, A. 2016. "Listening-touch: Affect and the Crafting of Medical Bodies through Percussion." *Body and Society* 22 (1): 31–61. https://doi.org/10.1177/1357034x15604031.

– 2020. *A Sensory Education.* Abingdon: Routledge.

Harvey, E., ed. 2003. *Sensible Flesh: Touch in Early Modern Culture.* Philadelphia: University of Pennsylvania Press.

Heelas, P., and A. Lock, eds. 1979. *Indigenous Psychologies.* London: Academic.

Hein, L., and M. Selden. 1997. "Commemoration and Silence: Fifty Years of Remembering the Bomb in America and Japan." In *Living with the Bomb: American and Japanese Cultural Conflicts in the Nuclear Age*, edited by L. Hein and M. Selden. New York: East Gate.

Heitmann, J. 2009. *The Automobile and American Life.* Jefferson, NC: McFarland & Company.

Heller-Roazen, D. 2007. *The Inner Touch: Archaeology of a Sensation*. Cambridge, MA: Zone Books.

Heller-Roazen, D. 2008. "Common Sense: Greek, Arabic, Latin." In *Rethinking the Medieval Senses: Heritage, Fascinations, Frames*, edited by G. Nichols, A. Kablitz, and A. Calhoun, 30–50. Baltimore: Johns Hopkins University Press.

Helmreich, S. 2015. "Transduction." In *Keywords in Sound*, edited by D. Novak and M. Sakakeeny, 222–31. Durham, NC: Duke University Press.

Henshaw, V. 2013. *Urban Smellscapes: Understanding and Designing Urban Smell Environments*. New York: Routledge.

Hertel, R. 2014. "The Senses in Literature, 1920–2000: From the Modernist Shock of Sensation to Postcolonial and Virtual Voices." In *A Cultural History of the Senses in the Modern Age, 1920–2000*, edited by D. Howes, 173–94. London: Bloomsbury.

Herzfeld, M. 2001. *Anthropology: Theoretical Practice in Culture and Society*. Oxford: Blackwell.

Hess, D.J. 1993. *Science in the New Age: The Paranormal, Its Defenders and Debunkers, in American Culture*. Madison: University of Wisconsin Press.

Heywood, I. 2017. "Introduction." In *Sensory Arts and Design*, edited by I. Heywood, 1–28. Abingdon: Routledge.

Heywood, I., and B. Sandywell, eds. 2011. *The Handbook of Visual Culture*. London: Bloomsbury.

Heywood, P. 2017. "The Ontological Turn." *The Cambridge Encyclopedia of Anthropology*. https://www.anthroencyclopedia.com/entry/ontological-turn.

Higgins, H.B. 2014. "Art and the Senses: The Avant-Garde Challenge to the Visual Arts." *A Cultural History of the Senses in the Modern Age, 1920–2000*, edited by D. Howes, 195–218. London: Bloomsbury.

Highmore, B. 2011. *Ordinary Lives: Studies in the Everyday*. London: Routledge.

Hinton, D., D. Howes, and L. Kirmayer. 2008. "Toward a Medical Anthropology of Sensations: Definitions and Research Agenda." *Transcultural Psychiatry* 45 (2): 142–62.

Hirschkind, C. 2006. *The Ethical Soundscape: Cassette Sermons and Islamic Counterpublics*. New York: Columbia University Press.

Hockey, J. 2006. "Sensing the Run: Distance Running and the Senses." *The Senses and Society* 1 (2): 183–201. https://doi.org/10.2752/174589206778055565.

Hockey, J., and J. Allen-Collinson. 2007. "Grasping the Phenomenology of Sporting Bodies." *International Review for the Sociology of Sport* 42 (2): 115–31.

Hoffer, P.C. 2005. *Sensory Worlds in Early America*. Baltimore: Johns Hopkins University Press.

Hollingham, R. 2004. "In the Realm of Your Senses." *New Scientist*, 31 January 2004, 181 (2432): 40–3.

Holtzman, J. 2009. *Uncertain Tastes: Memory, Ambivalence and the Politics of Eating in Samburu, Northern Kenya*. Berkeley: University of California Press.

Hooke, R. 1971. *The Posthumous Works of Robert Hooke*. Edited by R. Waller. London: n.p.

Hooper-Greenhill, E. 1994. *Museums and Their Visitors*. London: Routledge.
- 1995. *Museum, Media, Message*. London: Routledge.
Horgan, J. 2014. "Scientific Heretic Rupert Sheldrake on Morphic Fields, Psychic Dogs and Other Mysteries." *Scientific American*, July 14.
Howes, D. 1990a. "Controlling Textuality: A Call for a Return to the Senses." *Anthropologica* 32 (1): 55–73. https://doi.org/10.2307/25605558.
- 1990b. "Les techniques des sens." *Anthropologie et Sociétés* 14 (1): 99–116.
- ed. 1991. *The Varieties of Sensory Experience: A Sourcebook in the Anthropology of the Senses*. Toronto: University of Toronto Press.
- 2003. *Sensual Relations: Engaging the Senses in Culture and Social Theory*. Ann Arbor: University of Michigan Press.
- 2005a. "Architecture of the Senses." In *Sense of the City*, edited by M. Zardini, 322–31. Montreal: Canadian Centre for Architecture.
- ed. 2005b. *Empire of the Senses: The Sensual Culture Reader*. Abingdon: Routledge.
- 2005c. "HYPERAESTHESIA, or the Sensual Logic of Late Capitalism." In *Empire of the Senses*, edited by D. Howes, 281–303. Abingdon: Routledge.
- 2005d. 'Skinscape." In *The Book of Touch*, edited by C. Classen, 27–39. Abingdon: Routledge.
- 2006. "Charting the Sensorial Revolution." *The Senses and Society* 1 (1): 113–28.
- 2009. "Introduction: The Revolving Sensorium." In *The Sixth Sense Reader*, edited by D. Howes, 1–52. Oxford: Berg.
- 2010. "Oh Bungalow." In *Journeys: How Travelling Fruit, Ideas and Buildings Rearrange Our Environment*, edited by G. Borasi, 129–36. Montreal: Canadian Centre for Architecture.
- 2011. "Hearing Scents, Tasting Sights: Toward a Cross-Cultural Multimodal Theory of Aesthetics." In *Art and the Senses*, edited by F. Bacci and D. Melcher, 161–82. Oxford: Oxford University Press.
- 2012. "Re-visualizing Anthropology through the Lens of the Ethnographer's Eye." In *The Handbook of Visual Culture*, edited by I. Heywood and B. Sandywell, 628–47. Abingdon: Routledge.
- ed. 2014a. *A Cultural History of the Senses in the Modern Age, 1920–2000*. London: Bloomsbury.
- 2014b. "Introducing Sensory Museology." *The Senses and Society* 9 (3): 259–67. https://doi.org/10.2752/174589314X14023847039917.
- 2015a. "Anthropology of the Senses." In *International Encyclopedia of the Social and Behavioral Sciences*, 2nd ed., 615–20. Edited by J.D. Wright. Oxford: Elsevier.
- 2015b. "The Art of Scenting: On the Aesthetics and Power of Smell Across Cultures." In *Belle Haleine – The Scent of Art: Interdisciplinary Symposium*, 59–71. Basel: Museum Tinguely in association with Kehrer Verlag.
- 2015c. "The Science of Sensory Evaluation: An Ethnographic Critique." In *The Social Life of Materials*, edited by A. Drazin and S. Küchler. Abingdon: Routledge.

- 2016a. "Music to the Eyes: Intersensoriality, Culture and the Arts." In *Routledge Companion to Sounding Art*, edited by M. Cobussen, V. Meelberg, and B. Truax, 159–68. London: Routledge.
- 2016b. "Sensing Cultures: Cinema, Ethnography and the Senses." In *Beyond Text? Critical Practices and Sensory Anthropology*, edited by R. Cox, A. Irving, and C. Wright, 173–88. Manchester: Manchester University Press.
- 2019a. "Multisensory Anthropology." *Annual Review of Anthropology* 48 (1): 17–28. https://doi.org/10.1146/annurev-anthro-102218-011324.
- ed. 2019b. "Troubling Law's Sensorium: Explorations in Sensational Jurisprudence." Special issue, *Canadian Journal of Law and Society* 34 (2).
- 2022. "In Defense of Materiality: Attending to the Sensori-social Life of Things." *Journal of Material Culture* (OnlineFirst). https://doi.org/10.1177%2F13591835221088501.
Howes, D., and C. Classen. 1991. "Conclusion: Sounding Sensory Profiles." In *The Varieties of Sensory Experience*, edited by D. Howes, 257–80. Toronto: University of Toronto Press.
- 2014. *Ways of Sensing: Understanding the Senses in Society*. London: Routledge.
Howes, D., C. Geertz, and R. Lambert. 2018. "Boasian Soundings: An Interrupted History of the Senses (and Poetry) in Anthropology." *Amerikastudien/American Studies* 63 (4): 473–87.
Howes, D., and C. Salter. 2015. "Mediations of Sensation: Designing Performative Sensory Environments." *NMC Media-N* 11 (3). http://median.newmediacaucus.org /research-creation-explorations/mediations-of-sensation-designing-performative -sensory-environments/. Accessed 1 August 2018.
- 2019. "The Performance of Sensation: Dramaturgies, Technologies and Ethnographies in the Design and Evaluation of Performative Sensory Environments." In *Emerging Affinities: Possible Futures of Performative Arts*, edited by M. Borowski, M. Chaberski, and M. Sugiera, 127–48. Bielefeld: transcript Verlag.
Hsu, E. 2008. "The Senses and the Social." *Ethnos* 73 (4): 433–43.
Hsu, H.L. 2020a. "The Sensorial Bioaccumulation of Race." *The Senses and Society* 15 (2): 247–50.
- 2020b. *The Smell of Risk: Environmental Disparities and Olfactory Aesthetics*. New York: New York University Press.
Hughes, H.C. 2001. *Sensory Exotica: A World beyond Human Experience*. Cambridge, MA: MIT Press.
Huhtamo, E., and J. Parikka, eds. 2011. *Media Archaelogy: Approaches, Applications and Implications*. Berkeley: University of California Press.
Huizinga, J. (1919) 1996. *The Autumn of the Middle Ages*. Translated by R. Payton and U. Mammitzsch. Chicago: University of Chicago Press.
- (1929) 1984. "The Task of Cultural History." In *Men and Ideas: History, the Middle Ages, the Renaissance*. Princeton, NJ: Princeton University Press.
Hume, L. 2007. *Portals: Opening Doorways to Other Realities through the Senses*. London: Bloomsbury.
Huxley, Aldous. 1954. *The Doors of Perception*. London: Chatto & Windus.

IFF. 2017. *Avant-Garden*. Exhibition catalogue. New York: International Flavors and Fragrances Inc.

Illich, I. 2000. *H2O and the Waters of Forgetfulness*. London: Marion Boyars Publishers.

Ingold, T., ed. 1996. *Key Debates in Anthropology*. London and New York: Routledge.

– 2000. *The Perception of the Environment: Essays on Livelihood, Dwelling and Skill*. London: Routledge.

– 2004. "Culture on the Ground: The World Perceived through the Feet." *Journal of Material Culture* 9 (3): 315–40.

– 2011. *Being Alive*. London: Routledge.

– 2018. "Back to the Future with the Theory of Affordances." *HAU* 8 (1): 39–44.

Ingold, T., and D. Howes. 2011. "Worlds of Sense and Sensing the World." *Social Anthropology* 19 (3): 313–31. https://doi.org/10.1111/j.1469-8676.2011.00163.x.

Ingrassia, P., and J.B. White. 1994. *Comeback: The Fall and Rise of the American Automobile Industry*. New York: Touchstone.

Irving, A. 2016. *The Art of Life and Death: Radical Aesthetics and Ethnographic Practice*. Chicago: HAU.

Jackson, P. 2004. *Inside Clubbing: Sensual Experiments in the Art of Being Human*. Abingdon: Routledge.

Jaffe, R., E. Dürr, G.A. Jones, A. Angelini, A. Osbourne, and B. Vodopivec. 2020. "What Does Poverty Feel Like? Urban Inequality and the Politics of Sensation." *Urban Studies* 57 (5): 1015–31. https://doi.org/10.1177%2F0042098018820177.

James, W. (1898) 1969. *The Turn of the Screw*. Harmondsworth: Penguin.

Jay, M. 1993. *Downcast Eyes: The Denigration of Vision in Contemporary French Thought*. Berkeley: University of California Press.

– 2011. "In the Realm of the Senses: An Introduction." *American Historical Review* 116 (2): 307–15. https://doi.org/10.1086/ahr.116.2.307.

Jones, C.A. 2006a. "The Mediated Sensorium." In *Sensorium: Embodied Experience, Technology and Contemporary Art*, edited by C.A. Jones, 5–48. Cambridge, MA: MIT List Visual Arts Center and MIT Press.

– ed. 2006b. *Sensorium: Embodied Experience, Technology and Contemporary Art*. Cambridge, MA: MIT Press.

– 2006c. *Eyesight Alone. Clement Greenberg's Modernism and the Bureaucratization of the Senses*. Chicago: University of Chicago Press.

– 2017. *The Global Work of Art: World's Fairs, Biennials, and the Aesthetics of Experience*. Chicago: University of Chicago Press.

Jørgensen, H.H.L. 2013. "Sensorium: A Model for Medieval Perception." In *The Saturated Sensorium: Principles of Perception and Mediation in the Middle Ages*, edited by H.H.L. Jørgensen, H. Laugerud, and L.K. Skinnebach, 9–23. Aarhus, Denmark: Aarhus University Press.

Jørgensen H.H.L., H. Laugerud, and K.L. Skinnebach, eds. 2015. *The Saturated Sensorium: Principles of Perception and Mediation in the Middle Ages*. Aarhus, Denmark: Aarhus University Press.

Jungnickel, K., ed. 2020. *Transmissions: Critical Tactics for Making and Communicating*. Cambridge, MA: MIT Press.

Jütte, R. 2005. *A History of the Senses: From Antiquity to Cyberspace*. Cambridge: Polity Press.

Kagan, N., P. Daniels, and A. Horan, eds. 1987. *Psychic Powers*. Alexandria, VA: Time-Life Books.

Kahn, D. 1999. *Noise Water Meat: A History of Sound in the Arts*. Cambridge, MA: MIT Press.

– 2002. "Digits on the Historical Pulse." *PulseField*. https://cara.gsu.edu/pulsefield/kahn _essay.html. Accessed 15 August 2020.

Kalekin-Fishman, D., and K. Low, eds. 2010. *Everyday Life in Asia: Social Perspectives on the Senses*. Farnham: Ashgate.

Kane, B. 2015. "Sound Studies without Auditory Culture: A Critique of the Ontological Turn." *Sound Studies* 1 (1): 2–21. https://doi.org/10.1080/20551940.2015.1079063.

Kapralos, B., K. Collins, and A. Urube-Quevedo. 2017. "The Senses and Virtual Environments." *The Senses and Society* 12 (1): 69–75.

Kazubowski-Houston, H., and M. Auslander, eds. 2021. *In Search of Lost Futures: Anthropological Explorations in Multimodality, Deep Iinterdisciplinarity, and Autoethnography*. London: Palgrave Macmillan.

Keats, J. 1957. *The Crack in the Picture Window*. Boston: Houghton Mifflin.

Keeley, B. 2002. "Making Sense of the Senses: Individuating Modalities in Humans and Other Animals." *Journal of Philosophy* 99 (1): 5–28. http://dx.doi.org/10.2307/3655759.

Keifenheim, B. 1999. "Concepts of Perception, Visual Practice, and Pattern Art among the Cashinahua Indians (Peruvian Amazon Area)." *Visual Anthropology* 12: 27–48.

Keller. E.F., and C.R. Grontkowski. 1983. "The Mind's Eye." In *Discovering Reality: Feminist Perspectives on Epistemology, Metaphysics, Methodology and Philosophy of Science*, edited by S. Harding and M.B. Hintikka, 207–24. Dordrecht: Reidel.

Kelman, A.Y. 2015. "Rethinking the Soundscape: A Critical Genealogy of a Key Term in Sound Studies." *The Senses and Society* 5 (2): 212–34.

Kemp, S. 1990. *Medieval Psychology*. New York: Greenwood Press.

Kensinger, K. 1995. *How Real People Ought to Live: The Cashinahua of Eastern Peru*. Prospect Heights, IL: Waveland Press.

Kettler, A. 2020. *The Smell of Slavery*. Cambridge: Cambridge University Press.

Key, B. 1974. *Subliminal Seduction*. New York: Penguin.

Kihlstedt, F.T. 1983. "The Automobile and the Transformation of the American House." In *The Automobile and American Culture*, edited by D.L. Lewis and L. Goldstein. Ann Arbor: University of Michigan Press.

King, A.D. 1984. *The Bungalow: The Production of a Global Culture*. London: Routledge and Kegan Paul.

Kirshenblatt-Gimblett, B. 1998. *Destination Culture: Tourism, Museums and Heritage*. Berkeley: University of California Press.

– 1999. "Playing to the Senses: Food as a Performance Medium." *Performance Research* 44 (1): 1–30.

Kirton, J.F., and N. Timothy. 1977. "Yanyuwa Concepts Relating to 'Skin.'" *Oceania* 47 (4): 320–2.

Kivy, P. 2003. *The Seventh Sense: Francis Hutcheson and Eighteenth-Century British Aesthetics*. Oxford: Clarendon Press.

Knappett, C. 2007. "Materials *with* Materiality?" *Archaeological Dialogues* 14:20–3. https://doi.org/10.1017/S1380203807002140.

Kocur, Z. 2011. *Global Visual Cultures: An Anthology*. Oxford: Wiley-Blackwell.

Korsmeyer, C. 1999. *Making Sense of Taste: Food and Philosophy*. Ithaca, NY: Cornell University Press.

– ed. (2005) 2016. *The Taste Culture Reader: Experiencing Food and Drink*. London: Bloomsbury.

Korsmeyer, C., and D. Sutton. 2011. "The Sensory Experience of Food." *Food, Culture & Society* 14 (4):461–75. https://doi.org/10.2752/175174411X13046092851316.

Kramer, M.J. 2013. *The Republic of Rock: Music and Citizenship in the Sixties Counterculture*. Oxford: Oxford University Press.

Krmpotich, C., and L. Peers with the Haida Repatriation Committee and the staff of the Pitt Rivers Museum and British Museum. 2013. *This is Our Life: Haida Material Heritage and Changing Museum Practice*. Vancouver: UBC Press.

Kuhn, T.S. 1970. *The Structure of Scientific Revolutions. International Encyclopedia of Unified Science*. Vol. 2, no. 2. Chicago: University of Chicago Press.

Kuipers, J. 1991. "Matters of Taste in Weyewa." In *The Varieties of Sensory Experience*, edited by D. Howes, 111–27. Toronto: University of Toronto Press.

Kuriyama, S. 1999. *The Expressiveness of the Body and the Divergence of Greek and Chinese Medicine*. Cambridge MA: Zone Books.

Kurlansky, M. (2002) 2010. *Salt: A World History*. New York: Bloomsbury.

Kusahara, M. 2011. "The 'Baby Talkie,' Domestic Media, and the Japanese Modern." In *Media Archaelogy: Approaches, Applications and Implications*, edited by E. Huhtamo and J. Parikka. Berkeley: University of California Press.

Lafrance, M. 2012. "From the Skin Ego to the Psychic Envelope: An Introduction to the Work of Didier Anzieu." In *Skin, Culture and Psychoanalysis*, edited by S. Cavanagh, A. Failler, and R. Hurst. New York: Palgrave MacMillan.

– 2018. "Introduction: Skin Studies – Past, Present, and Future." *Body and Society* 24 (1–2): 3–30.

Lahne, J., and C. Spackman. 2018. "Introduction to Accounting for Taste." *The Senses and Society* 13 (1): 1–5.

Lamrani, M., ed. 2021. "Beyond Revolution: Reshaping Nationhood through Senses and Affects." Special issue, *Cambridge Journal of Anthropology* 39 (2).

Laplantine, F. 2005. *Le social et le sensible: introduction à une anthropologie modale*. Paris: Téraèdre.

– 2015. *The Life of the Senses: Introduction to a Modal Anthropology*. Translated by J. Furniss. Abingdon: Routledge.

Laughlin, C. 1994. "Psychic Energy and Transpersonal Experience: A Biognetic Structural Account of the Tibetan Dumo Yoga Practice." In *Being Changed: The Anthropology of Extraordinary Experience*, edited by D.E. Young and J.-G. Goulet, 93–134. Peterborough, ON: Broadview Press.

Law, L. 2005. "Home Cooking: Filipino Women and Geographies of the Senses in Hong Kong." In *Empire of the Senses*, edited by D. Howes, 224–44. Oxford: Berg.

Le Breton, D. 1990. *Anthropologie du corps et modernité*. Paris: PUF.

– 2017. *Sensing the World: An Anthropology of the Senses*. Translated by C. Ruschiensky. Abingdon: Routledge.

Le Guérer, A. 1992. *Scent: The Mysterious and Essential Powers of Smell*. New York: Random House.

Leahy, H.R. 2012. *Museum Bodies*. Farnham, Surrey: Ashgate.

– 2014. "Incorporating the Period Eye: Spectators at Exhibitions of Exhibitions." *The Senses and Society* 9 (3): 284–95. https://doi.org/10.2752/1745893 14X14023847039836.

Leder, D. 1987. *The Absent Body*. Chicago: University of Chicago Press.

Leenhardt, M. (1947) 1979. *Do Kamo: Person and Myth in the Melanesian World*. Chicago: University of Chicago Press.

Lende, D.H., and G. Downey, eds. 2012. *The Encultured Brain: An Introduction to Neuroanthropology*. Cambridge, MA: MIT Press.

Levent, N., G. Kleege, and J. Muyskens Pursley, eds. 2013. "Museum Experience and Blindness." Special issue, *Disability Studies Quarterly* 33 (3).

Levent, N., and A. Pascual-Leone. 2014. *The Multisensory Museum: Cross-Disciplinary Perspectives on Touch, Sound, Smell, Memory, and Space*. New York: Rowman & Littlefield.

Levin, D.M. 1997. "Introduction." In *Sites of Vision: The Discursive Construction of Sight in the History of Philosophy*, edited by D.M. Levin. Cambridge, MA: MIT Press.

Lévi-Strauss, C. (1962) 1966. *The Savage Mind*. Chicago: University of Chicago Press.

– (1969) 1979. *The Raw and the Cooked: Introduction to a Science of Mythology*. Vol. 1. Translated by J. and D. Weightman. New York: Octagon.

Lévi-Strauss, C., and D. Eribon. 1991. "Sensible Qualities." In *Conversations with Claude Lévi-Strauss*, translated by P. Wissing, 110–15. Chicago: University of Chicago Press.

Lindberg, D.C. 1981. *Theories of Vision from Al-Kindi to Kepler*. Chicago: University of Chicago Press.

Lloyd, S., and A. Tremblay. 2021. "No Hearing without Signals: Imagining and Reimagining Sonic Transduction through the History of the Cochlear Implant." *The Senses and Society* 17 (1): 259–77.

Llull, R. 1984. *Ars breuis, quae est de inuentione iuris, Dist. 5*. Edited by A. Madre. Corpus Christianorum Continuatio Mediaevalis 38. Turnhout, Belgium: Brepols.

– 2014. *Liber de sexto sensu, id est, de affatu, Prologue*. Edited by V. Tenge-Wolf. Corpus Christianorum Continuatio Mediaevalis 248. Turnhout, Belgium: Brepols.

Locke, J. 1975. *An Essay Concerning Human Understanding*. Oxford: Clarendon Press.

Longhurst, R., E. Ho, and L. Johnston. 2008. "Using 'the Body' as an Instrument of Research: Kimch'i and Pavlova." *Area* 40 (2): 208–17.

Longhurst, R., L. Johnston, and E. Ho. 2009. "A Visceral Approach: Cooking 'At Home' with Migrant Women in Hamilton, New Zealand." *Transactions of the Institute of British Geographers* 34:333–45. https://doi.org/10.1111/j.1475-5661.2009.00349.x.

Lorimer, H. 2005. "Cultural Geography: The Busyness of Being 'More-Than-Representational.'" *Progress in Human Geography* 29 (1): 83–94. https://doi.org/10.1191%2F0309132505ph531pr.

Lorimer, J. 2010. "Moving Image Methodologies and More-Than-Human Geographies." *Cultural Geographies* 17 (2): 237–58. https://doi.org/10.1177%2F1474474010363853.

Low, K.E.Y. 2009. *Scent and Scent-sibilities: Smell and Everyday Life Experiences*. Newcastle: Cambridge Scholars Press.

Luhrmann, T.R. 2014. "Can't Place That Smell? You Must Be American." *New York Times*, 5 September 2014.

Lupton, D., and S. Maslen. 2018. "The More-than-Human-Sensorium: Sensory Engagements, with Digital Self-tracking Technologies." *The Senses and Society* 13 (2): 190–202. https://doi.org/10.1080/17458927.2018.1480177.

Lupton, E., and A. Lipps, eds. 2018. *The Senses: Design Beyond Vision*. New York: Cooper Hewitt, Smithsonian Design Museum and Princeton Architectural Press.

Lynch K. 1960. *The Image of the City*. Cambridge, MA: MIT Press.

Lyng, S. 2004. *Edgework: The Sociology of Risk-Taking*. London: Routledge.

Lyon, D. 2007. *Surveillance Studies: An Overview*. Cambridge: Polity Press.

Maboungou, Z. 2005. *Heya … Danse! Historique, poétique et didactique de la danse africaine*. Montreal: Les Éditions de CIDIHCA.

MacDougall, D. 2005. *The Corporeal Image: Film, Ethnography, and the Senses*. Princeton, NJ: Princeton University Press.

– 2019. *The Looking Machine: Essays on Cinema, Anthropology and Documentary Filmmaking*. Manchester: Manchester University Press.

Mack, A. 2012. "The Politics of Good Taste: Whole Food Markets and Sensory Design." *The Senses and Society* 7 (1): 87–94. https://doi.org/10.2752/174589312X13173255802166.

Maillet, A. 2004. *The Claude Glass: Use and Meaning of the Black Mirror in Western Art*. Cambridge, MA: MIT Press.

Majid, A. 2015. "Cultural Factors Shape Olfactory Language." *Trends in Cognitive Sciences* 19 (11): 629–30. https://doi.org/10.1016/j.tics.2015.06.009.

– 2021. "Human Olfaction at the Intersection of Language, Culture and Biology." *Trends in Cognitive Sciences* 25 (2): 111–23. https://doi.org/10.1016/j.tics.2020.11.005.

Majid, A., and S. Levinson, 2011. "The Senses in Language and Culture." Special issue, *The Senses and Society* 6 (1).

Malinowski, B. 1929. *The Sexual Life of Savages in North-Western Melanesia*. New York: Harcourt, Brace and World.

– (1923) 1961. *Argonauts of the Western Pacific*. New York: E.P. Dutton.

Manalansan IV, M.F. 2006. "Immigrant Lives and the Politics of Olfaction in the Global City." In *The Smell Culture Reader*, edited by J. Drobnick, 41–52. Abingdon: Routledge.

Manning, E. 2009. *Relationscapes: Movement, Art, Philosophy*. Cambridge, MA: MIT Press.

Mansell, J. 2017. *The Age of Noise in Britain: Hearing Modernity*. Champaign: University of Illinois Press.

Margulies, A. 1985. "On Listening to a Dream: The Sensory Dimensions." *Psychiatry* 48 (4): 371–81. https://doi.org/10.1080/00332747.1985.11024298.

Marinetti, F.T. 2006. *Critical Writings: New Edition*. Edited by G. Berghaus. New York: Farrar, Straus and Giroux.

Marks, L.E., and C.M. Mulvenna. 2013. "Synesthesia on Our Mind." *Theoria et Historia Scientiarum* 10: 13–35.

Marks, L.U. 2000. *The Skin of the Film: Intercultural Cinema, Embodiment and the Senses*. Durham, NC: Duke University Press.

Martin, L., and K. Seagrave. 1988. *Anti-rock: The Opposition to Rock 'n' Roll*. Hamden, CT: Archon Books.

Masiello, F. 2018. *The Senses of Democracy: Perception, Politics, and Culture in Latin America*. Austin: University of Texas Press.

Massumi, B. 2014. *What Animals Teach Us about Politics*. Durham, NC: Duke University Press.

Mather, G. 2016. *Foundations of Sensation and Perception*. London: Taylor & Francis.

Matthews, M., and R. Roulette. 2018. "'Are All Stones Alive?' Anthropological and Anishinaabe Approaches to Personhood." In *Rethinking Relations and Animism: Personhood and Materiality*, edited by M. Astor-Aguilera and G. Harvey, 173–92. London: Routledge.

Mazzio, C. 2005. "The Senses Divided: Organs, Objects and Media in Early Modern England." In *Empire of the Senses*, edited by D. Howes, 85–105. Oxford: Berg.

McCormack, D. 2018. *Atmospheric Things: On the Allure of Elemental Envelopment*. Durham, NC: Duke University Press.

McCosh, J. 1875. *The Scottish Philosophy: Biographical, Expository, Critical, from Hutcheson to Hamilton*. London: Forgotten Books.

McHugh, J. 2012. *Sandalwood and Carrion: Smell in Indian Religion and Culture*. Oxford: Oxford University Press.

McKenzie, K. 2006. "Patria." *Canadian Encyclopedia*. https://www.thecanadianencyclopedia.ca/en/article/patria-emc.

McKibbin, R. 1998. *Classes and Cultures: England 1918–1951*. Oxford: Oxford University Press.

McLuhan, E. n.d. "(Herbert) Marshall McLuhan." Encyclopedia.com. https://www
.encyclopedia.com/people/social-sciences-and-law/education-biographies/marshall
-mcluhan.

McLuhan, M. 1962. *The Gutenberg Galaxy*. Toronto: University of Toronto Press.

– (1964) 1994. *Understanding Media: The Extensions of Man*. Cambridge, MA: MIT
Press.

McLuhan, M., and E. McLuhan. 1992. *Laws of Media*. Toronto: University of Toronto
Press.

McLuhan, M., and Q. Fiore. 1967. *The Medium Is the Massage: An Inventory of Effects*.
New York: Random House.

Merleau-Ponty, M. 1962. *Phenomenology of Perception*. London: Routledge and Kegan
Paul.

Midgley, A. 2012. "Cultural History and the World of Johan Huizinga." *Saber and Scroll*
1 (1): 109–22.

Miekle, J.L. 1995. *American Plastic: A Cultural History*. New Brunswick, NJ: Rutgers
University Press.

Miller, W.I. 1997. *The Anatomy of Disgust*. Cambridge, MA: Harvard University Press.

Milner, M. 2011. *The Senses and the English Reformation*. Farnham: Ashgate.

Mintz, S. 1985. *Sweetness and Power: The Place of Sugar in Modern History*.
Harmondsworth: Penguin.

Miodownik, M. 2013. *Stuff Matters: Exploring the Marvelous Materials that Shape Our
Man-Made World*. Boston: Mariner Books/Houghton Mifflin Harcourt.

Mitchell, W.J.T. (1992) 1994. "The Pictorial Turn." In *Picture Theory*. Chicago:
University of Chicago Press.

Miyarrka Media. 2019. *Phone & Spear: A Yuṯa Anthropology*. London: Goldsmiths Press.

Montagu, A. (1971) 1986. *Touching: The Human Significance of the Skin*. New York:
Harper and Row.

Montaigne, M. de. 1580. *Essays*. Harmondsworth: Penguin.

Moore, J. 2004. "Francis Hutcheson (1694–1746)." In *Oxford Dictionary of National
Biography*. Oxford: Oxford University Press.

Mopas, M., and E. Huybregts. 2020. "Training by Feel: Wearable Fitness-Trackers,
Endurance Athletes, and the Sensing of Data." *The Senses and Society* 15 (1): 25–40.
https://doi.org/10.1080/17458927.2020.1722421.

Munn, N. 1986. *The Fame of Gawa: A Symbolic Study of Value Transformation in a
Massim (Papua New Guinea) Society*. New York: Cambridge University Press.

Myers, N. 2015. "Conversations on Plant Sensing. Notes from the Field." *NatureCulture*
3:35–66.

Nash, A., and M. Carroll. (2006) 2018. "The Urban Sensorium." *The Senses and Society*
1 (2): 283–8.

Nedelsky, J. 1997. "Embodied Diversity and the Challenges to Law." *McGill Law Journal*
42:91–117.

Newhauser, R. 2007. *Sin: Essays on the Moral Tradition in the Western Middle Ages*. Aldershot: Ashgate Publishing.

– ed. 2014. *A Cultural History of the Senses in the Middle Ages, 1000–1400*. London: Bloomsbury.

Ngao, E. 2018. "Caribou Heard." *The Walrus*, 1 July 2018.

Niewöhner, J., and M. Lock. 2018. "Situating Local Biologies: Anthropological Perspectives on Environment/Human Entanglements." *BioSocieties* 13:681–97.

Nöe, A. 2006. *Action in Perception*. Cambridge, MA: MIT Press.

Norton, Q. 2006. "A Sixth Sense for a Wired World." *Wired*, 7 June 2006. http://www .wired.com/gadgets/mods/news/2006/06/71087.

Norton, R.E. 1990. *Herder's Aesthetics and the European Enlightenment*. Ithaca, NY: Cornell University Press.

Nudds, M. 2014. "The Senses in Philosophy and Science: From Sensation to Computation." In *A Cultural History of the Senses in the Modern Age, 1920–2000*, edited by D. Howes, 125–48. London: Bloomsbury.

Obrador-Pons, P. 2007. "Haptic Geography of the Beach: Naked Bodies, Vision and Touch." *Social and Cultural Geography* 18 (1): 123–41.

Off, C. 2006. *Bitter Sweet: Investigating the Dark Side of the World's Most Seductive Sweet*. Toronto: Random House.

Ogbar, J.O.G. 2004. *Black Power: Radical Politics and African American Identity*. Baltimore, MD: Johns Hopkins University Press.

Olofsson, J.K., and J.A. Gottfried. 2015. "The Muted Sense: Neurocognitive Limitations of Olfactory Language." *Trends in Cognitive Sciences* 19 (6): 314–21. https://doi.org /10.1016/j.tics.2015.04.007.

Ong, B.L. 2012. "Warming up to Heat." *The Senses and Society* 7 (1): 5–21. https://doi .org/10.2752/174589312X13173255801969.

Ong, W.J. 1967. *The Presence of the Word*. New Haven, CT: Yale University Press.

– (1967) 1991. "The Shifting Sensorium." In *The Varieties of Sensory Experience*, edited by D. Howes, 25–30. Toronto: University of Toronto Press.

– 1982. *Orality and Literacy: The Technologization of the Word*. New York: Methuen.

Onians, R.B. 1951. *The Origins of European Thought about the Body, the Mind, the Soul, the World, Time and Fate*. Oxford: Clarendon Press.

O'Rourke, D. 1988. *Cannibal Tours*. http://www.cameraworklimited.com/films/ cannibal-tours.html. Accessed 15 August 2020.

Ovenell, R.F. 1986. *The Ashmolean Museum, 1683–1894*. Oxford: Clarendon Press.

Palasmaa, J. 1996. *The Eyes of the Skin: Architecture and the Senses*. London: Academy Editions.

Panagia, D. 2009. *The Political Life of Sensation*. Durham, NC: Duke University Press.

Parisi, D. 2018. *Archaeologies of Touch*. Minneapolis: University of Minnesota Press.

Parr, J. 2010. *Sensing Changes: Technologies, Environments, and the Everyday, 1953–2003*. Vancouver: UBC Press.

Paterson, M. 2007. *The Senses of Touch: Haptics, Affects and Technologies*. Oxford: Berg.
– 2009. "Haptic Geographies: Ethnography, Haptic Knowledges and Sensuous Dispositions." *Progress in Human Geography* 33 (6): 766–88. https://doi.org/10.1177%2F0309132509103155.
– 2021. *How We Became Sensorimotor: Movement, Measurement, Sensation.* Minneapolis: University of Minnesota Press.
Pavsek, C. 2015. "*Leviathan* and the Experience of Sensory Ethnography." *Visual Anthropology Review* 31 (1): 4–11. https://doi.org/10.1111/var.12056.
Pearson, A. 1991. "Touch Exhibitions in the United Kingdom." In *Museums without Borders: A New Deal for Disabled People*, edited by Fondation de France and ICOM. London: Routledge.
Pearson, T. 2003, *All about the Sixth Sense: Exploring the Extrasensory World*. Hod Hasharon, Israel: Astrolog Publishing House.
Peers, L., and A.K. Brown. 2003. *Museums and Source Communities*. London: Routledge.
Pells, R. 2011. *Modernist America: Art, Music, Movies, and the Globalization of American Culture*. New Haven, CT: Yale University Press.
Pentcheva, B. 2006. "The Performative Icon." *Art Bulletin* 88 (4): 631–55. https://doi.org/10.1080/00043079.2006.10786312.
– 2010. *The Sensual Icon*. Philadelphia: Pennsylvania State University Press.
Pérez-Gómez, A. 2016. *Attunement: Architectural Meaning after the Crisis of Modern Science*. Cambridge, MA: MIT Press.
Peterson, M. 2016. "Sensory Attunements: Working with the Past in the Little Cities of Black Diamonds." *South Atlantic Quarterly* 115 (1): 89–111.
– 2021. *Atmospheric Noise: The Indefinite Urbanism of Los Angeles*. Durham, NC: Duke University Press.
Pettersson, I. 2017. "Mechanical Tasting: Sensory Science and the Flavorization of Food Production." *The Senses and Society* 12 (3): 301–16.
Pinard, S. 1991. "A Taste of India." In *The Varieties of Sensory Experience*, edited by D. Howes, 221–30. Toronto: University of Toronto Press.
Pinch, T., and K. Bijsterveld, eds. 2011. *The Oxford Handbook of Sound Studies*. Oxford: Oxford University Press.
Pink, S. 2004. *Home Truths: Gender, Domestic Objects and Everyday Life*. Abingdon: Routledge.
– 2006. *The Future of Visual Anthropology: Engaging the Senses*. London: Taylor and Francis.
– 2009. *Doing Sensory Ethnography*. London: Sage.
Pink, S., and D. Howes. 2010. "The Future of Sensory Anthropology/The anthropology of the Senses." *Social Anthropology* 18 (1): 331–40. https://doi.org/10.1111/j.1469-8676.2010.00119_1.x.
Pleij, H. 2004. *Colors Demonic and Divine: Shades of Meaning in the Middle Ages and After*. New York: Columbia University Press.

Plumb, C. 2015. *The Georgian Menagerie: Exotic Animals in Eighteenth-Century London*. London: I.B. Taurus.

Pocock, D. 1993. "The Senses in Focus." *Area* 25 (1): 11–16.

Poggi, C. 2008. *Inventing Futurism: The Art and Politics of Artificial Optimism*. Princeton, NJ: Princeton University Press.

Poli, A. 2017 "Soundwalking, Sonification and Activism." In *The Routledge Companion to Sounding Art*, edited by M. Cobussen, V. Meelberg, and B. Truax, 81–92. Abingdon: Routledge.

Pollan, M. 2002. *The Botany of Desire: A Plant's-Eye View of the World*. New York: Random House.

– 2018. *How To Change Your Mind*. New York: Penguin.

Porcello, T., L. Meintjes, M.A. Ochoa, and D.W. Samuels. 2010. "The Reorganization of the Sensory World." *Annual Review of Anthropology* 39: 51–66.

Porteous, J.D. 1990. *Landscapes of the Mind: Worlds of Sense and Metaphor*. Toronto: University of Toronto Press.

Porter, R. 2003. *Flesh in the Age of Reason*. New York: W.W. Norton and Co.

Postrel, V. 2003. *The Substance of Style: How the Rise of Aesthetic Value Is Remaking Commerce, Culture, and Consciousness*. New York: HaperCollins.

Power, N. 2018. "Sensing Things: Merleau-Ponty, Synaesthesia and Human-Centredness." In *Senses and Sensation IV*, edited by D. Howes, 357–67. Abingdon: Routledge.

Promey, S.M. 2006. "Taste Cultures and the Visual Practice of Liberal Protestantism, 1940–1965." In *Practicing Protestants: Histories of the Christian Life in America*, edited by L. Maffly-Kipp, L. Schmidt, and M. Vakeri, 250–93. Baltimore, MD: Johns Hopkins University Press.

– 2012. "Visible Liberalism: Liberal Protestant Taste Evangelism, 1850 and 1950." In *American Religious Liberalism*, edited by L.E. Schmidt and S.M. Promey, 76–96. Bloomington: Indiana University Press.

– 2014. "Religion, Sensation, and Materiality: An Introduction." In *Sensational Religion: Sensory Cultures in Material Practice*, edited by S.M. Promey, 1–22. New Haven, CT: Yale University Press.

Proust, M. 1984. *Marcel Proust on Art and Literature*. New York: Carroll & Graf.

Pursey, T., and D. Lomas. 2018. "Tate Sensorium: An Experiment in Multisensory Immersive Design." *The Senses and Society* 13 (3): 354–66. https://doi.org/10.1080/17458927.2018.1516026.

Pye, E., ed. 2007. *The Power of Touch: Handling Objects in Museum and Heritage Contexts*. Walnut Creek, CA: Left Coast Press.

Quiviger, F. 2010. *The Sensory World of Italian Renaissance Art*. London: Reaktion Books.

Ramachandran, V.S., E.M. Hubbard, and P.A. Butcher. 2004. "Synesthesia, Cross-Activation, and the Foundations of Neuroepistemology." In *The Handbook of Multisensory Processes*, edited by G. Calvert, C. Spence, and B.E. Stein, 867–84. Cambridge, MA: MIT Press.

Rancière, J. 2004. *The Politics of Aesthetics: The Distribution of the Sensible*. London: Continuum.

Randl, C. 2010. "Sensuality and Shag Carpeting: A Design Review of a Postwar Floor Covering." *The Senses and Society* 5 (2): 244–9. https://doi.org/10.2752/174589210X 12668381452926.

Rée, J. 1999. *I See a Voice: A Philosophical History of Language, Deafness and the Senses*. London: Flamingo.

– 2000. "The Aesthetic Theory of the Arts." In *From an Aesthetic Point of View: Philosophy, Art and the Senses*, edited by P. Osborne. London: Serpent's Tail.

Reichel-Dolmatoff, G. 1981. "Brain and Mind in Desana Shamanism." *Journal of Latin American Lore* 7 (1): 73–98.

Reynolds, D., and B. Wiseman, eds. 2018. "Methods of Aesthetic Enquiry across Disciplines." Special issue, *The Senses and Society* 13 (3).

Rhine, J.B. 1934. *Extra-Sensory Perception*. Boston: Society for Psychic Research.

Rhys-Taylor, A. 2017. *Food and Multiculture: A Sensory Ethnography of East London*. London: Bloomsbury.

Rice, T. 2013. *Hearing and the Hospital: Sound, Listening, Knowledge and Experience*. London: Sean Kingston Publishing.

Richards, J. 2010. *The Age of the Dream Palace: Cinema and Society in 1930s Britain*. London: L.B. Tauris & Co.

Riskin, J. 2002. *Science in the Age of Sensibility: The Sentimental Empiricists of the French Enlightenment*. Chicago: University of Chicago Press.

Ritchie, I. 1991. "Fusion of the Faculties: A Study of the Language of the Senses in Hausaland." In *The Varieties of Sensory Experience*, edited by D. Howes, 192–202. Toronto: University of Toronto Press.

Rivlin, R., and K. Gravelle. 1984. *Deciphering the Senses: The Expanding World of Human Perception*. New York: Simon & Schuster.

Robben, A., and J. Slukka, eds. 2007. *Ethnographic Fieldwork: An Anthropological Reader*. Oxford: Blackwell Publishing.

Robbins, D. 2019. *Audible Geographies in Latin America: Sounds of Race and Place*. New York: Palgrave.

Roberts, J.B., and P.L. Briand, eds. 1957. *The Sound of Wings: Readings for the Air Age*. New York: Henry Holt.

Roberts, L. 2005. "The Death of the Sensuous Chemist: The 'New' Chemistry and the Transformation of Sensuous Technology." In *Empire of the Senses*, edited by D. Howes, 106–27. Abingdon: Routledge.

Robertson, B.A. 2016. *Science of the Séance: Transnational Networks and Gendered Bodies in the Study of Psychic Phenomena, 1918–1940*. Vancouver: UBC Press.

Robinson, D., and K. Martin, eds. 2016. *Arts of Engagement: Taking Aesthetic Action in and beyond the Truth and Reconciliation Commission of Canada*. Waterloo: Wilfrid Laurier University Press.

Rodaway, P. 1994. *Sensuous Geographies: Body, Sense, and Place*. London: Routledge.

Röder, B., and R. Rösler. 2004. "Compensatory Plasticity as a Consequence of Sensory Loss." In *The Handbook of Multisensory Processes*, edited by G. Calvert, C. Spence, and B.E. Stein, 719–74. Cambridge, MA: MIT Press.

Rodriguez Mendez, M., and V. Preedy, eds. 2016. *Electronic Noses and Tongues in Food Science*. New York: Elsevier.

Roeder, G.H. 1994. "Coming to Our Senses." *Journal of American History* 81: 1112–22. https://doi.org/10.2307/2081453.

Romanielo, P., and T. Starks, eds. 2016. *Russian History through the Senses: From 1700 to the Present*. London: Bloomsbury.

Romberg, R. 2009. *Healing Dramas: Divination and Magic in Modern Puerto Rico*. Austin: University of Texas Press.

Roodenburg, H., ed. 2014. *A Cultural History of the Senses in the Renaissance, 1400–1650*. London: Bloomsbury.

Rorty, R. (1979) 2017. *Philosophy and the Mirror of Nature*. Princeton, NJ: Princeton University Press.

Roseman, M. 1993. *Healing Sounds from the Malaysian Rainforest*. Berkeley: University of California Press.

Roseman, M. 2008. "Blowing 'cross the crest of Mount Galeng': Winds of the Voice, Winds of the Spirits." In *Wind, Life, Health: Anthropological and Historical Perspectives*, edited by E. Hsu and C. Low, 51–64. Oxford: Blackwell Publishing.

Rourke, R. 2019. *A Sensory Sociology of Autism*. Abingdon: Routledge.

Rozin, P. 1982. "'Taste-Smell Confusions' and the Duality of the Olfactory Sense." *Perception and Psychophysics* 31 (4): 397–401. https://doi.org/10.3758/BF03202667.

Rudy, G. 2002. *Mystical Language of Sensation in the Later Middle Ages*. London: Routledge.

Ryan, E.J. 1951. "The Role of the 'Sensus Communis.'" In *the Psychology of St. Thomas Aquinas*. Carthagena, OH: Messenger Press.

Sacks, O. 2008. "An Auditory World: Music and Blindness." In *Musicophilia: Tales of Music and the Brain*, 171–6. New York: Vintage Books.

Said, E. 1983. "The Music Itself: Glenn Gould's Contrapuntal Vision." In *Glenn Gould Variations*, edited by V. McGreevy. Toronto: Macmillan.

Salter, C. 2015. *Alien Agency: Experimental Encounters with Art in the Making*. Cambridge, MA: MIT Press.

– 2018. "Disturbance, Translation, Enculturation: Necessary Research in New Media, Technology and the Senses." *Visual Anthropology Review* 34(1): 87–97. https://doi.org/10.1111/var.12156.

– 2022. *Sensing Machines: How Sensors Shape Our Everyday Life*. Cambridge, MA: MIT Press.

Sandburg, C. 1976. *The Complete Poems of Carl Sandburg*. New York: Harcourt, Brace, Jovanovitch.

Saussure, F. de. 1959. *Course in General Linguistics*. Translated by W. Baskin. New York: McGraw-Hill.

Schafer, R.M. n.d. *The Palace of the Cinnabar Phoenix*. Part 8 of the Patria Cycle. https://www.thecanadianencyclopedia.ca/en/article/patria-emc. Accessed 15 August 2020.

– 1977. *The Tuning of the World*. Toronto: McClelland and Stewart.

Schechner, R. 2001. "Rasaesthetics." *TDR* 45 (3): 27–50. https://doi.org/10.1162/10542040152587105.

Schifferstein, H.N.J., and C. Spence. 2008. "Multisensory Product Experience." In *Multisensory Product Experience*, edited by H.N.J. Schifferstein and P. Hekkert, 133–61. Amsterdam: Elsevier.

Schifferstein, H.N.J., and L. Wastiels. 2014. "Sensing Materials: Exploring the Building Blocks for Experiential Design." In *Materials Experience: Fundamentals of Materials and Design*, edited by E. Karana, O. Pedgley, and V. Rognoli, 15–26. Amsterdam: Elsevier Ltd.

Schivelbusch, W. 1992. *Tastes of Paradise: A Social History of Spices, Stimulants and Intoxicants*. New York: Pantheon.

– 1995. *Disenchanted Night: The Industrialization of Light in the Nineteenth Century*. Berkeley: University of California Press.

Schmidt, L. 2000. *Hearing Things: Religion, Illusion and the American Enlightenment*. Cambridge, MA: Harvard University Press.

Schneider, A., and C. Wright, eds. 2010. *Between Art and Anthropology: Contemporary Ethnographic Practice*. Oxford: Berg.

– eds. 2013. *Anthropology and Art Practice*. London: Routledge.

Schoch, R.M., and L. Yonavjak, eds. 2008. *The Parapsychology Revolution: A Concise Anthology of Paranormal and Psychical Research*. New York: Penguin.

Schulze, H., ed. 2021. *The Bloomsbury Handbook of the Anthropology of Sound*. London: Bloomsbury.

Schwartzman, S. 2011. *See Yourself Sensing: Redefining Human Perception*. London: Black Dog.

Seeger, A. 1975. "The Meaning of Body Ornaments: A Suya Example." *Ethnology* 14 (3): 211–24.

Sekimoto, S., and C. Brown. 2020. *Race and the Senses: The Felt Politics of Racial Embodiment*. Abingdon: Routledge.

Senior, M. 2004. "The Ménagerie and the Labyrinthe: Animals at Versailles, 1662–1792." In *Renaissance Beasts: Of Animals, Humans, and Other Wonderful Creatures*, 208–32. Champaign: University of Illinois Press.

Sennett, R. 1994. *Flesh and Stone: The Body and the City in Western Civilization*. New York: W.W. Norton.

– 2009. *The Craftsman*. New Haven, CT: Yale University Press.

Seremetakis, C.N. 1994a. "The Memory of the Senses – Marks of the Transitory: The Breast of Aphrodite." In *The Senses Still*, edited by C. Nadia Seremetakis, 1–18. Boulder, CO: Westview Press.

– ed. 1994b. *The Senses Still: Memory and Perception as Material Culture in Modernity*. Boulder, CO: Westview.

– 2019. *Sensing the Everyday*. London: Routledge.

Shapin, S. 2016. "A Taste of Science: Making the Subjective Objective in the California Wine World." *Social Studies of Science* 46 (3): 436–60. https://doi.org/10.1177%2F 0306312716651346.

Shaw-Miller, S. 2010a. "Disciplining the Senses: Beethoven as Synaesthetic Paradigm." In *Art, History and the Senses: 1830 to the Present*, edited by P. Di Bello and G. Koureas, xv–xxiv. London: Routledge.

Shaw-Miller, S. 2010b. *Eye hEar: The Visual in Music*. London: Routledge.

Sheets-Johnstone, M. 1999. *The Primacy of Movement*. Amsterdam: John Benjamins.

Sheldon, R., and R. Arens. (1932) 1976. *Consumer Engineering: A New Technique for Prosperity*. New York: Arno Press.

Sheldrake, R. 1981. *A New Science of Life: The Hypothesis of Formative Causation*. London: Blond & Briggs.

– 2009. "The Sense of Being Stared At." In *The Sixth Sense Reader*, edited by D. Howes, 247–66. Abingdon: Routledge.

– 2011. *How Dogs Know That Their Owners Are Coming Home*. New York: Penguin.

– n.d. "Morphic Resonance and Morphic Fields: An Introduction." https://www.sheldrake .org/research/morphic-resonance/introduction.

Shermer, M. 2005. "Rupert's Resonance." *Scientific American*, 1 November 2005.

Sherry Jr., J.F. 2006. "Sporting Sensation." *The Senses and Society* 1 (2): 245–8.

Shiga, J. 2017. "An Empire of Sound: Sentience, Sonar and Sensory Impudence." In *Sensing Law*, edited by S.N. Hamilton et al., 238–56. London and New York: Routledge.

Simmel, G. (1903) 1976. "The Metropolis and Mental Life." In *The Sociology of Georg Simmel*. New York: Free Press.

– (1907) 1997. "Sociology of the Senses." In *Simmel on Culture: Selected Writings*, edited by D. Frisby and M. Featherstone. London: Sage.

Skeates, R., and J. Day, eds. 2020. *The Routledge Handbook of Sensory Archaeology*. London: Routledge.

Smith, B.R. 1999. *The Acoustic World of Early Modern England*. Chicago: University of Chicago Press.

– 2004. "How Sound Is Sound History?" In *Hearing History: A Reader*, edited by M.M. Smith, 85–111. Athens: University of Georgia Press.

– 2009. *The Key of Green: Passion and Perception in Renaissance Culture*. Chicago: University of Chicago Press.

Smith, M.M. 2001. *Listening to Nineteenth-Century America*. Chapel Hill: University of North Carolina Press.

– 2006. *How Race Is Made: Slavery, Segregation and the Senses*. Chapel Hill: University of North Carolina Press.

– 2007a. "Producing Sense, Consuming Sense, Making Sense: Perils and Prospects for Sensory History." *Journal of Social History* 40: 841–58. https://doi.org/10.1353 /jsh.2007.0116.

- 2007b. *Sensing the Past: Seeing, Hearing, Smelling, Tasting and Touching History*. Berkeley: University of California Press.
- 2008. "The Senses in American History: A Round Table." Special issue, *Journal of American History* 95 (2).
- ed. 2019. *Smell and History: A Reader*. Morgantown: West Virginia University Press.
- 2021. *A Sensory History Manifesto*. Philadelphia: Pennsylvania State University Press.

Sobchack, V. 1991. *The Address of the Eye: Phenomenology of Film Experience*. Princeton, NJ: Princeton University Press.

Sontag, S. 1973. *On Photography*. New York: Picador.

Sormani, P., G. Carbone, and P. Gisler, eds. 2018. *Practicing Art/Science: Experiments in an Emerging Field*. London: Routledge.

Sparkes, A. 2017. *Seeking the Senses in Physical Culture: Sensuous Scholarship in Action*. London: Routledge.

Spence, C. 2018a. "Crossmodal Correspondences: A Synopsis." In *Senses and Sensation III*, edited by D. Howes, 91–132. Abingdon: Routledge.
- 2018b. *Gastrophysics: The New Science of Eating*. New York: Viking.
- 2021. *Sensehacking: How to Use the Power of Your Senses for Happier, Healthier Living*. New York: Viking.

Spence, C., and B. Piqueras-Fiszman. 2014. *The Perfect Meal: The Multisensory Science of Food and Dining*. Oxford: Wiley-Blackwell.

Spencer, D. 2012. *Ultimate Fighting and Embodiment*. London: Routledge.
- 2014. "Sensing Violence: An Ethnography of Mixed Martial Arts." *Ethnography* 15 (2): 232–54. https://doi.org/10.1177%2F1466138112471108.

Spigel, L. 1992. *Make Room for TV: Television and the Family Ideal in Postwar America*. Chicago: University of Chicago Press.

Spiro, M. 1982. *Oedipus in the Trobriands*. Chicago: University of Chicago Press.

Spock, B., and S. Parker. 1998. *Dr Spock's Baby and Child Care*. New York: Pocket Books.

Springgay, S., and S.E. Truman. 2019. *Walking Methodologies in a More-than-Human World: Walking Lab*. London: Routledge.

Stahl, A.B. 2008. "Colonial Entanglements and the Practices of Taste: An Alternative to Logocentric Approaches." *American Anthropologist* 104 (3): 827–45. https://doi.org/10.1525/aa.2002.104.3.827.

Staples, W.G. 2000. *Everyday Surveillance: Vigilance and Visibility in Postmodern Life*. Lanham, NY: Rowman & Littlefield.

Sterne, J. 2012. *The Sound Studies Reader*. London: Routledge.

Stevenson, R.J., and R. Boakes. 2004. "Sweet and Sour Smells: Learned Synesthesia Between the Senses of Taste and Smell." In *The Handbook of Multisensory Processes*, edited by G. Calvert, C. Spence, and B.E. Stein, 69–84. Cambridge, MA: MIT Press.

Stewart, K. 2007. *Ordinary Affects*. Durham, NC: Duke University Press.

Stoever, J.L. 2016. *The Sonic Color Line: Race and the Cultural Politics of Listening*. New York: New York University Press.

Stoller, P. 1989. *The Taste of Ethnographic Things: The Senses in Anthropology.* Philadelphia, PA: University of Pennsylvania Press.

– 1997. *Sensuous Scholarship*. Philadelphia, PA: University of Pennsylvania Press.

Stoller, P., and C. Olkes. 2005. "Thick Sauce: Remarks on the Social Relations of the Songhay." In *The Taste Culture Reader*, edited by C. Korsmeyer, 131–42. London: Bloomsbury.

Sturken, M., and L. Cartwright. 2008. *Practices of Looking: An Introduction to Visual Culture*. Oxford: Oxford University Press.

Sur, M. 2004. "Rewiring Cortex: Cross-Modal Plasticity and Its Implications for Cortical Development and Function." In *The Handbook of Multisensory Processes*, edited by G. Calvert, C. Spence, and B.E. Stein, 681–94. Cambridge, MA: MIT Press.

Surkis, J. 2012. "When Was the Linguistic Turn? A Genealogy." *American Historical Review* 117 (3): 700–22. https://doi.org/10.1086/ahr.117.3.700.

Sutton, D. 2001. *Remembrance of Repasts: An Anthropology of Food and Memory*. Abingdon: Routledge.

– 2010. "Food and the Senses." *Annual Review of Anthropology* 39 (1): 209–23. https://doi.org/10.1146/annurev.anthro.012809.104957.

Synnott, A. 1993. *The Body Social: Symbolism, Self and Society*. London: Routledge.

Synnott, A. 2005. "Handling Children." In *The Book of Touch*, edited by C. Classen, 41–7. Oxford: Berg.

Szczelkun, S., and B. Arning. 2006. "Touch This." *The Senses and Society* 1 (1): 149–54.

Tallis, R. 2011. *Aping Mankind: Neuromania, Darwinitis and the Misrepresentation of Humanity*. Durham: Acumen.

Taussig, M. 1993. *Mimesis and Alterity: A Particular History of the Senses*. London: Routledge.

Taylor, D.R.F., and T. Lauriault. 2013. *Developments in the Theory and Practice of Cybercartography: Applications and Indigenous Mapping*. Amsterdam: Elsevier.

Taylor, D.R.F., P.L. Trbovich, G. Lindgaard, and R.F. Dillon. 2018. "Cybercartography: A Multisensory Approach." In *Senses and Sensation I*, edited by D. Howes. Abingdon: Routledge.

Taylor, L., ed. 1994. *Visualizing Theory*. London: Routledge.

– 1996. "Iconophobia." *Transition* 69: 64–88.

– 1998. "Introduction." In *Transcultural Cinema*, edited by D. MacDougall and L. Taylor. Princeton, NJ: Princeton University Press.

Teil, G. 2019. "Learning to Smell: On the Shifting Modalities of Experience." *The Senses and Society* 14 (3): 330–45.

Thomas, P. 2012. *Listen, Whitey: The Sights and Sounds of Black Power, 1965–1975*. Seattle, WA: Fantagraphics Books.

Thompson, E. 2002 *The Soundscape of Modernity: Architectural Acoustics and the Culture of Listening in America, 1900–1933*, Cambridge: MIT Press.

Thompson, H. 2017. *Reviewing Blindness in French Fiction*. London: Palgrave.

– 2018. "Towards a Multisensory Aesthetic: Jean Giono's Non-Visual Sensorium." In *Senses and Sensation IV*, edited by D. Howes, 315–18. Abingdon: Routledge.

Throop, J. 2010. *Suffering and Sentiment: Exploring the Vicissitudes of Experience and Pain in Yap.* Berkeley: University of California Press.

Thurschwell, P. 2001. *Literature, Technology and Magical Thinking, 1880–1920.* Cambridge: Cambridge University Press.

Tichi, C. 1987. *Shifting Gears: Technology, Literature, Culture in Modernist Literature.* Durham, NC: University of North Carolina Press.

Tilley, C., W. Keane, S. Küchler, M. Rowlands, and P. Spyer, eds. 2006. *Handbook of Material Culture.* London: Sage.

Tillyard, E. (1942) 2011. *The Elizabethan World Picture.* London: Routledge.

Tomkis, T. 1607. *Lingua, or the Combat of the Tongue and the Five Senses for Superiority.*

Toner, J.P., ed. 2014. *A Cultural History of the Senses in Antiquity, 500 BC–1000 AD.* London: Bloomsbury.

Trnka, S., C. Dureau, and J. Park, eds. 2013. *Senses and Citizenships: Embodying Political Life.* London: Routledge.

Trower, S. 2012. *Senses of Vibration: A History of the Pleasure and Pain of Sound.* London: Bloomsbury.

Truss, L. 2003. *Eats, Shoots & Leaves: The Zero Tolerance Approach to Punctuation!* New York: Gotham Books/Penguin.

Tsing, A.H. 2015. *The Mushroom at the End of the World: On the Possibility of Life in Capitalist Ruins.* Princeton, NJ: Princeton University Press.

Tuan, Y.-F. 1974. *Topophilia: A Study of Environmental Perception, Attitudes and Values.* Englewood Cliffs, NJ: Prentice-Hall, Inc.

– 1977. *Space and Place.* Minneapolis: University of Minnesota Press.

– 1993. "Synesthesia, Metaphor and Symbolic Space." In *Passing Strange and Wonderful: Aesthetics, Nature, and Culture*, 166–77. Washington, DC: Island Press.

Tufte, E.R. (1983) 2001. *The Visual Display of Quantitative Information.* Cheshire, CT: Graphics Press.

Tullett, W. 2019. *Smell in Eighteenth-Century England: A Social Sense.* Oxford: Oxford University Press.

Turin, L. 2006. *The Secret of Scent.* London: Faber & Faber.

Turner, B.S. 1994. "Introduction." In *Baroque Reason: The Aesthetics of Modernity*, by C. Buci-Glucksmann. London: Sage.

Tuzin, D. 1980. *The Voice of the Tambaran: Truth and Illusion in Ilahita Arapesh Religion.* Berkeley: University of California Press.

Urry, J. (2003) 2011. "City Life and the Senses." In *The New Blackwell Companion to the City*, edited by G. Bridge and S. Watson. Oxford: Blackwell.

Van Campen, C. 2007. *The Hidden Sense: Synesthesia in Art and Science.* Cambridge, MA: MIT Press.

– 2014. *The Proust Effect: The Senses as Doorways to Lost Memories.* Translated by J. Ross. Oxford: Oxford University Press.

Vannini, P., D. Waskul, and S. Gottschalk. 2012. *The Senses in Self, Society and Culture: A Sociology of the Senses*. London: Routledge.

Vercelloni, L. 2016. *The Invention of Taste: A Cultural Account of Desire, Delight and Disgust in Fashion, Food and Art*. Translated by K. Singleton. Abingdon: Routledge.

Vila, A., ed. 2014. *A Cultural History of the Senses in the Age of Enlightenment*. London: Bloomsbury.

Vinge, L. 1975. *The Five Senses: Studies in a Literary Tradition*. Lund, Sweden: The Royal Society of the Humanities at Lund.

– 2009. "The Five Senses in Classical Science and Ethics." In *The Sixth Sense Reader*, edited by D. Howes, 107–18. Abingdon: Routledge.

Virilio, P. 1986. *Speed and Politics*. New York: Semiotext(e).

Vodvarka, F., S. Irish, and J.M. Malnar. 2006. "Millennium Park, Chicago: A Sensory Delight, Part I." *The Senses and Society* 1 (1): 93–103.

Von Hornbostel, W.M. 1927. "The Unity of the Senses." *Psyche* 7 (28): 83–9.

Von Uexküll, J. 1982. "The Theory of Meaning." *Semiotica* 42 (1): 25–82.

Watson, L. 1999. *Jacobson's Organ and the Remarkable Nature of Smell*. London: Penguin.

Watzlawick, P., J.B. Bavelas, and D.D. Jackson. 1981. *Pragmatics of Human Communication: A Study of Interaction Patterns, Pathologies and Paradoxes*. New York: W.W. Norton.

Weiner, A.B. 1976. *Women of Value, Men of Renown: New Perspectives in Trobriand Exchange*. Austin, TX: University of Texas Press.

Weiner, A.B. 1988. *The Trobrianders of Papua New Guinea*. New York: Holt, Rinehart and Winston.

Weiner, I. 2014. "The Senses in Religion: Pluralism, Technology and Change." In *A Cultural History of the Senses in the Modern Age, 1920–2000*, edited by D. Howes, 101–24. London: Bloomsbury.

Weinstein, D., and M. Weinstein. 1984. "On the Visual Constitution of Society: The Contributions of Georg Simmel and Jean-Paul Sartre." *History of European Ideas* 5 (4): 349–62. https://doi.org/10.1016/0191-6599(84)90041-X.

Weismantel, M.J. 1989. "The Children Cry for Bread: Hegemony and the Transformation of Consumptioon." In *The Social Economy of Consumption*, edited by B. Orlove and H. Rutz, 105–24. Lantham, MD: University Press of America.

Whatmore, S. 2006. "Materialist Returns: Practising Cultural Geography in and for a More-Than-Human World." *Cultural Geographies* 13: 600–9. https://doi .org/10.1191%2F1474474006cgj377oa.

White, D. 2017. "Affect: An Introduction." *Cultural Anthropology* 32 (2): 175–80. https://doi.org/10.14506/ca32.2.01.

White, F. 1998. *The Overview Effect: Space Exploration and Human Evolution*. Reston, VA: American Institute of Aeronautics and Astronautics.

Whitehead, A.N. (1925) 1987. *Science and the Modern World*. London: Macmillan.

Whorff, B.L. 1956. *Language, Thought and Reality*. Cambridge, MA: MIT Press.

Widdis, E. 2017. *Socialist Senses: Film, Feeling, and the Soviet Subject, 1917–1940*. Bloomington: Indiana University Press.

Wilkerson, M. 2006. *Amazing Journey: The Life of Peter Townshend*. Louisville, KY: Bad.

Williams, R. 1976. *Keywords: A Vocabulary of Culture and Society*. London: Fontana.

Wittgenstein, L. (1922) 2020. *The Tractatus Logico-Philosophicus*. London: Chiron Press.

Wober, M. 1991. "The Sensotype Hypothesis." In *The Varieties of Sensory Experience*, edited by D. Howes, 31–42. Toronto: University of Toronto Press.

Woolgar, C.M. 2006. *The Senses in Late Medieval England*. New Haven, CT: Yale University Press.

Yoshimizu, A. 2022. *Doing Ethnography in the Wake of the Displacement of Transnational Sex Workers in Yokohama: Sensuous Remembering*. Abingdon: Routledge.

Young, D. 2005. "The Smell of Green-ness: Cultural Synaesthesia in the Western Desert." *Etnofoor* 18 (1): 61–77. http://dx.doi.org/10.2307/25758086.

Young, K. 2021. "Synesthetic Gestures: Making the Imaginary Perceptible." *The Senses and Society* 16 (1): 89–101. https://doi.org/10.1080/17458927.2021.1873668.

Youssef, J., and C. Spence. 2021. "Náttúra by Kitchen Theory: An Immersive Multisensory Dining Concept." *International Journal of Gastronomy and Food Science* 24. https://doi.org/10.1016/j.ijgfs.2021.100354.

Zardini, M., ed. 2005. *Sense of the City: An Alternate Approach to Urbanism*. Montreal: Canadian Centre for Architecture.

Zika, F. 2013. "Color and Sound: Transcending the Limits of the Senses." In *Light, Image, Imagination*, edited by M. Blassnigg, G. Deutsch, and H. Schimek, 29–46. Amsterdam: Amsterdam University Press.

Index

linguistic, 4, 8, 46, 96, 121, 144, 191; extralinguistic, 45; model, 8, 209n6; turn, 4, 10, 206n2
Lipps, Andrea, 173, 175
listening, 30, 49, 92–3, 95, 117, 137, 139, 147, 183; listening-touch, 61–2; modes of, 157
literate, 38, 127–8, 138, 209n5. *See also* oral
Llull, Ramon, 70
Locke, John, 209n8
Lomas, David, 178–9
Lorimer, Hayden, 27, 28
Louis XIV, 201, 202
love, 89, 118, 135; "free," 119; magic, 134–5
Low, Kelvin, 10
Lupton, Ellen, 173–6
Lynch, Kevin, 150

Maboungou, Zab, 197, 200–3, 214n8
Magee, John Gillespie, 106
Maistre, Roy de, 179
Majid, Asifa, 96–7, 191, 192
male, 59, 70, 125, 132, 134; gaze, 60
Malinowski, Bronislaw, 126, 128, 130, 132, 134–6
Man in the Grey Flannel Suit, The, 109
Manalansan IV, Martin F., 37–8, 39
Maniq, 96
Mann, Thomas, 159
mapmaking, 28; multimodal, 41
maps, 4, 41, 42, 172, 174, 190
March on Washington for Jobs and Freedom, 117
Marchetti, Florencia, 201, 202
Margulies, Alfred, 92–3
marijuana, 54, 121; smell, 121
Marinetti, F.T., 104
Marks, Laura U., 154, 162, 211n3
Marks, Lawrence E., 99
Martin Gropius Bau, 186, 188

Masiello, Francine, 50
Massim, 128–39; a culture of kinetic, smooth, redolent, radiant, and resounding sensations, 130
Massumi, Brian, 95–6, 210n12
material, 5, 15–17, 36–7, 49, 56–7, 74, 88, 94, 105, 114, 115, 143, 145, 148, 149, 153–4, 157, 167, 170, 187, 188, 194, 206n15, 211n2; culture, 36, 55, 115, 124, 149, 152, 166, 170; experimentation, 15, 181; immaterial, 155, 167, 182, 188; synthetic, 103; turn, 5, 10, 36, 44
materialism, 115, 155, 171
materiality, 16–17, 36–7, 56–7, 90–1, 151, 153–4, 171, 205–6n7; of sound, 145, 177; of touch, 145
Matisse, Henri, 104
matter, 36, 193, 206n15; sentient, 36
McCord Museum, 167–8
McGurk effect, 84–6
McHugh, James, 10
McLuhan, Eric, 128
McLuhan, Marshall, 6, 13–14, 16, 17, 38, 52, 53, 60, 66, 76, 127–8, 138, 161, 204, 207n4, 208n5, 208n1, 209n7, 214n9
meal, 42, 98, 113, 115, 156, 211n6; Massim marriage, 134–6; the perfect, 97; quick, 115
meaning, 4, 5, 29, 30, 32, 39, 40, 46, 49, 63, 73, 82, 144, 152–3, 158, 167, 169–70, 190, 201, 205n6; meaningless, 194; meaning-making, 100; in motion, 158
measurement, 29, 32, 177
media, 14, 17, 32–3, 38, 51–2, 59, 76, 111, 114, 122, 127, 150, 154, 162, 182, 207n4; acoustic, 137; anthropology, 33; archaeology, 51; of communication, 6, 51, 55, 208n2; electronic, 182; new, 15, 162, 190. *See also* intermedia